Law in American History
(And in Mine)

Law in American History (And in Mine)

C. Evan Stewart

Twelve Tables Press

ISBN 978-1-946074-45-4

Twelve Tables Press
P.O. Box 568
Northport, New York 11768
www.twelvetablespress.com

10 9 8 7 6 5 4 3 2 1

The cover photograph is of Carl Newton performing magic tricks at the Donovan Leisure 1977 Christmas Dinner. The back cover photograph is of Ken Hart and the author, December 1985. Both photographs are from the author's collection.

To:

My Mother, my Father, my Sister, and my Daughter
–and–
My colleagues at Donovan Leisure, who made it such a special place: Ken Hart, Sam Murphy, Reg Koehler, Dan Murdock, Jim Hayes, John Baity, Jim Withrow, Owen McGivern, John Hendricks, Dave Versfelt, Louise Parent, Oscie Thomas, Bob Siverd, Jean Prewitt, Curt Gimson, Sara Moss, Meg Gifford, Cam Cowan, Tom Ahlf, Orin McCluskey, Peter Chaffetz, Lloyd Blankfein, John Schwolsky, Kristen Lewis, Tim O'Neil, Rose Suelt, Ann Papp, Al Borner, Bill Hancock, Chief Korves & Tracy Russell

Contents

Preface

I started law practice as a first-year associate on September 26, 1977, at the renowned law firm Donovan Leisure Newton & Irvine. The firm had been started in 1929 by then-titled Colonel "Wild Bill" Donovan, the most decorated veteran of World War I (and more recently the head of the U.S. Antitrust Division); he would later become Major General Donovan, founder of the Office of Strategic Services (the forerunner of the C.I.A.) during World War II. By 1977, Donovan Leisure was considered one of the country's leading litigation firms, with a specialty in large, complex antitrust cases.

I was a summer associate at the firm in 1976, and had gotten an offer of permanent employment at the end of my summer tenure. I felt honored to be joining this prestigious firm and, after trips to California and France (after the New York Bar Exam), I found a one-bedroom apartment to rent on East 57th Street and showed up early for work on the 39th floor of 30 Rockefeller Plaza on Monday morning, September 26.

This book contains—at its beginning—a number of chapters focused on Donovan Leisure, as well as some of my early experiences there. A few episodes are/were (in hindsight) pretty amusing, and I hope readers will find them so. Others were/are not so amusing, and I hope they will be instructive, especially to young lawyers at the outset of their careers.

One side benefit of my years at Donovan Leisure—besides receiving superb training which would help guide me through 47 years (plus) of my legal career—was that I began to write and publish articles on a wide range of topics. While many of those written addressed complicated legal topics, I also began to write and publish articles that examined significant episodes concerning the legal history of our country. Many of those articles were published in the *Federal Bar Council Quarterly*; and it is those articles that (in updated form) comprise the majority of this book's chapters. From famous/infamous trials to miscarriages of justice, examining famous historical figures' brushes with the law as well as looking at how well prominent politicians cut the mustard as practicing lawyers, these chapters cover a vast swatch of material that I hope readers will find new and interesting.

Law in American History (And in Mine)

CHAPTER I

The Law Firm of "Wild Bill" Donovan

Great law firms can begin for any number of reasons. One such firm (which, regrettably, is no more) had its origins in a political double-cross. That firm was Donovan Leisure Newton & Irvine.

A War Hero

Colonel William "Wild Bill" Donovan led New York's 69th Regiment (the "Fighting Irish") in World War I. And in so doing, he received not only his nickname but also the Medal of Honor, the Distinguished Service Cross, the Distinguished Service Medal, a Purple Heart (with two Oak Leaf Clusters), the Légion d'Honneur and Croix de Guerre (with Palm and Silver Star), and the Croci di Guerra. When the regiment marched up Fifth Avenue after the war, a band played "Gary Owen," and the mayor honored Donovan and his men, proclaiming: "History will tell of your gallantry and uncalculating indifference to life . . . !" Not surprisingly, returning as a famous, highly decorated veteran helped first to attract prominent clients (e.g., J.P. Morgan) to Donovan's Buffalo, New York, law firm, and thereafter push him into political life. With respect to the latter, the first stop on that ladder came when Donovan was appointed United States Attorney for the Western District of New York. And in the early 1920s, the main priority of Donovan's office was to enforce Prohibition, which he did with skill, enthusiasm, and vigor (even raiding a private club in which he was a member—much to the displeasure of his fellow club members).

The Department of Justice

In 1924, Harlan Fiske Stone was appointed Attorney General by President Calvin Coolidge. As Dean of the Columbia Law School, Stone had taken a personal interest in Donovan when he had been a law student there; and he now asked his friend of two decades to join him as his deputy, in the post of Assistant Attorney General. Stone's tenure was a brief one; he was sworn in as a Supreme Court Justice in March of 1925. Succeeding Stone was John Garibaldi Sargent, a modest man, who was frequently absent from Washington; this had the effect of often leaving Donovan in the position of being acting Attorney General. Given wide sway to pick his priorities, Donovan delegated responsibility for the Justice Department's Criminal Division to one of his colleagues, and took over day-to-day control of the Antitrust Division. There he met Ralston R. Irvine, a recent graduate of the Cornell Law School and one of the country's leading antitrust experts. Donovan and "Shorty" Irvine brought on 65 cases in 4 years; a number of them were landmark prosecutions (e.g., the *Trenton Potteries* case). Each of the six cases litigated up to the Supreme Court was argued by Donovan, and in each the government prevailed.

The Rise of Herbert Hoover

When President Coolidge announced that he did not choose to run for reelection in 1928, Herbert Hoover became the inevitable choice to lead the Republican Party. Donovan, at one point, received a "boomlet" for the vice presidential slot. His main contribution, however, was in the background, as one of Hoover's principal advisers. Donovan, for example, was the sole architect of Hoover's acceptance speech to the Republican Convention, and he and Hoover thereafter planned the campaign together on a five day fishing retreat in Oregon. For all this work (a quid) there was an explicit quo: that Donovan would be elevated in a Hoover administration to the position he had de facto occupied for much of the Coolidge administration—that of Attorney General.

Hoover won a massive victory in November, overwhelming New York Governor Al Smith by an Electoral College margin of 444 to 87 (the popular vote was 21 million to 15 million). The issues were economic: peace and prosperity under eight years of Republican leadership; and ugly: Smith was a Catholic, and the religious bigotry that was unleashed against the first Catholic to head a national party ticket was truly grotesque. This latter fact would play a critical role in Donovan's career ambitions.

In the period between the election and Hoover's inauguration on March 4, 1929, Donovan's promotion was floated out as a political trial balloon. Public opposition, however, was quickly interposed against Donovan. Why? Because he, like Smith, was a Catholic, and how, it was contended, could a Catholic Attorney General enforce Prohibition (since everyone knew that all Catholics were "wets"—i.e., against Prohibition). This "argument" was made in the face of Donovan's enforcement of Prohibition as a U.S. Attorney earlier in the decade.

Notwithstanding, a number of Protestant ministers, senators, and congressmen, and just plain wackos, publicly weighed in on the unsuitability of Donovan for such an important post. And while many prominent people weighed in strongly on Donovan's behalf (Emory Buckner, for example, then the U.S. Attorney for the Southern District of New York, issued a ringing endorsement of Donovan's capabilities), the political well had been poisoned.

Sticking in the Knife

On January 7, 1929, Hoover had a brief audience with Donovan, telling him that he could not make him Attorney General, but

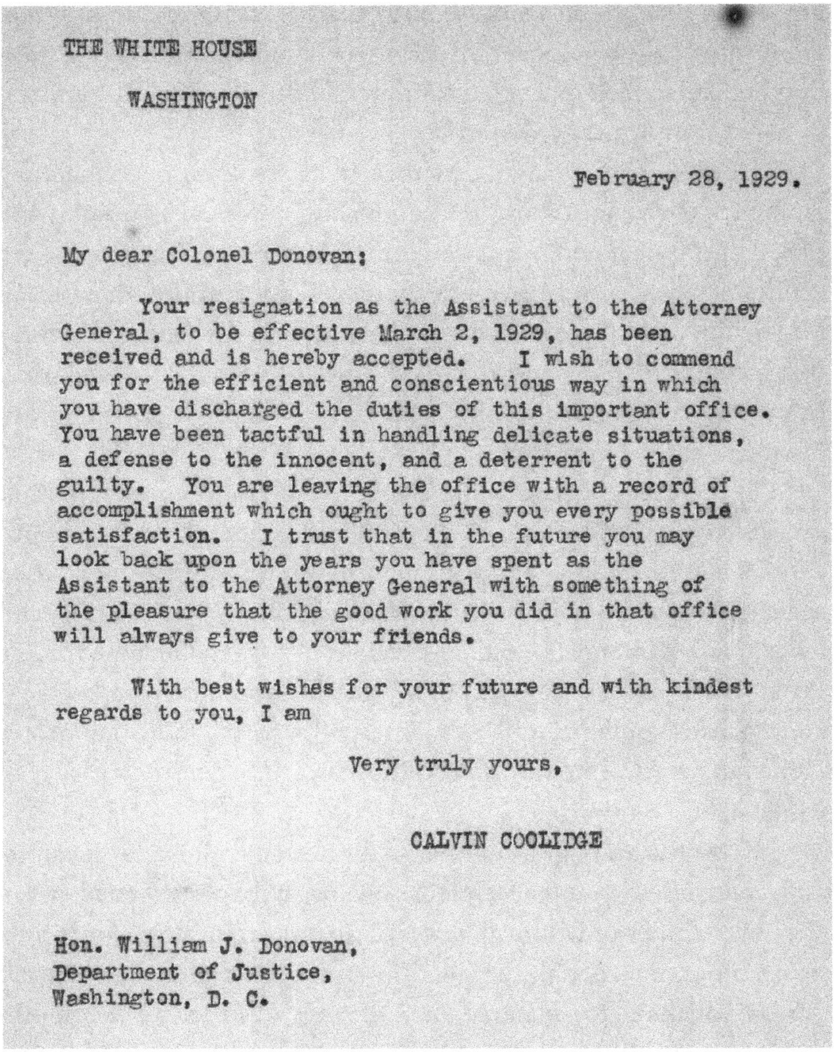

THE WHITE HOUSE

WASHINGTON

February 28, 1929.

My dear Colonel Donovan:

Your resignation as the Assistant to the Attorney General, to be effective March 2, 1929, has been received and is hereby accepted. I wish to commend you for the efficient and conscientious way in which you have discharged the duties of this important office. You have been tactful in handling delicate situations, a defense to the innocent, and a deterrent to the guilty. You are leaving the office with a record of accomplishment which ought to give you every possible satisfaction. I trust that in the future you may look back upon the years you have spent as the Assistant to the Attorney General with something of the pleasure that the good work you did in that office will always give to your friends.

With best wishes for your future and with kindest regards to you, I am

Very truly yours,

CALVIN COOLIDGE

Hon. William J. Donovan,
Department of Justice,
Washington, D. C.

Letter from President Coolidge to William Donovan (author's collection)

promising him a place elsewhere in the Cabinet. The position that seemed likely, and the one discussed, was that of Secretary of War.

Donovan was then called out to Santa Fe, New Mexico, on government business. In late February, a Hoover aide contacted Donovan and asked him to return to Washington immediately. Upon

William Donovan Consulting with a Client
(author's collection)

arriving, Donovan went directly to Hoover's Georgetown home. Hoover did not beat around the bush, telling Donovan that the job he wanted him to take was that of Governor-General of the Philippines. Donovan's immediate reaction was categoric and negative: "It is impossible." Hoover responded by pointing out that that post would be most useful "for [his] political career" (i.e., William H. Taft, Leonard Wood, and Henry Stimson had all held that post). Donovan was unmoved, however, and asked about the War Department. Hoover's reaction was terse: "You could work there, but I wouldn't suggest it."

Donovan was growing increasingly agitated and stated he was going to head back to Santa Fe. Hoover, in the hopes of averting a total break, suggested that he meet with some of Hoover's advisers before doing so. Those interviews did nothing to change Donovan's mind, however. Justice Stone even visited with him, attempting to make Donovan face, and come to terms with, the less than pleasant side of politics. Donovan would have none of it, finally asking Stone to tell Hoover: "I expected nothing from him but honesty, and that I have not received."

Justice Stone did arrange for Donovan to meet with Hoover one last time before the inauguration. Donovan did not go quietly: "I am used to dealing with equals.... If I have any use at all, it is to stay here in America and deal with my equals, ... you will need someone to stay here who can pull the sword for you." Dismissive of such talk, Hoover replied: "I don't think so, Bill." And that was that.

With his political career seemingly in shambles, Donovan resigned his post in the Justice Department, effective March 2, receiving (by Coolidge's standards) an effusive letter in response. Then he headed off to New York City to form a law firm of the first rank. Donovan attracted prominent alumni from Emory Buckner's U.S. Attorney's office (George Leisure, Carl Newton, and Edward Lumbard) to become name partners in the new firm. And when Lumbard went into public life (he ultimately became Chief Judge of the Court of Appeals for the Second Circuit), the firm's name was changed to Donovan Leisure Newton & Irvine.

Postscript

Hoover's double-cross of Donovan was well-known among political insiders. Indeed, in 1939 when President Franklin Roosevelt was contemplating bringing Donovan into his administration (ultimately Donovan became head of the Office of Strategic Services), FDR specifically referenced to Frank Knox (FDR's Secretary of the Navy) that he wanted Donovan ("an old friend of mine") "not only for his own ability, but also to repair in a sense the very great injustice done him by President Hoover in the Winter of 1929."

CHAPTER II

Sam Murphy: The John Wayne of Lawyerdom

What are the limits of zealous representation of a client? For one of the most famous lawyers of his generation, it meant being cited for contempt by a federal district court judge in a "bet your company" case.

Samuel W. Murphy Jr., in the words of one reporter, was "the kind of lawyer who instantly inspires confidence in clients." Closer to home, one of his law firm colleagues once said of him: "If John Wayne had been a lawyer, he'd have been Sam Murphy."

After graduating from the Harvard Law School, Murphy joined the Marine Corps and saw action during the Korean War. Thereafter, he joined the law firm of Donovan Leisure Newton & Irvine. A protégé of Ralston "Shorty" Irvine, Murphy rose to become the firm's preeminent litigator, representing such clients as Walt Disney, General Electric, Mobil Oil, American Home Products, and American Cyanamid in complex civil suits across the country.

The Development of Tetracycline

In the early 1950s, several drug companies made competing applications to the U.S. Patent Office for the broad spectrum antibiotic drug tetracycline. After much brouhaha, Pfizer ultimately prevailed in receiving a patent; Pfizer entered into licensing agreements with various other drug companies after, *inter alia,* infringement litigation.

The federal government did not believe the drug companies had dealt properly with the Patent Office; nor did it believe they had acted as true competitors thereafter. After bringing on a Federal Trade Commission proceeding (sort of successful) and a criminal antitrust case (unsuccessful), the government filed a three-count civil action in 1969 against Pfizer, Bristol Myers, Cyanamid, Olin, Squibb, and Upjohn.

By its suit, the government (1) sought to cancel Pfizer's patent on the ground that it was procured by fraud; (2) sought overcharge money damages against Pfizer, Cyanamid, and Bristol; and (3) charged all the defendants with violating the federal antitrust laws.

The action paralleled 153 private antitrust lawsuits, 93 of which had been settled; the remaining 60 actions were assigned to Judge Miles W. Lord in Minnesota, who also had the government's case. For the drug companies, this was "bet your company" litigation, and the government made it clear that it planned to play hardball. The best evidence of the government's attitude was its determination to get documents from the drug companies' law firms dating back to the 1940s; more specifically, the government wanted to get its hands on, *inter alia,* internal law firm legal memoranda and other attorney opinion work product. And to that end, the government petitioned Judge Lord to get all such attorney-related materials.

Donovan Leisure and Cyanamid

Donovan Leisure had been established in 1929 by William "Wild Bill" Donovan, one of World War I's greatest heroes and head of the government's Antitrust Division under President Coolidge (*see* Chapter I). The law firm quickly gained national preeminence in antitrust litigation (e.g., *Appalachian Coals; In re Humphrey's Estate; United States v. Socony-Vacuum*).

Since 1939, Donovan Leisure had been representing Cyanamid in numerous antitrust disputes; it had not, however, had anything to do with Cyanamid's dealings with the Patent Office. In the mid-1950s, as Cyanamid's legal problems mounted, Donovan Leisure created numerous internal analyses of Cyanamid's legal exposure in both current and anticipated litigation. Most significantly, the firm put some of its best minds to work preparing a "devil's advocacy" piece—that is, the very best case that could be prosecuted against Cyanamid by a "skilled and imaginative" adversary.

Three Masters and Their Lord

The government initially filed motions to get the law firm materials. To expedite the process, Judge Lord empaneled three masters to review documents and make preliminary discovery rulings. The drug companies' law firms agreed to give the masters in-camera access to all materials except internal files that had never been shown to or seen by their clients. Agreeing to that limitation by a stipulation executed at Donovan Leisure's New York office, the masters focused first on the documents the firms did make available for inspection.

On June 1, 1973, the masters delivered their first substantive ruling on attorney work product, issuing two legal opinions. The first was to limit work product only to materials generated in the litigation at hand; materials from terminated disputes would be protected only if they involved "substantially the same issues" as the current litigation.

The second opinion was not to accord "opinion work product" any special status—that is, it would be subject to Rule 26(b)(3)'s "substantial need" standard; as such, the masters ordered that all opinion work product be produced for in-camera inspection.

Lord adopted both opinions on the same day they were issued. But the drug companies' counsel were not cowed, continuing to insist that their internal work product was not fair game. Because the lawyers had also taken issue with the discovery demands themselves—on

Samuel W. Murphy Jr. (photograph courtesy of his daughter Connie Murphy)

the ground that they did not reach materials that were outside "the possession, custody, or control" of the drug companies, a determined Judge Lord thereafter issued Rule 45 subpoenas directly to each of the companies' law firms in January of 1975.

Donovan Leisure moved to quash its subpoena; while that motion was *sub judice,* the parties negotiated a revised subpoena. Over objections and without prejudice, Donovan Leisure thereafter provided in-camera access to the masters of responsive law firm files, while separately identifying in a privilege log those materials which constituted "hard core" work product and which it viewed as being absolutely protected from disclosure.

After their review, the masters issued rulings in February and March of 1976; these rulings were directed to addressing further "opinion" work product issues. Faced with the fact that their June 1973 views had been directly rebuked in the interim by the Fourth

Circuit (*see Duplan Corp. v. Moulinage et Retorderie de Chanvanoz*, 509 F.2d 730 (4th Cir. 1974), *cert. denied*, 420 U.S. 997 (1975)), the masters determined that *Duplan* had been "wrongly decided" and ordered Donovan Leisure (and the other firms) to turn over specifically identified opinion work product.

In the summer of 1976, the firms sought reconsideration, first from the masters, and thereafter from Judge Lord; both efforts were unsuccessful. And when Murphy, on behalf of Donovan Leisure, formally refused to accede to Judge Lord's order to produce the subpoenaed materials, the judge on September 22, 1976, entered a judgment of civil contempt against Murphy and his law firm.

Up to the Eighth Circuit

Perhaps the only obvious benefit of being cited for civil contempt is that such an order is appealable; thus, Murphy was able to take Judge Lord's order up to the Eighth Circuit immediately. And besides that timing benefit, Murphy was also a significant beneficiary of the Department of Justice having done a 180-degree turn regarding its position on *Duplan*.

Before the masters, the DOJ had argued that Duplan was "clearly erroneous and should not be followed." At the same time, however, the DOJ had been simultaneously representing to the Sixth Circuit that it was "committed" to the result in *Duplan*. *See United States v. Leggett & Platt, Inc.*, 542 F.2d 655 (6th Cir. 1976).

When all this came out, the DOJ recognized that its 180-degree turn "eviscerate[d] the central holding of the masters"; it was left to argue to the Eighth Circuit that disclosure was still appropriate because the attorney documents were prepared in furtherance of a crime or fraud.

Even with (or notwithstanding) the government's embarrassing posture, the Eighth Circuit recognized that this was a landmark case and that the court had an obligation to provide guidance not just to the contemnors before it but also to future litigants dealing with attorney work product permutations. And so, on August 12, 1977, the Eighth Circuit handed down *In re Murphy*, 560 F.2d (8th Cir. 1977).

The Eighth Circuit began its analysis with the Supreme Court's decision in *Hickman v. Taylor*, 329 U.S. 495 (1947). Unlike the masters who took the view that *Hickman* was a limited ruling, the Eighth Circuit believed that *Hickman* was a seminal decision that reconciled competing interests of liberalized discovery and attorney privacy, with attorney privacy ("without undue and needless interference") the clear winner. And, as the court further observed, *Hickman* became the basis for Rule 26(b)(3), which formally codified the attorney work product doctrine as a matter of federal procedure.

The Eighth Circuit then addressed several of the limitations imposed by the masters. First, the court determined that work product protections cover terminated litigation; to do otherwise would be directly contrary to *Hickman*'s policies. Similarly, the two litigations did not have to be "closely related"; again, the Hickman policies applied regardless of how related or unrelated the litigations might be.

The Eighth Circuit then moved on to the critical issue of what showing would be sufficient to get access to opinion work product. Based again upon *Hickman* policies, the court ruled that "opinion work product enjoys a nearly absolute immunity and can be discovered only in very rare and extraordinary circumstances." The Eighth Circuit did not want to go to an "absolute" position because there might be some highly unusual situation that could not be envisioned (citing the Nixon White House tapes situation).

The government urged that this was just such a circumstance because of the fraud that Cyanamid had committed on the Patent Office and the fact that the company violated the antitrust laws when they sought the advice of their law firm. With respect to the latter point, the court ruled that the government had not yet shown in prior litigation that Cyanamid had in fact violated the antitrust laws (*see* 367 F. Supp. 91 (S.D.N.Y. 1973); 384 F. Supp. 265 (E.D.N.C. 1974)).

As to fraud on the Patent Office, however, there had been prior litigation in which Cyanamid's wrongdoing vis-à-vis the Patent Office had been demonstrated (*see* 465 F.2d 545 (8th Cir. 1972)). But since Donovan Leisure had had no substantive role in Cyanamid's application to the Patent Office, there was no nexus between the client's fraud and the law firm's opinion work product reflecting its antitrust work and advice. As a result, the Eighth Circuit concluded that none of Donovan Leisure's opinion work product was discoverable and the court thus reversed the contempt orders against Murphy and his law firm.

Postscript

Beyond his outstanding litigation career on behalf of corporate clients, Murphy also received the Thurgood Marshall Award for his pro bono representation of death row inmates. He died on September 7, 2001.

Not only were Murphy and Donovan Leisure cited for contempt by Judge Lord, Merrill Clark (of Winthrop Stimson Putnam & Roberts) and Henry Zafian (of Fish & Neave)—counsel to Bristol—also were cited. Ultimately, their contempt orders were also purged by the Eighth Circuit.

When I was a summer associate at Donovan Leisure in 1976, I came upon an excited discussion among permanent associates about the proceedings before Judge Lord and the strong possibility that Sam Murphy could be cited for contempt. "Who is Sam Murphy?" I innocently asked. One associate looked at me dismissively and said: "Good luck getting a job here!"

CHAPTER III

Walter Mansfield: Lawyer, Judge, Warrior

Walter Roe Mansfield was a giant in the New York City Bar during the twentieth century. An outstanding trial lawyer, a distinguished jurist on both the Southern District bench and on the Second Circuit, Mansfield also had a fascinating military career during World War II. While this chapter will touch on his legal career, Mansfield's war experiences will be its focus.

Born and raised in Boston, Mansfield's father was a prominent lawyer, judge, and ultimately the mayor of Boston. Educated at Harvard for both his undergraduate (1932) and law (1935) degrees, Mansfield decided not to practice in Boston; as the son of the mayor, he was concerned that people either would assume any success was due to the influence of his father, or would attempt to use him as a conduit to influence the local government. Mansfield thus instead focused his job search on New York City.

Donovan Leisure Newton & Lumbard

Started by Colonel William J. Donovan in 1929 (*see* Chapter I), the law firm of Donovan Leisure Newton & Lumbard was a relatively small firm which Mansfield "fell in love with at first sight." That attraction was based on the sterling credentials of the firm's lawyers, the firm's growing renown in antitrust litigation, and the fact that

Major General William Donovan

Mansfield's starting salary was set at the "bonanza" level of $1,800 per annum.

Mansfield did a host of young lawyer jobs and participated in the firm's rapid growth. When J. Edward Lumbard was appointed a special prosecutor on an important criminal case, he asked Mansfield to join his staff. Working for Lumbard (later the U.S. Attorney for the Southern District and Chief Judge of the Second Circuit) turned out to be a great learning experience for the young lawyer, and it whetted his appetite for trial work. As a result, Mansfield began an aggressive campaign to join the U.S. Attorney's office. With the help of his father's friend, Joseph P. Kennedy, Mansfield ultimately secured a post as an Assistant U.S. Attorney in May of 1939. During his two and a half year tenure, Mansfield was given a number of important assignments (e.g., *United States v. Simm Davis, Inc.*; *United States v. Albert Mook*), for which he won high praise.

World War II

Mansfield returned to Donovan Leisure in 1941, but with the Japanese attack on Pearl Harbor, his legal career was put on hold. Mansfield enlisted in the Marine Corps. After completing parachute training ("All they do is throw you out of airplanes. Do five jumps, and you're a parachutist."), and thanks to Donovan's appointment by FDR to be the head of the Office of Strategic Services (OSS), Mansfield was transferred over to the OSS.

Mansfield's first real wartime assignment took place in Yugoslavia, which had been overrun by the Nazis in 1941 (supported by many Croats, who hoped for an independent nation state). Opposing the Nazis—but in distinct conflict with each other—were Josip Broz Tito's Partisans (break-off Croats, supported by the British) and the Serbian Chetniks, a group loyal to the in-exile Yugoslavian king and led by Dragoljub "Draža" Mihailović. The British were of the view that the Chetniks were Nazi collaborators; Donovan did not believe that and he wanted Mansfield to contact Mihailovich and his men to refute the British position and have the United States stand with the Chetniks. Of even greater importance was to maximize the anti-Nazi effort in Yugoslavia and tie the Germans down, given the imminence of the Allies' campaign in Italy.

And so, on August 19, 1943, Mansfield, by himself, parachuted out of a RAF Halifax bomber and into Yugoslavia. Jumping from 8,000 feet, Mansfield drifted away from the fires in the shape of a cross that constituted his target. When he hit the ground (he later wrote):

> I got out of my harness, hid my chute, drew my .45 and waited in the cold. Within ten minutes I heard voices yelling out in Serbian, "Zdravo! Zdravo! Priatelj!" ("Greetings! Greetings! Friend!") I answered and was soon surrounded

> by a small group of weird ragged-looking men, most of whom had black beards and hats bearing a skull and bones emblem. I told Lt. Perich, their leader, that I was an American, whereupon they all began to whoop, holler, and kiss me (black beards and all), shouting, "Zdravo, Purvi Americanec" ("Greetings, first American.") I mustered up my Serbian to reply, "Zdravo Chetnici."

The Robin Hood of Serbia

The happy group led Mansfield to Mihailovich (the "Robin Hood of Serbia"), who greeted him warmly (in French) and invited him to sit by the fire and share in a bottle of "rakia" (a vodka distilled from plums).

Mihailovich and his men looked quite disheveled (they had been living in mountains, and fighting the Nazis therefrom, for two years), but they quickly impressed Mansfield with their morale and "excellent discipline." These paid off when, in Mansfield's first combat experience, German troops attacked Mihailovich's camp. After driving off the attack, the General ordered a forced march in the rain further into the mountains. Mansfield would later write:

> After the first eight hours I became weary and stiff. Whenever I asked, "How much longer?" I would always receive the same reply, "Only two hours."

Once in a more secure location, Mansfield was eager to take some offensive action. He was ultimately successful in persuading a reluctant Mihailovich (who did not want to risk losing his lone American representative) to let him lead a group to take out the main railroad artery near the town of Vardište. This assignment was ultimately successful, but not without the usual confusion and miscommunications that occur in warfare.

Shortly after that foray, it was learned that the Italian Army had surrendered to the Allies (six days after the invasion of the Italian mainland). Mansfield was then directed to help facilitate the surrender of Italian forces based in Yugoslavia (five divisions); this was to be done notwithstanding the looming presence of two German divisions.

Mansfield was tasked with a group of about 300 Serbs to go to the town of Priboj, at which there was an Italian garrison of 1,800 men. After an eight-hour trek, he and his men arrived in the dead of night at a point overlooking the garrison. Not waiting for daybreak, Mansfield led a small patrol down near the garrison and convinced a Priboj man to take a surrender-demand note into the Italians. Before the local even got to the front gate, however, he was cut down by machine gunfire.

The next day, Mansfield sent another surrender-demand note, which received a more peaceful response by the Italian commander of "no surrender." Knowing that a frontal assault against protected superior numbers would be futile, Mansfield and his men bided their time. By the next day, the Italians sent a message that they would indeed be interested in talking about terms. And shortly thereafter, Mansfield's group marched into the garrison to accept their surrender.

Happily ensconced in the Italian garrison, Mansfield's men quickly separated out the Fascist "Blackshirts" from the regular Italian troops and then established for himself a "fantastic life": "Italian cognac, good food, white bread, [and] a bed to sleep in." At the same time, however, Mansfield was concerned as to what would happen "if the Germans came."

And come they did. Rather than make a stand against the large incoming German force, Mansfield decided to evacuate the garrison, take the great bulk of the Italians' armaments and ammunition, and leave the Italians to face their former allies. Ultimately, the Chetniks, led by Mansfield, reunited with Mihailovich's forces in the mountains.

Next up was an attack in October 1943 on a fortified German garrison in the town of Visegrád. Mansfield and the skilled Chetnik guerrillas quickly took the city, killing many of the enemy and driving out the remainder. Thereafter, they destroyed the city's railroad bridge.

At this point, geopolitical concerns came to the fore. Because of the great buildup Tito was receiving in the British media (and the obvious bias the Russians had in his favor), Mansfield decided to undertake a tour of the various Chetnik forces throughout Serbia so he could report to the U.S. government on the effectiveness of Chetnik attacks on German troops. Thereafter, and with the Gestapo in close pursuit, Mansfield ultimately made his way to the Adriatic Sea, met up with local guerrilla forces, and was able to contact U.S. officials in Cairo. After some false starts, Mansfield was able to arrange for a British PT boat to pick him up on February 15, 1944, and return him to Cairo.

Transfer to Asia

After reporting to OSS officials on the Chetniks' effective guerrilla tactics against the Nazis, Mansfield was promoted to Captain and transferred to the Pacific War. His first job was to establish a base for OSS operations in Southeast Asia. Once he had accomplished that (in the Mergui Archipelago), Mansfield was sent to China to train Chinese guerrillas to ambush the Japanese and disrupt their communications and supply lines. Unlike the highly skilled, disciplined, and motivated Serbs, the Chinese recruits that Mansfield had to work with were "a pretty poor lot." Even after a month's worth of hard training, "[m]ost of the Chinese had such poor eyes that they could not hit the side of a barn at 100 yards!"

In February 1945, Mansfield took his Chinese troops out for their first taste of combat with the Japanese. Ambushing a truck convoy, Mansfield "was disappointed in [his] men's ability to hold fire as they had been trained"; nevertheless, the results were good in terms of enemy killed, rifles and secret papers captured, and a bridge destroyed.

Other ambushes on Japanese troops followed, with some good successes (there would have been better results if the troops had better discipline and marksmanship skills). In another episode,

Mansfield directed seven B-25 bombers from the ground to take out a large Japanese truck dispersal area.

In June of 1945, Mansfield took on yet another assignment: parachuting into and liberating various prison camps located in China. On this last task, Mansfield's most important contribution was helping to effect the rescue of General Jonathan M. Wainwright, who had spent virtually the entire war in captivity—Douglas MacArthur having left him behind in the Philippines.

After the War: Donovan Leisure Redux

Mansfield pondered a number of options after the war, but ultimately decided to rejoin his old law firm. Trying cases all over the country, Mansfield took on increasingly key assignments for one of Donovan Leisure's most important clients, the American Cynamid Company. Cynamid had criminal and civil antitrust exposure, problems with the federal government (Department of Justice, Federal Trade Commission, Congress), and even international intrigue. Mansfield also argued a major corporate case in the U.S. Supreme Court on behalf of another Donovan client, the Alleghany Corporation. He prevailed by a four-to-three vote.

On the Bench

Having refused to entertain an invitation to go on the federal bench in 1961, Mansfield proved more amenable in 1966. Even though Mansfield was a Republican, President Lyndon B. Johnson nominated him. The Democratic Senate approved his appointment to the Southern District.

Judge Mansfield immediately found the bench "a much more satisfying way of using [his] talents than private practice." His most famous cases included his ruling that Muhammed Ali, who had been convicted of draft evasion, should be allowed a New York State boxing license (316 F. Supp. 1246). Mansfield also required McSorleys'

Ale House—a men's only bar for 114 years—to serve women (317 F. Supp. 593) (a year later, the owner of McSorleys' thanked the judge: his business had more than doubled).

In 1971, President Richard M. Nixon nominated Mansfield to the Second Circuit. Mansfield's jurisprudence on that court included the Pentagon Papers case, the Attica prisoner uprising, corporate disputes (e.g., Hanson-SCM, Texaco-Pennzoil), and the Bhopal case. Mansfield took senior status in 1981. On January 7, 1987, Walter Roe Mansfield died.

Postscript

Mansfield received a Bronze Star for his work in Yugoslavia. The Yugoslavian government in exile presented him with the Certificate of the White Eagle with Swords. And for his work in China, Mansfield received the Legion of Merit.

In a *New York Times* article on November 29, 1945, Mansfield was interviewed on the difficulties of adjusting to peacetime:

> It was far easier to locate a sniper in the jungles of China than to find an apartment in New York City or the vicinity.... I have been in four different hotels in the last five days and have to move again. Peace is hell ... finding a place to live in New York is more nerve-racking than anything the Japanese or Nazis had to offer.

The Russians took over on the ground in Yugoslavia. This allowed Tito to consolidate control as the USSR's proxy. Ultimately, Mihailovich was captured by Tito's men. After a show trial, Mihailovich was executed by a firing squad on a golf course.

Mansfield would have become President of the Federal Bar Council in 1966 had he not been nominated to the Southern District. Years later, in 1981, he accepted the FBC's Judge Learned Hand Award.

The Second Circuit paid special tribute to Judge Mansfield in an Extraordinary Session on April 7, 1987. In 1995, the Federal Bar Foundation published *Glimpses of Walter Mansfield*. Much of the material for this chapter was drawn from *Glimpses*. Among the many admirable traits that were reflected on in the personal tributes paid to Mansfield were his sense of humor and lack of pretense and self-importance. The best example of these comes in a story relayed by his law partner, Kenneth N. Hart:

> Another little story isn't really related to Walter's practicing as an attorney. Walter told this story at the firm's formal alumni dinner several years ago. During World War II, Walter had parachuted into Yugoslavia and was engaged in fighting the Germans with the Mihailovich freedom fighters. In those days they were living in caves in the mountains and fighting in the daytime, things that Walter really loved doing. They were robust men and they would come back at night and drink wine and give toasts. One toast they used to give all the time sounded something like "Agrura stollyanski peratroya." Years after the war was over, they had a big affair in Belgrade. The hundreds of guests included key people from the Yugoslavian government, lots of other important people, and a few representatives from the United States, including Walter, sitting at the head table. People were dressed up and wearing their medals. And of course, they were giving speeches. They called upon Walter, who thought he'd add a great touch and say the toast he remembered the Mihailovich freedom fighters giving during the war years. So, Walter stood up before the assembled audience at the formal dinner and said on behalf of the United States, "I'm proud to offer the toast, 'Agrura stollyanski peratroya.'" This elicited a mixed reaction in the hall. After Walter finished, the man sitting next to him said, "Did you know what you said?" Walter said, "No, what?" His dinner companion said,

"You have just wished, 'May your penis always have an erection.'" Walter told this story himself and thought it was extremely funny.

CHAPTER IV

The Associate's Dilemma: Joe Fortenberry, Mahlon Perkins, and the Kodak Antitrust Trial

In the December 1979 issue of *Esquire,* Steven Brill published an article ("When a Lawyer Lies"); it has become the widely accepted story of what went wrong in the most important antitrust trial of the 1970s: *Berkey Photo v. Kodak.*

The Conventional Wisdom

On April 20, 1977, Alvin Stein, Berkey's lead lawyer (a partner at Parker, Chapin, Flattau & Klimpl), was taking the deposition of Kodak's expert witness, Merton Peck, a distinguished professor of economics at Yale. Kodak's law firm was its long-standing outside counsel, Donovan Leisure Newton & Irvine, one of the country's leading litigation firms. And defending Peck at the deposition were Mahlon F. Perkins Jr. and Joseph Fortenberry.

Perkins, the son of a U.S. diplomat, was born in China, where he lived until he was 14. Thereafter, Perkins came to the United States to go to school, ultimately enrolling at Phillips Exeter Academy. After graduating from Exeter, Perkins matriculated at Harvard College. During World War II, he served in the Office of Strategic Services (toward the end of the war, he parachuted into Peking to assist in the release of POWs, for which he was awarded the U.S. Army Soldier's Medal for Valor and the Chinese Order of the Flying Cloud). After the war, Perkins entered Harvard Law School; and after graduation

Carl Newton performing magic tricks at the Donovan Leisure 1977 Christmas Dinner (author's collection)

he joined Donovan Leisure—the firm founded by the Office of Strategic Services's head, General William "Wild Bill" Donovan. At the time of the Kodak trial, Perkins (according to Brill) was "one of the firm's most respected partners."

Joe Fortenberry, originally from Mississippi, went to Harvard and then to Yale Law School. After clerking for a federal appeals court judge, he joined Donovan Leisure in 1970. At the time of the Kodak trial, Fortenberry (according to Brill) "was on the perfect big-time lawyer's career path": he was "not only ... brilliant but [was] also ...

engaging and enjoyable to work with"; he was "a well-liked, personable genius"; and his "prospects for being made a partner at the prestige firm the following year were excellent."

Peck was an important witness for Kodak. His task was to advance the narrative that Kodak's market domination was the result of its skill, hard work, and innovative products, and not because of other less honorable methods (e.g., illegal tie-ins, the acquisition of competitors). At his deposition, Stein pressed for all the materials Peck had generated and used in arriving at his conclusions, including everything Donovan Leisure had provided to him. Peck responded that he had shipped everything back to Donovan Leisure. At that point, Stein angrily demanded that Perkins immediately produce all of the documents. Perkins's response: that would not be possible, he had destroyed them.

That was not true. In fact, the documents were sitting in a suitcase in Perkins's office. Moreover (according to Brill), not only did Fortenberry know his boss was lying, he whispered in Perkins's ear about the suitcase (and the documents therein), but Perkins waved him off during the angry back and forth with Stein. Two weeks later, Perkins submitted an affidavit to the court in which he doubled down on his misrepresentations(s) vis-à-vis the "destroyed" documents.

In January 1978, the *Berkey v. Kodak* trial was winding down, with Peck as the final witness for Kodak. On cross-examination, Stein pressed Peck about the materials used to reach his conclusions. This led Judge Marvin Frankel to review the whole history of the "destroyed" documents. Faced with this new and intensive scrutiny of the episode, Perkins broke down and confessed his wrongdoing, which Stein then used before the jury to destroy Peck's credibility and thereafter secure a "spectacular $113 million verdict" (a verdict reversed on appeal because the measure of damages was improper; ultimately, Kodak settled the matter by paying Berkey a few million dollars).

Perkins was prosecuted and pled guilty to contempt of court; he was sentenced to one month in prison (which he served). Although he resigned from Donovan Leisure (on March 20, 1978), Perkins did not lose his law license.

Fortenberry was the real focus for Brill, however. Citing to the Code of Professional Responsibility (then DR 7-102(R) (reporting fraud on a tribunal), and then DR 8-102(A) and 8-103 (reporting another lawyer's "dishonesty, deceit, or misrepresentation"), Brill wrote: "Fortenberry was obligated to speak up when Perkins lied. Instead, he said nothing to anyone." Brill went on to quote an unnamed "close associate" of Fortenberry's: "What happened to Joe was that he saw Perk [Perkins's nickname at the firm] lie and really couldn't believe it. And he had no idea what to do. I mean, he knew Perkins was lying, but he kept thinking that there must be a reason. Besides, what do you do? The guy was his boss and a great guy."

The remainder of Brill's piece was an examination of the pressures on associates at large law firms and the quandaries facing them if they see wrongdoing (a Fortenberry "situation"). He concluded with a quotation from Judge Frankel: "There isn't any way for an associate to handle that problem."

The Real Story: Telling the Firm

Not surprisingly, the conventional wisdom (à la Brill) is not quite the whole (and more interesting) story. It turns out that I was also an associate at Donovan Leisure at the time (I was a summer associate in 1976; I started full time on September 26, 1977). I knew the principals of this story. And since the time I started teaching professional responsibility at the Fordham School of Law in 1996, I have devoted one class session to reviewing this tragic episode. (I have also taught it in my Cornell law class since 2006.)

On January 12, 1978, a memo from Donovan Leisure's Executive Committee was directed to "All Associates and Paralegals." We were to assemble at 3 p.m. the following day (Friday the 13th) in the Belvedere Suite on the 64th Floor of 30 Rockefeller Plaza. The next day at the appointed hour, I saw (and heard) Samuel W. Murphy Jr. for the first time.

Murphy was the firm's preeminent litigator and a legendary figure in the bar. I had not seen him before because he had mostly been in Minnesota defending himself (and the firm) against a contempt citation issued by a federal judge because of Murphy's strong defense of his client, American Cyanamid (*see* Chapter II) (the reversal of that contempt citation remains the leading decision on opinion work product; *see In re Murphy*, 560 F.2d 326 (8th Cir. 1977)).

Murphy succinctly detailed the unfortunate events at the trial's end (John Doar, Kodak's lead trial counsel, had just delivered his summation on January 11; the jury, after deliberating for nine days, would return its verdict on January 22), Perkins's inexplicable conduct, that the firm was being advised by ex-federal judge Simon Rifkind (of Paul, Weiss), and that the firm was doing everything it could to protect Kodak's interests (Murphy reported that he had deployed fellow partner Kenneth N. Hart to rally the shell-shocked Donovan Leisure trial team). Fellow Executive Committee member John E. Tobin then sought to assure the stunned assemblage that the firm would survive this unfolding tragedy and that we would all be needed to continue to work hard to service the firm's stable of other clients. We then shuffled out silently and took the elevators back down to our offices.

The Real Story: Three Document Issues

Right after Perkins had told Stein in Peck's deposition that he had destroyed Peck's documents, there was another major document problem. John Doar, a partner of the firm, had shown Peck the four trial notebooks he intended to use for Peck's testimony; they included all the questions he intended to ask, as well as all the *answers* he expected to receive. When Doar revealed this to Stein, Stein objected (*see* Rule 612, F.R.E.), but Doar claimed those materials were attorney work product and need not be produced. Stein raised Doar's blunder to Magistrate Sol Schreiber, who ordered Doar to hand over the notebooks. Doar appealed that order to Judge Frankel. This led to a May 5, 1977, hearing, a session that quickly turned its focus onto

Perkins's "destruction" of the Peck documents. Frankel ordered Perkins to submit an affidavit about the "destruction"; and it was that affidavit that constituted the basis for Perkins' criminal conviction. It is more than ironic that Perkins's deposition outburst obscured Doar's huge mistake—a mistake, in and of itself, that undoubtedly would have destroyed Peck's testimony and credibility. Amazingly, the judge did not order Doar to produce the notebooks (74 F.R.D. 613), although, as a matter of law, it was/is not even a close call (*see* "Positively 4th Street: Lawyers and the 'Scripting' of Witnesses," *NY Business Law Journal* (Summer 2014)).

The second document issue involved a letter Peck had written to Donovan Leisure in November 1974, early on in his work for Kodak. In that document Peck told the firm he was unable to conclude (at that point in his work) that a 1915 antitrust consent decree entered into by Kodak was not a contributing factor to Kodak's subsequent market dominance. Although Magistrate Schreiber had ordered the production of all expert reports, including "interim" ones, the trial team did not consider Peck's 1974 letter as falling into the "interim" category. Fast forward to Peck's testimony in January 1978. With Doar questioning Peck on the reason(s) for Kodak's preeminent market position, Stein argued to Judge Frankel that he should be able to inquire about the 1915 consent decree. Frankel took the matter under advisement and said he would rule the following day. Overnight, Doar and his trial team dug up the 1974 Peck letter and decided if Frankel ruled in Stein's favor it would have to be produced.

The next morning, however, Frankel ruled that the 1915 decree was too remote in time and would be too prejudicial. But Stein formed a different way to attack, asking Peck whether he had generated any relevant work product before 1975. When Peck answered in the affirmative, Stein demanded it, and the document was produced. This turn of events had two critical consequences. First, it allowed Stein to blow up Peck before the jury. An unprepared Peck could not explain how the seemingly contradictory letter jibed with the opinion he had offered in response to Doar's questions. As one Donovan

Leisure lawyer recounted: "[Peck] was completely at sea. He looked like a fool, he sounded terrible, he wasn't answering properly, he wasn't making any sense." In short, it was the 1974 document that was the tipping point in Peck's destruction as a witness.

The second consequence was that an incensed Judge Frankel ordered Doar to produce an affidavit explaining why the 1974 letter had not been produced earlier and for another affidavit to be submitted on Perkins's "destruction" of the Peck documents. When Perkins could not bring himself to lie under oath a second time, he confessed to his earlier perjury. That then allowed Stein—on Peck's last day as a witness—to drop the other hammer down on the now hapless Peck, ending his cross-examination with questions about the "destroyed" documents and Perkins's perjury.

The third document issue is perhaps the most bizarre. The documents in the suitcase in Perkins's office had virtually all been produced to opposing counsel and, in any event, had no real substantive impact on the trial. Perkins had lied for no reason (or had he?).

Why Did Perkins Lie?

Perkins was the wrong man, for the wrong job, at the wrong time. The business model that Donovan had established for his firm was unique. He did not want the firm to be made up of generalists; rather, he wanted his partners to have niche specialties. Thus, for example, there would be certain partners whose only job was to be brilliant, creative geniuses; they would sit in their offices, ponder their partners' most difficult questions, and then come up with impossible solutions. There would be other partners who, although called litigators, never went to court; their specialty was brief writing. That was Perkins's niche (conversely, in Murphy's words: "[Perk] doesn't get up on his feet."). In fact, he was generally considered to be the firm's best writer.

So, what was a lawyer, who had no real experience in sharp-elbow trial practice, doing heading up the critical expert witness phase of the most important, hotly contested antitrust trial of the 1970s? Donovan Leisure had been stretched to the limit, not only by its obligations to Kodak but also by a whole host of other major, complex cases (indeed, that was the reason Murphy was unable to take the lead in Kodak, as the client initially desired). As such, Perkins, being a good team player, agreed to step in to help out on Kodak. While that was admirable on one level, he would be entering an arena which was not only a war zone but also one with which he had no experience or aptitude.

Then there was an obvious culture clash. Perkins was not only from a genteel, upper-class, establishment world, he was also the most gentle man in Donovan Leisure's partner ranks (while he was not really one of the firm's "most respected partners" on a professional level, Perk was in fact one of the most revered—hence, the shock to most of us that, of all the partners, he would be the one to act unlawfully). Stein, on the other hand, was a Brooklyn born, street-fighter type, with years of in-the-trenches trial experience. Thus, when Stein angrily demanded that Perkins immediately bend to his will in the heat of the moment, Perkins got his back up, snapped, and lost his way. As Perkins later said to Judge Frankel: "that answer came into my head for some reason at the deposition. I had not planned to make that answer; I don't believe that I had really considered it." But having crossed this fateful Rubicon in a heated instant, Perkins thought he was trapped and did not seek counsel or consider correcting his obvious misrepresentation(s).

What About Fortenberry?

It is important to understand who Joe Fortenberry really was. Contrary to Brill, Fortenberry was not "brilliant," "engaging," "enjoyable to work with," "a well-liked, personable genius"; moreover, he would not have made partner. Fortenberry was smart, but a loner, nerd type, who affected a quirky, professorial persona (he smoked a pipe, nicknamed himself "El Lagarto" (the alligator)), and regularly published law review articles on esoteric subjects (I remember one on "hirsute jurisprudence"). Fortenberry appeared to believe his future at the firm was in the creative genius niche.

As for the "situation" in which Fortenberry found himself, the evidence is not compelling. Fortenberry at the time, and for the rest of his life, categorically denied that he knew about Perkins's misconduct or that he had whispered in Perkins's ear at the deposition about the suitcase. And initially, Perkins avowed that he "did not discuss [the documents] with Mr. Fortenberry," and that "Mr. Fortenberry had no knowledge … of the contents of [Perkins's] affidavit." But later, in what appeared to be an attempt to help Fortenberry, Perkins suddenly remembered that "Mr. Fortenberry … whispered in my ear, something to the effect … 'You have forgotten about the suitcase.'" When told about Perkins's refreshed memory, Fortenberry was startled and thus began his categorical denials. Regardless, Fortenberry's career at the firm was thereafter under the black cloud of the Perkins's debacle and, until his "All Hands" departure memo on July 27, 1979, Fortenberry walked around the office a beaten man with glazed eyes. Notwithstanding, the firm helped him get a job in the Antitrust Division at the Justice Department in Washington. Fortenberry died a few years later of a heart attack; I believe it was of a broken heart.

The Fortenberry "Situation"

The associate quandary posed in Brill's article was actually directly teed up by *In the Matter of Kristian Peters*, M-2-238 (S.D.N.Y. April 10, 2008). In that case, Kristian Peters, a seasoned litigator and a (then) partner at a well-known New York City law firm, had received deposition transcripts covered by a protective order in a case before Judge Harold Baer. On the eve of Peters voluntarily dismissing the Southern District of New York action and seeking to file an identical suit in Boston, Judge Baer ordered the return of all documentation covered by the order. To forestall part of that return, Peters instructed a first-year associate to "scribble all over" unmarked deposition transcripts; she believed (wrongly) that by so "scribbling" on the transcripts they would be converted into attorney work product and thus not be subject to being returned. The associate promptly reported the instruction to senior members of the firm, which then launched an investigation.

This incident was brought to Judge Baer's attention and an evidentiary hearing was conducted. Peters testified her instruction was merely a "joke" or that she was being "facetious" or "sarcastic." Questioned by Judge Baer, however, the associate testified: "It was absolutely not in jest." Peters received a multiyear ban from practicing in the Southern District.

Postscript

Two associates at Donovan Leisure directly benefited from Perkins's departure: a good friend of mine received responsibility for Perkins's client, the 4As (the leading trade association for advertising agencies); and I received responsibility for Perkins's client, the National Board of the YWCA USA.

John Doar's public career (first in the Justice Department's Civil Rights Division, and later as Chief Counsel for the House Impeachment Committee for President Richard Nixon) had been exemplary, but he was not exempt from criticism within the firm and in the numerous public accounts of the *Kodak* trial and the Perkins's affair. Because it was Doar's first complex trial of any kind—let alone the most important antitrust trial of the 1970s—it is no surprise that things did not go as planned, and that hindsight could be especially tough. Finding himself increasingly isolated, Doar announced to the firm on December 22, 1978, that he was leaving Donovan Leisure effective January 2, 1979. In his "All Hands" memo, Doar wrote that he wanted to practice law "independently" and had made his decision "some time ago."

I was lucky to work on a number of matters with Sam Murphy and on many trials and appeals with Ken Hart (whose autographed picture is in my office). They were great lawyers, great mentors, and great men.

Each of the "All Hands" memos referenced herein (including Fortenberry's "El Lagarto" departure memo) is in my DLN&I file. At one point during my tenure at the firm I was assigned to Fortenberry's old office; I found it a comfortable place in which to work.

So what is the "real" lesson of the unfortunate Kodak episode? In my view it is the following: when (not if) you make a mistake under pressure, do not internalize the problem and double-down on it (like Perkins did); instead, seek good counsel from someone whose judgment you trust so you can rectify/mitigate the damage.

CHAPTER V

The Associate's Dilemma: Regulation U

In Chapter IV, I examined the dilemma purportedly faced by Joe Fortenberry in 1977 on what to do when he saw his boss/partner lie about documents. In that same time period, another associate was faced with a different dilemma involving his boss/partner, but this time it was me.

Bright Eyed and Bushy Tailed

It was late October 1977, and I had been at Donovan Leisure Newton & Irvine about three weeks. Donovan Leisure, at that time, was the fourth largest firm in New York City, and I was proud to be one of the 27 first-year associates at one of the country's leading litigation firms.

At the beginning of the month, the firm held a reception for the biggest group of incoming lawyers in its history at the University Club. In the club's historic Council Room we were individually introduced to George Leisure Sr.—the oldest living founding partner. Hard of hearing, Leisure had a junior partner standing next to him who fed him a morsel of information about each young lawyer. When it came to my turn, the junior partner, not so *sotto voce*, whispered: "This is Evan Stewart; he played tennis for Cornell." Leisure nodded, graciously shook my hand and said: "I understand you are a tennis player, Mr. Stewart. In my day, I used to play with Fred Perry [a three-time Wimbledon champion] when he was in New York." Suitably impressed with that factoid, I passed the baton to the next in line.

Work-wise, I was quickly given a variety of litigation assignments for various partners involving a number of firm clients. It was exciting and heady stuff. But one assignment proved to be something for which I was not prepared.

Regulation U

At 9:15 a.m. that late October day, I was sitting at my desk in the office I shared with another first-year when my phone rang. It was Roger Kapp. Kapp was a 41-year-old corporate partner, helping out on a litigation matter because it had an important securities component. He was a short, spark-plug built man with an impatient, type A personality; he used to punch the elevator button at 30 Rockefeller Plaza a dozen or more times on the theory that that would make the elevator appear more quickly.

"Evan," he said, "can you come to my office right away?" "Yes, sir," I replied. I walked down the corridor on the thirty-eighth floor to Kapp's office and found him at his desk with his head down reading some legal tome. I knocked on the door, and he looked up at me with no recognition, so I said: "Mr. Kapp, you called and said you wanted to see me." He gestured to me to sit in one of the chairs in front of his desk and began to speak: "I have been giving some thought to this case and have concluded that Regulation U is the key to winning it. Spend the day in the library and report back to me before 5:30 on why I am right." "Yes, sir," I replied, and left his office, just as Kapp was resuming the position in which I had found him.

I immediately went to the law library on the thirty-ninth floor and sought out the firm's long-time librarian, Al Borner. "Mr. Borner," I began, "I just left Mr. Kapp's office." "Uh-oh," he glumly replied. "Mr. Borner, he has asked me to do some research on Regulation U and I have no idea what that is!" He gently responded: "Not to worry,

The author at the time he was researching Regulation U

that is a regulation created by the Federal Reserve and the set of those regulations is in that alcove" (pointing to one not far from where we were standing). I thanked Borner for being so helpful (and kind), but he just shrugged and said that was his job ("and please call me Al").

And so I ploughed into learning about Regulation U, curious as to how it was going to win our case. Unfortunately, when I read the text of Regulation U, it appeared to have absolutely nothing to do with anything in the litigation. At that point, I was wondering how I had graduated from law school, let alone gotten a job at Donovan Leisure. With my father a Wall Street lawyer (and most of his friends the same), I had grown up with an ingrained belief that partners in leading New York City firms were, if not gods, certainly never wrong in their legal judgments. So, I concluded, I was clearly missing something—perhaps if I read some cases interpreting Regulation U that would make clear what Kapp had in mind. Nope, that did not clear things up.

Perhaps leading law reviews on Regulation U would provide the answer? Nope, no help there either. Perhaps Kapp meant Regulation V, or Regulation T, or some other regulation close to Regulation U? Nope, nope, and nope.

Reporting My Research

With 5:15 fast approaching, I realized I needed to go report to Kapp on my research. Once outside his office, I saw him in exactly the same position from earlier in the day. So I once again knocked on his door, and (once again) he looked up at me with no recognition. "Mr. Kapp," I began, "you asked me to report on Regulation U and its applicability to our case." "Oh, yes," he replied, "tell me why I am right and how it will win the case." "Well, actually, Mr. Kapp, I have spent the entire day reading everything I could on Regulation U, as well as the Federal Reserve regulations that surround that regulation, and none of them have any application to this case."

After I delivered my conclusion, Kapp gave me a look I have never forgotten: he looked at me as if I was the dumbest person he had ever encountered. Scowling, he said ominously, "Be in my office tomorrow at 9:15 and we will call someone who will tell me why I am right about Regulation U!"

Kapp then returned his head to the legal tome he was reading, signaling my dismissal.

An All-Nighter

Pure terror filled me as I shrank away from Kapp's door: my budding legal career was going to end in approximately 16 hours. Maybe if I went back to the library and redoubled my efforts I would see the light and understand how Regulation U really could save the day?

So, as the sun set over Manhattan, I pored over the same ground from earlier in the day. Not only did an epiphany not occur, but as midnight approached my mind started to hurt as not finding the "right" answer was causing me to hallucinate.

Finally, at 2 a.m., I decided I needed to go back to my apartment, shave and shower, put on a new suit, and (hopefully) return to the law library refreshed (and refortified by coffee) to unlock the mystery(ies) of Regulation U.

Back at the library at 4 a.m., I gave it my last, best shot: What was I missing? Why was I so stupid? What jobs could I get at McDonald's? Unfortunately, this did not do the trick, and like a condemned man on death row, I watched as the clock moved inexorably from 6 to 7 to 8 and then to 9. At 9:10, wondering how I was going to explain to my father that my legal career had lasted not even four weeks, I grimly headed down to face my executioner.

Facing My Executioner

At 9:14 I knocked on Kapp's door. He was still positioned as he had been the prior day. Again, he looked up at me with no recognition. "Mr. Kapp," I said with fear and trepidation, "you told me to report to you and you would call someone about Regulation U." Channeling the same look he had given me the prior afternoon, Kapp pointed at me and then to the chair in front of his desk next to his speaker phone: "You, sit there!" As I sat in the chair my mind flashed to a scene in *Thunderball*, when the Spectre miscreant is electrocuted, his chair goes down under the floor, and then returns empty and sizzling. There would be no report to my father; rather, my charred remains would forever be entombed in the bowels of 30 Rockefeller Plaza!

With his type A style, Kapp quickly hit many buttons on the speaker phone. After a few rings, a disembodied voice came on the box: "Hello." Now, I was just a minute or two from my execution. Kapp replied: "Bob, Roger Kapp here. Bob, this isn't a social call. I'm calling, Bob, because you are the world's expert on Regulation U. You know more about that regulation than any man alive. Let's face it, you wrote the book on Regulation U!" In reply, Bob said: "Well Roger, you are gilding the lily a bit, but yes, I do know a lot about Regulation U." Kapp jumped in: "And that's why I'm calling, so let me tell you about our situation." He then went on to give Bob a truly brilliant precis about the litigation, as you would expect from a Wall Street law firm partner. When he had finished, Kapp then asked, "And so, how does Regulation U win the case for us?"

Now, I had only seconds before the electricity would enter my body. My terror was only enhanced by the seemingly long delay Bob took before proving Kapp right and me the dumbest ex-first-year associate ever.

"Uh, Roger," Bob intoned, "Regulation U has nothing whatsoever to do with your case." A long silence then ensued. Finally, Kapp broke the silence: "Well, thanks a lot Bob. I owe you a lunch. Talk soon." Then Kapp hung up and his head returned down to the same position he had been in the day before. So there I sat. Was this a good moment for me? I was not so stupid: I had been right; I had given Kapp the correct conclusion. But, here was my boss/partner humiliated and proven wrong in front of (and by) some nobody first-year associate. Maybe I was not going to die immediately, but I did not think Kapp would be inviting me out to lunch anytime soon. After what seemed to be an eternity, with me sitting in the almost-death chair and Kapp with his head down reading his tome, I found enough of my voice to blurt out, "Is there anything else you would like me to do, Mr. Kapp?" "No!" And so I tiptoed out of his office.

Postscript

Kapp subsequently left Donovan Leisure to become the general counsel of one of the firm's major pharmaceutical clients. His tenure in that position was cut short when it was discovered he had engaged in a long-standing practice of pretending to be a doctor, calling hospitals, and ordering enemas for female patients. *See Frig v. Lenox Hill Hospital*, 167 Misc.2d 42, 676 N.Y.S. 2d 971 (Sup. Ct. 1995). The *New York Post* ran several articles about him, dubbing him "Doctor Enema." Apart from his legal troubles over that behavior, Kapp also was accused of improperly diverting trust funds over which he was the trustee. Shortly after this latter issue became public, Kapp committed suicide.

I never told any Donovan Leisure partners of my near death experience with Kapp until years after I had left the firm. At lunch with Ken Hart, with whom I had worked closely on many matters over many years, something led to my recounting the foregoing story to my mentor. With his jaw out at half-mast during most of my retelling, Ken just shook his head when I finished: "I guess I now know why Kapp never liked you."

CHAPTER VI

The Associate's Dilemma: Obeying Dumb Orders

In the prior two chapters, I examined two serious dilemmas facing associates at large law firms. Now I will look at another real-life dilemma of an associate (me), this time feeling obligated to obey a really stupid order of his boss and the improbable consequences that flowed therefrom.

At the Beginning

Ralston "Shorty" Irvine had been then-Colonel William "Wild Bill" Donovan's protégé in the Antitrust Division under President Calvin Coolidge, and he had later been present at the creation of Donovan Leisure Newton & Irvine in 1929. Ultimately, Irvine came to head the firm and was principally responsible for some of the firm's most important clients, including Mobil Oil and Disney. With respect to Disney, Irvine's relationship with Walt Disney was such that Walt Disney delayed the opening of Disneyland by one day to accommodate Irvine's schedule.

Beyond handling Disney's antitrust work and the stealth buying of land in the Orlando area in advance of Disney World, the firm also branched out into the tax field for its client. Under the brilliant leadership of John Baity, the head of the firm's tax department, Donovan Leisure had crafted a strategy whereby Disney reaped such a humongous tax benefit on its used film stock that it warranted a footnote

1982 Donovan Leisure Christmas Dinner
(author's collection)

explanation in the federal budget! This landmark achievement did not go unnoticed by the other film studios; soon Baity and Donovan Leisure had been asked by other studio clients to perform similar miracles. And those developments then led Donovan Leisure to be the first major New York City firm to open a branch in the City of Angels.

Initially, the L.A. office had a small permanent staff. To make do on various matters, a few New York City associates were shuttled in for stints; in 1979, I spent approximately five very enjoyable months in Los Angeles. As I was wrapping up my tour of duty, the head partner in L.A. asked me if I wanted to stay full time; while I was flattered, I wanted to get back to New York and (I think) I politely declined.

Fast Forward to 1983

Four years later, I was now a sixth-year associate and fairly seasoned by dint of, *inter alia*, having worked on a number of significant antitrust matters. During a lull in one complex, multi-district litigation, I was pulled onto a new tax litigation initiated by Baity in Los Angeles on behalf of a major Hollywood studio. Interestingly, Baity's opposite number was Martin Ginsburg (Ruth Bader Ginsburg's spouse).

While Baity was the lead partner, another partner was responsible for the day-to-day operation of the case: Richard Sayler. Dick, who had been at the top of his class at Michigan Law School, went on to clerk for Whizzer White. His niche in the Donovan Leisure partnership was to ponder great issues and come up with brilliant solutions; he could usually be found in his office smoking a pipe and looking profound. In light of the foregoing, most (if not all) of the practical litigation work fell to me. A second-year associate (a former Supreme Court clerk) was added to the team to do "brilliant" tax research.

On to L.A.

As the case moved into high gear, the team left New York for Los Angeles. The highlight of my flight was sitting across the aisle from Jessica Lange, who had just won the Best Supporting Actress Oscar for *Tootsie* (while having also lost the Best Actress Oscar for *Francis*). Halfway through the flight I summoned up enough courage to walk over and clumsily offer my kudos for her affecting performance in *Francis* (she smiled and said "thank you," but seemed relieved that I quickly went back to my seat).

Ensconced in the Bonaventure Hotel in downtown L.A. near the office (it featured prominently in the Clint Eastwood classic *In the Line of Fire*), the team was working 14-hour days in preparation for a critical court appearance. Late one afternoon, Dick came into my office and said the team had been working really hard; we should take the night off and go to a fancy restaurant: "Evan, you know all the hot spots in L.A., pick one!" And so I did, making a reservation for the three of us at the best restaurant in Venice Beach.

From downtown L.A. to Venice Beach is a bit of a hike, but we three piled into my rental car at 7 p.m. and headed out. Forty-five minutes later, we arrived; I checked the car with the valet, and we strolled in on time for our reservation. The pretentious maître d' escorted us to our table, which was against the far wall, in a line of banquette arranged, cozy setups. Dick immediately ordered a martini (since I was responsible for getting us home, I did very little imbibing that night).

By the time Dick was on his second martini, it became clear that the banquette right behind me (just over my shoulder) held the most famous leading man in the movies at that time—first, because of the great success of *10* and, right on its heels, the mega success of *Arthur*. Four feet away, Dudley Moore was having dinner with his girlfriend, actress Susan Anton. They made a highly improbable looking couple: Moore was not a dashing, handsome matinee idol type (indeed, he was only five feet three—on a good day), while Anton was a stunning, Nordic goddess, who towered over him at six-feet tall (without heels). How did we know it was them? Because even in this very fancy, very expensive restaurant numerous patrons were constantly interrupting their dinner, shouting out "Hey, Arthur," and verbalizing various familiar lines from the *Arthur* movie.

A "Great" Idea

Now on his fourth (or fifth) martini, Dick slurred out words I have never forgotten: "Evan, I have a great idea!" He went on: "You know a lot about wine. Go order a fancy bottle and have it delivered to them with your business card. We'll probably land him as a client!" Oh boy, I thought to myself, what a really stupid idea. But to Dick, I said: "You bet, I'll be right back."

I immediately hightailed it over to the sommelier and asked for the wine list. He happily supplied it and I said this would not take long. Not knowing whether Moore and Anton were having fish or meat, I mentally crossed off red and white wines. Accordingly, I went to the champagne section of the list and quickly hit upon a vintage Dom Pérignon. I told the sommelier that I was ordering the Dom Pérignon and that it should be delivered promptly to the nice people seated right next to us who had been constantly interrupted and bothered by other patrons all during their dinner; and I also asked the sommelier to have my card accompany the champagne.

Returning to the table, a semiconscious Dick anxiously awaited. I assured my boss/partner that all was taken care of: I had ordered something that would surely impress the Hollywood big shots! After five minutes, however, nothing had arrived; and after ten, still nothing. Dick was onto his umpteenth martini and seemingly not too focused on the issue, but I was starting to get concerned.

Have you ever had that feeling in the back of your head that someone is staring at you? Well, I started to get that feeling, and my eyes slowly turned to my left and out toward the middle of the restaurant. There was a table about 10 to 15 feet away, and I saw an ice chest. Going higher, I saw the top of a vintage Dom Pérignon bottle in the chest. Going higher still, I saw two couples who had just been seated. In their hands were four champagne glasses, and they were toasting me for the wonderful gift a stranger had bestowed upon them!

Leaping to my feet I sped toward the sommelier. I told him of his obvious mistake and the need to *immediately* rectify it. Huffily, he informed me that that would not be possible. Not wanting to see my career derailed by such a screwup, I turned on my "I'm a New York lawyer" persona and detailed the various legal weapons at my disposal to render him and his restaurant naked, homeless, and without wheels. After a bit more back and forth along those lines, the sommelier ultimately relented and said he would bring another bottle of vintage champagne to Moore and Anton. With my blood pressure dropping back somewhat to normal, I returned to our banquette.

I had hardly caught my breath when the sommelier appeared. He had offered the champagne to our neighbors (the right ones), but they were just finishing their dinner and were not interested in champagne at that point. "Well," I replied, "could you see if they would like an after-dinner drink? Whatever they'd like!" It turned out that that was just fine by them, especially since this Venice Beach restaurant had one of the most extensive cellars of old, exotic liquors in California. And so Moore and Anton selected two after-dinner liquors that predated California's admission to the Union (and which cost a multiple of the Dom Pérignon).

As they were enjoying these priceless drinks, Susan Anton knelt on her seat and leaned over my shoulder to thank me for the tasty treats. Looking into her stunning face I said: "You wouldn't believe what I've had to go through to get those to you!" "Really?" she said: "Why don't you come over and tell us?" So I stood up and slipped into the neighboring banquette next to Moore and Anton. As I gave them a blow-by-blow recap of the "great" idea run amok, they broke into sustained laughter—they thought it was all hilarious! After I concluded, and we seemed to be on friendly terms, I asked Moore for a small favor. "Sure," he replied. "Well, you can do whatever you want with it, but I have to be able to tell my boss I gave you my business card. Would you be offended?" "Not at all," he graciously said, "who knows, maybe I'll need you some day." With that, I thanked them both, wished them a pleasant rest of the evening, and took my leave back to our banquette. "Dick," I told my sleepy boss, "mission accomplished." He smiled wanly, and then—as Moore and Anton left—we finished our dinner. Once we were done, I told my younger colleague that his job was to get Dick up and out of the restaurant and into my rental car; I would join them as soon as I had settled our debt(s) to the restaurant.

Are You European?

After I was sure that our tab did not include any Dom Pérignon, I calculated a generous tip and prepared to steel myself for the lengthy drive back to the hotel. But as I made my way across the restaurant an extremely attractive young lady walked up to me and asked: "Excuse me, are you European?" Mr. Smooth, instead of replying "mais oui," awkwardly stuttered: "Um, er, ah, no, I'm from New York." Unfazed, the woman pointed to the bar area and said: "My two friends [also quite attractive] and I were wondering if you and your friends would like to join us for a drink?" Never at a loss for witty repartee, Mr. Smooth responded: "I don't know. Let me check with my friends." With that, I quickly exited the restaurant where I found the rental car all set to leave, with Dick slumped in the shotgun seat and my younger colleague in the back. "Dick," I said in a fairly loud voice with my hand resting on his right shoulder, "there are three very attractive women in the bar who would like to have a drink with us. What should I tell them?" It was like a light switch had been tripped: Dick sat up straight and, with clear eyes and a steady voice, gave me our marching orders: "Let's go!"

So back inside we went, where we chatted up these lovely L.A. ladies for about two hours. It was never made clear to me, but I am pretty sure they had witnessed my interchange with Moore and Anton and assumed we were movie industry people who might be able to help them with their careers. In any event, after we had exhausted whatever topics we shared in common, we bade our new friends adieu, and once more Dick was helped out to the rental car. My memory is that we got back to the Bonaventure circa 2:45 a.m. Truly, a night to remember!

Postscript

Two Donovan Leisure alumni have served as Disney's general counsel: Joe Shapiro and Sandy Litvack (and numerous other alumni have served Disney in a variety of other capacities).

Outside of Irvine's office were a number of original "cels" from famous Disney animation movies. One day his secretary saw me admiring them. "Would you like one?" she asked. "Would I? Yes, ma'am!" Giving me my pick, I selected a cel from "Dumbo," with Walt Disney's autograph on the matting. Out of all the things I have acquired or collected over my lifetime, the "Dumbo" cel is the only thing my daughter wants.

CHAPTER VII

How to Handle Your First Pro Bono Matter?

As explained in prior chapters, there are many challenges that young associates at large firms must confront and overcome. In this chapter, another will be addressed: How does a novice lawyer handle his or her first pro bono case, where he or she is flying solo?

After I passed my Character and Fitness interview (which consisted of an elderly gentleman taking one look at my file and, upon seeing that I was at Donovan Leisure Newton & Irvine, standing up to shake my hand, saying, "Anyone good enough for Owen McGivern [legendary New York First Department jurist and then "of counsel" to Donovan Leisure] is good enough for me!") and was admitted to the bar, one of my top priorities was to take on some pro bono work. Although I was challenged and excited to be working for the firm's blue chip-paying clients, the work for someone at my level on the food chain tended to be (for the most part) doing legal research and reviewing lots and lots of documents. But with pro bono assignments, I could actually interact with clients, and maybe even try a case on my own (just like Perry Mason)!

And so I asked some sage veteran of the firm (a third-year associate) how to go about getting one of those plum assignments. I was told that the firm had a well-established pro bono program, and that the program was headed by a senior associate named Doris K. Shaw.

Doris, as I would later learn, was a fearsome personage. She was so tough that many of the firm's partners were scared of her. But when

I knocked on her door and introduced myself, she seemed quite pleasant and prepared to help me take this big step on becoming a "real" lawyer. She explained the firm's program, its connection to the Legal Aid Society, how the firm was assigned cases, and her oversight responsibility. All that sounded great to me, and so I asked her how I might get in the queue. Doris told me she would be back to me in short order with an appropriate assignment.

My First Case!

About a week later Doris called and told me that the Legal Aid Society had sent on a new matter that, if I was interested, I could work on. "I'll be right there," I replied, and hot-footed it to her office. Doris handed me the file and wished me luck.

Back in the office I shared with another first-year associate, I excitedly scanned the materials by which I would start to make my reputation as the lawyer of first and last resort. It was not what I expected. The matter was a criminal prosecution brought on by the Manhattan District Attorney's office against a middle-aged man with a Hispanic surname (for purposes of this article, he will be identified as Mr. Rodriguez). Mr. Rodriquez was accused of public indecency on a New York City subway—specifically, rubbing up against a woman who was unknown to him. This did not sound promising (did Edward Bennett Williams get his start on such cases?!).

Undeterred, I next went to the firm's law library to dig into the charge against *my* client and see what (if anything) I could find that would help me defend the case. Once I felt fairly comfortable with the legal side of things, I steeled myself and called Mr. Rodriguez at the telephone number in the Legal Aid file. On the third ring, a male voice answered. I identified myself and told Mr. Rodriguez that I had been assigned to represent him. He seemed grateful to have a young, hard-charging advocate on his side. We then arranged for him to come to the firm's offices at 30 Rockefeller Place to discuss his defense.

When Mr. Rodriguez arrived the following week, he was dressed in a suit and seemed a highly unlikely defendant of the crime for which he stood accused. Middle-aged and fairly nondescript (with a neatly trimmed mustache), *my* client greeted me with a firm handshake; I then escorted him to one of the firm's lavishly decorated conference rooms for our initial interview. During this meeting (and at each succeeding session in preparation for his defense), Mr. Rodriguez strongly protested his innocence. He had a responsible job at a bank in Harlem; he was happily married and had wonderful children. This charge was a blot on his impeccable reputation and he wanted to go to trial (if necessary) to clear his good name. I assured *my* client (then and thereafter) that I would vigorously defend his honor with every weapon at my disposal and would (of course) advocate his innocence at every opportunity. Together, we then started to map out a strategy for vindicating his good name, including him getting me a list of strong witnesses to attest to his upstanding character.

A Court Date

After several such sessions with *my* client, I felt prepared for the notification to appear at Centre Street for a settlement conference. This would be my first time (as a real lawyer) in court!

Together with Mr. Rodriguez (who was required by the notification to attend), we made our way to the vast forum for such events (later, I would learn that these were usually referred to as "cattle calls"). With hundreds of other lawyers (and their clients), we sat in the huge courtroom awaiting the clerk to call our case. Finally, we heard "People versus Rodriguez"—"counsel for the People?" (a female voice from far away answered "present"); "counsel for Rodriguez?" (I heard myself peep out "present"). "Will counsel please approach?"

Leaving Mr. Rodriguez, I made my way up to the clerk's station. There I met the Assistant District Attorney, a woman who was clearly a more senior member of the bar. The clerk instructed us to talk and report back when we were ready to speak with the judge. My adversary started by asking was I ready to discuss the terms of a settlement? "Oh no," I replied: "*My* client is innocent, and we are prepared to go to trial to vindicate his good name!"

She looked at me like I was the dumbest person she had yet to come across. "Go to trial?" she responded: "Are you kidding me? Do you know what kind of evidence we have?"

That did not sound good, so I asked her to share it with me. "Well, for starters, he has prior convictions for the same conduct. Plus, I have two police officers who were eye-witnesses and are ready to testify." At that point, I do not know whether my adversary saw my Adam's apple move and heard my big gulp, but suddenly it was clear that my best laid plans were not looking so good.

Notwithstanding, she went on to explain that if *my* client would agree to a number of mandatory items, including psychological counseling, the D.A.'s office would agree to a suspended sentence with no jail time. I responded that I would have to check with *my* client and I would get back to her promptly.

I made my way across the packed courtroom to meet with Mr. Rodriguez, who anxiously asked me: "How did it go?" "Well, the D.A.'s office will agree to no jail time if...." Mr. Rodriguez interjected: "Agreed!" "But don't you want to hear the rest?" I asked. And while I dutifully recited the other items that were part of the deal, *my* client had clearly checked out once he was assured he would not be prison bound.

Later that day, I was back at the firm and I ran into Doris, who knew I was going to be in court. "How did it go?" She asked with genuine interest. "Sorta mixed," I replied: "I got a really good settlement for *my* client with no jail time, but it is clear to me that he had been lying to me all this time about his innocence!" Doris looked at me with a look I still remember 48 years later, paused and said (with words I have also not forgotten): "I guess you just don't have what it takes to be a lawyer."

Postscript

Notwithstanding Doris Shaw's disdainful look and comment, I did go on to do a few other pro bono turns while I was with the firm.

In *McGuiness v. Jakubiak*, 106 Misc.2d 317, 431 N.Y.S.2d 755 (Sup. Ct. Kings Co. 1980), I represented the family of a young secretary at the firm who sued their landlord for extensive water damage in their apartment caused by roof leakage. That case made new law when our motion for summary judgment was granted based on a breach of the implied warranty of habitability (RPL § 235-b). *See Bender's Forms: Real Property Law* Section 235-b (Form 3).

As part of a program initiated by the Manhattan District Attorney, several large firms agree to "volunteer" associates to serve (in their "free time") as Special Assistant District Attorneys. In that role, I briefed, argued, and won several appeals in the First Department. Somewhere, in the bowels of the D.A.'s files, is a picture of me and a few other, eager beavers being sworn in by Robert Morgenthau.

I subsequently represented a Sing Sing inmate who prosecuted a § 1983 Civil Rights claim against the prison warden. After a four-day trial before Judge Leonard B. Sand, the jury awarded my client damages and punitive damages. Thereafter, Judge Sand awarded my attorney's fee application in full ($49,047). *See New York Law Journal* (July 14, 1986); *Attorney Fee Awards Reporter* (Vol. 9, No. 4) (August 1986).

CHAPTER VIII

Ken Hart: Extraordinary Lawyer, Legal Mentor, and Good Friend

Kenneth Nelson Hart was a great man; and he had a profound impact on my professional career and my life. Born to modest circumstances in Rhode Island, Ken attended Colby College, where he excelled academically. Thereafter he joined the Marines, where he served as a master sergeant—because of his imposing visage (he was six feet four (plus) and approximately 240 pounds), his picture was used on Marine Corps recruiting posters. Upon his honorable discharge, Ken enrolled at Boston University Law School, where he graduated first in his class. That accomplishment made him eligible for the U.S. Justice Department's Honors Program, where he served with distinction in the Antitrust Division for several years. Upon completing that program, Ken considered numerous attractive job options, ultimately agreeing to Ralston "Shorty" Irvine's request that he join one of the country's leading litigation firms: Donovan Leisure Newton & Irvine.

At Donovan Leisure, Ken worked for and with many of the firm's legendary litigators, including Walter Mansfield and Sam Murphy. Ken's intelligence, work ethic, good judgment, even temperament, and sense of humor earned him the respect and affection of colleagues and clients alike. Over the course of Ken's exemplary career, his clients would include Pfizer, Kodak, American Cyanimid, and the Penn Central Transportation Company.

My first exposure to Ken came as a result of his administrative task at the firm in the late 1970s: giving out substantive assignments to associates. As was his want, Ken would invariably end up his assigning some onerous task with a cheerful: "This will be a good experience for a young lawyer."

Off to Boston

My first real work with Ken was on an important criminal antitrust case that was going to trial in federal court in Boston. We were faced with an uphill job. Our client was a major, international conglomerate that had acquired a leading manufacturer of industrial screws several years before (as a stand-alone company, it had been called the Southern Screw Company—some "wit" had had business cards printed up with the logo: "There's no screw like a Southern Screw"). The screw industry in the United States at that time was under enormous pressure from foreign competitors. As a result, the trade association for the industry had not played fair under our antitrust laws. The association was led by a former FBI agent who convened meetings in Bermuda, where he assured company representatives it was permissible to discuss and agree on prices. To make matters worse, the case was assigned to Chief Judge Andrew Caffrey—an Irish politician turned judge, who was legendary for his temper (he was twice appealed to the First Circuit for prejudicial facial expressions made during testimony).

On the first day of jury selection, the judge assembled 70 potential jurors in his courtroom. Caffrey, whose flaming red hair of his youth had turned snow white, explained the nature of the case and said that it would likely take four weeks to try. Leaning over the bench, the judge sternly asked: "Will any of you have any difficulty serving for that long?" The large group, intimidated by the setting and the imposing judge, was silent … until one elderly gentleman in the back row meekly raised his hand. Caffrey leaned further over the bench and with an even more menacing stare intoned: "What would your problem be, sir?" The old gentleman squeaked out: "I have an ear appointment in two weeks." In response, Caffrey even more intensely probed: "And will that prevent you from serving on this jury?!" To that came the quiet reply: "What?" With the entire courtroom erupting in laughter, and with his face now scarlet vermillion and the veins on his neck visibly pulsing, Judge Caffrey screamed out: "You're excused!"

That singular light moment did not change the daunting assignment we faced. After two days of trying to see how we could possibly put on a defense through our client's principal witness, Ken worked out a *nolo* plea agreement with the Justice Department lawyers. The other defendants did not pursue that same path, however, and (not surprisingly) were found guilty of price-fixing by the jury.

Iron Ore Litigation

My next important job for Ken was in representing the Penn Central Transportation Company in a series of cases that went on for many years, and became known as the *Iron Ore Antitrust Litigation* (*see* 42 B.R. 657 (E.D. Pa. 1984); 771 F.2d 762 (3d Cir. 1985); 1982-83 Antitrust Trade Cases (CCH) ¶¶ 65,054 and 65,608 (N.D. Ohio 1983)). For our first pretrial conference in Cleveland before Judge William Thomas, we flew out the day before to meet with our local counsel, a leading partner at the Jones Day firm. He told us that Thomas was an old-school gentleman who put a particular premium on courtroom decorum; one insight I will never forget was the fact that Thomas took great umbrage at lawyers putting their briefcases on counsel tables in the courtroom.

Opposing us (and the litany of co-counsel representing the other co-defendants) was the plaintiff's lead counsel, Lawrence R. Velvel of Howrey & Simon. Velvel, as we would soon learn, was an intelligent and aggressive lawyer, but one who also had an extremely abrasive temperament that often did not serve him or his client (a dock company that transported iron ore to the railroads from the

Great Lakes) well. As the large group assembled in the majestic courtroom in downtown Cleveland, Judge Thomas entered to greet us. Before we could sit down, the first thing Thomas said (in a booming voice) was (to Velvel): "Get that briefcase off the table!" It was an auspicious beginning to many years of tough sledding.

And it did not take long to find that out. In the first deposition—which concerned Penn Central's production of documents—it got testy, very early. Ken objected to a question that began with the prologue: "As I understand it." Velvel jumped in: "You can continue if you wish with that kind of belaboring . . . , but I will tell you, sir, that you will pay for that." Just minutes later Velvel reacted to another objection: "Mr. Hart. . . ." Ken cut him off with: "You're not going to threaten me again with 'you'll pay,' are you?" Velvel: "Well, I think before the case is over you're probably going to write a very large check, Mr. Hart." Hart: "Mr. Hart is not going to write a very large check, Mr. Velvel. I have eight children to support. I will tell you right now, I am very fond of you, Larry. . . ." Velvel: "I only have two, three."

When Velvel then pressed his argument to Judge Thomas that Penn Central was hiding the ball in discovery, he again did not get off to a great start. When the judge asked how many copies of a key document should be made, Velvel answered: "I suppose about seven or eight copies, what we normally use, your Honor." Thomas replied: "[M]ake seven. We don't want this to be indefinite, like the number of children you have, Mr. Velvel. You said two or three."

The next step in the case (for me) was an assignment to go off to a document warehouse, review the millions of documents therein, collect all the "hot" documents, and then write up a fact memorandum that would be the "bible" for the duration of the case. When I asked Ken how long I should expect to be away on this project, he smiled and said: "until you're done." And, of course, he added: "This will be a good experience for you." And you know what, he was right!

Later came the substantive part of discovery: depositions of the key witnesses. Our co-counsel deferred to Ken, and he was asked to depose the CEO of Velvel's client, Maynard Walker. I came along to assist Ken with the "hot" documents (and whatever else he needed me to do). This was in the era of multiple-day depositions (or even weeks); and so we headed to Washington for the long haul within the D.C. offices of Howrey & Simon. In that one week I learned from watching Ken an enormous amount, both in substantive experience and how to conduct yourself as a professional.

Early on, Velvel was up to obstructionistic behavior. First, he objected to a question: "No foundation is laid." Ken calmly replied: "I didn't know you had to have a foundation for questions for a deposition. You may answer." Then Velvel objected: "Mr. Hart, what is the purpose of this line of question?" Ken (again) calmly replied: "I don't think I need to tell you what the purpose is. If you want to object on some ground recognized by the Rules of Civil Procedure, the record can so show." After Walker had difficulty estimating how much time he had spent preparing for his deposition, Ken said: "Why don't you try your best. I am sure being with Mr. Velvel every day is memorable." Velvel: "If only women thought the same thing, Mr. Hart." Hart: "I have been told a lot of them do." Velvel: "I wish to put on the record, Mr. Hart, I would certainly like to know your source of information." Hart: "That's privileged information. I have been instructed not to go any further."

As the deposition dragged on—and as Ken was eliciting favorable testimony for our promising statute of limitations defense—things got even more testy. Now, Velvel weighed in as follows: "Mr. Walker, I instruct you not to be browbeaten." Hart: "Don't be browbeaten, Mr. Walker." Walker: "That is a long hose you have."

Then Ken showed Walker a document and asked him to review it in advance of some questions. Velvel objected. Ken asked: "On what grounds?" Velvel responded that it was improper interrogation because it was a document neither authored by nor seen by Walker. At that point Ken stood up (all six feet four (plus)), leaned over the conference table (which meant he was towering over the elderly, diminutive Walker), and said in a commanding voice: "I can use a baseball bat, if I want to, to refresh Mr. Walker's memory!" This was

Ken Hart and the author, December 1985
(author's collection)

(and is) of course precisely so (and the image of the cowering Walker has never faded from my memory).

Toward the end of the deposition, Velvel's objections became even more fanciful—at one point he tried to cut off questioning because the "document speaks for itself." Hart: "That is why we are taking the deposition to get some information that is in Mr. Walker's head. If we had to look at the documents, Mr. Velvel, we could all go home. I can read these in my library in a nice comfortable chair with a fire going and my feet up and my good dog Ralph by my side." Velvel: "Tell me something, Mr. Ralph, . . ." The following day, Velvel went on the record to say he had not called Ken "Mr. Ralph." Ken replied: “I was just going to say that my dog Ralph was so offended that you called me by his name, and I thought that was probably a Freudian slip, that you think I am really a dog, Larry.” Velvel: “No sir; now whatever I may think I did not say, “Tell me, Mr. Ralph.”

A Lanham Act War

During a brief lull in the never-ending *Iron Ore* odyssey, Ken and I took on a new challenge. The New England Educational Institute (NEEI) had a temporary restraining order application filed against it by Yeshiva University in the Southern District. Yeshiva, which had run a summer vacation program for mental health professionals on Cape Cod for years, was extremely upset that NEEI had established a competitive program (also on Cape Cod). As such, Yeshiva initiated a Lanham Act prosecution aimed at shutting NEEI's program down.

Hired to deal with the temporary restraining order, Ken devised a not obvious, but brilliant, plan of attack. Rather than defend on the merits, we would take a dive and negotiate (using the good offices of the judge assigned to the case—Leonard Sand) a means to resolve any “confusion” that might exist between subscribers to the two programs. In the end we mailed registered letters to the hundreds of subscribers to the NEEI program, explaining the situation and offering them the opportunity (if they had been “confused”) to re-register in Yeshiva's program. The end result: two psychiatrists switched programs.

We thought that would be the end of it; but Yeshiva wanted its pound of flesh. And so we ultimately went to trial for a week before Judge Sand and a jury. Two highlights remain (for me). The first was my cross-examination of the plaintiff's expert on his survey “evidence,” which purported to reflect vast “confusion” on the part of the “validly” surveyed mental health professionals concerning the two programs. And while I thought I had done a good job, it paled in comparison to Ken's cross-examination of the plaintiff's expert on damages.

The plaintiff had hired the Dean of the NYU Graduate School to come up with a Rube Goldberg–like structure which resulted in monetary damages in the high seven figures (a lot of money in 1985). But after Ken spent time deconstructing the Dean's work, what he demonstrated on cross-examination was that (according to the Dean) *every year after* the registered letters had been sent the level of "confusion" as to the two programs (for some of the smartest people in America) would actually *increase*—thus, the "confusion" by year ten would be *ten times* worse than year one!

Following this vivisection, we asked Judge Sand to strike the Dean's testimony (and supporting evidence) in toto. Aware of what he had just seen, but reluctant to impose such a drastic sanction, the judge (outside the presence of the jury) admonished the Dean to reconsider his testimony and come back the next day with something more defensible. But when the next trial day began, the Dean dug in and would not change his story. Judge Sand, cutting the plaintiff a lot of slack, then told the jury to disregard *only* years three through ten of the Dean's damages model. Regardless, and needless to say, we prevailed at trial. *See* 229 USPQ 849 (March 13, 1986).

The Haunted House

The firm was retained to handle the appeal of an adverse antitrust ruling from a trial that had taken place in Oklahoma. To get a realistic understanding of what had happened (as well as to assess our client's chances on appeal), Ken and I flew to Oklahoma City. Arriving at the best hotel in town, I asked for restaurant recommendations. The Haunted House was the unanimous favorite, so I booked us there for our first night. It was a night to remember.

After we sat down to dinner, Ken ordered his usual cocktail and I had a glass of wine. Once we had refreshed both of our drinks we ordered the restaurant's specialty: sirloin steak with all the trimmings. When our meals arrived they certainly appeared to live up to their billing, so we dug in. As I was enjoying my steak I glimpsed across the table and saw something I had never seen—Ken had turned ashen and had a look of total fear on his face! "You're choking, aren't you?" I immediately asked. Ken nodded. "Stand up!" I ordered. So here I was up against Ken's back with my arms around his chest, feeling his large but slack body (and life) in my hands. I had never done the Heimlich maneuver before, but I started pounding his lower chest with all my might. Fortunately, within just a few poundings the large chunk of steak that had lodged in Ken's throat flew out of his mouth and on to the Haunted House's floor.

Both of us—for related but somewhat different reasons—sat back down with huge sighs of relief. Ken was, of course, grateful; but I was still somewhat shocked that I had reacted so quickly and effectively to save my boss's (and friend's) life. As we finished our dinner (making sure we cut each piece of steak into very small bites), I explained that my maternal grandmother had died under the same circumstances because she had been eating alone.

The End of Ken's Career

By odd timing, Ken was becoming head of Donovan Leisure just as I was leaving the firm. He had a big job ahead of him because a number of senior partners had recently jumped ship. By all accounts he did a fine job in calming the waters, but then fate intervened. Carol, his beloved wife (and mother of their eight children), was diagnosed with an extremely serious degenerative disease. As a result, Ken had to spend a considerable amount of time caring for her, especially as Carol's condition worsened. Always looking for a bright spot, Ken took over all cooking duties and ultimately published in 1994 *Home Cooking of the Hart Family* (a copy of which is in my office). Not long after, Carol died and Ken retired to his summer residence in Rhode Island. On December 24, 2014, Ken Hart died peacefully, surrounded by his family. Ken's son, Kevin (a noted antitrust lawyer in the federal government), called me to share the sad news at the express request of his father.

Ken and I stayed in close touch after I left the firm; and he took a strong interest in the professional milestones of my career. Every day in my office I look at his picture and draw strength from all my wonderful memories of that very special man.

CHAPTER IX

The Most Publicized Trial in History, and the Case with Perhaps the Most Legal Errors

Certainly every person who was *compos mentis* in America remembers his or her reaction when a Los Angeles jury, on October 3, 1995, acquitted O.J. Simpson of the murders of his ex-wife, Nicole Brown Simpson, and her friend, Ronald Goldman, at Simpson's ex-wife's home on June 12, 1994. The entire eight-month trial had been broadcast on television, with breathless 24/7 media commentary.

O.J. Simpson was a charismatic Hall of Fame football player turned actor. Knowing he was going to be arrested for the brutal double murders, Simpson had fled in a white Bronco, owned and driven by his friend A.C. Cowlings. Spotted on the Los Angeles freeways, the Bronco was soon converged upon by the city's police department.

Cowlings warned them not to do anything precipitous, shouting: "Put away your guns. He's in the back seat, and he's got a gun to his head." That led to an hours' long, freeway parade of the Bronco being followed by a string of police department squad cars in its wake—a spectacle that was broadcast live across the country and watched by an estimated audience of 95 million people.

During the "chase," a note just written by Simpson was publicly disclosed by a friend of his; it concluded with: "Don't feel sorry for me. I've had a great life, great friends. Please think of the real O.J. and not this lost person. Thanks for making my life special. I hope I helped yours."

Ultimately, the "chase" ended back at Simpson's home, with Simpson surrendering and saying: "I'm sorry, guys. The only person who deserves to be hurt is me." Inside the Bronco was Simpson's travel bag, in which was found his passport, a fake goatee and mustache, a supply of fresh clothes, and a fully loaded Smith & Wesson handgun. In addition, Cowlings had $8,750 in cash, which he said was Simpson's.

The Evidence

Simpson's conduct, his note, and his statement upon arrest all seemed to indicate consciousness of guilt. What else pointed to him being the murderer? Only, among other things, the following:

1. There was a long pattern of domestic abuse by Simpson on his wife: between 1985 and 1988, the police had been called to Simpson's home eight times (on one of them his wife was in a car, crying, with the windshield having been smashed by a baseball bat–wielding Simpson). In 1989, a 911 call brought police again to the house, where they found Nicole Simpson, who emerged from the bushes, with her lips cut and bleeding, a black-and-blue left eye, and a clear hand imprint on her neck ("He's going to kill me! He's going to kill me!") (for this incident, Simpson pled "no contest" to a misdemeanor of spousal abuse). In October 1993 (less than eight months before her murder), Nicole Simpson made another 911 call—while she pleaded for 13 minutes for the police to come, Simpson (who had broken down his ex-wife's door to gain entrance) was recorded as saying: "I'm leaving with my two fists is when I'm leaving."). And on June 7, 1994, five days before her murder, Nicole Simpson called the Sojourn Battered Women's Shelter in Santa Monica, asking for help because she was being stalked by her ex-husband,

O.J. Simpson (this report was ruled to be inadmissible hearsay, and the criminal jury never heard it).

2. Even without that last bit of evidence, the long pattern of abuse was highly relevant given the brutal nature of what was clearly a crime of passion: Nicole Simpson was stabbed seven times in her neck and scalp, with one of her wounds being a slash to her throat that nearly severed her head; Ron Goldman was stabbed approximately 30 times (and not only was there nothing taken from Nicole Simpson's home—her children were asleep in the house—only a very strong person could have inflicted such brutal and fatal injuries).
3. Simpson, who had no alibi, failed a polygraph test, and failed it spectacularly—with a score lower than –6 constituting lying, Simpson scored a –24 (this test, administered by his own legal team, was never before the trial court or jury).
4. Every drop of blood—at the crime scene, at Simpson's home, on and in Simpson's car, on two gloves (a matching pair, one found at the crime scene and one found at Simpson's house), and on Simpson's socks—belonged to Nicole Simpson, Ron Goldman, Simpson, or some combination of all three (e.g., Nicole Simpson's blood was found in Simpson's house, Ron Goldman's blood was in Simpson's car).
5. More specifically, of three blood drops next to footprints at Nicole Simpson's house, only one out of 240,000 people had a DNA match (and Simpson was one); of another blood drop at the same spot, only one in 170 million people had a DNA match (and Simpson was one); of blood found at the rear gate of Nicole Simpson's house, only one out of 57 billion people had a DNA match (Simpson again) (this data came from two different crime laboratories utilizing different techniques).

6. The black knit cap found at Ron Goldman's feet had hair fibers that matched Simpson's (as did hair found on Goldman's shirt).
7. Hair from the bloody glove found at Simpson's home matched Nicole Simpson's hair.
8. Fibers from the shirt Simpson wore the night of the murder were found on the same glove, on Simpson's socks, and on Goldman's shirt.
9. Carpet fibers from Simpson's car matched those found on the knit cap and on the bloody glove at Simpson's house.
10. The bloody gloves were an unusual style, sold only at Bloomingdale's in New York City—Nicole Simpson had bought two extra large pairs in 1990, and only approximately 200 had ever been sold in that size.
11. The bloody footprints of the killer were from size 12 Bruno Magli shoes—a type and size that Simpson wore.
12. The footprints were made by someone between six-feet and six-feet, four-inches tall and weighing approximately 200 pounds (Simpson: six feet, one inch, 210 pounds).
13. Simpson had no explanation for the deep cut to one of his left knuckles (Simpson did tell police he had cut himself on the night of the murder, but he had "no idea, man" how it happened; he also told them he had not cut himself the last time he said he had been at his ex-wife's home, a week earlier).
14. At the time of the murders a witness had had her car cut off by a car hastily leaving the crime scene, with the driver yelling: "Move your damn car! Move it! Move it!"—she recognized the driver as O.J. Simpson, took down the license plate number (Simpson's car), reported the incident to the police after learning of the murders, and testified about what she had seen to the grand jury.

What Went Wrong?

With all that (and a lot more), one might wonder how things turned out the way they did. As the title of this article suggests, the lawyers prosecuting the case made a lot of mistakes; the most material of those mistakes were venue, jury selection, evidence not used, the race card, and trying on the glove.

Venue

Prior to the Simpson case, the Los Angeles District Attorney (Gil Garcetti) and his office had lost a number of high-profile cases: the first Menendez brothers trial (accused of murdering their parents), the Michael Jackson trial (child abuse), the McMartin Preschool trial (child abuse), and the Rodney King trial (police brutality). With the plethora of evidence they possessed, perhaps the district attorney and his colleagues thought they could win anywhere. So, rather than conduct the trial in the Santa Monica District of Los Angeles County (where the murders occurred), Garcetti (up for re-election in 1996) decided that the trial would take place in the South Central District of the county—that is, in downtown Los Angeles, where the jury pool would be made up primarily of African-Americans, likely to be favorable for Simpson. Harshly criticized (especially in hindsight) for this venue decision, Garcetti gave a series of dissembling responses, most of them flat out false (e.g., the court had made the decision; trials lasting longer than two months had to be tried in the downtown courthouse). In any event, this fateful decision was then magnified by the process of jury selection.

Jury Selection

And it was not that the district attorney's office had been unaware of the downtown jury pool issue. With the help of a well-known jury consultant, the office had held a number of focus groups, demographically made up of the likely jury pool. The results were not good, to say the least: the African-Americans, for example, believed Simpson was innocent, notwithstanding the evidence; and the African-American women were particularly "vociferous" in their support of Simpson. Not only were they not affected by the history of domestic violence ("every relationship has these kinds of problems"), they also hated the lead prosecutor, Marcia Clark; as the jury consultant reported, they described her with such words as "shifty," "strident," and "bitch, bitch." The consultant reported all that to Garcetti, Clark, and others in the prosecutor's office, adding that the African-American women "saw [Clark] as a pushy, aggressive, white woman who was trying to bring down and emasculate a prominent black man."

Given that feedback, not only should the district attorney have reconsidered having Clark lead the trial team but the consultant's unwavering conclusion—that "black females were the worst conceivable jurors for the prosecution in the Simpson case"—should have been heeded. Instead, Clark, hating the messenger, banished the consultant and decided to follow her "gut"—that she "could talk to women, . . . reach them somehow. . . . White, Hispanic, Asian, Black, it didn't matter." The result? The jury ultimately selected to hear the evidence, deliberate, and decide Simpson's fate was comprised of eight African-American women, one African-American man (inexplicably, a former Black Panther), one Hispanic man, and two White women. Simpson's lead lawyer, Johnnie Cochran, reportedly had said: "Give me one black juror, and I'll give you a hung jury." Now he had nine. Even Clark herself (later) described the process as "this [expletive] jury pool from hell."

Evidence Not Used

With these seemingly insurmountable obstacles, was there any hope of gaining a conviction? Who knows; but one thing is sure: the prosecution continued to make matters worse, particularly in the trial itself by what incriminating evidence it did *not* present to the jury. Four stand out: First, the prosecution had a 32-minute police interview on tape with Simpson from the day after the murders (for some reason his then-lawyer allowed this to happen, and without him present!). While the interrogation was less than stellar interrogation, Simpson did make a number of extremely incriminating statements (e.g., cutting his hand the night before and bleeding in his car and in his house that night); things he said would also have made some of the police-racism conspiracy theories woven at trial impossible to be advanced. In addition, the jury would have heard Simpson's voice, contemporaneous with the murders (contradicting, changing answers, hesitant, ungrieving)—as opposed to the silent, yet well-rehearsed Simpson with whom the jury spent eight months. Finally, the jury learned of the police tape, but not having heard it allowed them to speculate that the tape exonerated Simpson (something Cochran invoked in summation).

Second, the prosecution (incredibly/inexplicably) failed to put in anything regarding Simpson's white Bronco "chase." As set forth above, Simpson's attempted flight from arrest, statements made both during (when he also called his mother and reportedly told her: "It was all her fault, Ma.") and after his arrest, the materials Simpson had in his possession, etc., were all powerful evidence of consciousness of guilt. Yet none of it was put before the jury.

Third, the prosecution never used Simpson's "farewell" note. Composed shortly before his flight to avoid arrest (during which he had placed a gun to his head), it sure sounded like further evidence of him acknowledging his guilt (and his desire not to face justice for his brutal actions). But the jury never saw it. (Simpson's note and the "chase"—Simpson's own actions—would also have gone far to undercut the defense's conspiracy theme of police racism.)

Last, and certainly not least, Jill Shively—the eyewitness of Simpson's driving away from his ex-wife's home at the time of the murders—did not testify! Because Shively had sold her story to a television tabloid show for $5,000, Clark (later calling it a matter of principle) angrily decided that Shively's action "made her personally useless to the government." Certainly Shively's action was ill-advised, but there were obvious ways to inoculate her from an obvious cross-examination attack. Instead, because of Clark's pique, the jury never heard this key piece of the puzzle.

The Race Card

Everyone knew that the Los Angeles Police Department's difficult history in race relations might well play an important role in the trial. Indeed, after the trial, one of Simpson's lawyers, Robert Shapiro, told Barbara Walters: "We not only played the race card, we dealt it from the bottom of the deck." And well before the trial started, it was clear that the focus would be on Detective Mark Fuhrman. Fuhrman had a well-documented history of racist statements, about which the prosecutors were aware. Moreover, Jeffrey Toobin had written an article in the July 22, 1994, *New Yorker*, in which he reported that Simpson's lawyers were going to portray Fuhrman as a racist who planted the bloody glove at Simpson's house.

With that as prologue, the prosecution moved to exclude any reference to racist bias on Fuhrman's examination under California's evidence code (Section 352). Judge Lance Ito correctly ruled that there could be nothing on that score unless the defense could offer proof that Fuhrman in fact did plant the glove (of which there was none). Three days later, however, Ito reversed himself and ruled that Fuhrman could be crossed on whether he had used the N-word at any point in the past ten years.

The trial was now at a critical crossroad because of Ito's error (unfortunately, just one of many); and the prosecution chose the wrong fork(s). Prosecutors could have sought an immediate appeal of Ito's second ruling. Fearing he would be mad at them, however, the prosecution decided not to appeal (even Clark later admitted that was a bad error in judgment). But with Fuhrman a key witness, and clearly going to be open to racist attacks, did Clark or her colleagues (knowing of Fuhrman's past statements) ever subject him to rigorous preparation, confront him with his various statements and other allegations of racist statements, and inoculate him from attack? They did not. So, Fuhrman went in unprepared and on cross-examination, lied:

> *Q*: And you say under oath that you have not addressed any black person as a n***** or spoken about black people as n***** in the past ten years?
> *A*: Yes, that is what I'm saying.
> *Q*: So that anyone who comes to this court and quotes you as using that word in dealing with African-Americans would be a liar, would they not, Detective Fuhrman?
> *A*: Yes, they would.
> *Q*: All of them, correct?
> *A*: All of them.

The defense could now show that Fuhrman was both a liar and a racist. And they did, most spectacularly with tapes a screenwriter had made in 1988 with Fuhrman; the tapes included a plethora of racist vulgarities from Fuhrman's lips, including the N-word 41 times.

With those tapes, the race card had truly been played. Fuhrman was immediately cut loose by the prosecutors; they refused to speak with him (or even return his phone calls). As such, when Fuhrman was called back by the defense—with no assurance that the prosecutors would attempt to rehabilitate him (which they could have—there were a number of Los Angeles Police Department minority officers who had worked with Fuhrman and were willing to testify that he was not a racist, that he had a police record free of racial bias, and that he was a good policeman who was scrupulous in handling evidence)—he took the Fifth Amendment to all the questions posed to him. This Fifth Amendment spectacle was, as Clark later wrote, a disaster; and she compounded the disaster by telling the jury she was "disgusted" with Fuhrman (a key witness for her case) and "wish[ed] there were no such person on the planet." But the whole mess (1) could have been avoided by taking an immediate appeal of Ito's improper ruling;

(2) could have been neutralized by proper witness preparation (i.e., admit to prior racist statements on direct, put them into some kind of context (that they applied only to hardened criminals), and cut-off a parade of impeaching defense witnesses on Fuhrman's past, including the tapes); and (3) could have been mitigated if the prosecution had recognized that it was their duty to rehabilitate Fuhrman.

Trying on the Glove

Last, but certainly not least, came the infamous glove demonstration, where the prosecutors had Simpson try on the bloody gloves—one found at the murder scene, the other at his home—in front of the jury.

At a sidebar, Clark had noted that there might be a problem: "He has to wear latex gloves underneath ... and they're going to alter the fit." Another problem was that the gloves, soaked in blood, had shrunk. A third problem was that the demonstration was being turned over to the control of Simpson himself. Thus, there was a terrible trifecta, underscoring what any first-year law student should know (let alone what every experienced trial lawyer does know): Never try a demonstration in front of a jury unless you know it is going to work. So Simpson, by now an experienced movie and television actor, walked over to the jury box as he "tried" to put on the gloves. Keeping his thumb bent at a right angle to his wrist (ensuring the glove could not fit on his hand), Simpson grimaced and testified in front of the jury (but not under oath) "too tight" (others heard him also say "they don't fit"). Clark (who had approved of this demonstration) later wrote that she said to herself: "That's it, we just lost the case." And, of course, this monumental screwup allowed Cochran to coin the most famous phrase of his legal career: "If it doesn't fit, you must acquit." And that is precisely what the jury did, "deliberating" for four hours. After the verdict was read, the former Black Panther juror, in open court, gave a Black Power salute!

Postscript

Simpson did not fully escape justice. He lost a civil wrongful death suit brought by the families of his ex-wife and Goldman. And, in 2008, he was convicted of armed robbery, kidnapping, and conspiracy in Nevada; Simpson was released from prison on October 1, 2017 (he died on April 10, 2024, never having found the "real" murderers). Oprah Winfrey once said that one way to delineate an inappropriate potential suitor is if the potential suitor believes Simpson did not do it. Of the mountains of material written on the Simpson case, the best continues to be Jeffrey Toobin's *The Run of His Life: The People v. O.J. Simpson* (Random House 1996). For those who want a detailing of all the errors by the prosecution, as well as those by Judge Ito (and the not-edifying tactics and strategies of Simpson's counsel), the best book is Vincent Bugliosi's *Outrage: The Five Reasons Why O.J. Simpson Got Away with Murder* (W.W. Norton 1996). An excellent overview of the whole imbroglio is a chapter in Glenn Altschuler and Faust Rossi's wonderful book *Ten Great American Trials: Lessons in Advocacy* (American Bar Association 2016).

When the Simpson criminal trial was first being teed up, I was speaking to a law school classmate who is a prominent lawyer in Los Angeles. I will never forget what he told me: Because of the venue decision and the basic incompetence of the local prosecutor's office, a hung jury would be the best result achievable. He was right.

CHAPTER X

Mrs. Palsgraf and the Long Island Railroad: Did Cardozo Get It Wrong?

The *Palsgraf* decision is one that has perplexed many, if not most, first-year law students. Written by legal genius and judicial legend Benjamin Cardozo, and hailed by wizened law professors, it is supposed to impart mystical insights into the complexities of the civil tort law system. Those law students who "get it" are destined to prosper at the bar; those who do not wait in fear that Professor Kingsfield will call them down in front of the class, hand them a dime, and instruct them to call their fathers and tell them they will be pursuing a more suitable career (e.g., flipping burgers, digging ditches).

What Happened to Lena Palsgraf?

On Sunday morning, August 24, 1924, Lena Palsgraf and her daughter stood on the station platform in East New York station, waiting for the Long Island Railroad to take them to Rockaway Beach. As Palsgraf waited for her train, another LIRR train started to pull out of the station. Two men, determined to get on that departing train, ran toward it; the first man jumped safely on. The second man, carrying a newspaper-covered package, also jumped on, but because it seemed like he might fall, two LIRR guards—one on the train who pulled him, and one on the station platform who pushed him—came to his rescue.

Unfortunately, in so pulling and pushing the second man, the guards' efforts led to the package falling onto the rails below. In the package were fireworks; they immediately exploded. The force of the explosion caused a large "penny" scale on the station platform, which Palsgraf was standing next to, to fall on her, causing numerous injuries.

Palsgraf decided to sue the LIRR, and for that task retained Matthew Wills Wood, a fairly prominent New York solo practitioner whose offices were in the "Cathedral of Commerce" (aka the Woolworth Building). Wood initiated a lawsuit in the fall of 1924, seeking the astronomical sum of $50,000 in money damages.

Assigned to defend the LIRR was William McNamara, a young attorney in the railroad's in-house legal department. Because of congestion in the Second Judicial District's trial calendar, Palsgraf's trial did not get underway until May 25, 1927.

The trial itself was pretty straightforward and simple. Palsgraf's testimony was the key event of the trial, and it basically came in unchallenged by McNamara.

Importantly for the later appellate opinions, there was no definitive evidence as to exactly how far she was from the package when it was dropped and then exploded; witnesses' testimony (and lawyers' interpretations thereof) differed—from "6 or 7 feet, "about 7 feet," "12 feet," "12 to 15 feet," "29 feet," "approximately 30 feet." Medical experts also testified about the nature and extent of Mrs. Palsgraf's physical and neurological injuries.

After Wood rested, McNamara did as well, renewing unsuccessfully his prior motion to dismiss. After summations and the court's instructions, the jury retired for two hours and thirty-five minutes (which included lunch); well fed, the jury thereupon returned a verdict for Palsgraf and awarded her $6,000 in damages.

The Appeal

The LIRR was viscerally disappointed with the verdict and almost immediately filed an appeal in the Appellate Division, Second

Department. Oral argument took place on October 21, 1927, with both Wood and McNamara appearing on behalf of their respective clients. Both sides focused on two key questions: (1) was the LIRR negligent?, and (2) if the LIRR was, did it proximately cause Palsgraf's injuries? Needless to say, each advocate answered those questions differently.

In a decision entered on December 19, 1927, the Second Department upheld the result in the trial court by a three-to-two vote. The majority was not impressed with the LIRR's stressing that the railroad guards were unaware of the explosives, ruling instead that the jury had found them negligent, that Palsgraf's status as a LIRR passenger meant that she was entitled to "the highest degree of care required by [the railroad]," and that the guards' negligence had proximately caused Palsgraf's injuries.

The dissent accepted that the guards were negligent; it also agreed that the guards' negligence caused the package to fall and explode. And while the dissent further agreed that the LIRR's negligence "was a cause" of Palsgraf's injuries, the dissent would not connect all of the dots, reasoning that her injuries were "too remote" from the negligence to be actionable.

The LIRR immediately appealed from the Second Department's ruling, and oral argument was conducted in Albany before the New York Court of Appeals on February 24, 1928.

Wood and McNamara again appeared as advocates for their clients. Wood argued that all factual issues had been resolved in favor of Palsgraf—indeed, not only had the jury weighed in as such but so had all *five* of the judges in the Appellate Division; he also argued that proximate cause was a factual issue, per prior Court of Appeals' precedent.

The LIRR's position before the Court of Appeals mirrored that which had been argued to the Second Department: the railroad could not be liable to Palsgraf given that the guards had no knowledge of the explosives in the package.

As to the Second Department's view that Palsgraf was entitled to the "highest degree of care," the LIRR contended that nothing within the control of the railroad (e.g., the cars, the rails, the roadbed) had a defect that caused Palsgraf's injuries.

Cardozo's Opinion

On May 29, 1928, the New York Court of Appeals handed down its decision: by a four-to-three vote, the court overturned Palsgraf's two lower court victories. Judge Cardozo wrote the opinion on behalf of the majority. Cardozo's opinion is famous for a number of opaque aphorisms:

- "Negligence is not actionable unless it involved the invasion of a legally protected interest, the violation of a right."
- "One who jostles one's neighbor in a crowd does not invade the rights of others standing at the outer fringe when the unintended contact casts a bomb upon the ground. The wrongdoer as to them is the man who carries the bomb, not the one who explodes it without suspicion of the danger. Life will have to be made over, and human nature transformed, before prevision so extravagant can be accepted as the norm of conduct, the customary standard to which behavior must conform."
- "The risk reasonably to be perceived defines the duty to be obeyed, and risk imports relation; it is risk to another or to others within the range of apprehension."
- "[W]rong is defined in terms of the natural or probable, at least when unintentional."
- "Negligence is not a tort unless it results in the commission of a wrong, and the commission of a wrong imports the violation of a right, in this case, we are told, the right to be protected against interference with one's bodily security. But bodily security is protected, not against all forms of interference or aggression, but only against some."

- "If the harm was not willful, [a plaintiff] must show that the act as to him had possibilities of danger so many and apparent as to entitle him to be protected against the doing of it though the harm was unintended. Affront to personality is still the keynote of the wrong."

Beyond the above-cited snippets of legal wisdom/jargon, what is the reasoning behind Cardozo's holding that Palsgraf did not have an actionable claim? To this first-year law student (plus 51 years), the opinion seems to have three bases.

The first is that Palsgraf only possessed a derivative claim with respect to the LIRR guards' negligence—the civil wrong was done to the package holder and only he would have had a direct claim vis-à-vis the guards' conduct. In such circumstances, the law should only give rights and remedies to those with direct claims.

The second is that where a negligent act is unintentional, a plaintiff must show that the act had possibilities of danger "so many and apparent." Given that the LIRR guards had no way of knowing what was in the package, their unintended negligence was not so inherently dangerous as to meet the standard articulated by Cardozo.

The third prong of Cardozo's opinion is perhaps the most problematic. Out of nowhere, without citation, and without any related text following thereafter, Cardozo pronounced: "The law of causation, remote or proximate, is thus foreign to the case before us." Why did he pen those words, especially after writing only a few paragraphs earlier that inquiry must be made into whether a wrong is "probable"?

One answer might lie in his frequently repeated factual determination—made *de novo*—that Palsgraf was "far away" from the negligent act. The more basic reason for Cardozo's declaration that proximate cause had nothing to do with the case is that, at an October 1927 meeting of the American Law Institute, the great judge had articulated a new theory that there should be no tort duty to an unforeseeable plaintiff. Thus, Palsgraf was perfectly timed for

Cardozo to establish that theory, one that by definition had to be "foreign" to the doctrine of proximate cause.

The Andrews Dissent

Chief Judge William Andrews did not agree with Cardozo, and wrote a dissent for which he got two judges on the Court of Appeals to agree with him.

Andrews took direct aim at Cardozo's new theory, arguing that his relationship-oriented duty was "too narrow a conception." Instead, Andrews wrote that the appropriate duty of care is that "[e]very one owes to the world at large the duty of refraining from those acts that may unreasonably threaten the safety of others."

Intent, foreseeability, danger zones, etc., should be irrelevant in considering whether Palsgraf had an actionable tort claim (to illustrate these points, Andrews used several scenarios in which a negligent driver caused multiple injuries). What was relevant, contended Andrews—citing precedent and "common sense"—was that (1) "[h]er claim is for a breach of duty to herself" (i.e., it was not a derivative claim), and (2) her injuries were indisputably caused by the negligent act.

As to the limiting factors on proximate causation, Andrews identified them as "remoteness in time and space." And since in this case, "[t]here was no remoteness in time, little in space," Palsgraf's jury verdict should have been upheld.

So, Who Is Right?

In my book, Andrews (and the majority of judges who passed on this case) got it right. The LIRR guards were in fact negligent and Palsgraf's injuries were obviously caused by the exploding package, notwithstanding the circuitous circumstances by which the scale ultimately fell on her. Tort law today, moreover, does not seem overly concerned with the foreseeability of plaintiffs (*see* Restatement (Third) of Torts: General Principles 6 (April 5, 1999)); loss causation, for example, is a much more important (and litigated) issue.

But even if one sides with Cardozo, it has been posited that the *Palsgraf* holding has had "no precedential importance" because of "its freakish facts." Of course, those "freakish facts" are premised on the assumption (as opposed to record evidence) that Palsgraf was virtually in the next county when the fireworks exploded. Clearly, that was not the case; but this key evidentiary gap (and the poor lawyering in failing to nail down that issue) allowed Cardozo to pioneer his new theory that still challenges 1Ls everywhere.

Postscript

For those wanting more on the *Palsgraf* case and its place in history, William Manz has written a splendid book entitled *The* Palsgraf *Case: Courts, Law, and Society in 1920s New York*" (2005). For scholarly considerations of the decision, see W. Prosser, *Palsgraf Revisited,* 52 MICH. L. REV. 1 (1953); R. Epstein, *Two Fallacies in the Law of Joint Torts,* 73 GEO. L. J. 1377 (1985); G. Calabresi & J. Cooper, *New Directions in Tort Law,* 30 VALPARAISO L. REV. 859 (1996); E. Weinrib, *The Passing of Palsgraf,* 54 VAND. L. REV. 803 (2001). For excellent biographies of Cardozo, see A. Kaufman, *Cardozo* (1998); R. Polenberg, *The World of Benjamin Cardozo* (1997); R. Posner, *Cardozo: A Study in Reputation* (1990).

CHAPTER XI

The Trial of Anthony Burns and the Coming of the Civil War

Although we do not like to admit it, the Founding Fathers wrote slavery into the United States Constitution. In some places it is somewhat obscure (e.g., Article I, Section 2—"other persons" (i.e., slaves) are to be counted as three-fifths of a person for purposes of congressional representation and federal taxation); in others, it is more explicit (e.g., Article IV, Section 2, Clause 3—"No person held to service or labor in one state, under the laws thereof, escaping into another, shall, in consequence of any law or regulation therein, be discharged from such service or labor, but shall be delivered up on claim of the party to whom such service or labor may be due."). This latter provision came at the insistence of Pierce Butler and Charles Pinckney of South Carolina, who proposed to the Constitutional Convention on August 28, 1787, that a clause be added to require "fugitive slaves and servants be delivered up like animals." The following day Butler moved to have the following language added to the Constitution: "If any person bound to service or labor in any of the United States shall escape into another state, he or she shall not be discharged from such service or labor in consequence of any regulation subsisting in the state to which they escape, but shall be delivered up to the person justly claiming their service or labor." The substance and sentiment of Butler's language was ultimately embodied in Article IV, Section 2, Clause 3.

The Fugitive Slave Acts of 1793 and 1850

Because Article IV, Section 2, Clause 3 provided no enforcement mechanism, Congress passed the Fugitive Slave Act of 1793, which President George Washington signed into law on February 12, 1793. By that legislation, slave owners/catchers were (1) allowed into every state and all territories owned by the United Sates, and (2) upon written or oral proof to an official therein, permitted to reclaim their "property." The legislation also made it illegal to "knowingly and willingly" interfere with slave owners/catchers and/or to "harbor or conceal . . . a fugitive from labor," with punishment thereof by payment of $500.

The 1793 law was not vigorously enforced in the northern states, much to the consternation of the staunch advocates of the South's "Peculiar Institution." In fact, many northern states passed "personal liberty laws," designed to inhibit federal enforcement of the 1793 law. In New York, for example, Governor William Henry Seward helped enact numerous protections for fugitive slaves, including (1) a right to a jury trial, (2) a requirement that state lawyers intervene on the fugitive slave's behalf, and (3) the right of the governor to name agents to go to southern states to negotiate for and free Blacks captured and sold into slavery.

One state's personal liberty law was litigated up to the U.S. Supreme Court: *Prigg v. Pennsylvania*, 41 U.S. 539 (1842). In *Prigg*, the Court (via seven separate opinions) struck down Pennsylvania's statute as unconstitutional, as well as being trumped by the 1793 law under the Supremacy Clause. At the same time, however, Justice Joseph Story's "majority" opinion observed that states were under no obligation to use any of their own resources to enforce the 1793 law. To many southern "Fire-Eaters" that dictum constituted a breach of faith to the South, rendered its "property utterly insecure," and (at a minimum) violated the "spirit" of the Constitution. By the late 1840s, according to Senator John Calhoun, "the attempt to recover a slave, in most of the Northern States, cannot now be made without the hazard of insult, heavy pecuniary loss, imprisonment, and even of life itself."

Those concerns (and the ever-increasing Underground Railroad) led to the Fugitive Slave Act of 1850. It was part of an omnibus set of bills Senator Henry Clay designed (and Senator Stephen Douglas later skillfully guided through Congress) to deal with the huge swatches of land acquired as a consequence of the Mexican-American War. As a part of the Compromise of 1850 (which was hailed by many as the "final" answer to controversies over slavery), the Fugitive Slave Act (1) required all law enforcement offices throughout the country to arrest an alleged runaway slave (failure to do so brought a fine of $1,000), (2) forbade anyone from helping an alleged runaway slave (with punishment of six months in jail and a fine of $1,000), (3) forbade a runaway slave from testifying on his or her own behalf, (4) barred jury trials, and (5) required only that the owner swear under oath as to his ownership of the runaway slave. Debate over the statute was heated and intense. In his famous Seventh of March Speech, Senator Daniel Webster—pleading for compromise between the two sections—declared that on the issue of fugitive slaves: "the South is right, and the North is wrong." Ultimately, the 1850 Act passed the Senate by a vote of 27-12 (with 20 Senators registering as not voting); it passed the House by a vote of 109-76 (with 42 Congressmen registering as not voting). President Millard Fillmore signed the bill into law on September 18, 1850.

Once in place, the 1850 Act played out in various states throughout the North in a way that made Harriet Beecher Stowe's *Uncle Tom's Cabin* chillingly real: in Ohio, the cases of Margaret Garner, Rosetta Armstead, and George McQuerry; in Syracuse, New York, the case of Jerry Henry; in New York City, the case of Stephen Pembroke; in Wilkes-Barre, Pennsylvania, the case of William Thomas; the "Christiana Massacre" in Southeastern Pennsylvania (three Blacks were killed, as well as the White owner-claimant); in Boston, the cases of William and Ellen Craft, Shadrach Minkins, and Thomas Sims. But none of these incidents was as significant to the fate of the nation as the case of Anthony Burns.

The "Trial" of Anthony Burns

Anthony Burns was a Virginia born slave who, against state law, learned to read and write; he was also a lay minister in his slave community. Hired out by his master, Charles Suttle, to another man, William Brent, in Richmond, Burns was able to save some money doing odd jobs and ultimately stowed away on a boat to Boston in February of 1854. After working as a cook and a window cleaner, Burns was able to find a steady job in a clothing store.

Unfortunately, Burns wrote a letter back to one of his brothers, who was still enslaved in Richmond. Suttle came into possession of the letter and went into state court in Virginia to start the process of recovering his slave. On May 16, 1854, the Virginia court declared that Suttle had demonstrated "satisfactory proof" that Burns was his slave and was a fugitive. Suttle and Brent then set sail for Boston to reclaim Suttle's "property."

On May 24, 1854, Suttle appeared before Edward Greely Loring, who, in addition to being a Massachusetts state probate judge and a Harvard Law School professor, was also a commissioner for the federal district court in Boston. Faced with the Virginia court determination and Section 10 of the Fugitive Slave Act of 1850 (said determination constituting "full and conclusive evidence of the fact of escape, and that service or labor of the person escaping is due to this party in such record mentioned"), Loring issued an arrest warrant for Burns. He was apprehended outside his shop and "escorted" by a large group of men to the courthouse. Brought upstairs to the jury room, Burns was confronted by Suttle and Brent:

> *Suttle*: "How do you do, Mr. Burns? Why did you run away?
> *Burns*: "I fell asleep on board the vessel where I worked and, before I woke up, she set sail and carried me off."

Suttle: "Haven't I always treated you well, Tony? Haven't I always given you money when you needed?"
Burns: "You have always given me twelve and one-half cents once a year."

After this exchange, Suttle and Brent confirmed to the United States Marshal that Burns was in fact the fugitive slave they sought. Burns was then compelled to spend the night in the jury room, with a hearing as to Suttle's claim on his "property" to take place the following day before Loring.

By the next morning (May 25), news of Burns's arrest had spread throughout Boston. Already outraged by Congress's passing of the Kansas-Nebraska Act on May 22 (which opened up those territories to the possibility of slavery, thus nullifying the Missouri Compromise of 1820), many prominent abolitionists showed up in Loring's courtroom, including well-known attorney Richard Henry Dana. Initially, Burns seemed intent not to put up a fight; but after Dana's intervention on his behalf and Loring's advising him of his right to counsel and that he did not have to make any decisions right away, Burns said he would like more time; Loring then declared: "then you shall have it." The hearing date, first set for the next day (May 26), was ultimately reset for three days thereafter: Monday, May 29.

On Friday evening (May 26), a large crowd (between 2,000 and 5,000) gathered in Faneuil Hall to hear protest speeches (e.g., "if [Anthony Burns] leaves the city of Boston, Massachusetts is a conquered State.") Whipped into a frenzy, several hundred people left Faneuil Hall and headed to the courthouse determined to free Burns. Using a battering ram, protesters breached the building. In the melee that ensued, a temporary deputy federal marshal was killed. Ultimately, the protesters were driven off, with eight men arrested.

After the events of Friday night, Boston's mayor ordered the state militia to guard the courthouse. The U.S. Marshal also brought in two separate contingents of Marines to assist; and he thereafter sent a telegram to President Franklin Pierce, telling him what had happened, but that "[e]verything is quiet now. The attack was repulsed by my own guard." The President's response: "Your conduct is approved. The law must be executed."

At 11:00 a.m. on May 29, the rendition hearing (i.e., the legal process for judging whether a fugitive slave would be returned to his or her master) began. Brent was the first witness, testifying first about his knowledge of and experience with Burns in Virginia (inexplicably, he swore he had last seen Burns in Richmond on March 20—a physical impossibility that opened up an evidentiary door for Burns's defensive team). He then was asked to recount the May 24 colloquy between Burns and Suttle. At that point Burns's counsel objected, citing Section 6 of the 1850 Act, which prohibited any testimony of an alleged fugitive slave at a rendition hearing. Suttle's counsel's responded that confessions and/or admissions uttered outside a courtroom did not constitute "testimony." Loring overruled the objection, but noted he might reconsider his decision at a later point. After Brent related the two men's exchange, his account was corroborated by a second man who had been present in the jury room. Suttle's counsel thereafter put into evidence the Virginia court determination and then rested.

When it was the defense's turn, a second lawyer, Charles Ellis, made an incendiary opening argument ("if you send [Burns] hence..., he goes to the block, to the sugar or cotton plantation [and] to the lash"), attacked the bona fides of the Virginia proceeding under the 1850 Act, and contended that the Massachusetts court was not in a position to give "full faith and credit" to that proceeding (per Article IV, Section I of the Constitution).

The following day (which happened to be the same day President Pierce signed the Kansas-Nebraska Act into law), Ellis resumed his offensive, now rearguing about the admissibility of the May 24 exchange between Burns and Suttle. He also contended that to be a "fugitive," a slave had to intend consciously to escape, and (even assuming the admissibility of the May 24 exchange) the only evidence in the record was that Burns's escape was inadvertent. Ellis concluded by making a full, frontal assault upon the constitutionality of the 1850 Act (unfortunately, most of his arguments had been previously vetted and rejected by the Massachusetts Supreme Judicial Court in *In re Sims*, 7 Cush. (61 Mass.) 285 (1851)).

The defense then called William Jones, a free African-American, who testified that he had worked with Burns cleaning windows in early March; this, of course, contradicted a key portion of Brent's testimony. Jones's testimony about Burns being in Boston in early March was then corroborated by eight other witnesses. Suttle's lawyer subsequently tried to rebut the testimony regarding Burns's location with some additional witnesses, but was not very effective.

In their closings, both parties' counsel made impassioned pleas, repeating many of the same legal points previously argued to Loring. Suttle's lawyer, among other things, praised the city of Boston, glad "that order was supreme; that Faneuil Hall, cradle of law and liberty, was closed today against treasonable and insane speech." Dana, closing for Burns, appealed to Loring's better angels:

> You recognized, Sir, in the beginning, the presumption of freedom. Hold to it now, Sir, as to the sheet-anchor of your peace of mind as well as [Burns's] safety. If you commit a mistake in favor of the man, a pecuniary value, not great, is put at hazard. If against him, a free man is made a slave forever. If you have, on the evidence or on the law, the doubt of a reasoning and reasonable mind, an intelligent misgiving, then, Sir, I implore you, in view of cruel character of this law, in view of the dreadful consequences of a mistake, send him not away, with that tormenting doubt on your mind. It may turn to a torturing certainty. The eyes of many millions are upon you, Sir. You are to do an act which will hold its place in the history of America, in the history of the progress of the human race. May your judgment be for liberty and not for slavery, for happiness and not for wretchedness; for hope and not for despair.

At 9 a.m. on June 1, with Boston now under martial law, Loring entered a packed courtroom to read his decision. Suttle and Brent, however, were not present—they had repaired to the *United States Revenue Cutter Morris,* which had been sent to Boston to assist in the rendition of Burns (President Pierce had directed the Secretary of War, Jefferson Davis, and officials in Boston that "any expense deemed necessary" should be used to enforce the 1850 Act). Loring dismissed all of the constitutional arguments raised because of the *Sims* precedent that bound him (thus, it was not his job, he opined, to strike down a constitutional law that some/many considered "so cruel and wicked").

Loring then turned to sole issue that remained: was Burns in fact a fugitive slave. Acknowledging the "complete and irreconcilable" conflict between witnesses "whose integrity is admitted," Loring looked instead to Burns's own words on May 24 and found that they constituted a legal admission that had not been the result of "hope or fear." As such, Loring ruled that Burns was the fugitive slave identified by the Virginia court and ordered that he be returned to Suttle.

The Return to Virginia and Bondage

At 2:30 p.m. on that same day, Burns was escorted out of the courthouse on foot by (1) a group of the Boston Lancers; (2) a U.S. Army company of infantrymen; (3) two Marine companies; (4) an artillery group, which had with them a nine-pound cannon (filled with grapeshot); (5) approximately 100 U.S. Marshals and deputies; and (6) the entire Boston police force. The streets, which had been closed to traffic for over two hours, were jammed with 50,000 people, (yelling, among other things, "kidnappers") as Burns was led to the wharf. At one point, some of the military were pelted with cayenne pepper, vitriol, and cowitch (an extract from a plant that causes skin rashes and extreme itching). As the crowd surged forward, a horse was killed by one of the military personnel and an order was given to fire on the crowd. Thankfully, the order was quickly canceled and the unruly protesters were pushed back without any fatalities (but with many having sustained severe injuries).

Burns, who was dressed up in elaborate finery given to him by his jailers, finally reached the wharf. Taken first to a steamer, the *John Taylor,* he was later transferred to the *Morris* and the trip to Virginia began.

Back in Richmond, Burns spent four months in an eight-square-foot cell, with his hands and feet bound. Ultimately, he was placed up for auction, where he was sold to David McDaniel, a slave trader from North Carolina. Once relocated to North Carolina, Burns was identified to a friend of McDaniel's wife as the slave who had been at the center of the great controversy in Boston. This news made its way back to Amherst, Massachusetts, where a minster, G.S. Stockwell, thereupon contacted McDaniel about purchasing Burns. McDaniel was amenable, at a price of $1,300. Stockwell then reached out to Leonard Grimes, a Boston-based minister who had earlier tried to purchase Burns's freedom during the trial. This ultimately led to an agreement for the deal to be closed in Baltimore on February 27, 1855. Not without difficulties along the way, Grimes met McDaniel (with Burns in tow) in Baltimore that day and $1,325 was exchanged (McDaniel demanded an extra $25 for his expenses). Grimes then left with Burns on a train headed north (but only after having to put up a $1,000 bond to the railroad, which feared liability for transporting a fugitive slave).

Free at last, Burns received a scholarship to study at Oberlin College. Ultimately, he resumed his religious career, becoming a minister, first in Indiana, and later at a Black Baptist Church in Ontario, Canada. Burns died in 1862, at the age of 28 years old.

Postscript

Three individuals were tried for the May 26 death of the temporary deputy federal marshal at the Boston courthouse. One man was acquitted; the two others kept getting hung juries. Ultimately, the federal government got the message that no Boston jury was going to convict any of these individuals and the charges were dropped.

At Harvard, Judge Loring (whose southern law students had vowed to protect him from physical harm) was stripped of his appointment by Harvard's Board of Overseers. An effort was also made to remove him from his position as a probate judge (based on his conduct as a federal commissioner, acting under the authority of the Fugitive Slave Act of 1850). Richard Henry Dana led the effort to defend Loring, arguing that judicial independence was at stake and that Loring had "been considerate and humane" in executing a law held by Massachusetts' highest court to be constitutional. A majority of the Massachusetts legislature's committee charged with this inquiry, however, ruled that Loring's handling of Burns's case had "outrage[d] the sense of the people." Both the Massachusetts' House (by a vote of 206-111) and Senate (by a vote of 27-11) voted for removal. Governor Henry Gardner, however, rejected the legislature's action.

At the same time Governor Gardner was rejecting the legislature's attack on Loring, that body enacted the most radical personal liberty law of any northern state (the terms of which ensured that no southern claimant could ever prevail in a Massachusetts court). One add-on provision, unmistakably directed at Loring, dictated that no Massachusetts state judge could also serve as a commissioner for the federal courts. When Loring ignored that provision and continued in both offices, a new initiative was launched to remove him. The two legislative bodies again voted that Loring had to go; and with a new governor (Nathaniel Banks) in place, removal was effected on March 19, 1858. Less than two months later, however, President James Buchanan nominated Loring to the federal Court of Claims, and the Senate approved his nomination on May 6, 1858, by a vote of 27 to 13. Loring served on that court until he retired in 1877.

Needless to say, people in the South and North tended to react to these events very differently. With respect to the Burns trial, the *Worcester Spy* opined: "[T]he law of God, written in the people's hearts and the law of man, written in the Constitution, were against the rendition of [Burns] to slavery; but the law of Virginia, sustained by the bayonets of the militar ... was in favor of it, and of course, everything had to give way before the omnipotent edict of the Slave Power." The

Richmond Examiner, however, took a different tack: "[S]uch an execution of the Fugitive Slave law as that which we witness in Boston is a mockery and an insult[; it must] awaken the South to a sense of its position and the necessity of an independent and exclusive policy.... A few more such victories, and the South is undone."

Of Governor Gardener's refusal to strip Loring of his judicial post, the *Worcester Spy* wrote that it "detaches him from the support of his own citizens of Massachusetts [and] attaches him to the proslavery citizens of Virginia." The *Daily South Carolinian*, however, praised the Governor's "heroic acts [which] stand out in bold relief [as] a beautiful contrast to the black fanaticism which pervades the body politic of his State"; the *Fayetteville Observer* added that "we are happy that the authorities in Massachusetts are not all traitors and madmen."

Of Loring's ultimate removal in 1858, the *Richmond South* opined: "to her eternal disgrace, Massachusetts is the first State in the Confederacy whose Legislature, too cowardly to assert its fancied rights against the national government by secession or otherwise, wreaks its vengeance against the individual sworn to execute the law, and endeavors to set the interests of the man in opposition to his official duty." Surprisingly, many house organs of the Republican party also criticized Loring's removal.

Beyond the media, individuals in the South quickly perceived that the intense furor the Burns case fueled in the North would make enforcing the Fugitive Slave Act of 1850 going forward near impossible, at best (e.g., the new "personal liberty law" passed by the Massachusetts legislature in 1855); this made the idea of secession much more palatable, even to Union-loving men in the South. At the same time, the words of Amos Adam Lawrence, a Conscience Whig in Massachusetts, captured the sentiments of many in the North: "We went to bed one night old-fashioned, conservative, compromise Union Whigs & waked up stark mad Abolitionists."

For those who want to know more about Burns and related matters, see Albert J. von Frank, *The Trials of Anthony Burns* (Harvard University Press 1998); Gordon S. Barker, *The Imperfect Revolution:*

Anthony Burns and the Landscape of Race in Antebellum America (Kent State University Press 2010); Earl M. Maltz, *Fugitive Slave on Trial: The Anthony Burns Case and Abolitionist Outrage* (University Press of Kansas 2010). For those interested in the legal issues surrounding the Fugitive Slave laws, see H. Hyman & W. Wiecek, *Equal Justice Under Law* (Harper & Row 1982); Barbara Holden-Smith, "Lords of Lash, Loom, and Law: Justice Story, Slavery, and *Prigg v. Pennsylvania*," 78 CORNELL LAW REVIEW 1086 (1993).

CHAPTER XII

The Supreme Court Gets It Right (Twice): The Trials of the "Scottsboro Boys"

On March 25, 1931, as a freight train crossed the Alabama state border, a fight broke out between a group of Whites and Blacks. The Blacks won and forced all the Whites (save one) off the train. The de-trained Whites reported to local authorities that they had been assaulted by a gang of Blacks; and at the next station a deputized posse corralled nine Black males (their ages ranged from 12 to 20 years). Also found on the train, dressed in men's overalls with caps on their heads (covering their hair), were two White girls (Victoria Price and Ruby Bates). Price and Bates were unemployed mill workers who said they had traveled on the train in search of work. As the nine males were being restrained, one of the girls said that they had been raped by all of them. Later, at the jail (in Scottsboro), Price identified six out of the nine as her rapists. It did not take long for local Whites to assemble at the jail demanding vigilante "justice"; and the local press quickly reported that the arrested males were guilty of "a heinous and unspeakable crime that savored of the jungle."

Twelve days after their arrest, the nine were put on trial. They had no lawyer(s) representing them, although a Tennessee real estate lawyer (Stephen Roddy) volunteered to advise them (and an elderly trial lawyer from Alabama said he was willing to advise Roddy). After Roddy met with the nine for a 25-minute consultation, the proceedings commenced.

There were actually four trials—the two oldest were tried first; and the youngest (the 12 year old) was tried last. Price and Bates testified at each trial, as did two local doctors, both of whom testified as having found semen within the women. Roddy not only did not cross-examine the doctors, he called each of his "clients" to testify—without any preparation! Some of the defendants, while denying their own guilt, gave contradictory accounts, pointing fingers at various others in the group.

After three days, all of the trials were completed. The jury verdicts for eight were guilty, with the death penalty. For the 12 year old, there was a hung jury because the prosecutor had only asked for life imprisonment—a majority of that jury held out for the death penalty. The eight guilty verdicts were appealed to and affirmed by the Alabama Supreme Court (although the Alabama Chief Justice strongly dissented, believing that the eight had not received fair trials). The United States Supreme Court thereafter took the case and reversed the convictions of the "Scottsboro Boys": *Powell v. Alabama,* 287 U.S. 56 (1932).

The Supreme Court—Part I

Although the petitioners raised multiple constitutional challenges to the trials, the Court considered only one: Were they denied the right of counsel in contravention of the Sixth Amendment via the due process clause of the Fourteenth Amendment? Justice George Sutherland, for the majority, first noted that the "ignorant and illiterate" defendants "were not asked whether they had, or were able to employ, counsel, or wished to have counsel appointed." Sutherland then went on to recite the lengthy colloquy between the trial judge and Roddy, in which:

1. Roddy did not accept designation as trial counsel,
2. He acknowledged he had "not prepared this case for trial,"

3. He further acknowledged that he was "not familiar with the procedure in Alabama," and
4. He also offered his opinion that "the boys would be better off if I step entirely out of the case."

Nonetheless, with the local lawyer telling the trial judge that he was "willing to go ahead and help Mr. Roddy," that was enough; in Sutherland's words, "in this casual fashion the matter of counsel in a capital case was disposed of."

Sutherland next moved to the constitutional issue. Recognizing that the Alabama Supreme Court had found the trial met the standards of the Alabama State Constitution, he wrote that that determination had no binding effect on the Court's purview of the federal Constitution. Clearly influenced by the factors in play (it was a capital case, the defendants were minors and illiterate, there was no time to prepare, the existing public hostility, etc.), the Court ruled that the Sixth Amendment's right of counsel applied to the states for the first time in the country's history—via the Fourteenth Amendment.

Justice Pierce Butler (joined by Justice James McReynolds) dissented. Not only did Butler believe the record did not support the notion that the defendants had not gotten an eminently fair trial, he also objected to the extension of federal authority into a field hitherto occupied exclusively by the several states. Thus, it was his view that "[t]he record wholly fails to reveal that petitioners have been deprived of any right guaranteed by the Federal Constitution."

More Trials

Unfortunately for the Scottsboro Boys, all that meant was they would be retried in Alabama state court. Fortunately for the group, it was arranged (by the Communist Party) that going forward they would be represented by one of the leading criminal defense lawyers in the country: Samuel S. Leibowitz of New York City.

Once more, there would not be a group trial. Rather, the first trial to go forward was against the young man (Haywood Patterson) whose physical appearance seemed to meet the most deep-seated prejudices of Alabama Whites. For the prosecution, Alabama Attorney General Thomas Knight stepped into the first chair (he had also argued *Powell* in the U.S. Supreme Court). Leibowitz initially moved to dismiss the indictment on the ground that Blacks had been barred from both the grand jury and the pool of potential jurors. Spending a day with witnesses who proved that point without dispute would provide an issue for appeal, notwithstanding his motion's defeat.

In the trial, Liebowitz went on a frontal assault against Price. Armed with evidence, *inter alia*, that both women had had sex with other men the night before the alleged rapes, that Price (21 years old) was twice married and had been convicted of adultery and fornication, that Price's description of her injuries was not supported by the doctors, Leibowitz systematically destroyed Price's credibility. But that destruction was double-edged because, to the southern ear, Leibowitz (an alien from New York City) had violated basic "Southern chivalry" by portraying her as "white trash." In the words of one local newspaper: "Mr. Liebowitz's brutal cross-examination makes one feel like reaching for his gun while his blood boils to the nth degree."

With respect to the first doctor's testimony, Leibowitz was more strategic. Not only was Price's story not supported by the physical evidence, there was barely any semen found (notwithstanding her claim of multiple rapes only hours before); moreover, the semen found was immobile or dead (thus, most likely to have been there for day(s) prior). Based on those facts, the doctor agreed that Price's story about successive rapes on the night alleged was unlikely. As to the second doctor, Leibowitz did not get a chance to question him—he refused to be a prosecution witness, privately telling the judge: "these women were not raped." And although the judge urged him to testify, he refused because he believed it would destroy his local medical practice.

Then came the kicker: Ruby Bates, who had disappeared before trial and could not be called by the prosecution, suddenly appeared in court to testify for the defense. Bates recanted her entire story. She had agreed to lie because Price had convinced her that they would be arrested. Further, she corroborated other testimony about both women having had consensual sex the day before the alleged rapes.

Unfortunately, the prosecution's cross-examination of Bates played well to the jury (and the broader southern audience). Bates admitted that her fancy new clothes, her trip to New York (where she had disappeared), her expenses, etc., had all been paid for by the Communist Party. Eek! This cavalcade of bad news then allowed the assistant prosecutor to urge the jury in summation to "[s]how them, show them that Alabama cannot be bought and sold with Jew money from New York."

After getting the case in the afternoon, the jury took just a few minutes to agree that Patterson was guilty. But it took then until the next morning to agree on death in the electric chair, only because one juror held out for a while for life imprisonment.

This was Leibowitz's first loss in 79 trials. Undeterred, he moved to set aside the verdict. The trial judge, after agonizing over the matter (and undoubtedly his future) for weeks, ultimately granted the motion after a meticulous review of the physical evidence and Price's credibility. (Not surprisingly, the trial judge lost his re-election bid.)

Attorney General Knight then decided to retry the same defendant (Patterson), together with another one of the Scottsboro Boys (Clarence Norris), but this time before a new, and more compliant, judge. Leibowitz made his same dismissal motion because of the jury pool. But that motion, along with anything else that might help the defendants, was denied. In fact, most of the evidence so damning to the prosecution in the prior trial was excluded. This new judge was so in the tank that he actually told jurors the form they should use to find the defendants guilty! And, of course, that is what happened, with both defendants being given the death penalty.

The Supreme Court—Part II

After the Alabama state court appeals proved unfruitful, the United States Supreme Court again granted certiorari and again overturned the convictions: *Norris v. Alabama*, 294 U.S. 587 (1935). Writing for a nearly unanimous Court (Justice McReynolds did not hear arguments and did not participate in the decision), Chief Justice Charles Evans Hughes ruled that the systematic and arbitrary exclusion of Blacks from juries violated the equal protection guarantees of the Fourteenth Amendment. While the Court had established this principle in earlier cases, Norris was the first case where the Court not only rejected the factual determination found by the Alabama courts that there had been no such wholesale exclusion of Blacks from the jury(ies), but also found—as a matter of record and testimonial evidence—that there had been well-qualified Blacks in the Alabama jurisdiction who had never been called to serve on a jury.

Oral argument before the Court was also significant. After the aforementioned trials (and the record of exclusion Leibowitz had established), some Alabama official(s) had added the names of six Black men to the jury rolls. When Leibowitz identified this as a fraud coopered up by the state, he was asked at oral argument: "Can you prove it?" Replying, "Yes, your Honor," Leibowitz then handed up to the Court the doctored 1931 Alabama county jury roll, with the six names hastily scrawled into a small spot on the last page of the roll. Leibowitz paused his oral presentation while each of the justices reviewed the document with a magnifying glass. Observers said it was a critical inflection point in the argument; moreover, it would appear that this was the first time the Supreme Court was presented with (and reviewed) evidence during oral argument.

The Unfortunate Aftermath

The state of Alabama was undeterred. Ultimately, it prosecuted three of the Scottsboro Boys for the alleged rapes and got convictions (but without the death penalty); another defendant was convicted for assaulting a police officer. But even the Alabama prosecutors had limits—they publicly dropped charges against the remaining defendants because the physical evidence was indisputable that they could not have committed the alleged rapes (of course, this came after years of incarceration).

Ultimately, all the imprisoned Scottsboro Boys were paroled (except Patterson, who escaped from prison). In 1976, Norris (the last living Scottsboro Boy) was pardoned by the state of Alabama; the pardon was signed by Governor George Wallace. On April 19, 2013, Governor Robert Bentley issued a posthumous pardon to all of the Scottsboro Boys ("This has been a long time coming. But it's never too late to do the right thing.").

Postscript

The right to counsel precedent created by the Powell decision would, of course, be expanded by later Supreme Court jurisprudence. *See, e.g.*, *Gideon v. Wainwright*, 372 U.S. 355 (1963); *Escobado v. Illinois*, 378 U.S. 478 (1964); *Miranda v. Arizona*, 384 U.S. 436 (1966).

The Scottsboro Boys served as an inspiration to Harper Lee for her book *To Kill a Mockingbird*.

Sheila Washington, who was the catalyst for the creation for the Scottsboro Boys Museum and Cultural Center, as well as a major force in winning the 2013 pardons, died on January 29, 2021.

For those wanting to dig deeper into this tragic story, the best first stop is a two-part article by Faust F. Rossi, Samuel S. Leibowitz Professor of Trial Techniques, Emeritus, at Cornell Law School: "'The First Scottsboro Trials: A Legal Lynching," CORNELL LAW FORUM (Winter 2002 & Spring 2003). Also recommended is Dan T. Carter's *Scottsboro: A Tragedy of the American South* (LSU Press 2007).

CHAPTER XIII

New York at Its Nadir? The Trial of Bernhard Goetz

Rampant crime; open drug use in the streets; homeless people lying on the sidewalks; the subways not safe, even in the daytime—common complaints by New Yorkers today (the ones who have not de-camped to Florida). But in the late 1970s and early 1980s, New Yorkers feared those problems on steroids. One legal proceeding seemed to capture that era more than any other: *People v. Goetz.*

The Subway Vigilante

On Saturday, December 22, 1984, Bernhard Goetz left his apartment in the West Village and got on a subway car at approximately 1:00 p.m. In the subway car were 20 other passengers, including four Black teenagers, who were sitting near Goetz. One asked Goetz: "How are you?" Another approached Goetz and twice demanded $5. With that, Goetz pulled out a Smith & Wesson .38 revolver and shot each of the young men. Thereafter, he went over to one of them and said: "You seem to be [doing] all right; here's another"; that fifth bullet severed the young man's spinal cord, leaving him paralyzed.

Goetz then (relatively calmly), left the subway car, telling the conductor: "They tried to rip me off." He subsequently headed to New England to avoid arrest; on December 31, however, he walked into a police station in Concord, New Hampshire. Goetz was thereafter turned over to the New York City police on January 3, 1985. After spending a few days at Rikers Island, he was released on $50,000 bail (with a fairly large swatch of public support for his Charles Bronson–style delivery of "justice" to the young men, all of whom had criminal records, and who had been described by witnesses as "boisterous" prior to Goetz's appearance on the subway).

The Legal Process Begins

On January 25, a 23-person grand jury was convened. It heard Goetz's various taped confessions and the few witnesses who voluntarily came forward; it did not hear from any of the victims. Goetz was subsequently indicted, but only on three counts of gun possession.

The next month, as more of Goetz's racist past was reported in the media (and the police report of Goetz's conduct was made public, including his "You seem to be [doing] all right, here's another."), the Manhattan District Attorney (Robert Morgenthau) petitioned Acting Supreme Court Justice Stephen Crane to convene a second grand jury; Crane granted that petition. This time Morgenthau's office put on a more aggressive case in the star chamber proceeding (including granting two victims immunity). That resulted in 10 new charges (e.g., attempted murder, assault, reckless endangerment), to join the three gun-possession charges.

During that second grand jury's deliberations, Morgenthau's deputy, Gregory J. Waples, gave an explanation of self-defense that caused a major legal hiccup. At issue was whether Goetz "reasonably believed" (1) that he was about to be killed or robbed, and (2) that it was necessary to use deadly force. Was that a subjective test (what Goetz himself believed) or an objective test (what a "reasonable person" would have believed)? Waples, on this key point (on which the grand jury focused with great particularity), instructed them that they "should consider whether the defendant's conduct was that of a reasonable man in the defendant's situation." At that time, however, there were a number of cases in the Appellate Division, First Department that had rejected an objective standard and had, instead, endorsed a subjective test.

Justice Crane, in his review of the grand jury minutes, recognized that Waples had not properly instructed the grand jury on the First Department's standard. When Crane released relevant portions of the minutes to Goetz's defense team, they promptly moved for a dismissal of all charges relating to the improper instruction.

On January 16, 1986, as required by the First Department precedent, Justice Crane dismissed nine counts of the indictment (leaving reckless endangerment and the three possession charges). That was a correct (and courageous) decision by Crane—the latter adjective apt because he was pillorized in the press as "soft on crime" (with other, even less savory phrases also employed). The result looked like a huge victory for the defense; but it proved only in the short run, for it allowed the Manhattan D.A.'s office to appeal Justice Crane's decision.

Not surprisingly, the Appellate Division, First Department saw fit to approve its prior decisions on the proper standard. Before the Court of Appeals, however, it was a different story. The prosecution argued that allowing a subjective test to be the law would be giving "a license to kill for any subway rider like [Goetz] who is asked for money—or the time—by black youths, simply because he honestly, but totally unreasonably, believes that every such encounter with young members of a racial minority is potentially life-threatening." In a unanimous decision, the Court of Appeals agreed, determining that New York State's public policy required the objective standard for self-defense. (The court never grappled with the thorny issue of resolving how the objective standard—a test grounded in tort law—squared with criminal law, which has a fundamental requirement of *mens rea*.) Perhaps this is because New York law provides for negligent assault and negligent homicide. In any event, the nine dismissed counts were now reinstated, and the prosecution's burden became infinitely lighter.

The Trial Begins: Picking a Jury

On December 12, 1986, the trial of *People v Goetz* officially began; but not really. The first several months were devoted to pre-screening potential jurors. Ultimately, over 300 New Yorkers were whittled down to 135 potential jurors in advance of the public *voir dire,* which began on March 23, 1987. That phase was not concluded until a jury was impaneled on April 6. *Voir dire* proved challenging for both sides. The prosecutors wanted (1) politically left "Greenwich Village types," and (2) those who had not been victims of a crime(s). While the first criteria was fairly easy to meet, the second was near impossible—too many New Yorkers had been victims of a crime! (At various points, Justice Crane would ask groups of 18 potential jurors if they had been victims of a crime(s); and when so many hands went up, he would reverse the question: raise your hand if you have not been a crime victim!). This problem for the prosecutors obviously pleased the defense team, which was faced with a different challenge: what to do about Black jurors? New York law at the time (even with *Batson v. Kentucky,* 476 U.S. 79 (1986)) did not bar the defense from making a concerted effort to prevent Blacks from serving on juries (i.e., prosecutors were barred, but defense counsel were not (yet)). Being sensitive to the media, however, the defense team actively sought to have some Black jurors who (they hoped) would be sympathetic to the victims of street crime theme (ultimately, the defense accepted a police department administrative aide and a mid-50s bus driver).

At the end of the process, the jury selected thus had 10 Whites and 2 Blacks. Both sides had tried out various trial themes over the course of selecting this last-standing group (e.g., the objective standard of self-defense, the presumption of innocence, the distinction between possession and use of a gun). Even Justice Crane got involved when a defense lawyer asked if the jurors would allow their feelings to trump legal instructions they received; the judge jumped in to shut down any notion of jury nullification—he told them if Goetz were guilty on the law he instructed, they must convict. Once the twelfth juror was agreed to, a visibly relieved Justice Crane said: "We have a jury. Mazel Tov. Thank you." On April 27 (after Easter and Passover), the trial of *People v. Goetz* began in earnest.

The Trial

Several things happened during the trial that seem to have influenced its outcome. The first related to the prosecution's calling the two victims with immunity. Victim one testified without incident, and he appeared not to have helped or hurt either side. The second victim—James Ramseur—was a different story. On May 5, he was escorted into court in prison garb (in May of 1985—after being released from the hospital for his gunshot wound—he had held a gun while a friend raped, sodomized, and robbed a pregnant 18-year-old woman; he subsequently was sentenced to 8½ to 25 years in prison). Ramseur was a young man angry at the world and, although he had been granted immunity, his presence boded ill for the prosecution. In front of the jury, he twice refused to take the stand and testify. With Goetz's defense team milking this drama for all it was worth, Justice Crane finally held Ramseur in contempt and had him physically removed from the courtroom.

For reasons that remain unclear, the judge offered Ramseur a chance to vitiate his contempt citation; so he was back in court on May 19 (this time in a coat and tie). His testimony for the prosecution was straightforward—none of his group had threatened Goetz. But on cross, Ramseur turned back into the surly, angry (and potentially violent) young man the jury had seen two weeks before. He taunted and attempted to fence with Goetz's lawyer (at one point asking: "When was the last time you got a drug dealer off?"). Thereafter, Ramseur removed one of his shoes and various police guards moved toward him to ensure he would not hurl it. With his anger and frustration growing, Ramseur, when asked about his whereabouts days before the shooting, simply shut down and refused to answer any more questions. Justice Crane implored him not to stonewall such innocuous questions, but Ramseur replied: "Take me out of here."

Faced with this situation, Crane again cited Ramseur for contempt. At his May 22 sentencing hearing, the judge made clear to Ramseur how damaging his conduct had been:

> [You] conveyed viciousness and selfishness more efficiently than words could.... Your conduct has played right into the hands of Mr. Goetz's lawyer. He owes you a vote of thanks.... The jurors saw your contemptuous conduct. That can never be erased from their minds.

Besides fining Ramseur $1,500 and adding six months to his jail time, Justice Crane would also have to strike all of Ramseur's testimony (since Goetz's lawyer was unable to finish his cross-examination), and so informed the jury of that fact.

A sort-of counterbalance came with respect to another one of the other victims, Barry Allen. Allen had not been given immunity and it was believed likely that he would plead the Fifth Amendment if called to testify (fearing a risk of prosecution for conspiracy to rob Goetz). Justice Crane therefore ruled that Allen must first come into court—without the jury present—and answer questions. When Allen appeared (sans jury) and took the Fifth to every question, the judge ruled that the jury would not be allowed to see the spectacle of Allen pleading the Fifth.

This was a seeming victory for the prosecution. But the Goetz defense team pressed Crane to compel the prosecutors to grant immunity to Allen (an unsympathetic character who had a criminal record, which only got longer after the subway shooting). The judge declined that "novel" theory, but later did instruct the jury that (1) Allen was a "missing witness," (2) the absence of whom the prosecution had failed "adequately to explain," and (3) the jury could infer Allen's likely testimony would not have been helpful to the prosecution.

Then came three important evidentiary rulings by Crane regarding hearsay. The defense wanted a paramedic to testify about a statement a non-testifying victim had made to him on the way to the hospital ("The guys I was with were harassing this guy, asking him for money. The guy threatened us and then shot us."). They argued this hearsay should come in on the "penal interest" exception and/or the "excited utterance" exception. Crane correctly ruled that neither exception applied (1) because it was not an express admission of that victim's guilt, and (2) it took place an hour after the shooting and thus it was not close enough in time to the event.

The prosecution then sought to have two victims' "exculpatory" statements made to a subway passenger admitted ("He shot me for nothing. I didn't do anything, I only asked for five dollars"; and "I didn't do anything, he shot me for nothing."). Before those were allowed to come in, however, Goetz's lawyer skillfully elicited from the subway passenger her agreement that the statements were "clear and concise" and that "the people you spoke to were coherent and of sound mind and were out of the state of incident and were able to talk to you." With that testimony and given his prior ruling on the statement to the paramedic, Justice Crane declined to allow the hearsay statements to come in before the jury.

That left the "punks" testimony. Andrea Reid and her husband Garth Reid (both Black) were on the subway; and before the shooting, she said to her husband: "Look at those punks bothering that white man." While that statement, in and of itself, was not relevant to the issues at trial, the defense team desperately wanted the jurors (for obvious reasons) to hear it. When the prosecution called Garth Reid, the defense on cross asked a leading question: "Isn't it true that the reason you took notice of those four individuals is because someone said, 'Look at those four punks bothering that man'?" The prosecution jumped up and objected and Crane appeared sympathetic to that objection (at first). But prior questioning by the prosecution into the subway passengers' state-of-mind now proved a double-edged sword; the judge (upon reflection) ruled that the door was now "open and [defense counsel is] going into it." Thus, the jurors heard the "punks" hearsay from a Black man (via his wife).

The Jurors Decide

While the lawyers focused mightily over the charges to the jury (especially on self-defense), the legal nuances between the objective and subjective tests likely were of little moment given what actually happened in open court. As such (and not surprisingly), the jurors found Goetz not guilty of the most serious of the crimes charged. At the same time, Justice Crane went ahead with his "must" instruction, and the jurors did convict Goetz of criminal possession of a weapon in the third degree. That "must" instruction was upheld on appeal. Goetz ultimately served eight months in prison.

Postscript

Darrell Cabey, the young man paralyzed by Goetz's last bullet, did not testify. But he later filed a civil suit against the "Subway Vigilante." A jury awarded him $43 million; Goetz never paid a penny.

Goetz, after leaving prison, ran for New York City Mayor (in 2001) and Public Advocate (in 2005). On *Larry King Live,* he claimed that his conduct had made the city safer. It is statistically true that, as of 2006, New York City was one of the safest cities in the country.

Notwithstanding the political and public heat he took presiding over the trial, Acting Justice Crane was subsequently elected a Justice of the Supreme Court in Manhattan. He later served as Administrative Judge of that court; and in 2001, he was appointed an Associate Justice in the Appellate Division, Second Department. In 2008, he retired from the bench to join JAMS; since that time, has been one of the country's leading mediators. I am honored that Stephen Crane has been my friend for many decades.

For those wanting more details on *People v. Goetz,* please consult George Fletcher's *A Crime of Self-Defense: Bernhard Goetz and the Law on Trial* (The Free Press 1990).

CHAPTER XIV

The Trials of "Scooter" Libby: Justice Run Amok?

On July 6, 2003, a retired American diplomat Joseph C. Wilson IV published an op-ed piece in the the *New York Times,* challenging President George W. Bush's assertion that Saddam Hussein had sought to acquire nuclear materials for his regime in Iraq. That essay triggered a Rube Goldberg–like series of events that, frankly, confound me to this day.

Novak's Column

A week later, on July 14, 2003, well-known, national journalist Robert Novak published his regular column. In it, Novak wrote (among other things) that Wilson's earlier mission to Niger to investigate claims that Iraq had made plans to buy and transport uranium from Niger had been a result of his wife's suggestion. Wilson's spouse was publicly identified: Valerie Plame, an employee of the Central Intelligence Agency. Novak did not specify his sources, other than to reference "senior administration officials."

Novak's initial and primary source for his Wilson-Plame story was Richard Armitage, the Deputy Secretary of State (and a critic of the Iraq War); it was subsequently confirmed to Novak by Karl Rove, a key presidential aide, and Bill Harlow, the CIA's Director of Public Affairs. Armitage also leaked the Wilson-Plame story to Bob Woodward of the *Washington Post.*

The Intelligence Identities Protection Act of 1982 makes it a federal crime to disclose publicly the identity of a "covert" intelligence agent; and the CIA considered whether the Novak column triggered this concern. After its investigation, the CIA concluded that there was "no evidence" that the disclosure of Plame had harmed any CIA operation, any agent in the field, or "anyone else, including Plame herself." Indeed, by 2003, Plame was *not* a "covert" agent (as defined by the statute); furthermore, according to the CIA's acting general counsel, "dozens, if not hundreds of people in Washington" knew Plame was a CIA employee before the publication of Novak's column.

Let's Appoint a Special Counsel

Notwithstanding, the Novak column and the "leak" of Plame caused a political firestorm; it appeared to reflect a (clumsy) attempt by the Bush administration to punish opponents of the Iraq war. Attorney General John Ashcroft recused himself from any investigation into the matter out of an "abundance of caution," so it fell to his deputy, James Comey. Comey, in short order, appointed his good friend (and godfather to one of his children), Patrick Fitzgerald, as a Special Counsel. Fitzgerald promptly convened a grand jury and went to work.

After hearing from a bevy of witnesses, the grand jury indicted no one for violating the 1982 statue (not surprisingly). But, I. Lewis "Scooter" Libby, chief of staff to Vice President Dick Cheney, was indicted on October 25, 2005, on multiple counts for lying about his communications with journalists (other than Novak) regarding when and what he said to them about Plame in 2003. According to the indictment, Libby lied about discussions he had with Tim Russert (NBC News), Matthew Cooper (*Time* magazine), and Judith Miller (*New York Times*)—lied insofar as he *denied* he leaked Plame's CIA status to Cooper and Miller, and lied when he said he remembered first learning about Plame in a conversation with Russert on July 10,

2003. At his press conference announcing Libby's indictment, Fitzgerald accused Libby of having harmed national security, said that Libby had thrown "sand . . . in his eyes," and called the charges of lying quite serious because "truth is the engine of our judicial system."

On March 6, 2007, after deliberating for 10 days, a District of Columbia jury convicted Libby on 4 felony counts, while acquitting him on another. Still proclaiming his innocence, Libby was sentenced to 30 months in jail, fined $250,000, and subjected to 2 years of supervised release after the end of his prison term (this was based on Fitzgerald's sentencing recommendation that Libby's "falsehoods were central to issues in a significant criminal investigation").

On July 2, 2007, President Bush commuted Libby's prison sentence; but—not withstanding Vice President Cheney's imploring—he refused to pardon Libby. On November 3, 2016, the District of Columbia Court of Appeals reinstated Libby as a member of the D.C. Bar. And on April 13, 2018, President Donald Trump pardoned Libby.

I Am Confused

Almost immediately after having become Special Counsel, Fitzgerald learned what Comey already knew: the actual, primary leaker was Armitage. So why not go after him? Apparently, because (as set forth above) there was in fact no violation of the 1982 statute. So why did the investigation not end then and there, with the Special Counsel closing up shop? (Instead, Fitzgerald instructed both Armitage and Novak *not* to go public with the fact that Armitage was the primary source for Novak.) And why go after Libby, (1) who indisputably was not the leaker to Novak (and thus did not throw "sand . . . in [Fitzgerald's] eyes" on that score), and (2) the alleged "illegality" was Libby's lying about (misremembering) a call with Russert (that it was Russert who brought up Plame's name) and lying about leaking Plame's name to Miller and Cooper (notwithstanding that neither published the "leak" *prior* to Novak's column)?

The answer seems to be that Fitzgerald was after a bigger fish than Libby. According to Libby's lawyer, Fitzgerald twice offered to drop all charges against Libby if he would "deliver" Vice President Cheney to him on a silver platter. Exactly what crime Cheney supposedly committed was/is unclear (Fitzgerald did say in his closing argument to the jury: "There is a cloud over the vice president. He sent Libby off to [disclose Plame's identity to Miller]."—Fitzgerald also told the jury that CIA agents could have died because of Plame's "outing": "[Hostile foreign governments] could arrest them. They could torture them. They could kill them."). When Libby declined the twice-offered "deal," Fitzgerald settled for prosecuting him.

What Was the "Evidence"?

Russert's initial recounting to the Feds of what happened in the July 10, 2003, phone call with Libby was quite equivocal—he could not remember whether or not he had mentioned Plame's name to Libby (but would not rule it out). At the trial in 2007, however, Russert was unequivocal. Now (undoubtedly, with the help of governmental horseshedding), he was absolutely *certain* that Plame's name had *not* been discussed on the call. Standing alone, this difference in the two men's recollections of a phone call from years before seems to be of little moment—certainly not for meeting the burden of proving a crime. But what about Libby's interactions with the other reporters?

As for Cooper, it turned out that his work papers and notes *supported* Libby's version of his conversation with the *Time* reporter. (Karl Rove, in fact, turned out to be Cooper's source for Plame.) Consequently, the jury acquitted Libby of lying to the FBI about his conversation with Cooper.

This made Libby's interactions with Miller in June and July of 2003 pretty darn important to Fitzgerald's case. Indeed, in his summation to the jury, Fitzgerald called her testimony "critical" to his prosecution of Libby. At the close of the government's case, Libby's defense team moved to dismiss the allegation that Libby lied to Miller *after* the Novak column was public—the government did not oppose the motion, and the court granted it. This left a discussion between Libby and Miller on June 23, 2008, as the fulcrum on which hung the jury's conviction of Libby.

Miller originally went to jail (where she spent 85 days) rather than testify before Fitzgerald's grand jury about her confidential communications with Libby. She was freed from her contempt order after Libby contacted her and specifically released her from any obligations of confidentiality. Miller then testified before the grand jury twice; the second appearance was the most consequential because she had found her notes of her 2003 conversations with Libby, and Fitzgerald used those notes both to refresh her memory and prompt her testimony. With respect to the June 23 meeting, Miller's notes included the following: "(wife works in Bureau?)." And in her notes of a July 8 Libby-Miller conversation there was an untethered reference to "Valerie Flame [sic]." Based on those notations, Miller told the grand jury she was "certain that Libby and I discussed Wilson's wife . . . . [But that I] couldn't remember if that [June 23] was the first time I heard that she works for the CIA."

At Libby's trial, Miller was one of 10 journalists called to testify; she was the *only* one who testified that Libby had talked about Wilson's wife. Her testimony mirrored that of her second grand jury appearance (based on the above-quoted June 23 notes); at the same time, she also testified that she "did not recall Libby's having mentioned Plame's name, the fact that her job was secret, or that she had helped send her husband to Niger for the CIA." Nonetheless, Miller's testimony about her June 2003 conversation with Libby could not be squared with what Libby had said about his July 10 call with Russert, and that served to corroborate Russert unequivocal testimony. Thus, Miller's testimony was, as Fitzgerald told the jury, "critical" to Libby's conviction.

Innocent and Not So Innocent Mistakes

In the same year as Libby's conviction, Plame published her account of her "outing": *Fair Game: My Life as a Spy, My Betrayal by the White House* (Simon & Schuster 2007) (which later became a movie starring Naomi Watts as Plame). In 2011, at Libby's suggestion, Miller read *Fair Game* and a lightbulb went off. Plame had written that, during the time when she was in fact a covert agent overseas (years before 2003), her covers had been various "Bureau" jobs at the State Department. As Miller subsequently wrote in her memoirs (*The Story: A Reporter's Journey* (Simon & Schuster 2015)), if Libby had been her source on Plame as a CIA operative, "he would not have used the word *Bureau* to describe where Plame worked," since the CIA (unlike the State Department) is organized by divisions. *Someone else* had thus been Miller's source about Wilson's wife working at the "Bureau" ("one of the twenty or more nonproliferation experts I routinely spoke to")!

In her prep sessions with Fitzgerald (and before the grand jury), he had asked Miller several times what Libby had meant when he said "Bureau"—"Did he mean FBI?" Miller replied no; that Libby had only been talking about the CIA. But Fitzgerald, in steering Miller to the CIA conclusion, knew that Plame had had prior cover jobs in the State Department's "Bureaus." He nonetheless failed to provide that information to Miller; and given that it constituted exculpatory evidence vis-à-vis Libby, Fitzgerald never informed Libby's lawyers of Plame's State Department "Bureau" jobs (even though such background information on Plame had been sought by Libby's lawyers).

With this new insight into Plame's cover jobs at the State Department, Miller then re-reviewed her notes from the entire June-July 2003 period. She concluded that *none* of the Plame references came from Libby. In her memoirs she wrote:

> My heart sank as I closed the notebooks. What if my testimony about events four years earlier had been wrong? Had I misconstrued my notes? Had Fitzgerald's questions about whether my use of the word *Bureau* meant the FBI steered me in the wrong direction?
>
> Though I felt certain before the trial that Libby and I had discussed "the wife," if only in passing, my memory

may have failed me. Rereading those elliptical references and integrating them with what I had learned since trial and with the information about Plame's cover that Fitzgerald had withheld, it was hard not to conclude that my testimony had been wrong. Had I helped convict an innocent man?

The Aftermath of a Refreshed Memory

On November 3, 2016, the District of Columbia Court of Appeals granted Libby's petition for reinstatement to the D.C. Bar. That action was based on a report by the D.C. Bar's Office of Disciplinary Council, which, *inter alia*, wrote that (1) Libby had consistently maintained his innocence; (2) he never denied the seriousness of the charges for which he was convicted; and (3) Miller, as a "key prosecution witness ... has changed her recollection of the events in question."

In response to President Trump's 2018 pardon of Libby, Valerie Plame wrote that that act "hurts all of us." (Plame later ran for Congress in New Mexico, unsuccessfully.) Fitzpatrick, now a partner at Skadden Arps in Chicago, said the pardon was ill-considered, and to the extent the decision "purports to be premised on the notion that Libby was an innocent man convicted on the basis of inaccurate testimony caused by the prosecution, ... [t]hat is false."

The man who appointed Fitzgerald, James Comey, also weighed in on the Libby pardon, calling it "an attack on the rule of law ... There's no reason that's consistent with justice to pardon him." Of course, this is the same James Comey who, after telling the President of the United States: "I don't do sneaky things, I don't leak, I don't do weasel moves," promptly leaked seven internal FBI memos to a friend at Columbia Law School, so that he would in turn leak them to the *New York Times* and trigger the need for a Special Counsel to investigate Russian interference with the 2016 presidential election. (Comey also shared those FBI documents with his personal lawyer, Patrick Fitzgerald.) On August 29, 2019, the Justice Department's

Inspector General issued a 79-page report, citing Comey for willfully violating Justice Department/FBI internal policies and procedures in leaking those memoranda, and finding that Comey's actions were in an effort "to create public pressure for official action, ... [which] set[s] a dangerous example" for every FBI employee. The *New York Times* characterized the report as a "stinging rebuke"; Comey's response on Twitter was as follows: "I don't need a public apology from those who defamed me, but a quick message with a 'sorry we lied about you' would be nice."

CHAPTER XV

Edward Bennett Williams's Last Great Trial

Edward Bennett Williams was, without a doubt, one of the twentieth century's greatest advocates. As detailed in Evan Thomas's definitive biography (*The Man to See*), Williams had unsurpassed forensic skills in the courtroom, which he exercised on behalf of a wide range of clients (e.g., Joe McCarthy, Frank Costello, the *Washington Post*, Jimmy Hoffa, and Michael Milken). Williams's last great trial was his 1975 defense of John Connally, who was charged with accepting a $10,000 bribe in his capacity as Secretary of the Treasury in the Nixon administration, in exchange for advocating higher price supports for the milk industry.

The case was brought by the Watergate Special Prosecutor's Office, and Connally was at great risk of being caught up in the same eddy that had consumed a coterie of Nixon men. Connally's indictment was handed up barely a week before President Nixon resigned. And some of the evidence the prosecutors believed to be highly probative were tape recordings from the Oval Office, purporting to display Nixon and Connally cryptically talking about the benefits that would flow to the 1972 re-election effort from raising the price support levels. Lastly, the trial was to take place in Washington, D.C.—not thought to be favorable ground for a conservative Democrat who had recently switched to the Republican Party in a fairly transparent attempt to succeed his most recent political mentor, Richard Nixon.

On April 1, 1975, the case went to trial before Judge George L. Hart, an Eisenhower appointee. The empaneled jury was comprised of seven women and five men; nine were Black, three were White; all were at or below moderate income means (three were unemployed; two were retired).

The technical quality of the tape evidence was quite poor, and Judge Hart refused to let the jury use the prosecutors' transcript thereof. This had the effect of neutralizing the tapes, and putting the burden on the only witness who was prepared to give direct evidence against Connally.

The Dairy Lawyer

Jake Jacobsen was a lawyer for the dairy industry lobby, and a long-time hanger-on in Texas Democratic politics. In 1974, attempting to mitigate criminal exposure, Jacobsen had cut a deal with the government, telling the Watergate grand jury that in 1971 he had given Connally $10,000 in exchange for his influence.

Jacobsen's direct testimony took little more than an hour. The *Wall Street Journal* observed that the prosecutor "seemed at times to be a bit ashamed of his key witness, rushing through his testimony as a result." Other observers described Jacobsen during the trial as "peering warily, cowering almost," and as "an astonished lizard." As Williams's cross-examination demonstrated, he had good reason to be so described.

Williams's cross-examination is a classic, more in its restrained completeness, rather than in its histrionics. As Connally admiringly put it: "[Williams] was not a flamboyant questioner, as some trial lawyers are. He didn't win his cases by theatrics in the manner of Perry Mason. He won them ... with a tireless attention to detail." Williams had been handed an enormous amount of detailed ammunition as a result of the fact that over several years, Jacobsen had been interviewed repeatedly by prosecutors (and their notes had been produced to the defense), that Jacobsen had testified and submitted sworn statements in prior civil proceedings, that Jacobsen's proffer to the Watergate Special Prosecutor had been produced to the defense, and that Jacobsen's numerous grand jury appearances (both before and after his deal with the government) had been produced to the defense. From this dense web of information Williams proceeded to demonstrate methodically that Jacobsen had repeatedly modified or altered prior testimony and statements in an attempt to have his bribery accusation against Connally hang together in a somewhat coherent fashion.

Williams's Cross

Williams started his cross with a long series of procedural questions relating to the times Jacobsen had met with prosecutors since he struck his immunity deal in March 1974. Williams took Jacobsen through each of the 17 meetings, and emphasized that the preparation centered on "inconsistencies or possible inconsistencies in your testimony," with the prosecutors pretending to be Williams and asking Jacobsen "a lot of hard questions."

Williams then went into Jacobsen's extremely complicated business connections with a series of Texas banks. After leaving a low-level staff position in the Lyndon B. Johnson White House, Jacobsen had been "deeply in debt," but subsequently became a senior officer and/or director at a number of banks and had, at one point, 15 separate bank accounts and numerous safe deposit boxes. At the start of 1972, Jacobsen had listed his net worth at $3 million; by mid-1972, however, his net worth was a minus $8 million. Williams took Jacobsen through his bankruptcy petition in June 1972, and various sworn statements he had made at that time (including averments that certain safe deposit boxes, where he subsequently testified he stashed various amounts given to and from Connally, had been empty for two years prior to the bankruptcy).

Jacobsen's February 6, 1974, indictment by a federal grand jury in Texas was then fully aired in front of the jury. When Jacobsen professed not to be "familiar with the indictment," Williams was allowed to go through each of the seven felony counts that addressed the alleged four-year bank fraud conspiracy, and to ask Jacobsen about each; these charges, for which the punishment was 35 years in jail, were dropped as a result of a formal agreement reached with the Watergate prosecutors on May 21, 1974.

Williams then took Jacobsen through the second of two indictments returned against him in February 1974: that which was returned in Washington on February 21, 1974 (this was a perjury charge, based on his testimony that he had not touched the money provided by the milk lobby from his receipt thereof until January 1974).

Jacobsen's Meetings

Williams then was ready to move to the "substance" of the case against Connally: Jacobsen's meetings with Connally in March 1971 regarding the Nixon administration's position on price levels for milk. Williams developed a great tempo that undercut the notion that a bribe (of any amount) was necessary:

> Q: "You thought, did you not, Mr. Jacobsen, that he was the only person in the Nixon administration who understood the dairymen and the cattlemen and the farmer to whom you could talk?"
> A: "To whom I could talk; yes sir."
> Q: "There was no one else to whom you had access who would understand this problem as did Secretary Connally?"
> A: "No, sir."
> Q: "And you knew, did you not, from your association with him that he had been sympathetic over the years to the plight of the dairyman and the cattle farmer?"
> A: "Yes, sir."

Q: "And the agricultural community in this country? Is that right?"
A: "Yes, sir."
Q: "You didn't have any problem in convincing Connally of the fact he should help, did you?"
A: "No, sir."
Q: "He didn't resist in any way?"
A: "No, sir."
Q: "He expressed his willingness to help in any way that he could?"
A: "Yes, sir."

Having established the basic facts surrounding the March meetings, Williams proceeded to demonstrate that Jacobsen's direct testimony regarding the purported bribe made thereafter was at odds with a plethora of statements made and testimony given prior to Jacobsen's plea agreement.

With respect to Connally's reaction(s) to Jacobsen's alleged proffer of $10,000, Williams took Jacobsen through some specific grand jury testimony that predated the plea agreement:

Q: "Then what did you do with it?"
A: "Well, then I left it there and talked to Secretary Connally about whether or not he wanted to give money to someone or what he wanted to do with it and he said he didn't have anybody he wanted to give any money to, so he didn't use it."

* * *

Q: "Are you saying on the second occasion you asked Secretary Connally if he wanted the money?"
A: "Yes."
Q: "And again he said no?"
A: "That is right."

Ervin Committee

Having admitted to that prior testimony, Jacobsen then was forced to concede that he had given a consistent account of Connally's refusals to lawyers for the Senate Watergate Committee (the Ervin Committee). And in the course of this testimony Jacobsen also allowed, as he had previously testified under oath, (1) that he had received only $10,000 from the milk lobby (and not any subsequent funds), (2) that he had changed the $100 bills himself into smaller denominations ("thinking that a lot of people don't like to take the big bills"), and (3) that he had never reported back to the milk people that Connally had not accepted the $10,000 but instead had himself kept the money for over three years!

After the lunch break, Williams went right back to prior Jacobsen testimony, highlighting first that Jacobsen in a 1972 civil deposition had been insistent that Connally had never taken any milk money. Jacobsen's 1973 testimony before the Ervin Committee was next, focusing on the following facts: (1) that Connally's refusal to take money was consistent with other pre-agreement recounting ("He did explain why, I think. Briefly he said I am a Democrat in a Republican administration and I do not want to be giving money to Democrats since I am in a Republican administration, and I do not want to be giving money to Republicans since I am a Democrat, so I would just rather not give anything."), (2) that Jacobsen had previously changed the $100 bills himself (without any involvement by Connally), and (3) that Jacobsen had procured $10,000 from the milk lobby only once for such purposes.

Williams next moved on to Jacobsen's January 1974 grand jury testimony. Taking Jacobsen through that testimony, Williams put before the jury (1) that Jacobsen pre-agreement (and prior to his dual indictments) had freely testified (once again) that Connally had not accepted the money proffered, (2) that Jacobsen had himself changed this money into smaller denominations, and (3) that he had never made any use of the money in the intervening period, but

(4) that he had never returned the money to the milk lobbyists ("I was just very negligent.").

The Interview

Williams next reviewed an interview Jacobsen had had with lawyers for the milk lobby on February 7, 1974, the day after Jacobsen's first indictment. Once again, Williams elicited from the witness that he had explicitly stated that Connally had twice refused him ("I was never a party to giving any money whatever to Secretary Connally and I have no knowledge of milk money going to Secretary Connally.").

Having now repeatedly shown to the jury Jacobsen's pre-plea agreement, Williams turned to what Jacobsen testified to on his direct examination, as well as in his post-plea grand jury testimony and his 17 interviews with the prosecutors. Williams then reviewed Jacobsen's proffer to the Special Watergate Prosecutor's Office, which was in material disagreement on key points with his direct testimony at trial; this elicited the incredible and unbelievable response that what his lawyer put in the proffer was not based on information provided by Jacobsen! (*Q*: "But your testimony here in court is that you never told Mr. McNalie, your lawyer, that?" *A*: "No, sir." *Q*: "You never mentioned that to him?" *A*: "No, sir.")

Williams then reviewed twice-given testimony, once before the grand jury and then before the Ervin Committee, in which Jacobsen had stated without qualification that he had not received an additional $5,000 from the milk lobby in the fall of 1971. But after the plea agreement prosecutors had shown Jacobsen that he had received $5,000 on November 10, 1971. When confronted with that, Jacobsen had been quoted by the prosecutors in their notes as saying he now had "an inkling" of an additional $5,000 payment to Connally. Unable to resist, Williams then spent three full pages of trial transcript using the "inkling" to full use, ridiculing Jacobsen's evident attempts to make this square peg fit into a round hole.

Houston Meeting

A vivid part of Jacobsen's direct testimony related to his visit to Connally's Houston law offices in October 1973, a few days after Jacobsen was subpoenaed to appear before the Ervin Committee. In prior post-plea agreement testimony he had described Connally bringing the money to Jacobsen in a cigar box with a rubber glove on top; at trial, however, he testified that it was "a rubber or rubber gloves." Williams honed in on why the change. Jacobsen explained that it was "[j]ust this logic of it being gloves instead of glove." Again, Williams had fun at the witness's expense, making Jacobsen explain to the jury how "the logic of it" had revealed itself to him (and, again, allowing the jurors to reach their own conclusions).

The Age of the Money

Another key issue was the age of the money. Much had been made (albeit in a most confusing fashion) about whether money was taken out, first replaced with money that post-dated Connally's tenure as Secretary of the Treasury, and then hurriedly replaced later, with money that would be consistent with a 1971 bribe. Williams not only muddied these waters so totally that no juror could possibly have followed (beyond a reasonable doubt) the dated money trail (while making Jacobsen look like the political bag man he was by making him count each of the 280 bills in front of the jury, so as to determine that 49 post-dated Connally's tenure), he then had Jacobsen explain to the jury how he had thereafter kept the $10,000 in cash in "a little nightstand" by his bed from November 1973 until after his indictments in February 1974.

With Jacobsen's credibility in complete ruins, Williams ended with a nice touch:

> *Q:* "Do you remember, Mr. Jacobsen, that in April of 1972 you said to Secretary Connally that it occurred to you that you had never really expressed your gratitude to

him and that doing so was exceptionally difficult for you, that in all your life you had never had anyone in high position treat you as kindly as he did, and you said to him there was no possible way for you to express your real gratitude, although you knew when you talked to him he must feel it, and that the purpose of this communication was to tell how deeply grateful you are to him, and express the hope that in some small way you could merit his kindness and friendship? Do you remember saying that to him?"

A: "I don't remember saying that, but I may have said it."

* * *

Q: "I hand you Defendant's Exhibit Number 19, and I ask you whether that is a letter written by you on April 28, 1972, to Secretary Connally, signed by you, and whether it does not state precisely what I asked you in my question."

A: "Yes, sir."

Q: "Is that your signature?"

A: "Yes, that's my signature."

Q: "And you wrote the letter?"

A: "Yes, I did."

Q: "And you sent that letter?"

A: "Yes, I did."

Williams: "I have no further questions, Your Honor."

A Character Witness

Williams's cross-examination was not the only thing that helped the jury return its verdict in six hours. He also made skillful use of character witnesses, such as Claudia Alta "Lady Bird" Johnson, Congresswoman Barbara Jordan, and Reverend Billy Graham, who Williams had to be talked into using. The initial interchange between Williams and Graham is a classic:

Williams: "What is your work at the present time, sir?"
Graham: "I am an evangelist, preaching the gospel of Jesus Christ all over the world."

As soon as Graham gave his answer, an elderly Black woman in the jury box (who had once carried a Bible into the courtroom) said in a voice that carried throughout the courtroom: "A-a-men." Williams later allowed to reporters: "I thought that 'A-a-men' was a good sign."

CHAPTER XVI

The Trials of Alger Hiss

The 1997 biography of Whittaker Chambers by Sam Tanenhaus (Random House) rekindled many of the ideological flames ignited by Chambers's naming of Alger Hiss (among others) as a Soviet spy eight decades ago. Covered in Tanenhaus's biography, but subject to little comment in the multitude of reviews, is what transpired in the two criminal trials of Hiss in the Southern District.

The first was presided over by Judge Samuel Kaufman and resulted in a hung jury (8-4 for conviction); the second was before Judge Henry Goddard and resulted in a conviction. Assistant U.S. Attorney Thomas Murphy prosecuted both cases; Lloyd Paul Stryker was Hiss's principal lawyer in the first trial, with Claude Cross lead counsel in the second trial.

The trials contain many fascinating vignettes. Below are just a few:

- Stryker's opening statement made clear that the main thrust of Hiss's defense was to highlight the vast chasm in "lifestyles" between Hiss and his accuser, making the issue for the jury a simple one: Would it believe Hiss (with his stellar résumé) or Chambers? Chambers, Stryker intoned, was "[n]ot only a criminal but an atheist ... a confirmed liar [and] a blasphemer[, having] written a filthy despicable play about Jesus Christ." He summed up Chambers's life as being one of "atheism, destruction of religion, lies, stealing." As a *Time* magazine reporter wrote, "[Stryker] had keyed the jury to expect a witness whom you couldn't believe even if God were holding his right hand."

- Stryker's attempts to portray Chambers in an unflattering light knew few bounds as this snippet of transcript shows:

  Stryker: Lest I leave any unjust aspersion on anyone, your mother is a respectable and decent woman, is that not true?

  Chambers: I need scarcely answer that.

  Stryker: I am glad to state it for you.

  Judge Kaufman: Please, Mr. Stryker.

  Stryker: All right. Tell me ... do you not think it was a lowdown, scoundrel thing for you to bring a woman not your wife in and foist her in your mother's home?

- Hiss had many famous character witnesses testify, particularly in the first trial. They included Supreme Court Justices Felix Frankfurter and Stanley Reed, John W. Davis, Adlai Stevenson, and Philip Jessup. Before Justices Frankfurter and Reed took the stand, Judge Kaufman, in front of the jury, left the bench to shake each's hand! Murphy subpoenaed John Foster Dulles as a rebuttal character witness.
- Murphy's cross-examination of Hiss in the first trial, although it highlighted numerous inconsistencies between his trial testimony and prior statements, was not particularly effective in its overall impact. Repeatedly, he addressed Hiss as "Mr. Witness," but was unable to unnerve Hiss or make him sway from his basic theme of denial. In fact, Hiss seemed to enjoy the thrust and parry with Murphy, on occasion correcting Murphy's English and once even rephrasing one of his questions.

- Murphy's cross-examination of Mrs. Hiss, however, was effective in not only pointing up material inconsistencies from various, prior statements, but in leaving her rattled. One observer stated that her eyes were as "dead as raisins in a circle of dough," and her son later quoted his father as having said she "went into a panic" upon leaving the witness chair.
- In the second trial, Dr. Carl Binger, a psychiatrist working for the Hiss team, was allowed to testify as to Chambers's "psychopathic personality," notwithstanding that he had never met with or personally examined Chambers. One of the symptoms cited by Binger in support of his diagnosis was Chambers's trait of often looking up at the ceiling while testifying. Murphy's devastating cross-examination included the following question:

  > Now, Doctor, we made a count this morning of the number of times that you looked at the ceiling, and during the first 10 minutes you looked at the ceiling 19 times; the next 15 minutes, 20 times; and the next 15 minutes, 10 times; and the following 10 minutes, 10 times; making a total in 50 minutes of 59 times, and I was wondering, Doctor, whether that had any symptoms of a psychopathic personality?

  Adjusting himself in the witness chair, Binger responded: "Not alone."
- Murphy's closing statement in the second trial, like his second cross-examination of Hiss, was superior. In addressing Hiss's character witnesses, Murphy challenged the jury: "[W]hat kind of a reputation does a good spy have? Of course, it must be good. The fox barks not when he goes to steal the lamb." As to the famous pretrial confrontation between Hiss and Chambers at which Hiss finally identified Chambers as someone he

said he had previously known as George Crosley based solely upon his examination of Chambers's teeth, Murphy used a story about a giraffe (Hiss) and a hippopotamus (Chambers):

> The giraffe says to the hippopotamus "I don't remember you at all." The hippopotamus says, "You must remember me. We were in the jungle together, the two of us; we were friends."
>
> He says, "No, I don't remember you."
>
> But he says, "You must. We lived together. We ate together."
>
> No.
>
> So the giraffe says, "Let me see your teeth."
>
> So he looks and he says, "Oh, George Crosley, I know you."
>
> "George Crosley my aunt."

- Aside from the character and credibility attacks (which constituted much of both trials), the physical and documentary evidence was undoubtedly the key to the ultimate outcome. The damning evidence of the rug given to Hiss by Chambers, Hiss's $400 loan to Chambers, and the transfer of Hiss's car to an individual who, when called to testify, pleaded the Fifth Amendment, were all vital parts of the government's case. And the evidence of the State Department papers unearthed from the famous pumpkin having been typed on the Hisses' typewriter—a fact on which the experts all concurred (and Hiss's counsel conceded)—was the final nail in the coffin.
- After the guilty verdict, Judge Goddard thanked the jurors for reaching a "just verdict" and stated that he believed Hiss had received "an eminently fair trial." Before sentencing him, Judge Goddard allowed Hiss to make a statement. After denying his guilt, Hiss stated:

"I am confident that in the future the full facts of how Whittaker Chambers was able to carry out forgery by typewriter will be disclosed." Sentenced to five years in prison, Hiss appealed twice to the U.S. Supreme Court. The second appeal was based on the "forgery by typewriter" thesis. Both appeals first were rejected by the Second Circuit, with the Supreme Court denying certiorari in each instance.

- Fifteen days after Hiss's sentencing (as well as Secretary of State Acheson's "I do not intend to turn my back on Alger Hiss" sound bite), Senator Joseph McCarthy addressed the Ohio City Women's Republican Club of Wheeling, West Virginia, citing 205 known Communists "still working and shaping the policy of the State Department."

CHAPTER XVII

Alger Hiss (Redux)

Alger Hiss left the moderate-level security federal prison in Lewisburg, Pennsylvania, on November 28, 1954, having served approximately three-and-one-half years of a five-year sentence. His conviction had been based upon two perjury counts: one for lying about whether he had known Whittaker Chambers (an admitted former intelligence agent for the Soviet government) after 1936; the other for lying about whether he had given Chambers secret government documents. The conviction meant that the jury had concluded beyond a reasonable doubt that Hiss was a traitor (the statute of limitations for treason had expired so Hiss could not be charged directly with that crime).

Almost literally from the day he left prison, until he died on November 15, 1996, Hiss worked with great energy and ingenuity in an attempt to rehabilitate himself, recast his reputation, and establish his innocence. A major (and critical) part of that effort was to have his 1950 conviction overturned. To do that, Hiss prepared a *coram nobis* petition.

Hiss's Petition

A *coram nobis* petition is a process whereby a court is petitioned to vacate a prior judgment because of errors (as Hiss would later write) "so egregious that they command the attention of the courts no matter how many years have gone by." Based on approximately 150 documents Hiss received from the government upon a Freedom of Information Act request, in 1978 he moved in the Southern District of New York (the same court where he was convicted) to vacate that earlier conviction. Victor Rabinowitz represented Hiss. The government was represented by John Martin, then the Southern District's U.S. Attorney, and Mary Daley, who later became Dean of the St. John's Law School.

Judge Richard Owen, who drew the case, was asked by Rabinowitz to recuse himself, in place of "a scrupulously fair and unbiased judge." Judge Owen declined to do so. Hiss's petition was grounded on five points: (1) he had been deprived of effective assistance of counsel (the prosecutors having had improper contacts with a member of his defense team); (2) the government had suppressed three statements by Whittaker Chambers (the principal witness against Hiss); (3) the government had suppressed evidence that a Woodstock typewriter produced by the defense was not in fact the typewriter upon which the documents were typed; (4) the government had knowingly used perjured testimony; and (5) the government's lead lawyer had misled the jury in his summation.

After a lengthy process, Owen handed down his decision in July of 1982. He denied Hiss's petition in its entirety, finding that the jury's verdict was "amply supported by the evidence—the most damaging aspects of which were admitted by Hiss," that the issues raised in Hiss's *coram nobis* petition "considered singly or together ... raised no real question whatsoever, let alone reasonable doubt, as to Hiss's guilt," and that the original trial had been a "fair one by any standard." *See In re Hiss*, 542 F. Supp. 973, 999 (S.D.N.Y. 1982).

Hiss's *coram nobis* strategy and the "evidence" he used in support thereof highlight many of the differences between litigation strategy and writing history. An analysis of the petition and Owen's opinion are telling.

Effective Assistance of Counsel

Horace Schmahl was an investigator hired by one of Hiss's lawyers to locate the typewriter once owned by the Hisses. In the pre-indictment phase, Schmahl had been explicitly authorized to cooperate with the government—the defense team was proceeding on the theory (based on what Hiss had told them) that the typewriter would prove to be critical *exculpatory* evidence. Right after the indictment, Schmahl had two follow-up contacts with the government relating to the same matters he had previously discussed with the government.

In addition to the context of that prior cooperation, the government received no substantive knowledge from the two post-indictment contacts, and, therefore, the contacts had no impact on the first trial (which had resulted in a hung jury that voted 8 to 4 for conviction). More importantly, as noted by Judge Owen, any government intrusion into the defense camp simply "invalidates the trial at which it occurred." As to the second trial, it was in no way impacted by Schmahl's non-substantive contacts years before. No harm, no foul.

Chambers' "Suppressed Statements"

Hiss's petition posited that, had the defense been in possession of three statements by Chambers at trial, the defense would have "decimate[d] the prosecution's case and its star witness, Chambers." Judge Owen initially reviewed the trial transcript and concluded that the notion that the U.S. Attorney suppressed statements made by Chambers was not quite so (in fact, it constituted "a gross distortion of what actually occurred"). Judge Owen then turned to the three statements Hiss had put at issue: (1) an FBI draft of interviews it conducted with Chambers in 1949, (2) an FBI report of a specific interview in 1946, and (3) a handwritten note by Chambers written after Hiss's indictment regarding Chambers's homosexuality.

Noting that both of the Hiss trials took place before *Jencks* (the 1957 Supreme Court decision requiring the government to tum over any relevant "statement" by a witness—at the time of Hiss's trials, a defendant had to establish by cross-examination a prior inconsistent statement in order to get said statement), Owen also observed that Hiss's trial counsel consistently had not asked for any statements after August of 1948. Thus, as to "statements" (1) and (3), he ruled that it was hard to now fault the government.

As to statement (1), the cited "decimating" evidence was pretty slim pickings. The central piece was that the FBI in 1949 wrote that Chambers's recollection had been that Hiss had advanced him $500 to buy a car; at trial, Chambers testified that the loan was $400. Chambers's trial testimony was accurate, and Owen ruled the inconsistency as "minor in the extreme." The other allegedly inconsistent statements were either not, in fact, inconsistent, or were "so minimal, if not specious, as hardly to require comment" (i.e., the correct name/pseudonym of the person who took pictures of the spy materials Hiss had given to Chambers).

With respect to the only possibly relevant document asked for by Hiss—the 1946 FBI report—the only pertinent "fact" in that document (which, of course, was not a "statement" signed by Chambers) had to do with Chambers's comment to the FBI that he had left the Communist Party in 1937. That "fact," however, was contained in numerous other statements, and Chambers was cross-examined on this point at trial.

Finally, as to Chambers's note about his own sexuality, which was given to the government after the indictment, Judge Owen noted several things: (1) it is indisputable that Hiss well knew of Chambers's sexuality "long before trial"; (2) Chambers's "tortured" personality had been "fully explored on cross-examination"; (3) one psychiatrist, Dr. Carl Binger (whose effectiveness, if any, was destroyed on cross-examination; see Chapter XVI), had not been improperly questioned on this subject; and (4) one question and answer in the testimony of a second psychiatrist, Dr. Henry Murray, had not been proper in light of the government's knowledge of Chambers's sexuality. As to this one error, Hiss's lawyer did not argue that it was material ("I would be the last one to argue that homosexuality has anything at all to do with credibility"), and Judge Owen ruled that the "error" did not affect "the verdict in the slightest."

The Woodstock Typewriter

The gravamen of this claim was that the Woodstock typewriter found and produced by Hiss's trial team was not, in fact, the Hisses, and that the FBI "knew" that the provenance of the typewriter (originally given by Mrs. Hiss's father to her in the early 1930s), as well as its chain of custody after it left the Hisses possession, were fuzzy, at best.

Whether the Woodstock was made in 1927, 1928, or 1929 (and the FBI's knowledge thereof), however, was not critical in light of two material facts: (1) both Mr. and Mrs. Hiss testified at trial that the Woodstock the Hiss team uncovered was indeed their typewriter, and (2) regardless of the machine itself, it was not in dispute (and Hiss conceded prior to trial) that the typed notes reflecting espionage matched other typed documents that the Hisses had produced. Because of these facts, Hiss had argued at trial that years after the fact Chambers somehow had gotten access to the Woodstock and he himself had typed the espionage documents. The U.S. Attorney blew through that argument by a series of rhetorical questions at trial: Did Chambers go to the sons of the Hisses' maid (who last had the typewriter)? Did he have on a Woodstock repairman cap? Did he tell the sons to let him in to repair the Woodstock? Did he then sit down and type 40-some-odd documents evidencing espionage? Upon that construct, the U.S. Attorney turned to Hiss's lawyer and said: "You['ve] gotta do better than that."

These facts and circumstances reduced Hiss to arguing on his petition something he had already argued (based on essentially the same evidence) when he had sought a new trial in 1952: that Chambers had committed forgery by typewriter—that he had built a second typewriter—an exact replica of Hiss's Woodstock at some point circa 1948. Nothing had changed in the intervening 30 years, however. What Judge Henry Goddard wrote in 1952 was equally applicable in 1982:

> If this be so, it would mean that he [Chambers] constructed in three months a machine that has taken the defense's several experts at least one year to produce and that still falls short of being a perfect duplication. Moreover, there is not

> a trace of any evidence that Chambers had the mechanical skill, tools, equipment or material for such a difficult task It is quite unlikely that Communist friends constructed it or provided the material, etc. for Chambers, as the defense suggests, because at that time his relationship with them was far from friendly. If Chambers had constructed a duplicate machine how would he have known where to plant it so that it would be found by Hiss? In planting a duplicate typewriter he would subject himself to the risk of the real Hiss machine being found and his entire case being destroyed.

The "second" typewriter theory remains today just that—a theory based on no evidence.

Perjured Testimony

According to the Hiss petition, Edith Murray (the Chambers's maid in the mid-1930s) and George Roulhac (someone who once had visited the home of the Hisses' former maid in 1938) committed perjury. At trial, the elderly Murray had identified Mr. and Mrs. Hiss as being the only people who visited the Chambers; she also testified that she had not been told the names of the Hisses prior to trial. By Hiss's FOIA request, he had uncovered that prior to trial the government had told her the names of the Hisses (via a statement signed by Murray).

Judge Owen found this was not the government's knowing use of perjured testimony, but at best a prior inconsistent statement that would have hardly "cast any serious doubt" on the central part of Murray's testimony. Moreover, Hiss's trial counsel knew that Murray had signed a pretrial statement, but had made no request to examine it for inconsistencies.

As to Roulhac (an Air Force sergeant), whose testimony was in conflict with the Hisses as to the date they gave the typewriter to their maid, Hiss charged perjury relating to his testimony about how many times he had visited the U.S. courthouse prior to trial.

Roulhac's testimony was that there had been three or four visits. In a 1949 letter the prosecutor sent to the U.S. Marshall's office, however, the prosecutor justified the witness fee payments based on having seen Roulhac daily for a month. But that letter, obviously written for one purpose, was, in any event, not Roulhac's, was never shown to Roulhac, and could not support a charge of knowing use of perjured testimony.

As to Roulhac's other supposed perjury, it was not, in fact, inconsistent (or in conflict) with anything Roulhac had said. When he was first interviewed by the FBI while on duty in Alaska, he gave general comments as to the typewriter. His recollection was far more specific when he later picked out the Woodstock from among seven different typewriters "without hesitation." As noted by Judge Owen, refreshed recollection does not equal perjury.

Misleading Summation

Hiss's petition focused on an FBI report that an expert could not testify with metaphysical certainty that Priscilla Hiss had typed all the documents in question. From that, Hiss argued it was error for the U.S. Attorney to focus the jury on similar errors and/or idiosyncrasies between the typed materials showing espionage and other typed documents the Hisses had produced. Judge Owen, in response to that argument, however, found that an inability to testify as to Mrs. Hiss's typing was not the same thing as the "conclusion implicit in the prosecutor's comment that whatever his or her identity, the same person typed all the documents."

The Second Circuit

A panel of judges, Ellsworth Van Graafland, Thomas Meskill, and William Timbers, heard the appeal from Judge Owen's order. On February 16, 1983, the Second Circuit summarily affirmed that order, and the Supreme Court denied certiorari later that year.

Thus, the 1950 trial verdict had gone up on appeal and been upheld. The request for a new trial two years later had been rejected and upheld on appeal. And a third bite at the apple 30 years later was similarly unavailing. Hiss's attempts at judicial vindication were over.

Hiss and History

Hiss was devastated by the judicial rejection of his *coram nobis* petition. He later wrote that Judge Owen had "decided against me even before he read the petition." As for the Second Circuit panel that summarily rejected his appeal, Hiss wrote that "[I was] more shocked by [their] unreasoning hostility than I had been by the verdict thirty-three years earlier," and (somewhat incredibly) said that their ruling was "the most depressing experience of [my] life." Nonetheless, Hiss soldiered on, seeking nonjudicial redemption until his death.

At least two questions remain: (1) In the face of overwhelming evidence of his guilt (which has become even more compelling with the collapse of the Soviet Union and scholars' access to files of the USSR's military intelligence), why did Hiss continue to lie and maintain his complete innocence? (2) Why did anyone believe him (and why do some people even today)?

The first question is examined in some detail by G. Edward White in his book *Alger Hiss's Looking-Glass Wars* (Oxford University Press 2004); see also "Alger Hiss's Campaign for Vindication," 83 B.U.L. Rev. 1 (2003).

Hiss's motivation to join the Communist Party in the 1930s is not at all that difficult to understand. Having grown up in "circumstances of shabby gentility" (famed journalist Murray Kempton's words), Hiss found the economic dislocations of the 1930s best addressable by the Soviet "experiment"—when, before the Stalin purges, many "liberals" thought it was an experiment for good. It became more than that, however: Hiss (in the words of Sidney Hook (NYU professor and expert on the Communist Party)) became a "true believer"; and that allowed him to cross over to espionage against his country.

But why did he continue to lie about his role until his death? The head of Special Tasks for Soviet intelligence wrote in 1994 that it was because Hiss's "behavior followed instructions he may have learned in the 1930s: never admit anything." In the 1950s, Whittaker Chambers gave another reason:

> Alger Hiss is one of the greatest assets that the Communist Party could possess. What is vindication for him? It is the moment when one of the most respectable old ladies ... in Hartford ... says to another of the most respectable old ladies ... 'Really, I don't see how Alger Hiss could brazen it out that way unless he really were innocent.' Multiply Hartford by every other American community. For the CP that is victory.... And all that Alger has to do for this victory is to persist in his demands.

Professor White tries to answer this same question through the prism of Hiss allowing "his friends and family to go on carrying the awful burden of [his] lie." He believes that Hiss was motivated by a "complex jumble of elements." Those elements included: (1) a "fascination with secrecy," (2) an eager embracing of risk-taking, (3) an ability to compartmentalize unpleasant and/or irreconcilable events, and/or (4) a desire for "power; self-control, and self-confidence." White concludes:

> Alger Hiss's campaign for vindication ... seems best understood as a determined struggle to preserve a secret existence in order to gain self-fulfillment.... If people ended up believing that he had been innocent, Hiss would not merely have been exonerated, but, as he consistently put it, vindicated. His vindication would demonstrate the power of the ideological convictions that drove him to proceed secretly

to make a better world. It would also demonstrate his own power to shape his own life, including his legacy.

As to the second question, John Kenneth Galbraith opined some time ago that the reason so many people could not face up to the evidence was that "thousands of intellectuals, reflecting on their past sympathies, actions, or organizations, find themselves personally involved with it." Other explanations undoubtedly include(d), as White has written, the fact that "[h]is enemies included the unstable Whittaker Chambers, the megalomaniacal Richard Nixon, the fanatical anti-Communist right wing, and the corrupt J. Edgar Hoover." I would surmise at least another, related reason, which was brilliantly articulated years ago by Pulitzer Prize–winning historian Richard Hofstadter in his book *The Paranoid Style in American Politics*. There has always been a deep-seated strain in American history of societal groups who believe in conspiracies (of many kinds), regardless of the evidence. Hiss, having never proclaimed his guilt, tapped that "paranoid style," with some percentage of the public who simply refuse to believe him guilty, even now. Maybe that is not so inexplicable, after all. Some people think O.J. Simpson was still out looking for the real killers before he died.

CHAPTER XVIII

McCarthyism Meets the Law, and Loses

One of the great examples of legal advocacy in the twentieth century did not take place in a courtroom. Rather, it took place on June 9, 1954, in a Senate hearing room during the "Army-McCarthy" hearings. Special counsel for the Army, Joseph N. Welch, sucker punched Senator Joseph R. McCarthy into an exchange that still reverberates today; indeed, I was once a witness to one lawyer attack on another lawyer in a deposition with the following: "Jesus Christ. Have you never seen the Army McCarthy hearings? Have you no decency, sir?"

Tail-Gunner Joe

McCarthy was elected to the Senate from Wisconsin in 1946. He had run as a member of the energetic, World War II generation, embellishing greatly his insubstantial war record ("Tail-Gunner Joe"). Once in the Senate, McCarthy found himself overwhelmed. He exercised little influence over his colleagues and had no legislative achievements to speak of.

Groping for an issue that would help his re-election bid in 1952, McCarthy was invited to speak before the Ohio County Republican Women's Club of Wheeling, West Virginia, in February of 1950. Fifteen days after Alger Hiss's sentencing for perjury (for lying about engaging in espionage on behalf of the Soviet Union while a State

Department official), McCarthy charged that there were 205 known Communists "still working and shaping the policy of the State Department." Although that number varied thereafter (sometimes it was 57, sometimes it was 81; he ultimately identified four), he had caught the wave of a huge issue.

Fueled by the growing rivalry with the Soviet Union, the fact that there was in fact evidence of Soviet espionage, the sagging political fortunes of the Truman administration, and the conspiratorial tradition in American history (Richard Hofstadter would subsequently term this the "paranoid style" of our politics), McCarthy became an incredibly powerful force. Politicians he supported were elected (e.g., Richard Nixon, John F. Kennedy), and those he openly opposed lost (e.g., Millard Tydings, William Benton). His popularity was so strong that when Dwight Eisenhower ran for president in 1952 and appeared on a campaign swing in Wisconsin, Ike specifically deleted from a speech a reference in defense of his mentor, George Marshall; McCarthy had previously denounced Marshall as having "propounded a foreign policy . . . of craven appeasement," having turned the Korean War "into a pointless slaughter," and being the man responsible for the loss of China (not stopping there, McCarthy also linked Marshall to a Communist conspiracy "so immense as to dwarf any previous such venture in the history of man"). (President Harry S. Truman, who believed that Marshall was the greatest living American, never forgave Eisenhower for his acquiescence to political realities.)

At the height of his political power, McCarthy addressed an adoring crowd at the 1952 Republican National Convention. And after the band had finished playing "The Halls of Montezuma," he set forth a famous litany:

> I say one Communist in a defense plant is one Communist too many.
>
> One Communist on the faculty of one university is one Communist too many.

One Communist among the American advisors at Yalta was one Communist too many.

And even if there were only one Communist in the State Department, that would be one Communist too many.

The Beginning of the End

McCarthy's drinking, which had always been heavy, now (as one of his biographers has noted) "began to spiral out of control." And although he won re-election, McCarthy had political problems as well. He now was faced with an executive branch that was in the hands of the Republican Party for the first time since 1932; more importantly, it was run by a man of whom Richard Nixon later said: "He [Eisenhower] was far more complex and devious than most people realized, and in the best sense of those words."

Even before Eisenhower could use his "hidden-hand Presidency" to good effect vis-à-vis McCarthy, however, the Senator himself took a fateful turn: he hired Roy Cohn as chief counsel to the Senate's Permanent Subcommittee on Investigations (PSI).

While in many ways a talented lawyer, Cohn had poor political judgment, and turned out to be a disastrous choice. Also hired as part of the PSI staff were Robert F. "Bobby" Kennedy (just out of Virginia Law School) and David Schine, a young friend of Cohn's. It was an odd ensemble. Kennedy, like his father, Joseph P. Kennedy Sr., admired McCarthy greatly; he and Cohn, however, grew to have a visceral hatred of each other (they almost came to blows in the Capitol). Schine's only qualification appeared to be his bond with Cohn; and McCarthy became heavily dependent on Cohn.

In the meantime, McCarthy started to go after the "wrong" targets. For example, he attacked nominees of the Eisenhower administration, with spectacular failure. He attacked the CIA, which was being run by Eisenhower's chief of staff from World War II, Bedell Smith; he had to back down from that fight as well. After more (and similar) setbacks in his attempts to uncover and/or expose America's enemies, McCarthy settled on a new target: the U.S. Army!

Cohn and McCarthy became convinced that a spy ring existed on an Army base at Fort Monmouth, New Jersey (indisputably, the security procedures at the base were very poor). In the midst of both branches of government trying to figure out how best to deal with this matter, Schine was drafted and inducted into the Army. Cohn immediately began lobbying the Secretary of the Army for preferential treatment for Schine. These pressures continued over time, and ultimately presented the administration and its allies in the Senate with ammunition to go after Cohn and, by extension, McCarthy (who refused to part with his "indispensable" counsel). While all this political in-fighting was playing out inside "the Beltway" (which did not yet exist), the court of public opinion started to shift. Edward R. Murrow's March 9, 1954, *See It Now* broadcast was a broadside against McCarthy and his tactics—McCarthy's actions "have caused alarm and dismay amongst our allies abroad and given considerable comfort to our enemies." Murrow's show was widely seen and very influential; he concluded the show with: "This is not the time for men who oppose Senator McCarthy to keep silent."

And as many respected voices came forth in response, the newspapers got a hold of the evidence of Cohn's efforts on behalf of Schine. That led to the Senate Democrats on the PSI to press for an investigation of the Army's charges against Cohn (and, by extension, McCarthy). McCarthy, as PSI's Chairman, agreed, thinking he would be able to expose the Army's perfidy. He also agreed to one of Cohn's worst ideas: that he and Cohn would act as their own lawyers.

The Army-McCarthy Hearings

The circus-like hearings began on April 22, 1954, and lasted longer than the congressional investigation into Pearl Harbor. Senate Democrats (led by Lyndon Johnson) believed that the key to the hearings would be live television, calculating that McCarthy and his tactics would not survive such public scrutiny. (Interestingly, the western half of the United States did not get live coverage because NBC decided not to provide it.)

Also appreciative of the unusual nature of the proceedings and the likely impact of television was the man the Army had hired to represent its interests: Joseph N. Welch, a very experienced trial lawyer from Hale & Dorr in Boston. When Welch was hired in early April, he announced that two of his firm's young associates, James D. St. Clair and Frederick C. Fisher Jr., would be joining him on behalf of the Army. Two weeks later, Welch (after consulting with White House officials) dropped Fisher from the team upon learning that Fisher had once belonged to the National Lawyer's Guild (a target of, among others, the House Un-American Activities Committee). Welch told the *New York Times* and other members of the media: "I didn't want a diversionary affair."

As his own lawyer, McCarthy was a disaster. His incessant use of the phrase "point of order" as a means to object, interrupt, or merely attempt to bully a witness or fellow Senator, came to symbolize all that was wrong with his methods and tactics (*Point of Order* became the title of a "documentary" film of the hearings). One example will suffice:

> *McCarthy*: "May I finish my point of order?"
>
> *Mundt*: "Counsel advises the Chair that the senator is engaging in a statement or cross-examination rather than a point of order."
>
> *McCarthy*: "I am getting rather sick of being interrupted in the middle of a sentence."
>
> *Symington*: "I would like to say if this is not a point of order it is out of order. The counsel says it is not a point of order and it is not a point of order, if the counsel says it is not a point of order. "
>
> *McCarthy*: "Oh, be quiet."
>
> *Symington*: "I haven't the slightest intention of being quiet. Counsel is running this committee, and you are not running it."

McCarthy: "Mr. Chairman, do I have the floor?"

Mundt: "The Chair has the floor, and nobody is endeavoring to determine whether or not Senator McCarthy is speaking to a point of order. Will you state your point of order and then speak to it?"

McCarthy: "Mr. Chairman, may I suggest that when I start to say something, I not be interrupted in the middle of a sentence, and that Mr. Symington and no one else have the right to interrupt unless he addresses the Chair, and unless the Chair recognizes him. I am getting awfully sick of sitting down here at the end of the table and having whoever wants to interrupt in the middle of a sentence.

* * *

"Call it a point of order or call it what you may, when counsel for Mr. Stevens, and Mr. Hensel, and Mr. Adams makes a statement and he is allowed to do it without interruption, and if that statement is false, do I have a right to correct it, or do we find halfway through my statement that Mr. Welch should not have made his statement and therefore I cannot point out that he was lying?"

In contrast, Welch (who has been described as a "man by turn Pickwickian, avuncular, puckish, stern and righteous") went slowly but surely about his work, giving McCarthy gentle, and not so gentle, needles so as to exasperate the thin-skinned bully into further public tantrums. An example of the latter type of needle came when Welch was examining one of McCarthy's staff and he cleverly introduced a subtext that was constantly just below the surface of the hearings the unusually close "friendship" of Cohn and Schine:

Welch: "You did know what hung on Schine's wall when that was handed to you, sir."

Juliana: "I did not know what hung on Schine's wall."

Welch: "Did you think this came from a pixie? Where did you think this picture that I hold in my hand came from?"

Juliana: "I had no idea."

Mundt: "Senator McCarthy says he couldn't hear the question. It will be reread."

McCarthy: "Will counsel for my benefit define—I think he might be an expert on that—what a pixie is?"

Welch: "Yes. I should say, Mr. Senator, that a pixie is a close relative of a fairy. Shall I proceed sir? Have I enlightened you?"

McCarthy: "As I said, I think you may be an authority on what a pixie is."

In the midst of all this brouhaha came a serious matter that threatened to sidetrack or halt the hearings. It became known that the White House, through Sherman Adams, Eisenhower's chief of staff, and the Attorney General's office had orchestrated the accumulation of evidence regarding Cohn's efforts on Schine's behalf with the Army. When pressed by the Committee for details, Eisenhower issued a directive that none of the individuals would be allowed to testify or be interviewed, citing something that theretofore had never existed: executive privilege. This threatened the hearings themselves, and seemed to generate sympathy for McCarthy.

Unfortunately for McCarthy, however, the decision was made to plow ahead. And next into the witness chair came Roy Cohn, who, by his own assessment, was "a disaster." During a break in his ordeal, Cohn and Welch cut a deal: Welch would not bring up Cohn's avoidance of military service if Cohn did not raise Fisher's membership in the National Lawyers Guild; McCarthy agreed to this trade-off.

On June 9, Welch was grilling Cohn on the lengthy delay in actually disclosing the names of Communists at Fort Monmouth, sarcastically asking him to do so "before sundown," and then adding: "May I add my small voice, sir, and say whenever you know about a subversive or a Communist or a spy, please hurry. Will you remember those words?" At that, McCarthy snapped:

McCarthy: "Mr. Chairman, in view of that question . . . ."

Mundt: "Have you a point of order?"

McCarthy: "Not exactly, Mr. Chairman, but in view of Mr. Welch's request that the information be given once we know of anyone who might be performing any work for the Communist party, I think we should tell him that he has in his law firm a young man named Fisher whom he recommended, incidentally, to do work on this committee, who has been for a number of years a member of an organization which was named, oh, years and years ago, as the legal bulwark of the Communist party, an organization which always swings to the defense of anyone who dares to expose Communists. I certainly assume that Mr. Welch did not know of this young man at the time he recommended him as the assistant counsel forth is committee, but he has such terror and such a great desire to know where anyone is located who may be serving the Communist cause, Mr. Welch, that I thought we should just call to your attention the fact that your Mr. Fisher, who is still in your law firm today, whom you asked to have down here looking over the secret and classified material, is a member of an organization, not named by me but named by various committees, named by the Attorney General, as I recall, and I think I quote this verbatim, as 'the legal bulwark of the Communist party.'"

(As McCarthy launched into this, Cohn mouthed "no, no" to him, and even passed up a note to remind McCarthy of their deal with Welch. But McCarthy went on.)

McCarthy: "I am not asking you at this time to explain why you tried to foist him on this committee. Whether you knew he was a member of that Communist organization or not, I don't know. I assume you did not, Mr. Welch, because I get the impression that, while you are quite an actor, you play for a laugh, I don't think you have any conception of the danger of the Communist party."

Mundt tried to interject, but Welch interposed a "personal privilege" to speak, to which Mundt assented.

Welch: "Until this moment, Senator, I think I never really gauged your cruelty or your recklessness. Fred Fisher is a young man who went to the Harvard Law School and came into my firm and is starting what looks to be a brilliant career with us.

"When I decided to work for this committee I asked Jim St. Clair, who sits on my right, to be my first assistant. I said to Jim, 'Pick somebody in the firm who works under you that you would like.' He chose Fred Fisher and they came down on an afternoon plane. That night, when he had taken a little stab at trying to see what the case was about, Fred Fisher and Jim St. Clair and I went to dinner together. I then said to these two young men, 'Boys, I don't know anything about you except I have always liked you, but if there is anything funny in the life of either one of you that would hurt anybody in this case you speak up quick.'

"Fred Fisher said, 'Mr. Welch, when I was in law school and for a period of months after, I belonged to the Lawyers Guild,' as you have suggested, Senator. He went on to say, 'I am secretary of the Young Republicans League in Newton with the son of Massachusetts' governor, and I have the respect and admiration of my community and I am sure I have the respect and admiration of the 25 lawyers or so in Hale & Dorr.'

> "I said, 'Fred, I just don't think I am going to ask you to work on the case. If I do, one of these days that will come out and go over national television and it will just hurt like the dickens.'
>
> "So, Senator, I asked him to go back to Boston.
>
> "Little did I dream you could be so reckless and so cruel as to do an injury to that lad. It is true he is still with Hale & Dorr. It is true that he will continue to be with Hale & Dorr. It is, I regret to say, equally true that I fear he shall always bear a scar needlessly inflicted by you. If it were in my power to forgive you for your reckless cruelty, I will do so. I like to think I am a gentleman, but your forgiveness will have to come from someone other than me."

McCarthy, not willing to quit when he was being routed, kept on.

> *McCarthy*: "Mr. Welch talks about this being cruel and reckless ... He was just baiting; he has been baiting Mr. Cohn here for hours. . . ."
>
> *Welch*: "Senator, may we not drop this? We know he belonged to the Lawyers Guild, and Mr. Cohn nods his head at me. I did you, I think, no personal injury, Mr. Cohn."
>
> *Cohn*: "No, sir."
>
> *Welch*: "I meant to do you no personal injury, and if I did, I beg your pardon.
>
> "Let us not assassinate this lad further, Senator. You have done enough. Have you no sense of decency, sir, at long last? Have you left no sense of decency?"

Welch's electrifying confrontation with McCarthy did not end with the hearings; they dragged on for another week, and a report was ultimately issued on August 31 (which was critical of everyone, ranging from the Army to McCarthy). More important was the fact that the process of censuring McCarthy had been jump-started. To McCarthy's peers he had committed the ultimate sin of bringing the Senate into disrespect. On December 2, by a vote of 67 to 22, McCarthy was censured by the Senate. McCarthy's immediate reaction was: "I wouldn't exactly call it a vote of confidence, but I don't feel I've been lynched." In fact, he had been. His final years in the Senate were meaningless, and he died a broken man in 1957.

Welch's performance was praised by many (including Eisenhower, who personally thanked him). It was hardly an extemporaneous oration, however. His welling-up eyes and flowing tears while he defended "this lad" were widely commented on and written about, but as Welch left the hearing room with the tears still flowing, he looked over at a young reporter and winked!

CHAPTER XIX

Litigating *Profiles in Courage*

There were few things in the political arena that John F. "Jack" Kennedy took personally. At the 1960 Democratic National Convention, for example, Lyndon B. Johnson called Kennedy's father an appeaser of Hitler (when Joseph P. Kennedy had been U.S. ambassador to England in the 1930s); JFK sloughed it off and a few days later named LBJ as his vice presidential running mate (Robert F. "Bobby" Kennedy, on the other hand, was infuriated and never forgave Johnson).

JFK was very sensitive on one subject, however: his authorship of the book *Profiles in Courage,* for which he won a Pulitzer Prize in 1957. When his Harvard classmate Blair Clark kidded him about it at the 1956 Democratic National Convention ("Jack, I'm going to deny forever that I wrote [JFK's first book] *While England Slept*"), Kennedy became engaged.

The Mike Wallace Interview

The authorship issue reached a head when ABC television broadcast an interview in December 1957, between Mike Wallace and powerful Washington journalist Drew Pearson. The relevant part of the interview was as follows:

> *Pearson*: "Jack Kennedy is ... the only man in history that I know who won a Pulitzer Prize on a book which

JFK during 1960 campaign
(author's collection)

was ghostwritten for him, which indicates the kind of public-relations buildup he's had."

Wallace: "Do you know for a fact, Drew—"

Pearson: "[Speaking over Wallace] Yes, I do—"

Wallace: "… that the book, *Profiles in Courage,* was written for Senator Kennedy—"

Pearson: "I do."

Wallace: "… by somebody else—and he has never acknowledged that fact?"

Pearson: "No, he has not. You know, there's a little wisecrack around the Senate about Jack, who is a very handsome man, as you know. Some of his colleagues say: 'Jack, I wish you had a bit less profile and more courage.'"

The Senator and His Father

On Monday, December 9, 1957, Jack Kennedy called his lawyer (and Washington power broker), Clark Clifford, and asked for an immediate meeting. Arriving shortly thereafter in Clifford's office,

JFK told Clifford about the Wallace-Pearson interview and said: "I cannot let this stand. It is a direct attack on my integrity and my honesty." As Kennedy and Clifford were discussing the pros and cons of various legal strategies to deal with the problem (which included filing suit in New York against Wallace, Pearson, and ABC), the phone rang. It was Ambassador Kennedy; he wanted to speak to his son.

Clifford would later describe listening as "the old man screamed at Jack." After a while, JFK "calmly" handed the phone to his attorney, saying: "I will let you talk to Clark, Father." Before Clifford could even clear his voice, he heard Joseph P. Kennedy's distinctive voice: "I want you to sue the bastards for fifty million dollars. Get it started right away. It's dishonest and they know it. My boy wrote the book. This is a plot against us." Clifford, who had just finished advising JFK against such a tack, replied that he was instead planning "to go to New York and sit down with the people at ABC."

The elder Kennedy's response was blunt: "Sit down with them, hell! Sue them, that is what you have to do, sue them!" Clifford responded to these shouted (and repeated) demands by telling the Ambassador that "we may have to do that, but first we want to try to see if there isn't some other solution."

JFK watched this interchange "with a faint air of amusement." And when the call ended, he evenly said to Clifford: "Well, that's just Dad. Let's deal with this thing." As his client and he were now on the same page on how best to proceed, Clifford started to work—*dealing with this thing.*

Clifford tasked Kennedy with pulling together everything he could that would prove the provenance of the book. He then contacted ABC's chairman, Leonard Goldenson, and set up a meeting for Thursday (December 12) in New York City.

On that day (in the midst of a snowstorm and citywide subway and bus strikes), Kennedy and Clifford schlepped over to ABC's offices. They first met with Goldenson, but were quickly passed on to ABC's lawyers and other ABC personnel. To this latter group, Clifford made his presentation of proof, which included:

- JFK's handwritten drafts.
- A statement from the book's editor, Evan Thomas (son of the famous socialist, Norman Thomas, and father of Washington journalist and historian, Evan Thomas). He affirmed that he had "personally [seen] Mr. Kennedy writing parts of the manuscript in longhand. . . ."
- A statement from Arthur Krock (*New York Times* columnist and long-time Kennedy family retainer). Krock avowed that he had seen JFK (recovering from back surgery in Palm Beach) "lying flat on his back on a board with a yellow pad on which he was writing the book." He further attested that he "had read enough of those pages at the time to know that the product was his own."

Upon finishing his presentation, Clifford demanded that ABC issue a retraction on Wallace's next show. The ABC officials' response was to pick up the phone and call Drew Pearson in Washington. Pearson did not back down, but instead named the "ghostwriter": JFK's closest aide, Ted Sorenson. Kennedy and Clifford were prepared for this moment and responded as follows:

- The preface of the book in fact acknowledged JFK's "greatest debt" to Sorenson "for his invaluable assistance in the assembly and preparation of the material upon which this book is based."
- JFK revealed that Sorenson had received $6,000 in royalties directly from the publisher. [Clifford quickly chimed in that this was not an admission as to Sorenson's authorship.]
- Clifford had Sorenson standing by at a nearby hotel, and offered to have him submit a sworn affidavit denying authorship. The ABC officials asked instead to meet with Sorenson; that request was quickly agreed to, and Sorenson affirmed to the ABC lawyers that he was not the author of *Profiles in Courage*.

At this point, Clifford reiterated his earlier demand: an immediate, televised retraction, or the Kennedys "would be obliged to start legal proceedings." After huddling among themselves, the ABC team caved. Clifford then drafted out in longhand the retraction language, which (with only minor tinkering by the ABC lawyers) was what was read at the beginning of Wallace's December 14 broadcast:

> This company has inquired into the charge made by Mr. Pearson and has satisfied itself that such charge is unfounded and that the book in question was written by Senator Kennedy. We deeply regret this error and feel it does a grave injustice to a distinguished public servant and author and to the excellent book he wrote, and to the worthy prize that he was awarded. We extend our sincere apologies to Senator Kennedy, his publishers, and the Pulitzer Prize Committee.

Dealing with Pearson

In the course of the negotiations, Clifford had told ABC that the Kennedys would not hold the network accountable for Drew Pearson; they would deal with him separately.

Given the columnist's prominence (and, in Clifford's words, his "dangerous and influential sting"), JFK's attorney advised him to allow things to cool down a bit and then see if he could work some of the Senator's "dazzling personality and charm" on Pearson. It was good advice. On January 14, 1958, the two met at JFK's office. And a month later Pearson put a small item in his column acknowledging Kennedy's authorship of *Profiles in Courage*. Pearson's diary entry on the meeting shows the persuasive power of JFK one-on-one:

> Talked to [Kennedy] for about an hour. He showed me his original notes, and unquestionably he did conceive the idea of his book *Profiles in Courage* . . .
>
> Sometimes I'm a sucker for a nice guy who presents an appealing story. He didn't ask for a retraction, but I think

> I shall give him one. He got a whale of a lot of help on his book. I'm still dubious as to whether he wrote too much of it in the final draft language.... But he showed enough knowledge of the book, had lived with the book, made the book so much a part of him, that basically it is his book.... "Ted [Sorenson] did an awful lot of work," he said.

Who Wrote *Profiles in Courage*?

There is no doubt that the idea for the book germinated in JFK's brain sometime in 1954, just as the Senate was grappling with the fate of Joe McCarthy. The young Senator was interested in Senate history, and intrigued with legislators who had made "hard and unpopular decisions necessary for our survival." It also appears he was influenced by Herbert Agar's *The Price of Union,* as well as by his wife's American History course at Georgetown University with Jules Davids.

With input from various sources as to the individuals to be featured, Sorenson contacted Davids to see if he would work with Sorenson and Kennedy to put the project together for a modest fee. Sorenson, by this point, was spending long hours on the project, taxing the resources of the Library of Congress, and engaging the services of several clerical assistants.

By 1955, with Kennedy recuperating from back surgery in Florida, a book contract had been inked with Harper and Brothers, and Evan Thomas had signed on as the book's editor (possible titles at this time were "These Great Men," "These Brave Men," and "The Patriots"). Draft chapters, critiques, and suggestions were actively solicited and offered by various academics (Professors James Landis, Arthur Schlesinger, Walter Johnson, James MacGregor Burns, Allan Nevins, Arthur Holcombe), in addition to the ongoing work being done by Sorenson and Davids.

While Kennedy was in Florida, Sorenson often shuttled back and forth from Washington. Flat on his back, JFK would (in Sorenson's words) "take all the material, mine and his, pencil it, dictate the fresh copy in his own words, pencil it again—he never used a typewriter."

By the time Kennedy returned to Washington, the book was mostly done. At that point, JFK's focus was on polishing the first and final chapters. Working titles now included "Men of Courage," "Eight Were Courageous," "Call the Roll," and "Profiles in Courage." Ultimately, Harper chose the last one.

As Joe Kennedy was critiquing the book's prose as lacking polish, Sorenson was going through it one more time—to Thomas's satisfaction: "[T]his book reads like Jack Kennedy, and damn good, too."

Herbert Parmet, in his book *Jack: The Struggles of John F. Kennedy*, has done the most comprehensive (and undisputed) work on the provenance of *Profiles in Courage*. His conclusion is as follows:

> [Kennedy] served principally as an overseer or, more charitably, as a sponsor and editor, one whose final approval was as important for its publication as its birth. At the working level, research, tentative drafts, and organizational planning were left to committee labor, with such talents as Professor Davids making key contributions. But the burdens of time and literary craftsmanship were clearly Sorenson's, and he gave the book both the drama and flow that made for readability.

Postscript

Although publicly rebutting Pearson's charge was very important to JFK's long-term plan to become president (as he later informed Clifford), it did not completely put the matter to bed during Kennedy's lifetime. When JFK, as President-elect, met with Robert McNamara to talk about his becoming Secretary of Defense, for example, the threshold issue for McNamara was: "[D]id you really write *Profiles in Courage* yourself?"

Almost 50 years later, Mike Wallace remained bitter about ABC's capitulation to the Kennedys. In his memoir, *Close Encounters,* Wallace called the retraction "a craven gesture and an insult to Pearson." ABC, he wrote, should have had the "fortitude to call [JFK's] bluff."

One mystery that has never been successfully solved is why and how JFK was awarded the Pulitzer Prize. Nowhere among the five books recommended for the "Biography" prize by a distinguished panel of historians was *Profiles in Courage.* And yet the Pulitzer Advisory Board ignored their recommendations. Why? There is evidence that Arthur Krock aggressively lobbied some of his friends on the advisory board. There is much speculation (but no evidence) that the heavy hand of Joseph P. Kennedy reached into the deliberations. Least convincing, but the publicly released explanation, is that one member of the board announced to his colleagues that his 12-year-old grandson had been "absolutely fascinated" by the book, and it was that anecdote that turned the tide in Kennedy's favor. It seems we will never know the true story. But when the award was announced, Torby MacDonald—one of JFK's oldest and closest friends, and a Democratic congressman—sent a telegram: "Congratulations. Understand the committee in charge of running the Irish Sweepstakes has named you winner. And recently discovered land grant deeds to the states of Texas and California show you to be the rightful owner. More coming."

Much of the foregoing story, as it relates to communications between the Kennedys and Clifford and their legal strategy, is drawn from Clifford's memoir *Counsel to the President.* And while it is fascinating history, query whether Clifford was violating his professional responsibility vis-à-vis his obligations to client confidentiality. *See Swidler & Berlin v. United States,* 524 U.S. 399 (1998).

CHAPTER XX

The Twentieth Century's Most Infamous Crime: Solved Without a Trial

In his book *Reclaiming History* (W.W. Norton 2007), former Los Angeles prosecutor Vincent Bugliosi purported to set the record straight—for the first time—as to the assassination of John F. Kennedy. Going on for almost as long as the Warren Commission itself (whose legal staff was headed up by J. Lee Rankin, and included such legal talent as Francis W.H. Adams, Melvin A. Eisenberg, Wesley S. Liebeler, and Norman Redlich, all of whom were—or would become—prominent New York lawyers), *Reclaiming History* ends up supporting the basic, central conclusions of the Warren Commission.

Many of the evidentiary puzzles unanswered by the Warren Commission (mostly because of technology yet to be discovered) were later filled in by other investigators (the 1978 House Select Committee on Assassinations) and other authors (e.g., John Lattimer, Gerald Posner) long prior to Bugliosi.

For some, this historic and tragic event may seem challenging because the "conventional" wisdom (or whatever you want to label that of filmmaker Oliver Stone) is that JFK's murder has gone unsolved since November 22, 1963. That is not so, however. Lee Harvey Oswald killed the President, and he did it alone. The evidence has always been overwhelming and conclusive.

The Evidence Against Oswald

What is the evidence against Oswald? Not much, only that: (1) the gun that shot JFK was owned by Oswald; (2) both bullets that hit JFK came from Oswald's gun; (3) Oswald's fingerprint was on the gun (his finger and palm prints were also on the boxes surrounding the sniper's nest); (4) fibers from Oswald's shirt were on the gun; (5) eyewitnesses saw a man fitting Oswald's description firing from the sixth floor of the Texas School Book Depository; (6) Oswald worked in that building and was indisputably there before, during, and just after the assassination; and (7) Oswald, the only worker to leave the depository, indisputably killed police officer J.D. Tippit—a murder that had no motive other than to escape capture (a police wire had been sent out with a description of someone similar to Oswald just prior to Tippit stopping him).

Additional Medical and Scientific Evidence

Both bullets that struck the President came from behind (the bullet holes in JFK's back and skull are indisputably entry wounds) and from an angle that computer analysis tracks back to the sixth-floor window of the depository. The bullet fragments recovered from both JFK and Governor John Connally came from the bullets fired from Oswald's gun. The X-rays of JFK's skull, in the words of the doctor who was the chief pathologist at the President's autopsy, "disclosed fine, dust-like metallic fragments from back to front, where the bullet traversed the head before creating an explosive exit wound."

What Happened in Dallas

Oswald, having seen the President's motorcade route depicted in a Dallas newspaper days before, arrived at the depository the morning of November 22 with a large package that he said contained "curtain rods." Ultimately, he secreted himself on the sixth floor behind a wall of boxes so no one could see him. Just as the motorcade turned

1964 Democratic Convention souvenir of JFK in a rocking chair (author's collection)

onto Elm Street right below the depository, Oswald fired his first shot (it missed—some fragments of the bullet splintered a tree; others hit a sidewalk and were deflected, drawing blood from an onlooker's face).

The second shot—approximately three-and-a-half seconds later—hit JFK in the upper back, exited through his throat, and then hit Connally (this bullet almost fatally wounded the Texas governor).

The third shot came approximately five seconds later, with JFK still propped up because of severe bracing to alleviate his back pain; this bullet hit JFK in the back of his head, causing a massive loss of brain tissue and bone and ending his life (although the doctors at Parkland Hospital did not pronounce him dead until an hour later).

What About All the "—"?

Since 1964, conspiracy theorists have bilked millions of dollars from people with such "theories" as the President's body was somehow altered before the autopsy was performed (and X-rays taken). Well, we also live in a country that supports supermarket tabloids that report aliens among us. But as Lincoln observed, you cannot fool *all* the people *all* the time!

The most widely discussed conspiracy shibboleth is the so-called pristine bullet, magic bullet, or the single bullet theory. Because Oswald's gun fired only three rounds, and because his first shot clearly missed, *if* JFK and Connally were *not* both hit by the second bullet then there had to have been a second gunman in Dealy Plaza.

First of all, the "magic" bullet is not "pristine"—it is bent, deformed, and is missing a material amount of lead—some of which was indisputably in Connally's body. As to the often repeated charge that the bullet had to take an impossible zig-zag-zig path to hit both men, that is simply wrong.

Based on the most famous home movie of all time by Dallas businessman Abraham Zapruder and subsequent (and indisputable) computer analysis, JFK and Connally were perfectly aligned for Oswald's second bullet. Furthermore, all of Connally's wounds matched that of a bullet tumbling after it exited JFK's throat (e.g., the entry wound in the Governor's back was one-and-one-quarter inches long—the exact length of the bullet). That a high velocity, full-metal-jacketed bullet went through one man and slammed into another just two feet in front of him is of no surprise to anyone familiar with weaponry and the experience of soldiers beginning from the middle of America's Civil War.

Other "Theories" Raised (And Disposed Of)

Conspiracy theorists say Oswald was not a good enough shot to do it. In fact, his Marine Corps rifle scores show he was perfectly competent to hit his target that day in Dallas. The distance, moreover, was only approximately 200 feet away with Oswald's 4X telescope, JFK appeared only 25 yards away at the time of the third shot. And from a timing standpoint, Oswald had ample time to work his rifle and do what he did. That Oswald was not part of a larger conspiracy is demonstrated by his attempt (in early 1963) to kill General Edwin Walker, a local anti-communist figure. Before he left on his mission to assassinate Walker, Oswald left a note for his wife, telling her what to do with his body and possessions if he was caught or killed. What sort of conspirators (according to filmmaker Stone, the group included the CIA, the Pentagon, the Mafia, LBJ, etc.) would have permitted Oswald to freelance, endanger the more important plan, and subject them all to disclosure under questioning?

Moreover, what high-powered conspirators would have sent Oswald off with a $12 rifle that could be traced to Oswald within hours (by the purchase order, pictures, etc.)? Oswald fits the historical profile of political assassins: ideological, malcontented misfits with violent streaks, who yearn for historical greatness (Oswald, who had failed at everything in his young life—even in his defecting to the USSR, kept what he called a "historic diary").

Then there is the "Grassy Knoll." No evidence of any kind links that piece of Dealy Plaza real estate to the Kennedy assassination: there are no bullet paths from that location shown in the X-rays; there is no evidence whatsoever of a fourth, fifth, or __ bullet; and it would have been a crazy spot from which to try to shoot at the motorcade (as opposed to the perfect sniper's nest Oswald chose).

Even more telling, Zapruder was standing right in front of the Grassy Knoll. Had someone fired a high-powered rifle directly behind him, Zapruder would have jumped and lost control of his camera. The "definitive" acoustical evidence of a fourth shot, which was debuted by the 1978 House Assassination Committee, was shortly thereafter indisputably demonstrated to show nothing of the kind.

But what about the movement of JFK's head after the impact of the third bullet? It went backward and to the left (and as Jacqueline

Kennedy jumped up, the President slumped down to the car seat)—does that not prove that the fatal bullet came from the front and left? No. In fact, as Lattimer has demonstrated, over and over, based on the work of Nobel Prize–winning physicist Luis Alvarez regarding the "jet effect" of a rear-impacting bullet, "that is exactly what happens when you reproduce the head shot, knowing the true point of impact of the bullet."

The "ultimate" proof of conspiracy is said (by some) to be the killing of Oswald by Jack Ruby on November 24, 1963. Not so. Oswald was supposed to have been moved from the Dallas police station at approximately 10:30 a.m. that morning, and Ruby did not leave his apartment until 11:00 a.m.; but because of some unexpected, additional questioning of Oswald, the transfer was delayed.

By sheer happenstance, Ruby went to the Western Union across the street and was wiring money to one of his employees at 11:17 a.m. when he saw the police activity; the "hit man" then wandered down the rear ramp of the building and shot Oswald at 11:21 a.m. Obviously, if the conspirators had ordered Ruby to kill Oswald, he would have been down in the basement well before 10:30 a.m.

Indeed, if this was a premeditated act, why did Ruby, who had been in the police station over the weekend within feet of Oswald on a number of occasions, not shoot him at any of those more opportune times? Ruby was an emotionally volatile and violent man. At the time Oswald was supposed to have been transferred, Ruby was reading newspaper articles about the Kennedy children and the likelihood of Mrs. Kennedy having to return to Dallas to testify at Oswald's trial and became extremely upset.

Postscript

Oliver Stone's movie (*JFK*) suffers from the same problems that Mary McCarthy identified in the works of Lillian Hellman ("every word, including 'and' and 'the,' is a lie"). For anyone wanting to know what did not happen that day in Dallas, feel free to rent the movie.

For those who want to see an intentionally fictional take on the assassination, I would highly recommend the wonderful 1979 movie made by William Rickert (*Winter Kills*), which is based on the equally wonderful book of the same name by Richard Condon, who also wrote *Prizzi's Honor* and *The Manchurian Candidate,* and which has an all-star cast, including, among others, Jeff Bridges, John Huston, Anthony Perkins, Elizabeth Taylor, Toshio Mufume, Eli Wallach, and Ralph Meeker. The person behind the *Winter Kills* conspiracy is revealed at the end of the movie, but will not be revealed here.

Bugliosi did make an important contribution to the provenance of the single-bullet theory. Theretofore, based mainly on the public efforts of the then senior senator from Pennsylvania, Arlen Specter, the authorship of that theory has been tagged to a young Warren Commission staff lawyer from the Third Circuit (Philadelphia): Arlen Specter. Through some dogged investigation, Bugliosi demonstrated that Rankin and other Commission lawyers from New York led that effort with Specter's participation.

CHAPTER XXI

Bobby Kennedy's Department of Justice: RFK and His Greatest Nemesis

After John F. Kennedy won the presidency in 1960 by a wafer-thin margin (and, in the words of Chicago Mayor Richard Daley, "with a little bit of luck and the help of a few close friends"), he turned to trying to figure out who would staff the New Frontier. First was the issue of Robert F. Kennedy, who had brilliantly managed his brother's campaign, and to what job he would be assigned.

Becoming Attorney General

Joseph P. Kennedy, Jack and Bobby's father, wanted Bobby to become Attorney General ("Nobody's better qualified," said Joe to Jack). JFK was not enthusiastic, however, given the likely negative public/political fallout (e.g., nepotism, his 35-year-old brother had never practiced law); and Bobby Kennedy was, at best, torn about his father's wishes. As various trial balloons were being floated on the possible appointment (to almost universally negative reactions), Jack Kennedy contacted Clark Clifford, his personal lawyer and legendary Democratic insider, and asked for a private meeting.

At the President-Elect's Georgetown home, JFK explained that while he and Bobby saw various problems with such an appointment, their father was insistent ("I want Bobby to be Attorney General."). JFK then gave Clifford an unusual task: go to New York, meet with Joe and persuade him that having RFK as Attorney

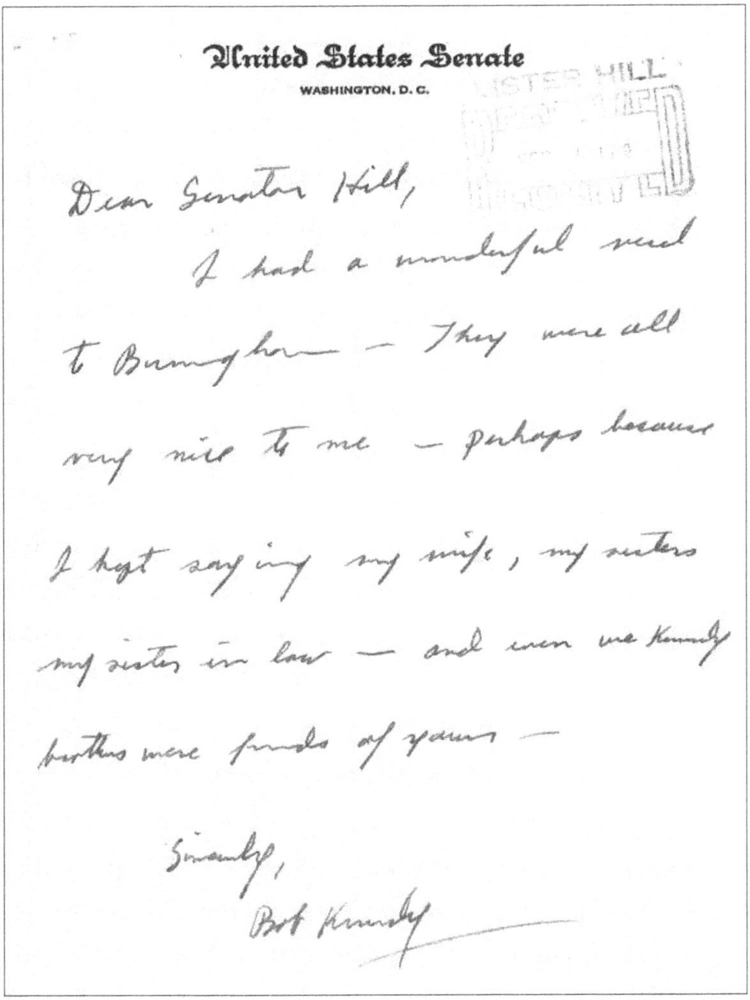

United States Senate
WASHINGTON, D. C.

Dear Senator Hill,

I had a wonderful visit to Birmingham — They were all very nice to me — perhaps because I kept saying my wife, my sisters my sisters in law — and even the Kennedy brothers were friends of yours —

Sincerely,
Bob Kennedy

1958 RFK letter to Senator Hill (author's collection)

General was a bad idea. Clifford agreed to take on this "truly … strange assignment."

Clifford prepared for his meeting with the Ambassador as if he were going to argue a case in the Supreme Court, studying up on the historical precedents of presidential appointments of family members and political operatives. "Steeled for the main event," Clifford traveled to New York to meet with the Ambassador, who invited Clifford into his private office for the oral argument (without interruption) as to "why it was not in the best interests of the new President, the Kennedy family, the entire administration and Bobby himself to take the post." Pleased with his persuasive presentation, Clifford sat back as Joe Kennedy, without rancor, thanked him for his views. The Ambassador then locked his cold blue-gray eyes on Clifford and concluded the meeting with the following: "I do want to leave you with one thought ... one final thought. *Bobby is going to be Attorney General.*"

Once *that* was settled came the next issue: how to get the Senate to "advise and consent" on this controversial appointment. JFK gave that assignment to the most powerful Senate leader in history: his soon-to-be vice president, Lyndon Johnson. LBJ bemoaned to his Senate colleagues that he had to pass this litmus test with the President-Elect or else he would have no influence of any kind in the new administration. And so, pulling in a lot of long overdue chits, LBJ was able to get the Senate Judiciary Committee to report out RFK's nomination unanimously; on the floor of the Senate there was a lone "nay" vote: Gordon Allott (R-Colorado).

On the evening of JFK's inaugural (and the day before RFK would be sworn in), JFK joked at a dinner of family and friends: "I don't know why people are so mad at me for making Bobby Attorney General. I just wanted to give him a little legal practice before he becomes a lawyer." After dinner, a much perturbed younger brother confronted the President: "Jack, you shouldn't have said that about me." JFK, who always took a cynical approach to politics, tried to deflect his brother's anger by explaining: "Bobby, you don't understand. You've got to make fun of it, you've got to make fun of yourself in politics." But Bobby would have none of that: "You weren't making fun of yourself. You were making fun of me."

RFK's Department of Justice

With this rocky lead-up, many predicted that Bobby Kennedy's reign at the Justice Department would be a failure—indeed, a disaster. But RFK confounded his critics by bringing on probably the most impressive and deepest bench of talent in the history of the DOJ, and then giving them wide latitude to do what was right and best for the country. First and foremost of this group was Byron "Whizzer" White as the Deputy Attorney General (White, later JFK's first nominee to the U.S. Supreme Court, held the unique distinction of having led the National Football League in rushing in the same year (1940) he finished first in his class at the Yale Law School). Other key members of RFK's team included Archibald Cox (Solicitor General), Nicholas Katzenbach (Office of Legal Counsel), Jack Miller (Criminal Division), Burke Marshall (Civil Rights Division), Mitchell Rogovin (Tax Division), William Orrick (Antitrust Division), and Edwyn Silberling (Organized Crime and Racketeering). And all that talent (along with other, soon-to-be famous lawyers, including John Doar, William Hundley, James Neal, Harold Greene, G. Robert Blakey) was necessary given that, in addition to the usual portfolios of issues, RFK's DOJ had to deal with the explosive social problem of enforcing civil rights, as well as tackling RFK's principal new focus: organized crime. Kennedy's antipathy to organized crime had its origin in his long-standing pursuit of Teamster boss Jimmy Hoffa.

Get Hoffa (Part I)

In 1957, a special Senate Committee (the Select Committee on Improper Activities in the Labor or Management Field, aka the "Rackets Committee") was empaneled, with Senator John McClellan of Arkansas as its chairman. Bobby Kennedy was chief counsel to the Rackets Committee.

The initial, principal focus of the committee and RFK was Dave Beck, the high-living head of the Teamsters. The Teamsters was the country's largest and richest union—an organization rife with corruption, including strong ties with the Mafia. At that point in time, Jimmy Hoffa, a former warehouseman based in Detroit, was seen as being in a position to assist the committee in its investigation of Beck. Hoffa, by undermining Beck, hoped to succeed him. Brought together for the first time by a Washington middleman, RFK and Hoffa took an immediate dislike to one another. Hoffa was unimpressed by Kennedy's weak handshake ("He's a damn spoiled jerk") and bragged: "I do to others what they do to me." RFK's take on Hoffa was that he was "a bully hiding behind a façade."

Having reviewed wiretaps that showed Hoffa doing business with the mob, RFK viewed Hoffa as "absolute evilness" and was not about to work with him. And when Hoffa was caught in March 1957 stuffing $2,000 in cash into the hands of an FBI double agent in exchange for an envelope, Kennedy was waiting for him at the courthouse for his midnight arraignment, an event that quickly became a media circus. An angry Hoffa challenged "Bobby" to a testosterone-charged duel about who could do more push-ups. With his Irish up, Kennedy told the assembled press that he would "jump off the Capitol dome" if Hoffa beat the bribery charge.

Unfortunately for Kennedy, Hoffa did beat the rap. With Edward Bennett Williams as his counsel, and with Williams using all of his forensic tricks (e.g., having boxing legend Joe Louis come into court and warmly greet Hoffa in front of the mostly black jury), Hoffa walked free and Williams publicly offered to give Kennedy a parachute.

Instead of "jump[ing] off the Capitol dome," Kennedy summoned Hoffa before the Rackets Committee. If RFK hoped for a Perry Mason moment (or even something out of *Godfather Part II*), he must have been sorely disappointed. Hoffa, in responding to "Bob's" questions, feigned a poor memory to almost every substantive question. ("I have to stand on the answers that I have made in regards to my recollection and I cannot answer unless you give me some recollection other than I have answered.") Frustrated, Kennedy would often just stare at Hoffa, and Hoffa would just stare right back. After minutes of silence, Hoffa would seize the high ground, giving RFK a stage wink. They went on this way for several days (and multiple sessions thereafter), with neither man yielding. Finally, in September 1958, over a year after Hoffa's first appearance, Senator McClellan publicly called off the dogs. RFK was visibly embarrassed, and Hoffa triumphantly pointed at his rival: "Look at him, look at him! He's too tired. He just doesn't want to go on."

Get Hoffa (Part II)

With that background (and with Hoffa beating the rap in two other trials in the late 1950s), when RFK became Attorney General he promptly commissioned a special task force known inside DOJ as the "Get Hoffa Squad." Heading up the squad was Walter Sheridan, an FBI-trained operative who had been the lead investigator of the Rackets Committee; he was aided by a staff of approximately 20 dedicated lawyers, and assisted by other DOJ lawyers, as well as by a variety of FBI agents and other investigators. As with Don Corleone's instruction to Luca Brasi, the squad was charged with finding out what Hoffa had "under his fingernails." Effectively, Hoffa came under a 24/7 surveillance. That Bobby Kennedy was intimately involved in the squad's activities is best shown by the fact that, in the midst of the Cuban Missile Crisis, RFK was in daily strategy sessions with Sheridan concerning his on-going efforts to get "the man."

All of these efforts led to various cases brought by the Kennedy Justice Department against Hoffa. This chapter will focus on the first trial, brought in Nashville (the *Test Fleet* case), and then a following trial in Chattanooga.

The *Test Fleet* trial centered on whether Hoffa had violated Taft-Hartley by setting up a truck-leasing business in 1949 under various people's names, including his wife's. The alleged conduct was, if proven, a conflict of interest; it was a misdemeanor, and punishable with up to a year in jail. The best and the brightest within the DOJ helped assemble the case and strategize its prosecution; in the words of one historian, "[n]ever in history had the government devoted so much money, manpower and top level brainpower to a misdemeanor case." After a two-month trial, the jury deadlocked at seven to five for acquittal; ultimately, the judge declared a mistrial on December 23, 1962.

Irrespective of the *Test Fleet* outcome, Sheridan's squad had bagged a bigger fish: in advance of the trial they had turned an unhappy Teamster, Edward G. Partin, into a government informant. Partin, who had a 20-year rap sheet (e.g., rape, manslaughter, embezzlement), reported to the squad that Hoffa had said: "I've got to do something about that son of a bitch Bobby Kennedy"; and that, in that context, Hoffa had asked Partin what he knew about plastic explosives. A skeptical Sheridan wanted to give Partin a lie detector test, to which RFK responded: "What do we do if that fellow passes the test?"

In any event, Partin was physically present in the Hoffa camp during the *Test Fleet* trial and documented to Sheridan several instances of jury tampering. And while the evidence thereof did not come in at the Chattanooga trial always smoothly (or consistently), the sheer volume of it was sufficient to have Hoffa found guilty of a felony, sentenced to eight years in prison, and fined $10,000. Hoffa appealed all the way to the Supreme Court, mostly attacking Partin's background and reliability, as well as the government's alleged misuse of him and improper dealings with him. Only Chief Justice Earl Warren was moved by those arguments, however, and as a result Hoffa entered Lewisburg Federal Prison in March 1967. A decade's-long crusade had finally borne fruit.

Postscript

The starting point for understanding RFK's legacy at the Department of Justice has to be Victor Navosky's excellent *Kennedy Justice* (Atheneum 1971). For the most balanced biography on Robert Kennedy (i.e., one not written by a family insider or friend), the best place to go is Evan Thomas's *Robert Kennedy: His Life* (Simon & Schuster 2000).

When Hoffa was told that RFK had turned his car around and returned to his Washington office upon passing Teamsters headquarters one night and seeing Hoffa's lights still on, Hoffa regularly thereafter left his office lights on, regardless of whether anyone was working. ("I used to love to bug the little bastard.")

When JFK became President, his Senate seat was given to a Harvard classmate (Benjamin Smith) to keep warm until his younger brother, Edward "Teddy," was eligible to run in 1962 (he would turn 30 only after the November election). Teddy had been kicked out of Harvard for cheating (later readmitted), and had no substantive qualifications for the world's greatest deliberative body, other than the fact that his brothers were the two most powerful men in the U.S. government. Given the flack that had accompanied RKF's appointment, as well as the bad feelings being generated among local Massachusetts pols, both the President and the Attorney General began to have second thoughts about the wisdom of a Senate race for their younger brother—concerns that they shared with their father. The elder Kennedy, however, was adamant: "You boys have what you want now, and everyone else helped you work to get it. Now it's Ted's turn." Later, when asked by the press what problems Teddy might have in winning his brother's Senate seat, his father succinctly replied: "None." The Ambassador proved correct.

After over four years in prison, Hoffa was pardoned by President Nixon and released on December 23, 1971, subject to the condition that he not seek the Teamsters' presidency before 1980. On July 30, 1975, Hoffa was scheduled to meet Anthony "Tony Pro" Provenzano and Anthony "Tony Jack" Giacalone at the Machus Red Fox Restaurant in Bloomfield Township, Michigan. Hoffa was never seen again, and was pronounced legally dead in 1982.

RFK was so distraught after his JFK's death that he took no public delight in Hoffa's 1964 conviction or upon his entering prison in 1967. In fact, according to Robert Morgenthau (a close friend and then U.S. Attorney in the Southern District of New York) RFK never talked about and took no interest in going after organized crime subsequent to November 22, 1963.

CHAPTER XXII

Chappaquiddick: Did the Justice System Work?

Many trees have died since July 18-19, 1969, quite a few devoted to exploring what really happened when Mary Jo Kopechne perished in Senator Edward Moore Kennedy's Oldsmobile Delmont 88, when it drove off Dike Bridge and was submerged in Poucha Pond on Chappaquiddick Island, in Edgartown, Massachusetts. That accident occurred during the latter stages of a party on Chappaquiddick for six "Boiler Room Girls" (young women who worked on Robert F. Kennedy's 1968 presidential campaign) and six middle-aged men, five of them were married (including Kennedy). Most of the reporting has been devoted to Kennedy's two accounts—his volunteered account on the morning of July 19 to the local police chief, and his July 25 televised statement (authored by his brother's principal speechwriter, Theodore Sorensen). Those two accounts are in material disagreement; furthermore, both have been shown—by countless analysts—to be false and misleading on numerous key points.

This chapter will not relitigate that well-trod ground. Rather, the focus will be on how well the justice system handled what has been called the "most famous traffic fatality of the (twentieth) century."

The Police Investigation

The only real "evidence" uncovered by the Edgartown police (which had jurisdiction over the investigation) was the account proffered by Kennedy to the police about one hour after he first reported the incident (nine to ten hours after it occurred). It was handwritten by his friend Paul Markham (a former U.S. Attorney for Massachusetts and a participant in the prior evening's party), and its text is as follows:

> On July 18, 1969, at approximately 11:15 p.m. in Chappaquiddick, Martha's Vineyard, Mass., I was driving my car on Main Street on my way to get the ferry back to Edgartown. I was unfamiliar with the road and turned onto Dike Road instead of bearing hard left on Main Street. After proceeding for approximately one half mile on Dike Road, I descended a hill and came upon a narrow bridge. The car went off the side of the bridge. There was one passenger with me, one Miss Mary ________, a former secretary of my brother, Senator Robert Kennedy. The car turned over and sank into the water and landed with the roof resting on the bottom. I attempted to open the door and the window of the car but have no recollection of how I got out of the car. I came to the surface and then repeatedly dove down to the car in an attempt to see if the passenger was still in the car. I was unsuccessful in the attempt. I was exhausted and in a state of shock. I recall walking back, to where my friends were eating. There was a car parked in front of the cottage, and I climbed into the back seat. I then asked for someone to bring me back to Edgartown. I remember walking around for a period of time and then going back to my hotel room. When I fully realized what had happened this morning, I immediately contacted the police.

The victim's name was left blank because neither Kennedy nor Markham knew how to spell her last name. At no time thereafter did Kennedy provide any other information to the police; and he refused to answer any questions. The five remaining single women at the party were whisked off the island on July 19 before the police knew they had been at the party (or that there had even been a party). None of the four other married men who attended the party—besides Kennedy—(including Markham and Kennedy's cousin, Joseph Gargan) were questioned; the sixth man at the party—Kennedy's aide and often chauffeur, John Crimmins—later offered a conclusory, tersely written statement that moved the evidentiary needle not one whit. Kopechne's body was flown off the island to Pennsylvania by another Kennedy aide on July 20 (he had been directed to do so on July 19, *before* Kennedy notified the police of his involvement). There had been only a cursory review of her body, with no autopsy or official statement as to the cause of death.

For multiple reasons—including the fact that nine or ten hours had passed since the incident, and that Kennedy seemed uninjured, was perfectly calm, and in full command of his faculties on the morning of July 19—the Senator was not subjected to any testing for alcohol. Nonetheless, it was later established that he had had numerous cocktails in the latter part of the afternoon of July 18 (along with a beer or two—all before the party), that he had (at least) several more drinks at the party, and it was widely known (in Washington circles) that he had had a serious drinking problem since RFK's 1968 assassination. Also unknown to the police was the fact that the small house on the island where the party took place had been stocked with three half-gallon bottles of vodka, four fifths of scotch, two bottles of rum, and two cases of beer (and two of the men present—Crimmins and Gargan—drank no alcohol that night); all evidence of what was in the house was quickly vacuumed up on July 19 by Kennedy aides. Finally, Kopechne—known as a very moderate drinker—was found (after nine or ten hours of being submerged in cold salt water and then several more hours after having been removed from the car) to have had an alcohol content in her blood of 0.09—the equivalent of having had 5 or 6 drinks in the hour before her death (i.e., she was "legally drunk"). None of the foregoing played any part in the police investigation.

Then there was the question of liability. Under Massachusetts law, "[a]ny person who wantonly or in a reckless or grossly negligent manner did that which resulted in the death of a human being was guilty of manslaughter, although he did not contemplate such a result." In meeting that standard, besides factoring in whether Kennedy was impaired when he drove off the bridge (which went unexplored), another key question would have been to determine how fast the car was going when it drove off the bridge. The police, however, made no effort to answer that question. Then there was the issue of Kennedy's driving history. Two facts complicated that subject: first, his driver's license had expired, and second, Kennedy had at least three reckless driving convictions in Virginia (and two other Virginia charges for driving without a license). The local authorities judged the former fact (when it was belatedly brought to their attention) of no importance; as to the latter fact(s), the police were (and remained) unaware.

A Deal and Then a Plea

Based on the "investigation," the local police and special prosecutor for the county concluded that there was "no criminal negligence" on Kennedy's part, nor was there any evidence "to indicate excessive speed or reckless driving." But what about the inescapable matters of Kennedy's leaving the scene of the accident (after causing a death) and not reporting it until nine or ten hours later? The police chief felt compelled to file a misdemeanor application, charging the Senator with that crime; the statute provided a sentence of two months to two years (with a mandatory 20 days in jail).

A few days later the local prosecutor met with Kennedy's lawyers to discuss a deal. Kennedy's team asked, if he pleaded guilty, what would the local prosecutor recommend to the judge in the way of a penalty. The response was "for any first offender," it would be a suspended sentence. [That, of course, posed a problem given Kennedy's Virginia offenses.] Would the judge go along? The local prosecutor could not make any such representation. The Kennedy team, without authority to commit to anything, said they had to go back and check with the people "calling the shots."

The dangers in not taking a guilty plea were significant: (1) a public trial; (2) a presentation of evidence; (3) party attendees could be subpoenaed to testify; (4) Deputy Sheriff Christopher "Huck" Look would undoubtedly be a witness, and he posed great problems for central tenets of Kennedy's story: (a) he had seen Kennedy's car (with a man and woman in the front seat) at *12:45 a.m.* on July 19; (b) Look, in his police uniform, had stopped his car and walked to within 20-30 feet of the Kennedy car, which had also stopped—but it then turned quickly on to Dike Road and drove away at a fast speed; and (c) Look would also testify that the male driver appeared "lost" and "confused"; (5) Kennedy would be subject to cross-examination; and (6) based on what transpired at such a trial, evidence sufficient to justify a manslaughter charge might well be developed. And as the Kennedy camp contemplated those items, the public/media pressure for the Senator to make some statement as to what happened had reached a mega boiling point (since the accident, Kennedy had holed up, incommunicado, at his family's Hyannisport compound with a bevy of advisors trying to figure out what to do). Ultimately, those two conflicting considerations won out, and Kennedy's legal team met again with the local authorities to seal the deal: Kennedy would agree to waive a hearing, plead guilty to leaving the scene, and a suspended sentence would be jointly proposed to the judge.

At 8:58 a.m. on Monday July 25, Kennedy and his legal team sat in Judge James Boyle's Edgartown courtroom. The charge of leaving the scene was read aloud and Kennedy was asked: "How do you plead? Guilty or not guilty?" With more than a little difficulty, Kennedy was able to offer a whispering "guilty." Then, after a summary of the "evidence," Judge Boyle asked if the defendant had made a "deliberate effort" to conceal his identity. The police chief answered: "Not to my knowledge, your honor." Kennedy (who had spent nine to ten hours after the accident concealing his culpability) offered no response. Both sets of lawyers then proposed a suspended sentence. Before ruling, Judge Boyle asked whether there was any prior "record." When told there was "none" (which was not true), Judge Boyle agreed to a suspended sentence, "[c]onsidering the unblemished record of the defendant and insofar as the Commonwealth represents that this is not a case where he was really trying to conceal his identity...."

And with that seeming to end his legal problems, Kennedy went on national television that night to read the Sorensen speech. It saved his political career with the Massachusetts voters; but it also served to exacerbate the many inexplicable, unanswered questions that remained regarding the death of Kopechne and his own conduct.

The Inquest

Kennedy's legal problems were not in fact over, however, because another prosecutor, the District Attorney for the Southern District of Massachusetts, Edward Dinis, also had jurisdiction. And on the same day Kennedy returned to the Senate (July 31), Dinis requested an inquest into Kopechne's death. On August 8, Judge Boyle agreed to that request, setting the inquest to take place on September 3. Fearing the public nature of an inquest (and the potential for such a proceeding exposing Kennedy to a charge of manslaughter), Kennedy's legal team petitioned the Massachusetts Supreme Judicial Court on September 2 for a temporary restraining order to stop the inquest. On October 30, the court not only ordered the press and public be barred from the inquest (because of all the publicity that had already accompanied the accident, further media coverage might "make it difficult, if not impossible,... to [e]nsure a defendant a fair trial in any criminal proceedings which may follow."), it also inexplicably ordered that the entire record from such a proceeding be impounded until *after* any prosecution of Kennedy's conduct could be undertaken. With those guidelines, Judge Boyle re-scheduled the inquest to begin on January 5, 1970.

While the injunction petition was pending, Dinis brought on his own petition (in Pennsylvania), seeking the exhumation and autopsy of Kopechne's body (citing evidence of blood on her body and clothing). Mr. and Mrs. Kopechne (after allegedly receiving counseling from an old Kennedy family friend, Cardinal Cushing) judicially intervened and opposed the disturbance of their daughter's body. On October 20-21, a Wilkes-Barre judge held a hearing on the petition. Notwithstanding testimony from witnesses (including a Kopechne expert) that Kopechne was alive and breathing for some period while trapped in the car underwater (which could have supported the notion that Kopechne suffocated, as opposed to having drowned), the judge on December 1 ruled that there was "[n]o evidence [that] anything other than drowning had caused the death of Mary Jo Kopechne." As such, there would be no exhumation and autopsy of her body.

Before the inquest could begin, yet another odd thing happened: the lead detective for the District Attorney's office contacted and later met twice with key Kennedy advisors to give them detailed "heads-ups" about what evidence and testimony the District Attorney intended to put on at the inquest. The detective (Bernie Flynn) wanted to help the Senator (who he thought not only had clearly lied in his television speech, but had also been "in the bag" when he was driving on the night of July 18-19): "My main purpose is, I don't want Ted Kennedy to get caught in a big lie that could really make him go down the drain." Risking his entire professional career to have the Senator (and the Kennedy machine) owe him one, Flynn did his best to put the Kennedy advisors' "mind[s] at ease that there weren't going to be any surprises [at the inquest]. And they seemed to like that."

On January 5, contrary to the order of witnesses proposed by Dinis, Judge Boyle required that the Senator testify first. Kennedy, under oath, was then allowed to present essentially a rambling monologue that tried to accommodate as best he could his two prior (inconsistent) versions, anticipate Look's (and others') testimony (based on Flynn's "heads-ups"), refute any notion that he was not "absolutely sober" at the time of the accident, and negate any suggestion that he was driving recklessly (Kennedy swore he was driving at 20 miles per hour). Dinis—a Democrat, who was running for re-election that year, and thus understood well the dangers of taking on Kennedy—allowed the Senator to bob and weave, not answering and/or filibustering different questions. When he thought he could, Kennedy flat out lied (for example, he keyed the time of when he asked Gargan and Markham to help him rescue Kopechne to a clock in a rental car back at the party house; the *Boston Globe* later proved the car had no clock). When asked about his numerous telephone calls on the morning of July 19 (before he notified the police of his involvement), he dissembled, with good reason—one of the calls was to his mistress in Florida. When Dinis tried to act like a lawyer and impeach Kennedy's testimony with his volunteered statement to the police on July 19, Judge Boyle stopped him (the statement "speak[s] for itself"); and when Dinis pursued it further with leading questions, the judge pronounced: "There is no cross-examination in this inquest!" After three hours, the Senator walked out of the courthouse "satisfied I responded in the most complete way possible to all the questions put to me by the judge and the district attorney."

Now all the Kennedy team had to worry about was the other 25 listed witnesses. The party participants—even with enormous coaching on how to hew to the Kennedy story (and their lawyers paid for by Kennedy money)—did not do such a great job. But Dinis and Judge Boyle did not do much in identifying various holes/inconsistencies in their stories and drilling down on them. For example, Ray LaRosa (a Kennedy campaign worker) confirmed that he and two of the "Boiler Room Girls" (while doing a "conga line" in the middle of the main street after midnight) had interacted with Huck Look driving *from* the direction of the ferry (right after Look had seen Kennedy's car); and just before meeting up with Look, LaRosa and the women had been passed by another car heading *toward* the ferry (i.e., where Look had just seen it). Notwithstanding this obvious bombshell to Kennedy's time line and version of events, neither Dinis nor Boyle pursued it.

Another Kennedy aide, Charles Trotter, also made a hash out of Kennedy's time line. And this had a significant personal consequence to him. Trotter—a married man—had taken two extended midnight "walks" with one of the "Boiler Room Girls." By this testimony, Kennedy's walk back from the accident to seek help from Gargan and Markham would have had him meeting up with them on at least one of their "walks." This hole in Kennedy's story went unpursued.

Gargan and Markham did their best to follow the televised Kennedy version of events (which had, *inter alia,* revealed for the first time that Kennedy enlisted their help after the accident and they had made repeated attempts to save Kopechne). Unfortunately, the two men (neither of whom could claim "shock" etc.) were not pressed on why they had not summoned help, or (as officers of the court) had not reported the accident at once. Both dissembled about the extent of Kennedy's drinking. And Gargan was never asked whether a frantic Kennedy had discussed that night offering up alternative explanation(s) for the accident—which he had: e.g., Kopechne was driving alone in the car (Gargan was prepared to answer—if asked—that "that was discussed, but not acted upon."). Nor was either man asked in detail about what happened when they confronted a calm and unconcerned Kennedy at 8:00 a.m. on July 19, and why it had taken the Senator almost an additional two hours to report the accident.

As for the witnesses who interacted with a calm and dressed-for-yachting Kennedy the morning of July 19, the District Attorney did not develop a full record. For example, the man who spent 30 minutes with the Senator was not questioned on several key matters he told investigators. Another man who had witnessed Kennedy's serious imbibing the afternoon before was not even called to testify. When the "Boiler Room Girls" testified, their prepackaged performances were so unpersuasive that Judge Boyle took over much of the questioning, with numerous sarcastic and pointed inquiries that reflected frustration at their collusive testimony.

Deputy Sheriff Look's testimony came in as advertised. And while he could not swear with metaphysical certainty that it was Kennedy's car he interacted with at 12:45 a.m. on July 19, his identification of the type of car and the license plate letters and numbers left little doubt that it was the Senator's car (it was later proven with metaphysical certainty, but Dinis decided not to put that evidence into the inquest record). The diver who recovered Kopechne's body from the car was severely limited as to what he was allowed to testify (i.e., that the position of Kopechne's body in the car meant she was gasping into an air bubble at the back of the car; that she did not drown, but suffocated; and that she could have been saved if he (or another professional diver) had been called immediately after the accident).

The inquest ended with a whimper on January 8. Left uncalled as witnesses included (1) the residents of the houses right near the bridge, whose testimony would have directly contradicted Kennedy's (i.e., the existence of house lights being on—which Kennedy denied emphatically), and (2) a next-door neighbor to the party house, who would have testified to "yelling, music[,] and general sounds of hell-raising" until 1:30 a.m. on July 19.

Upon his return to Washington, Kennedy told reporters: "I'm glad it's over.... I am hopeful now of getting back to the business of the Senate." But before that could really be the case, Judge's Boyle's inquest report would have to be factored in.

On February 18, the judge filed his report and the transcript of the inquest under seal with the Edgartown Superior Court clerk. The documents were subsequently brought to the Boston Superior Courthouse for safekeeping. Despite the not-so-perfect inquest's search for the truth, the report contained a number of bombshells, none good for the Senator. First, Boyle found that the testimony of the witnesses contained a great number of "inconsistences and contradictions." Second, he placed the accident as "between 11:30 p.m. on July 18 and 1:00 a.m., on July 19" (not resolving the conflict between Kennedy and Look's testimony). Third, he expressly rejected Kennedy's sworn claim that he had mistakenly taken a 90° turn on to the dirt road leading to the bridge (and beach beyond): "Kennedy and Kopechne did *not* intend to drive to the ferry slip and his turn onto Dike Road had been intentional." Fourth, that (1) driving at 20 miles per hour (as Kennedy testified to) was "at least negligent and possibly reckless"; (2) if Kennedy knew of the hazard ahead of him (i.e., the bridge), such driving would constitute criminal intent; (3) because the Senator had twice driven over the bridge earlier on July 18, the judge concluded that it was "probable" that Kennedy knew of the hazard; and (4) in light of the foregoing, "[t]here is probable cause to believe that . . . Kennedy operated his motor vehicle negligently . . . and that such operation appears to have contributed to the death of Mary Jo Kopechne."

Although what Judge Boyle laid out constituted a basis for the issuance of an arrest warrant for manslaughter, he did nothing; in fact, he retired from the bench two days later on February 20. The matter was left on the doorstep of Dinis. Upon Dinis's return to Massachusetts from a vacation abroad, he was stunned ("son of a bitch!") to read Boyle's (still confidential) report. Recognizing he was now between a rock (Boyle's report) and a hard place (prosecuting Kennedy), Dinis froze. He would soon find a group of people who would try to unfreeze him.

The Grand Jury

The grand jury of Dukes County, Massachusetts, had been pursuing Dinis to investigate the accident/death; but it had been persuaded to hold off until after the inquest. On March 17, the grand jury foreman wrote Joseph Tauro, Chief Justice of the Superior Court, requesting that the panel be reconvened in order to investigate Kopechne's death. Nine days later, Tauro judicially green-lighted the grand jury to convene on April 6 to hear evidence on the matter. Given Boyle's report, this looked like a moment of maximum danger for Kennedy's political career, as well as his liberty.

Fortunately for Kennedy, the case was assigned to Judge Wilfred J. Paquet; he was not only an old-time Democratic machine politician (and Kennedy stalwart), he was also a former client of the Senator's lawyer. At the outset of their April 6 session, the grand jury heard a 90-minute oration by Paquet about how limited their function was in investigating the matter. And to make that directive crystal clear, he told the jurors they would not be permitted to see any of the inquest materials or Judge Boyle's report. Furthermore, they would not be permitted to subpoena anyone who had testified at the inquest; instead, they would be permitted only to subpoena "other" witnesses and could consider only what the judge or district attorney showed them, or what they knew "personally" about the accident. Compounding the judge's erroneous directions, Dinis told the jurors that there was nothing in the inquest transcripts or Judge Boyle's report that would support any criminal charges against Kennedy.

Faced with these astonishing (and improper) roadblocks, the grand jury called four inconsequential witnesses, who testified for a total of 20 minutes. Thereafter, frustrated, but stymied by Paquet and Dinis, the jurors threw in the towel and were dismissed by the judge.

Kennedy was now truly free from criminal exposure. The inquest record and Boyle's report were subsequently made public on April 29, 1970. And although they caused a media firestorm (and greatly inflamed the grand jurors), Kennedy's stonewall stood firm. As to Boyle's findings, the Senator issued a statement: "I reject them." He added: "I plan no further statement on this tragic matter." And for the rest of his life, that is where Kennedy let things stand (e.g., "I've answered all the questions.").

Did the justice system work vis-à-vis Kennedy and Kopechne's death? I will let the reader(s) decide. That said, let me add what Dinis stated long after Kennedy was free from criminal exposure: "There's no question in my mind that the grand jury would have brought an indictment against Ted Kennedy for manslaughter, if I had given them the case."

Postscript

In November of 1970, Kennedy was re-elected to the Senate (where he served until his death in 2009). Dinis, on the other hand, lost his bid for a fourth term as District Attorney. Although he did not think Kennedy had "a direct role" in his defeat, Dinis did ruefully observe: "The girl died. And I got defeated."

The Massachusetts Motor Vehicles Registry concluded in May of 1970 that Kennedy had been speeding and was "at serious fault" for the accident. Nonetheless, it has refused since then to release its report without written authorization from Kennedy (which was never forthcoming during his lifetime). A subsequent analysis of what happened that night by one of the county's leading experts on car accidents concluded that Kennedy's account of his speed (20 miles per hour) was in error. The expert's analysis was that the car was traveling at "a minimum speed outside of 30 mph; it could have been going as fast as 38 mph."

The *Boston Globe* and *Reader's Digest* have both done significant investigatory reporting on Chappaquiddick, and that excellent work can be accessed via the internet for those who wish a more fulsome account of what actually took place in July of 1969 and thereafter. The leading (and best) book on the subject is Leo Damore's *Senatorial Privilege: The Chappaquiddick Cover-Up* (Regnery Gateway 1988). *See also Spy* magazine (November 1987) ("Experts Decide: Will Teddy Go to Hell?"). The 2017 movie *Chappaquiddick* (Apex Entertainment) is not sympathetic to Senator Kennedy or his conduct; at the same time, it is not wholly consistent with the known, undisputable facts (let alone in attempting to resolve the innumerable inconsistencies in testimony and disputed facts).

In response to President Gerald Ford pardoning his predecessor, Richard Nixon, in 1974, Kennedy posed this rhetorical question on the floor of the U.S. Senate: "Do we operate under a system of equal justice under law, or is there one system for the average citizen, and another for the high and mighty?"

CHAPTER XXIII

Attorneys in the White House

Billy Wilder, the brilliant screenwriter and director, was not a good historian. In Wilder's wonderfully funny movie *The Fortune Cookie*, shyster lawyer "Whiplash Willie" Gingrich, played by Walter Matthau, utters a classic line: "Lincoln—great president, lousy lawyer."

In my view, Abraham Lincoln was indisputably a great lawyer (and, of our presidents, the most able trial lawyer) (*see* Chapter XXV). But what about our other presidents who were also lawyers? Out of 47 presidents (including the current president), 27 were admitted to the Bar (with five more who studied law, but decided not to pursue a legal career).[1] Which lawyers were great presidents, and which presidents were great lawyers?

Lawyers as Presidents

To answer the first question, we can look to two surveys. The first was conducted by Arthur Schlesinger in 1996, the second was conducted by the Federalist Society and the *Wall Street Journal* in 2000; their methodologies were essentially the same—polling

[1] Since both Presidents Barack Obama and Joe Biden never had real law practices of any sort prior to entering politics, they have not been included in this chapter.

prominent scholars and collating the responses. Set forth below are the two surveys, with our legal brethren highlighted:

1996 Survey

Great:

1. G. Washington
2. **A. Lincoln**
3. **F. Roosevelt**

Near Great:

4. **T. Jefferson**
5. **A. Jackson**
6. J. Polk
7. T. Roosevelt
8. **W. Wilson**
9. H. Truman

Above Average:

10. **J. Adams**
11. **J. Monroe**
12. **G. Cleveland**
13. **W. McKinley**
14. D. Eisenhower
15. J. Kennedy
16. L. Johnson

Average:

17. J. Madison
18. **J.Q. Adams**
19. **M. Van Buren**
20. **R. Hayes**
21. **C. Arthur**
22. **B. Harrison**
23. **W. Taft**

24. **G. Ford**
25. J. Carter
26. R. Reagan
27. G.H.W. Bush
28. **W. Clinton**

Below Average

29. J. Tyler
30. Z. Taylor
31. **M. Fillmore**
32. **C. Coolidge**

Failure:

33. **F. Pierce**
34. **J. Buchanan**
35. A. Johnson
36. U.S. Grant
37. W. Harding
38. H. Hoover
39. **R. Nixon**

2000 Survey

Great:

1. G. Washington
2. **A. Lincoln**
3. **F. Roosevelt**

Near Great:

4. **T. Jefferson**
5. T. Roosevelt
6. **A. Jackson**
7. H. Truman
8. R. Reagan
9. D. Eisenhower

10. **J. Polk**
11. **W. Wilson**

Above Average:

12. **G. Cleveland**
13. **J. Adams**
14. **W. McKinley**
15. J. Madison
16. **J. Monroe**
17. L. Johnson
18. J. Kennedy

Average:

19. **W. Taft**
20. **J.Q. Adams**
21. G.H.W. Bush
22. **R. Hayes**
23. **M. Van Buren**
24. **W. Clinton**
25. **C. Coolidge**
26. **C. Arthur**

Below Average:

27. **B. Harrison**
28. **G. Ford**
29. H. Hoover
30. J. Carter
31. Z. Taylor
32. U. Grant
33. **R. Nixon**
34. **J. Tyler**
35. **M. Fillmore**

Failure:

36. A. Johnson
37. **F. Pierce**

38. W. Harding
39. **J. Buchanan**

[Note: The terms of J. Garfield and W. Harrison were so brief that they were not ranked.]

Presidents as Lawyers

In assessing the legal skills and careers of our former political chief executives, they seem to fall into four basic categories.

1. *Admitted, but with little or no law practice because of their political careers.* Into this category go presidents Jefferson, Monroe, Tyler, Polk, Fillmore, Pierce, Buchanan, Coolidge, and Clinton. Wilson, who left the practice of law after one year to pursue a Ph.D., should also be placed in this group.
2. *Admitted, but with a small hometown practice that served as the basis for their political careers.* Into this category go presidents Van Buren, Hayes (the first president to graduate from law school), Cleveland, McKinley, and Ford.
3. *Studied law, but were never admitted.* Into this category go presidents Madison, T. Roosevelt, Harding, Truman (he went to the Kansas City School of Law while a sitting judge!), and L. Johnson.
4. *Presidents who had distinguished legal careers (or who did some interesting things as lawyers).* Into this category go presidents J. Adams, J.Q. Adams, Jackson, Lincoln, Garfield & Harrison, Arthur, Taft, F. Roosevelt, and Nixon. Because Lincoln and Nixon have already been reviewed (*see* Chapter XXV and *The Worst Supreme Court Decisions Ever (And Related Tales)* (Twelve Tables Press 2024)), the other presidents' legal careers will be highlighted below.

John Adams

John Adams was admitted to the Massachusetts Bar in 1758, and soon built a thriving practice. In 1769, for example, he successfully defended John Hancock against charges that he had illegally smuggled wine into Boston. Adams's most famous case, however, was in representing British soldiers in the aftermath of the Boston Massacre. On March 5, 1770, British soldiers stationed in Boston were being taunted by an angry mob; the taunting escalated, with multiple objects being picked up and thrown. As tensions became acute, one British soldier suddenly fired his gun, and others followed suit. Three Americans were killed, with eight wounded. The British soldiers were arrested and charged with murder. Finding a colonial lawyer to defend them proved problematic, until Adams stepped forward and agreed to be their trial counsel. He did so knowing that he would be heavily criticized by his friends and neighbors, and notwithstanding his publicly articulated criticisms of British rule.

The soldiers' commanding officer was tried first, and separately. This proved fortuitous because Adams was able to demonstrate at trial that the soldiers had fired spontaneously without any orders or directive from their officer. Adams thus won his acquittal.

Next came the soldiers, who were tried en masse (eight in all). Adams's skill in jury selection resulted in all prospective jurors from Boston being excused; they were replaced by a jury panel consisting entirely of men from rural Massachusetts who were not as inflamed about the "massacre." Adams countered the prosecution's case by painting a lurid picture of the mob: "a motley rabble of saucy boys, Negroes, and mulattoes, Irish teagues and outlandish jack tars … shouting and hazzaing [sic] and threatening life … whistling, screaming and rending an Indian yell … throwing every species of rubbish they could pick up in the street." And he asked the jurors to stand in the shoes of the soldiers who had been subjected to all forms of verbal and physical abuse: "You expect he should behave like a stoic philosopher, lost in apathy?" After Adams was finished, the jury acquitted six of the soldiers, and found the other two guilty of manslaughter (for which they received brandings on the thumbs and were then released).

Adams, in standing up for a basic tenet of our profession, was vilified by many. For his services at both trials, Adams received a total of 40 guineas.

John Quincy Adams

John Quincy Adams, upon being admitted to the Massachusetts Bar in 1790, opened a law office in Boston. Unlike his father, he attracted few clients and was not a rousing professional success. Fortunately, because of his political activities and his political lineage (his father was vice president at that time) he left the law by dint of his appointment as Minister to the Netherlands (1794-1797).

That appointment led to a succession of increasingly important posts: Minister to Prussia (1797-1801), Massachusetts State Senator (1802), U.S. Senator (1803-1808), Minister to Russia (1809-1814), Chief Negotiator of Treaty of Ghent (1814), Minister to Great Britain (1815-1817), and Secretary of State (1817-1825). In that latter position, Adams was undoubtedly one of our country's most distinguished leaders (e.g., he was the author of the Monroe Doctrine).

Following his controversial election as president in 1824, Adams's presidency was not a great success (witness his ranking), notwithstanding his superb preparation. After losing the rematch against Andrew Jackson in 1828, he went home to Massachusetts. In 1830, Adams became the only former president to be elected as a U.S. congressman (John Tyler was elected to the Confederate Congress). He served with great distinction until he collapsed on the floor of the House in 1848 (he died two days later).

Adams's principal leadership came in the fight against the "gag rule," which had been adopted in 1836; the gag rule tab led without debate any petition critical of slavery. After an unrelenting eight-year battle by Adams, the rule was repealed in 1844.

As part of that effort came Adams's most significant contribution as a lawyer. Adams was persuaded to argue before the Supreme Court on behalf of slaves who had mutinied on a Spanish ship (the *Amistad*) that was transporting them from Africa; the ship ended up on Long Island. Abolitionists took up their cause in opposition to the Van Buren administration, which maintained that the slaves had to be returned to their Spanish owners under the provisions of a 1795 bilateral treaty.

A trial was held in federal court in New Haven (the slaves had been taken to New London, Connecticut). While much of the pretrial maneuverings had been over procedural issues (e.g., if the alleged mutiny took place in international waters, did the U.S. court have jurisdiction), the district judge ruled at trial that the slaves had been born free in Africa, that they had been kidnapped, and therefore they were not "legally" slaves who could be returned as Spanish "property." After that ruling was (basically) upheld by the court of appeals, the Van Buren administration sought review by the Supreme Court (a majority of its justices were, or had been, slave owners).

At that point, Adams, together with a future Connecticut governor, Roger Baldwin, argued for the appellees. Baldwin argued in support of the technical merits of the trial court's ruling, with Adams painting on a broader canvass. More specifically, Adams undertook to ridicule the geopolitical basis of the administration's position, especially its interpretation of the 1795 treaty. He also used passionate language (invoked a decade later by Seward and Lincoln in the political arena) to suggest that the Declaration of Independence could not be reconciled with a result of finding against the slaves.

The Court, in contradistinction to its abominable decision in 1857 in the *Dred Scott* case, issued a narrow ruling (7-1) in favor of the slaves (40 U.S. 518 (1841)). The linchpin of the Court's ruling was that the 1795 treaty did not define property to include human beings; as such, under international law, the United States had no obligation to return the slaves to Spain. In November of 1841, the slaves sailed back to Africa (the trip was financed by abolitionists).

The Spanish government sought, and continued to seek, compensation from the United States until 1860, when the election of Lincoln made the issue moot.

Andrew Jackson

When Andrew Jackson was reading the law in the office of Spruce McCay in Salisbury, North Carolina, he got a reputation as "the most roaring, rollicking, gamecocking, horse racing, card playing, mischievous fellow that ever lived in Salisbury." One example of his mischief was his invitation to the town prostitutes to attend the town's Christmas ball—a "joke" for which he received a severe reprimand. Notwithstanding, Jackson was admitted to the North Carolina Bar in 1787, having been adjudged to be of "unblemished moral character." A year later he became the public prosecutor for the western part of the state, before moving onto neighboring Tennessee where his political career flourished. He became Tennessee's first congressman in 1796, and was later elected by the legislature to the U.S. Senate.

Jackson, however, missed his wife and was bored by the pace of the upper body; he resigned after five months. The legislature then appointed him to the Tennessee Superior Court—the state's highest court. Despite his mercurial nature (duels and threatened duels were a regular part of his life at this point), as well as his nonclassical education, Jackson proved to be a highly effective and widely praised jurist over his six-year tenure (1798-1804). Besides writing opinions (only five of which have survived), Jacksonian justice on the frontier came in many forms. On one occasion while he was "riding the circuit," an indicted man refused to submit to being arrested, and the sheriff was too intimidated to force the issue. Jackson adjourned court for 10 minutes. He went outside and found the man, who was vowing to kill anyone who attempted to take him in. Jackson walked up to him with a pistol in each hand and said: "Now, surrender, you infernal villain, this very instant, or I'll blow you through." Thus confronted, the man relented: "It's no use, I give in." Days later when asked why he had given in so meekly to Jackson after holding off the sheriff and his posse, the prisoner said: "Why, when he came up, I looked him in the eye, and I saw shoot, and there wasn't shoot in nary other eye in the crowd; so I says to myself, says I, hoss, it's about time to sing small, and so I did." While on the court, Jackson was elected major general of the Tennessee militia; and that provided the segue into the military career that ultimately placed him in the White House. When he did become president, a Salisbury woman was incredulous: "Jackson? Andrew Jackson? . . . Well, if Andrew Jackson can be president, anybody can!"

James Garfield and Benjamin Harrison

James Garfield was admitted to the Ohio Bar in 1860 (while president of a college—the Western Reserve Electric Institute). Benjamin Harrison was admitted to the Indiana Bar in 1854. What each man shares is a role in the important Supreme Court case of *Ex Parte Milligan,* 71 U.S. 2 (1866) (*see* Chapter XVII, *The Worst Supreme Court Decisions, Ever!* (Twelve Tables Press 2024)).

During the Civil War, Union army officers in Indiana arrested Lambdin Milligan (and other prominent antiwar Democrats), charging a conspiracy to seize munitions and free Confederate prisoners. The defendants were tried before a military commission and found guilty; they were sentenced to hang.

On appeal to the Supreme Court, Milligan was represented by Garfield (then a congressman). It was Garfield's first case in any court, and he was the first lawyer to argue his first case before the Court. And he won! All nine justices (for a host of disparate reasons) agreed that the military commission lacked jurisdiction, and that any prosecution should have proceeded in federal civil court. Milligan et al. were thus freed. (This was a controversial decision in the Reconstruction era, especially with respect to ensuring the civil rights of ex-slaves in the southern states.)

In 1871, President Ulysses S. Grant appointed Harrison as counsel to the army personnel who were being sued by Milligan in light of the Court's 1866 ruling. With liability issues already established, Harrison was left to challenge Milligan's entitlement to money damages. As a result of his persuasive advocacy, Harrison limited Milligan's award to $5 (out of $100,000 sought).

Chester Alan Arthur

Chester Alan Arthur was admitted to the New York Bar in 1854, joining the firm of Culver & Parker (he read the law under Erastus Culver). Culver was a well-known lawyer, particularly because he was one of the principal advocates in the *Lemmon* case. In 1852, Mr. and Mrs. Lemmon had arrived in New York on a ship along with eight slaves, whom they planned to transport from Virginia to Texas. Culver argued on a petition for a writ of habeas corpus that their presence in New York rendered them free from bondage, and the trial judge agreed. This controversial ruling was clearly at odds with a key tenet of the Compromise of 1850—the Fugitive Slave Law—by which the southern states expected the northern states to return runaway slaves.

Arthur shared Culver's political views, and was thus excited when a group of African-American men retained the firm in 1855 to represent the interests of Lizzie Jennings. Jennings had been forcibly removed from a Brooklyn streetcar upon the vociferous demands of a white passenger. The case was put in Arthur's hands, and he brought suit against the streetcar company for the actionable conduct of the streetcar's conductor, who had been principally responsible for her actual removal and the injuries she sustained thereby. Arthur won a verdict in which his client was awarded $500 in money damages. More important, the case became the impetus for the desegregation of public transportation throughout New York City.

William Howard Taft

William H. Taft graduated from the University of Cincinnati Law School in 1880 and was admitted to the Ohio Bar in that same year. He became the assistant prosecutor of Hamilton County in 1881, and assistant solicitor of that same county in 1885. Taft's ambitions (and aptitude), however, lay in the judicial arena. Taft was appointed judge of Cincinnati's Superior Court in 1887, U.S. solicitor general in 1890, and a judge on the U.S. Circuit Court of Appeals for the Sixth Circuit in 1892 (while a Sixth Circuit judge he also served as a professor of law and dean at the Cincinnati Law School).

Although Taft seemed primed to fulfill his lifelong ambition of serving on the Supreme Court, his wife had other ideas. Nellie Herron Taft was fiercely ambitious for her husband, but in the political arena. Taft left the bench in 1900 to become Commissioner and then Governor-General of the Philippines; while in those important posts, he twice declined offers from President Theodore Roosevelt to be appointed to the Court. In 1904, he agreed to succeed Elihu Root as Secretary of War; and during the four years of Roosevelt's last term, he also served as Acting Secretary of State for a time (during John Hay's illness), as well as declining again a Supreme Court appointment.

With the 1908 election looming, and TR not a candidate, Taft was backed by TR (and Nellie). One night in the White House library, Roosevelt pretended to fall into a trance, saying: "I am the seventh son of a seventh daughter and I have clairvoyant powers. I see a man weighing 350 pounds. There is something hanging over his head. I cannot make out what it is.... At one time it looks like the presidency, then again it looks like the chief justiceship." Nellie's prompt response ("Make it the presidency") was quicker than Taft's ("Make it the chief justiceship'").

So, Taft became TR's successor, had an unhappy four years in office, was challenged by his former friend, and ultimately came in third in a three-way race for re-election in 1912. Taft rebounded quickly, however; he was appointed the Kent Professor Of Law at Yale, where he lectured and taught for eight years.

Then, in 1921, President Warren G. Harding appointed Taft Chief Justice of the U.S. Supreme Court, with the next nine years being the happiest professional period Taft experienced. Among his numerous opinions (he wrote approximately one-sixth of all the Court's decisions during his tenure) was *Myers v. United States*, 272 U.S. 52 (1926), which struck down the Tenure of Office Act of 1867 (the principal basis for the impeachment of President Andrew Johnson). And his dissent in *Adkins v. Children's Hospital*, 261 U.S. 525 (1923), foresaw the Court's tortuous relationship with the New Deal legislation coming a decade later. The majority had struck down a minimum wage provision for women in the District of Columbia; Taft's dissent forcefully asserted that "it is not the function of this court to hold Congressional acts invalid simply because they are passed to carry out economic views which the court believes to be unwise or unsound."

Franklin Delano Roosevelt

Instead of going to the Harvard Law School (as did his father), FDR enrolled at the Columbia School of Law at the request of his mother ("You ought to be in your own city and get to be known among the best men, also be nearer to Hyde Park."). He did not enjoy studying law, was frequently absent, and had few friends (outside of those he already knew from Groton and Harvard). And his academic record reflected all of the foregoing. One of his law professors many years later offered this evaluation of FDR: "[He] was not much of a student and nothing of a lawyer afterwards.... He didn't appear to have any aptitude for law, and made no effort to overcome that handicap by hard work."

In the summer after his second year, FDR took the New York State Bar exam. Before he learned he had passed (the following February), he had decided not to finish up at Columbia; FDR thus never got an LLB degree.

Besides his general boredom with law school, FDR had a growing family and thought he needed a job. With the intervention of his mother, he was offered a position at the venerable firm of Carter, Ledyard & Milburn (one of the senior partners was an old colleague of FDR's father). The offer letter was typical for that day: the first year would be "without salary," the second year's wages "would necessarily be rather small."

Carter Ledyard was handling a number of major antitrust cases on behalf of American Tobacco Company and Standard Oil of New Jersey. FDR, as the most junior lawyer in the firm, had nothing to do with those cases. His status was reflected in that he sat with the other junior clerks in one large room, which was notable principally for the presence of a large, stuffed seal—a litigation exhibit from a long prior dispute involving Bering Strait sealing rights.

After his first year, which constituted little in the way of practicing law, he was promoted to managing clerk and was paid $10 a week. At that point FDR started to go into the municipal courts, mostly representing American Express on various small claims disputes. The principal benefit from these experiences seems to have been that FDR was exposed to the ethno-cultural diversity of New York City for the first time. His most significant work came on a pro bono criminal case assigned to him by the court, arising out of an assault in the mostly German-American neighborhood of Yorkville; FDR won the case on a directed verdict.

The practice of law, however, was not for Roosevelt, and vice versa (Ledyard had already informed FDR's mother that "it was of no use"). Fortunately, at about the same time FDR's long-term plan to enter politics kicked in—the Democratic nomination for a seat in the New York State Senate representing Hyde Park was available and he leapt at it. This was consistent with what he had already previously shared with his fellow law clerks (who included Grenville Clark) as part of his plan to become president: first he would get elected to the state legislature, then be appointed assistant secretary of the Navy, and then become governor of New York (this proposed career path, of course, traced TR's, his distant cousin). After that, he had explained: "Anyone who is Governor of New York has a good chance to be President, with any luck."

Nineteen years later (in 1929), then-Governor Roosevelt (having served in the legislature, and having been Assistant Secretary of the Navy) was honored as the guest speaker at the Columbia Law School's alumni dinner. During the dinner Columbia University's President, Nicholas Murray Butler, said to FDR that he would "never be able to call [himself] an intellectual until [he came] back to Columbia and pass[ed] [his] law exam." FDR laughingly tossed his head back in his famous fashion and replied: "That just shows you how unimportant the law really is."

CHAPTER XXIV

FDR's "Trial" of Jimmy Walker

Upon his inauguration as president in March 1933, Franklin D. Roosevelt was described by Oliver Wendell Holmes as having a "second-class intellect, but a first-class temperament" (according to his law clerk, Alger Hiss). Walter Lippman, well before the election, had been harsher, declaring that Roosevelt was "a pleasant man who, without any important qualifications for the office, would very much like to be President." By any measure of historical standards, FDR certainly proved them wrong.

Pre-presidential endeavors by FDR make it clear that his talent for dealing with significant and complex problems was well developed prior to his defeat of Herbert Hoover. One such incident is detailed in Herbert Mitgang's book, *Once Upon a Time in New York: Jimmy Walker, Franklin Roosevelt, and the Last Great Battle of the Jazz Age* (Free Press, 2000). Mitgang's book examines how FDR, as governor of New York, dealt with a hydra-headed legal-political public relations nightmare that threatened to derail his bid for the Presidency.

Mayor Walker

James "Jimmy" J. Walker was an aspiring songwriter in Tin Pan Alley (his biggest hit was entitled "Will You Love Me in December as You Do in May?") until he turned his considerable schmoozing talents to New York City Democratic politics. Rising up the ranks as a protégé of Alfred E. Smith, Walker was elected Mayor of New York City in 1925 by a sizable plurality; and he was returned to office by a larger margin four years later.

Walker was a skilled politician, but he cared little for the nuts and bolts of municipal government. He far preferred the social whirl (he was called the "Night Mayor of New York"), frequent trips to his tailor, equally frequent trips outside the city to foreign hot spots, greeting visiting dignitaries, and leading parades. Notwithstanding, Walker was immensely popular; he seemed to epitomize the anything-goes style of the city's pre-Depression era.

Walker came from a long line of Tammany Hall politicians best embodied by George Washington Plunkitt. Plunkitt, who coined the term "honest graft" in the 1880s, believed that a "politician who steals is worse than a thief' because there were "grand opportunities all around" for anyone who kept his eyes and pockets open. Plunkitt's everyday philosophy was simple: "I see my opportunities and I take them." Walker lived (and profited) by a similar credo.

The Seabury Investigation

Mayor Walker's high-flying days were threatened in 1930 by a decision by the Appellate Division of the New York Supreme Court to name retired Court of Appeals Judge Samuel Seabury to investigate the city's judicial system. In the early stages of his investigation, Seabury's classic examination of Thomas Farley as to how, on an annual salary of $8,500 as sheriff of New York County, Farley had accumulated $500,000 in six years, demonstrated the depth and breadth of municipal corruption:

Seabury: "Where did you keep these moneys that you had saved?"
Farley: "In a safe-deposit box at home in the house."
Seabury: Whereabouts at home in the house did you keep this money that you had saved?"
Farley: "In the safe."
Seabury: "In a safe."

Farley: "Yes."
Seabury: "In a little box in a safe?"
Farley: "A big safe."
Seabury: "But a little box in a big safe?"
Farley: "In a big box in a big safe."

* * *

Seabury: "When you first drew it, Sheriff, was the box then crowded or very full?"
Farley: "Well, it was full and plenty in it."
Seabury: "More and plenty?"
Farley: "Yes."
Seabury: "And, Sheriff, was this big box that was safely kept in the big safe a tin box or a wooden box?"
Farley: "A tin box."
Seabury: "Is it the type of tin boxes that are specially manufactured and designed to serve as a receptacle for cash?"
Farley: "It is."

* * *

Seabury: "Kind of a magic box."
Farley: "It was a wonderful box."
Seabury: "A wonderful box. What did you have to do—rub the lock with a little gold, and open it in order to find more money?"
Farley: "I wish I could."

With the "tin box" as a recurring headline, it did not take long before the New York State Legislature expanded Seabury's mandate to include every official in the city's government. Walker's lifestyle (and the finances needed to support it) quickly became a target.

Seabury Versus Walker

In the spring of 1932, as New York Governor Roosevelt's political machine was going full tilt to secure the Democratic nomination, Seabury served a comprehensive subpoena duces tecum on Walker.

Walker subsequently appeared as a witness for two days before a special legislative committee. Seabury was intent on making a record of Walker's financial history; Walker played to the crowds and the press. At first it appeared that Walker had the upper hand, making wisecracks ("This fellow Seabury would convict the Twelve Apostles if he could"; "life is just a bowl of Seabury's"; etc.), getting favorable editorials, and having 18,000 people turn out for a rally at Madison Square Garden. And, of course, national politics loomed large.

The Democratic National Convention was about to open, and Roosevelt did not have quite enough delegates to ensure his nomination (at that time, the nominee had to achieve a two-thirds total). Al Smith had the largest bloc of non-FDR delegates, and most of them were Tammany Hall men. With one week to go before the opening gavel, Seabury delivered Walker's transcript (with an accompanying analysis) to FDR (who, under the state constitution, had the power to remove any public official for good cause); Roosevelt sent a copy to Walker, who responded that he would reply after the convention. FDR was thus placed in a difficult spot, as Walter Lippman ruefully noted: "[FDR] has displayed a singular petulance toward everybody who has had any part in putting him in a position where he might have to make a decisive choice between breaking with Tammany and surrendering to it."

At the convention, Walker made a point of publicly casting his vote for Smith; but that act had no effect of galvanizing the "Happy Warrior's" prospects. Ultimately, a deal was brokered (in large part by Joseph P. Kennedy) whereby the Speaker of the House of Representatives, John Nance Garner, became FDR's running mate in exchange for the California and Texas delegations. Even with those votes putting FDR over the top, however, Smith's supporters (including Walker) were bitter and refused to make the nomination unanimous.

Walker Versus Roosevelt

On July 29, 1932, Walker submitted to FDR a 27,000-word "answer" to Seabury's "charges"; as noted by many editorial writers, the response addressed little of the evidence, instead focusing on the purported political vendetta directed against the mayor, and the fact that his enemies (Seabury et al.) were attempting to reverse the popular will of the electorate. This left the ball squarely in FDR's court. Trapped, he called for a "trial" in Albany, at which he would preside and pass judgment on the evidence.

When it came time for Walker to testify at the end of August, he left by special train from Grand Central Station, where 5,000 people had come to see him off. When he arrived in Albany, he was met by another large crowd, a brass band, and the sight and sound of exploding aerial bombs. When informed that Walker had received this reception, Seabury's tart retort was: "So did [Boss] Tweed."

Knowing the importance of the "trial" to his political fortunes, FDR studiously prepared, working closely with his legal counsel (the most important of whom was Samuel Rosenman). Walker's counsel, while an experienced trial lawyer, ignored Walker's advice (don't get "Frank's Dutch up") and attempted to run roughshod over the proceeding (perhaps assuming that FDR, given his less-than-imposing legal career, could be placed on the defensive). Roosevelt would have none of that, however, and at one point admonished Walker's lawyer: "Don't try to instruct me about the difference between putting a thing into evidence and marking it for identification."

While FDR and Walker's counsel had numerous tussles over legal and evidentiary issues, FDR was scrupulously cool and even-tempered in his handling of Walker. Walker's testimony was basically a replay of his prior testimony. Rather than address squarely questionable transactions by which he and his associates had pocketed large wads of cash, Walker focused on other areas in which he felt more comfortable, such as his long public service, that he was being railroaded, and that he had little direct involvement in or knowledge of the transactions themselves. When FDR asked him about a slew of governmental contracts that had been awarded to dubious entities, Walker gave a lengthy soliloquy on "the executive mind." When FDR probed about a secret brokerage account that had netted Walker $246,000 (this came from a man who was vying for a major municipal contract), Walker tried to obfuscate matters by complaining that he was being put on trial for his use (misuse) of the word "beneficence"! After taking Walker through all the points previously established by Seabury, FDR concluded his examination:

> *Roosevelt*: "I think that concludes the direct examination of the Mayor by me."
> *Walker*: "What? What direct examination?"
> *Roosevelt*: "Direct examination of the Mayor by me."
> *Walker*: "I never want to be cross-examined if that was direct."

Most observers gave FDR high marks for his impartial and judicious oversight of the hearings. The proof of the pudding, however, still lay in what his decision would be. As noted in the *New York Times*, "the political consequences [are] enormous. If he removes the Mayor, he runs the risk of being knifed by the Democratic machine in New York City.... If he does not remove the Mayor, the Republican orators will ascribe his negative act to Presidential politics and picture Mr. Roosevelt as a trimmer and low type of politician."

As FDR mulled over his unpleasant options, the political bosses went to work. Jim Farley, who was FDR's political fixer and would soon become Chairman of the Democratic Party, acted as a middleman between FDR and Tammany Hall; his report back to the political bosses was negative—the thing was just too hot a potato and could not be settled quietly. Tammany was thus compelled to make a rational political judgment: power and future patronage were more important than a single officeholder (especially one whose openly adulterous lifestyle was starting to upset the Catholic Church). It was left to Al Smith to give Walker the bad news: "Jim, you're through. You must resign for the good of the party." And so Walker did.

The rest, as they say, is history. Tammany leaders were invited to a friendly meeting at the Executive Mansion in Albany to smooth things over, FDR went off on an historic barn-storming campaign trek via the rails throughout the country, and the Democratic ticket crushed the Republicans in November, losing only six states.

Postscript

Notwithstanding the broad public investigation into municipal corruption, not a whole lot changed in New York City. The mayor elected after Walker was asked by a reporter who his police commissioner would be. His response: "I don't know—they haven't told me yet."

In 1959, a hit Broadway musical comedy was based on the life and times of another New York City mayor, Fiorello La Guardia. Entitled *Fiorello!*, one of the play's show-stopping songs was "Little Tin Box."

CHAPTER XXV

Lincoln: A Great Lawyer (And Our Greatest President)

To the extent most Americans have a picture of Abraham Lincoln's professional life as a lawyer, it has been formed by John Ford's 1939 film *Young Mr. Lincoln,* starring Henry Fonda. Lincoln is portrayed as a naive and idealistic advocate, with Fonda uttering the classic line: "I may not know so much of law, ... but I know what's right or wrong." Besides the fact that the "facts" depicted by Ford are either wholly false or widely inaccurate, the overall image conveyed of Lincoln and his legal practice is simply at odds with the far more complex (and interesting) historical truth.

Honest Abe

It is true that Lincoln came from poverty and had a limited education. As such, after he read the law in John Todd Stuart's office and was admitted to the Illinois Bar in 1837, he was not immediately a skilled professional. Notwithstanding, he quickly developed into a shrewd opponent; as one who rode the Illinois circuit with Lincoln observed: "Any man who took Lincoln for a simple-minded man would soon wake up with his back in a ditch." In addition to his developing forensic skills, Lincoln built a reputation among his peers of absolute honesty. And by that reputation he became known as "Honest Abe" (or by his younger colleagues "Honest Old Abe").

Especially in the decade before he was elected president, Lincoln was one of the leading corporate litigators in Illinois; indeed, in David Herbert Donald's magnificent biography *Lincoln* (Simon & Schuster 1995), Donald describes Lincoln as being "at the head of his profession in [his] state." A review of some of Lincoln's leading cases—which interweave with his two unsuccessful bids for the Senate (in 1855 and 1858), his crucial role in the development of the new Republican Party in the aftermath of the Kansas-Nebraska Act, and his second-place finish for the Republican nomination for vice president (in 1856)—confirms his prominence within the Illinois Bar (although perhaps not elsewhere).

Railroad Law

Lincoln was retained by the Alton & Sagamon Railroad Company to enforce commitments of capital made to the railroad for its expansion by certain subscribers. *The Collected Works of Abraham Lincoln,* edited by Roy P. Basler, document Lincoln's meticulous efforts to demonstrate (1) that the railroad had been properly organized and had complied with its internal corporate procedures, (2) that the individual obligations had been undertaken legally, and (3) that the company was within its rights to enforce by legal means the capital commitments. The case went up to the Illinois Supreme Court, where Lincoln and his client's position was upheld. The case served as an important landmark in corporate law, and quickly established Lincoln at the forefront of one of the then most complex areas of corporate practice: railroad law.

Hurd v. Rock Island Bridge

The Rock Island Bridge Company built and owned a bridge that spanned the Mississippi River; the bridge's purpose was to carry the tracks of the Chicago, Rock Island, and Pacific Railroads. Rock Island was sued by the owner of the steamboat *Effie Afron,* which had struck part of the bridge and had gone up in flames. Because the case put in conflict the navigation interests of St. Louis (and the other port cities) against those of Chicago and the railroads, this was a landmark piece of litigation featuring some of the leading lawyers in the West; Lincoln was Rock Island's trial counsel.

Lincoln's papers contain a detailed summary of his two-day summation to the jury, in which he not only gave a bravura marshaling of the evidence in support of his client, but stressed the larger political vision of which he had been an exponent since his days as an acolyte for Henry Clay ("[T]here is a travel from East to West, whose demands are not less important than that of the river. It is growing larger and larger, building up new countries with a rapidity never before seen in the history of the world.")

The jury came back deadlocked at nine for the bridge and three for the plaintiff, and was discharged. Litigation went on in other forms for a number of years, culminating in 1862, when the Supreme Court set aside an order of the district court to remove part of the bridge.

McCormick v. Manny

Cyrus McCormick, who had invented the reaper, filed a patent infringement action against John Manny, who was building similar machines. Given the economic importance of breaking McCormick's legal monopoly on this vital agricultural machine, many key industrial concerns funded Manny's defense. With such a war chest, he went out to hire the country's best patent lawyers.

As lead counsel, Manny chose George Harding, who was a prominent Philadelphia lawyer. When it seemed likely that the case would be tried in the federal court in the Northern District of Illinois, Harding sought out local counsel.

Lincoln was not Harding's first choice, but he nonetheless was hired at a $400 retainer, with the ultimate fee set at $1,000. Lincoln clearly misunderstood the limited role envisioned for him, however, because he quickly attempted to learn all he could about the record (even though his attempts to gain pertinent documents from the Manny defense team went unheeded). When the case was transferred to the federal court in Cincinnati, no one even contacted him as to when the matter was to be heard.

Undeterred, Lincoln hopped on a train to Cincinnati, and on arriving called on Harding (whom he had never met). The meeting was not fruitful. Harding sized up Lincoln as "a tall rawly boned, ungainly backwoodsman, with coarse, ill-fitting clothes." Another defense team member, Edwin Stanton, was even more incredulous; he harangued Harding with: "Why did you bring that damned long armed Ape here ... he does not know anything and can do you no good."

Lincoln, who gamely remained in Cincinnati for the entire hearing, was little more than a spectator. He was so unhappy at his treatment that he initially refused the balance of his fee, keeping it only after a second check had been sent with the insistence that he had earned it. It is evidence of Lincoln's famed stoicism that only to his junior partner did he even hint at this blow to his professional pride, saying just that he had been "roughly handled by that man Stanton."

Charter Challenge

The Illinois Central Railroad's state charter, which exempted it from county taxes, was challenged by McLean County. Lincoln believed that this litigation posed "the largest law question that can now be got up in the State," and was determined to be involved.

After doing what lawyers today would call a conflicts check with a similarly situated county, Lincoln offered his services to the railroad and was retained. The case worked its way up to the Illinois Supreme Court, where it was twice argued over successive terms. Ultimately, the court ruled for Lincoln and his client.

Although his retainer ($250) had been modest, Lincoln believed the case (and result) to be of such significance (saving the client a half a million dollars a year in taxes) that he asked the railroad for $2,000.

In rejecting Lincoln's request, one Illinois Central official was dismissive: "This is as much as Daniel Webster himself would have charged. We cannot allow such a claim." Not easily put off, Lincoln consulted a number of his peers about the relative value of his services in relation to the result achieved, and then submitted a revised bill for $5,000.

When that request went unheeded, Lincoln filed suit for the amount. He not only prevailed, but the railroad continued to retain him on important matters!

Postscript

The foregoing is only a brief glimmer of Lincoln's legal career. Let me add three postscripts.

Edwin Stanton later served Lincoln as his second Secretary of War. Shortly before he was assassinated, Lincoln put his hands on Stanton's shoulders and told him: "You have been a good friend and a faithful public officer." And it was Stanton who had not only brought some measure of order to the chaos that reigned in the hours as Lincoln lay dying, he also was the one who gave the memorable eulogy after Lincoln was pronounced dead: "Now, he belongs to the ages."

Not all of the Lincoln-Douglas debates in 1858 focused on the great issues of the day (popular sovereignty, etc.). Stephen A. Douglas and his supporters suggested that Lincoln was under the thumb of large corporate interests, usually citing the Illinois Central Railroad and the "big fee" he received from the McLean case. As a result, Lincoln in numerous stump speeches had to explain the details of the case and the fact that he had had to sue the railroad for his fee. As he concluded before the people of Carthage on October 22, 1858: "This is the whole truth about the fee, and what tendency it has to prove that I received any of the people's money, or that I am on very cozy terms with the [railroad], I do not comprehend."

For archival research into Lincoln's legal career, see *The Papers of Abraham Lincoln: Legal Documents and Cases*" (University of Virginia Press 2008); see also John J. Duff's *A. Lincoln: Prairie Lawyer* (Bramhall House 1960).

CHAPTER XXVI

William Henry Seward: A Great Lawyer (And Great Statesman)

Although little remembered today, William Henry Seward was one of the nineteenth century's foremost Americans: first as New York's governor, later as its senator, the preconvention favorite for the 1860 Republican presidential nomination, and finally Abraham Lincoln and Andrew Johnson's Secretary of State. In that latter post, historians have judged Seward to be one of the nation's preeminent statesmen: he not only played a crucial role in ensuring that the Confederate States failed to gain diplomatic recognition from foreign nations, he also paved the way for America's expansion into the Pacific with the acquisition of the Guano Islands and Midway, as well as the purchase of Alaska from Russia for $7.2 million (aka "Seward's Icebox," "Seward's Folly," etc.).

What is even less known about Seward is that he was one of the leading lawyers of his era.

After graduation from Union College in 1820 (he was elected into Union's first Phi Beta Kappa class in his junior year), Seward read the law in various offices in New York, and quickly established himself as a rising star. Upon passing the bar, he shopped his services throughout the state, ultimately being offered the princely annual sum of $500 to join Judge Elijah Miller as his partner in Auburn, starting on January 1, 1823.

Seward tried all of his own cases from day one, and his reputation quickly grew and more than justified his guarantee by generating large fees to the partnership. And although he did not always find the practice of law in those years to be stimulating, there were offsetting benefits: Seward and Miller's daughter, Frances, fell in love and were married in 1824.

As Seward's practice grew, so did the firm. One of Seward's new law partners (Nelson Beardsley) recounted a matter with which many of us can identify.

"One day, just as [we] were closing [our] labors, a client came in with a case in which success was hopeless unless an injunction could be obtained before 11 o'clock the next morning from Judge Mosely, at Onondaga Hill; and to obtain it would require a review of the entire case, and an analysis of the papers, which his lawyer had told him would occupy at least a week.

Seeing the situation of the affair at once, Seward said, "Beardsley, did you sleep well last night?"

"Tolerably well," was the answer. "Why do you ask?"

"Because I think you will have to sit up all night tonight."

Lighting the candles, and closing the doors, the two partners set vigorously to work, Seward drafting, and Beardsley engrossing, until daybreak found them completing the last pages. A hasty breakfast and cup of coffee followed; and then, taking a horse and buggy, Seward drove 25 miles to Onondaga Hill, obtained the injunction, and saved his client's case.

Complex Litigation

After two terms as governor, Seward returned to Auburn and private practice in 1843. While he predicted to his political adviser Thurlow Weed that he hoped to earn $5,000 that year, he also acknowledged "[a]s yet I have no business; but my friends are around me so warm-hearted and affectionate that I have no fears about the future."

One of his first cases came in the form of defending his then political ally, Horace Greeley (editor of the *New York Tribune*), in two libel cases brought on by James Fenimore Cooper. Cooper seems to have been fairly litigious, because Seward was soon defending Weed (also editor of the *Albany Evening Journal*) in a similar action. His approach in such cases was as follows:

> I defend slander and libel suits always by delay as far as practicable. There is nothing for a plaintiff ... like haste; nor is there any advantage for a defendant like time; that diminishes the grievance complained of.

Seward's litigation skills also led him into the new field of patent law. With the burgeoning Industrial Revolution, American inventors were (1) seeking to protect their commercial interests, and/or (2) eager to challenge the legal monopolies of other inventors that blocked those same commercial interests.

In the summer of 1843, James G. Wilson, the owner of a patent on a "planing machine" (a method for processing prepared lumber), heard Seward successfully argue a case in federal court in Albany and offered to retain him to protect his interests in the patent. Seward, overcoming some reluctance due to a lack of experience and general ineptitude when it came to machinery, agreed to represent Wilson.

Seward's first step was to file an action in the Northern District of New York to solidify Wilson's claim to the patent. In advancing that claim, Seward embraced a new approach to advocacy. Rather than basing his argument strictly on patent law precedents, Seward asked the court to cast its net more broadly, consider the socioeconomic policy considerations of the matter before it, and implement the intention of Congress to foster genius and reward merit. Perhaps not surprisingly, this argument neatly coincided with the political philosophy espoused by Seward the politician (and his first mentor, John Quincy Adams):

> The American continent, from its icy boundaries on the north, to undefined latitude within the tropics, seems to be rapidly falling under the political sway of our confederacy. The habitations of a hundred million people, and of how

> many more I dare not conjecture, are to be erected by our artisans. The machine in question reduces, in the proportion of nine-tenths, the labor and expenses of a necessary part of every structure, whether it be raised for use or ornament.

The *Wilson* case went up to the U.S. Supreme Court in 1846. Consolidated with a number of related cases for purposes of argument, Seward found himself teamed with Daniel Webster as part of the "grand array of counsel"; arguing on the other side was Thaddeus Stevens. Seward found the Court to be "a very dignified and imposing tribunal"; at the same time, however, he wrote to Weed: "I have looked upon the faces of the [Justices] and they are of clay." Notwithstanding Seward's initial reaction to the Justices, a month later they handed down a decision not only in his client's favor but also adopting the policy rationale(s) he advocated.

This case and victory led to Seward being retained to litigate patent cases throughout the United States, and made him and his firm increasingly prosperous. One example of how successful Seward's patent practice quickly became is in the form of an affidavit that was filed on behalf of a new client:

> On the seventh day of March, one thousand eight hundred and forty-eight, personally came before me Samuel F.B. Morse, of Poughkeepsie, Dutchess County, in the State of New York, and being duly sworn, deposeth and saith: That he verily believes he was the original, true and first inventor of the American Electro Magnetic Telegraph, and the improvements in the same, described in the re-issued Letters Patent therefore, bearing date the fifteenth day of January eighteen hundred and forty-six, and the eleventh day of April eighteen hundred and forty-six.

Wyatt and Freeman

Not all of Seward's practice was aimed at promoting commercial interests. In 1846, he defended two Black men, Henry Wyatt and William Freeman, each separately accused of murder. Wyatt, while awaiting trial in Auburn Correctional Facility, sent a message to Seward requesting help. Seward agreed to represent Wyatt, even though the fact that Wyatt had committed the murder was clear. Believing Wyatt to be insane, Seward planned to assert that defense and retained medical experts to testify in support thereof. After an eight-day trial in February 1846, however, the jury rejected the defense; a second trial on the merits was scheduled for June.

In the interim, Freeman was arrested for killing an Auburn farmer and his family; Freeman seemingly had no motive and was said to have laughed when caught. The public's reaction was fever pitched, with numerous threats of lynching.

The farmer's minister called for Freeman's blood, and warned of the tricks of "adroit counsel" by which "law may be perverted, and jurors bewildered." Rumors quickly grew that Seward, away from Auburn on other business, would represent Freeman—a "fact" that led to intense anger being directed toward the absent Seward.

In the midst of all this, Seward returned to Auburn and was met at the railroad station by friends who feared for his safety and accompanied him in a quasi-security detail to his home. Against the wishes of his partners (some of whom had assured people that Seward would decline the case), Seward appeared on Freeman's behalf and asserted a plea of insanity.

The second Wyatt trial was initiated at this inauspicious moment, notwithstanding Seward's requests for a change of venue and postponement. Once impaneled, the jury listened to Seward's ten-hour legal argument in support of the insanity defense. After the judge's contrary legal instructions, however, the jury found against Wyatt in fewer than 30 minutes. Upon the judge's sentence, Wyatt was subsequently hanged.

Thereafter, the Freeman case proceeded with a preliminary trial to determine the legal issue of sanity or insanity. After two weeks of testimony, much of it by medical experts called by Seward in support of his client's lack of sanity, the jury (after an initial hesitancy, countered by the judge) came back with a verdict that Freeman was

William Henry Seward
(author's collection)

"sufficiently sane, in mind and memory, to distinguish between right and wrong." Seward termed the verdict a compromise verdict, "which implied that the prisoner was at least partially insane."

Over Seward's objections, a trial on the merits then began. Seward was allowed to present testimony as to Freeman's sanity at the time of the murders, but was barred from introducing testimony as to Freeman's state of mind at the time of trial, because it had just been determined he was then sane (notwithstanding the fact that Freeman was by this point evidencing "great mental confusion, if not imbecility").

Seward's summation, later termed by Charles Francis Adams as rising "to the uppermost region of eloquence," laid out the insanity defense, while also urging the jurors to reject racial considerations: "he is still your brother, and mine. Hold him to be a man." The jury quickly convicted Freeman, however, and the judge sentenced him to death.

Seward, appealing quickly, won a reversal, based on judicial errors in both trials. A new trial was ordered, but a different court found that Freeman was incapable of standing for the trial. Freeman died in jail in 1847 of consumption, with an autopsy of his brain revealing "the appearance of a chronic disease."

Seward emerged from these cases "exhausted in mind and body, covered with public reproach, stunned with duns and protests." There were also significant benefits, however. The arguments he presented on Freeman's behalf were published in a volume that went through four editions in one year. Seward's arguments have been cited as essential in establishing the insanity defense in American law.

And the attendant publicity further enhanced Seward's political reputation in antislavery circles throughout the North and led to an explosion in new legal business to Seward and his firm.

The Fugitive Slave Law

In 1842, an Ohio farmer, John Van Zandt, was sued by a Kentucky slave owner, Wharton Jones, for violating the Fugitive Slave Act of 1793. Van Zandt had been caught transporting ten of Jones's slaves; nine were captured. Jones was suing for compensation for the one slave who escaped, as well as for statutory damages allowed by the law. Salmon P. Chase, a young Ohio lawyer and leader of the fledgling Liberty Party (an antislavery organization), represented Van Zandt at trial. Van Zandt lost and was assessed $1,500 damages.

Ultimately, the case was appealed to the U.S. Supreme Court, and for that stage Chase sought out Seward to join the Van Zandt team. Chase's reasons were undoubtedly complex: they reflected Seward's growing national reputation as a politician and an advocate, their shared opposition to the "Locofocos" (a wing of the Democratic Party that espoused radical policies, such as free trade), and Chase's restless political ambition and his attempts to broaden his network of helpful alliances. Seward accepted the assignment, undoubtedly hoping that associating with a rising political figure in Ohio might be of future use to him, as well.

In light of a Supreme Court decision that had shortly before upheld the constitutionality of the Fugitive Slave Act, Seward and Chase had an uphill fight from the outset. Seward's arguments expanded on the policy considerations he had been developing both in legal and political contexts: that the country's economic progress and well-being should not and could not be stunted by outdated laws.

First, he contended that Van Zandt could hardly be held accountable at law for merely providing "shelter, comfort and sustenance" to a slave. "Such exiles have a national right to demand protection and charity. That right is sustained by divine laws."

Seward next argued that slavery was a system at odds with American and technological industrial political economy, citing that slavery existed only in "rude communities" as vestige of "the loss of feudal villenage," and would disappear when "intellectual and moral agencies are fully developed."

Finally, he posited that stare decisis "must be abandoned in every case where it is found, upon full and deliberate consideration, under the guidance of practical experience, or upon further development of essential facts, that the decision insisted upon, however time honored it may be, is erroneous."

Chase's arguments were more rhetorical and pushed farther out the envelope vis-à-vis the political ramifications that underlay the case. Notwithstanding the able efforts of both men, however, the Court upheld the lower courts without much concern for the public policy issues raised. (Van Zandt died before the case was finally resolved, and his heirs ultimately had to pay the judgment.)

Postscript

Seward's developing philosophy, partly based on his legal practice, had important implications for his political career after he stopped the active practice of law. (When he went to the Senate in

1849, he did continue to handle some matters for his firm, including arguing important cases in the U.S. Supreme Court.)

In the crucial debate over Henry Clay's compromise proposals in 1850 to preserve the Union, Seward rose in opposition. Declaring that "there is a higher law than the Constitution," Seward stated that slavery in the territories would be incompatible with "the security of natural rights, the diffusion of knowledge, and the freedom of industry." By this one speech, Seward became a leader of antislavery forces in the North, anathema to pro-slavery forces in the South, and a radical in the eyes of many in the country who wanted some sort of political compromise by which this moral issue could be resolved without turmoil, disunion, and bloodshed. It was Seward's radical image that did much to hurt his chances for nomination at the 1860 Republican Convention.

Seward and Chase became bitter rivals in Lincoln's cabinet (Chase served as Secretary of the Treasury). Wanting to force Seward from his post as Secretary of State (and thus give himself preeminence in the cabinet and a clear run at the presidential nomination in 1864), Chase forced a showdown in 1862. As depicted in David Herbert Donald's biography *Lincoln* (Simon & Schuster 1995), Lincoln brilliantly finessed Chase's Machiavellian maneuverings, got both Seward and Chase to submit their resignations, and then refused them both, with the resulting effect that he was able to moderate their behavior (and excesses) for the remainder of his presidency. *See also The Worst Supreme Court Decisions, Ever! (And Related Tales)* (Twelve Tables Press 2024).

Seward's law firm was a direct predecessor of Cravath, Swaine & Moore. Indeed, much of the first volume of Robert T. Swaine's *The Cravath Firm and Its Predecessors* details Seward's legal and political career and his importance to the development of that firm.

For the definitive biographies on Seward, readers should consult Glyndon G. Van Deusen's 1967 book *William Henry Seward* (Oxford University Press) and Walter Stahr's *Seward: Lincoln's Indispensable Man* (Simon & Schuster 2012).

CHAPTER XXVII

A Friendship That Helped Win the Civil War

Abraham Lincoln and William Henry Seward met only once prior to 1860. In September 1848, both men (Lincoln, a little known Congressman from Illinois, and Seward, twice elected New York's governor and soon to be sent to the Senate by the New York legislature) spoke at a Whig campaign rally for Zachary Taylor in Boston. The following night they shared the same bedroom in Worcester, Massachusetts, where they talked late into the night about the "slavery question."

Competitors

Later, in 1860, they were rivals for the presidential nomination of the Republican Party. Seward, the heavy favorite, was undone by a variety of factors; Lincoln, the second choice of many delegates, was nominated on the third ballot. Seward was devastated by the loss, but hid his disappointment from the public. Prompted by his political patron, Thurlow Weed, Seward undertook a vigorous speaking tour throughout the country on behalf of Lincoln's candidacy. (Lincoln, by tradition, stayed home in Springfield and made no public speeches.)

Seward's wildly successful tour took him to Illinois, and his train stopped in Springfield. Lincoln came on board to greet his new advocate; as one observer noted, Lincoln was "very awkward in manner; as if he felt out of place, and had a realizing sense that properly the positions should be reversed."

1860 Republican Presidential Candidates
(author's collection)

After the election, Lincoln moved quickly to offer the preeminent cabinet position, Secretary of State, to Seward. Because there had been rampant public speculation about whether Lincoln would offer the post to Seward, whether Lincoln really wanted Seward on his team, whether Seward wanted to work under Lincoln, among other things. Lincoln showed brilliant instincts in how to deal with super-sized egos. He deputized Senator Hannibal Hamlin (soon to be the vice president) to deliver *two* letters to Seward in Washington.

Returning to Washington, Hamlin tracked Seward down and orally broached the subject. Seward pooh-poohed it, but Hamlin cautioned him not to say anything more until he read what Lincoln had sent on.

Hamlin first presented Lincoln's terse, formal note, setting forth Lincoln's intention to nominate Seward. Unimpressed with what seemed to be an unenthusiastic offer, Seward was then handed Lincoln's second letter. That letter, labeled "private and confidential,"

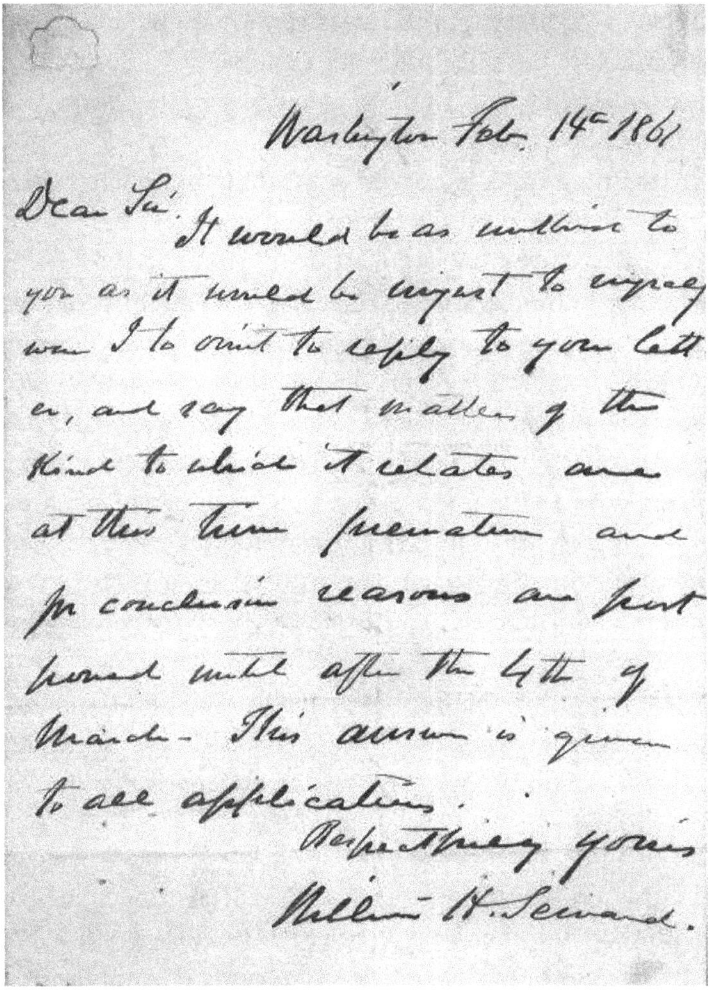
Washington Feb. 14th 1861

Dear Sir:

It would be as unkind to you as it would be unjust to myself were I to omit to reply to your letter, and say that matters of the kind to which it relates are at this time premature and for conclusive reasons are postponed until after the 4th of March. This answer is given to all applications.

Respectfully yours

William H. Seward.

Seward letter regarding incoming Lincoln administration (author's collection)

directly addressed and laid to rest all the rumors. In effusive prose, Lincoln assured Seward that he had been his choice since the nominating convention and that Seward's "position in the public eye, [his] integrity, ability, learning, and great experience, all combine to render it an appointment preeminently fit to be made."

Lincoln's skillful approach was rewarded. According to Hamlin, Seward's face became "pale with excitement," and he exclaimed: "This is remarkable, Mr. Hamlin." After playing coy for a few days, Seward formally accepted Lincoln's offer.

By the time Lincoln arrived in Washington in late February of 1861, much had changed. The Deep South had seceded. In Lincoln's absence, Seward, who everyone assumed would be the "premier" of the incoming administration, had been trying mightily to moderate passions in Washington and conciliate Unionists in the Upper South.

One of the first things Lincoln said to Seward was "there is one part of my work that I shall have to leave largely to you. I shall have to depend upon you for taking care of these matters of foreign affairs, of which I know so little, and with which I reckon you are familiar."

Lincoln also asked for Seward's input on his inaugural address. As one presidential historian has written, Seward "had the largest impact on [that] address" and his "revisions are evident in nearly every paragraph."

Most important was Seward's contribution to the conclusion of the speech. Lincoln originally envisioned a bellicose challenge to the states that had left the Union. Seward drafted a much different, conciliatory ending:

> I close. We are not we must not be aliens or enemies but fellow countrymen and brethren. Although passion has strained our bonds of affection too hardly they must not, I am sure they will not be broken. The mystic chords which proceeding from so many battlefields and so many patriot graves pass through all the hearts and all the hearths in this broad continent of ours will yet again harmonize in their ancient music when breathed upon by the guardian angel of the nation.

Lincoln adopted Seward's approach, but poetically edited it into the famous language Americans know so well:

> I am loth [sic] to close. We are not enemies, but friends. We must not be enemies. Though passion may have strained, it must not break our bonds of affection. The mystic chords of memory, stretching from every battlefield, and patriot grave, to every living heart and hearthstone, all over this broad land, will yet swell the chorus of the Union, when again touched, as surely they will be, by the better angels of our nature.

At the same time Lincoln and Seward seemed to be working together, discord was brewing. First came Seward's unhappiness that he had been unable to block Salmon Chase's appointment as Secretary of the Treasury. When it was clear that Lincoln was committed to having both Seward and Chase in the cabinet, Seward sent Lincoln a note in which he sought release from his earlier acceptance. Lincoln saw the power play for what it was, telling an aide: "I can't afford to let Seward take the first trick."

Waiting until he was inaugurated, Lincoln gently confronted Seward and asked him to reconsider—both in light of the national crisis and because of Lincoln's personal importunings. Again, Lincoln knew the right buttons to push and Seward relented (he told his wife, "I did not dare go home, or . . . leave the country to chance.").

A little over three weeks later, Seward, still chafing at his subordinate position, presented Lincoln with one of history's more amazing documents entitled, "Some thoughts for the President's consideration."

Seward, contending that Lincoln had basically left the country drifting both domestically and in foreign policy since March 4 (the inaugural), proposed a number of initiatives in both fields. He then laid down a challenge to the President: Either Lincoln or a member of the cabinet must energetically prosecute "whatever policy we adopt." And although he declaimed it was "not in my especial province," Seward ended with: "I neither seek to evade nor assume responsibility."

Faced with this brazen challenge to his presidency, Lincoln sat down and wrote a reply. In a polite, but direct, style, Lincoln took issue with the notion that his administration did not have "a policy, either domestic or foreign." After then addressing the substantive points in Seward's memo, Lincoln made clear to his Secretary of State that, as far as leading the administration, "if this must be done, I must do it."

The letter was never sent, and was never even seen until it was found in Lincoln's papers several decades later. Historians have speculated that in lieu of sending it, Lincoln chose to meet with Seward mano a mano. Whatever took place, there was never again any question as to who was the boss. Shortly thereafter, in fact, Seward was reporting to his wife that the "President is the best of us"; at the same time he could not help himself, adding that Lincoln "needs constant and assiduous cooperation."

Collaborators

Seward, in the view of most historians, was one of America's greatest Secretaries of State. Notwithstanding Lincoln's comment to him in February 1861, however, he did not conduct foreign policy without Lincoln's input and influence.

The first diplomatic crisis that confronted the Lincoln administration was how to deal with the British government, which in May 1861 declared its neutrality in the American Civil War, an action that acknowledged the South's status as a belligerent entity. This was a short step to formal recognition of the South, the effects of which could well have proven fatal to the North's attempts to restore the Union.

In response, Seward drafted Dispatch Number 10; that famous document included some stem language, not the least of which was an explicit threat that if England were to recognize the South: "We from that hour shall cease to be friends and become once more, as we have twice been forced to be, enemies of Great Britain."

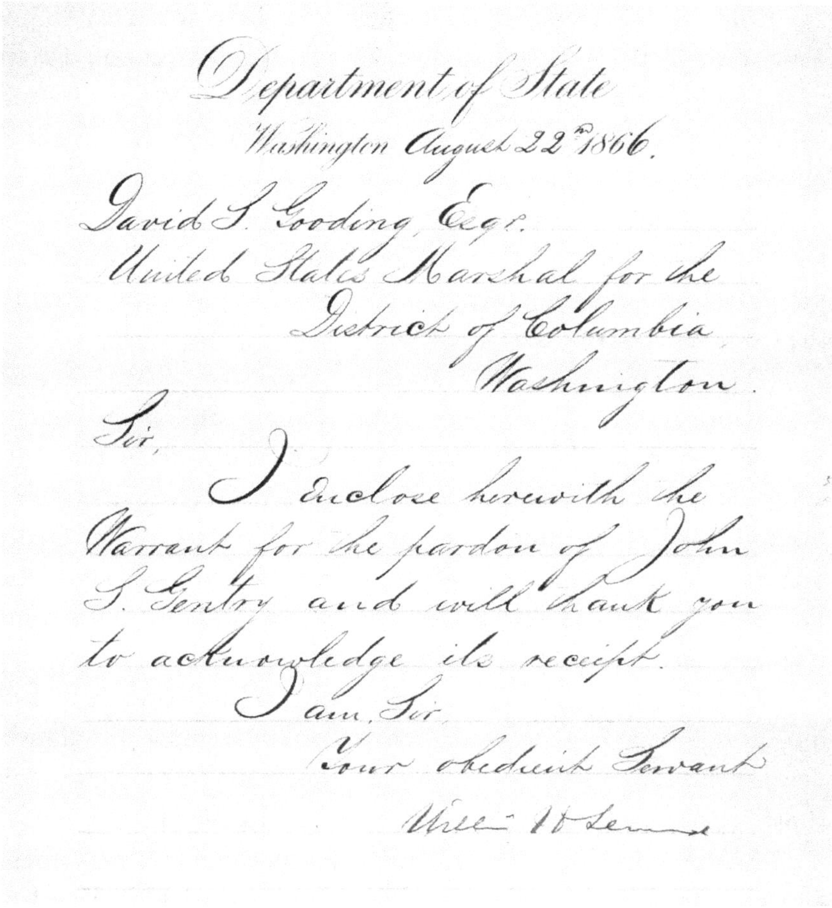

Department of State
Washington August 22d 1866.

David S. Gooding Esqr.
United States Marshal for the
District of Columbia
Washington.

Sir,

I enclose herewith the Warrant for the pardon of John S. Gentry and will thank you to acknowledge its receipt.

I am, Sir,
Your obedient Servant
William H Seward

Pardon issued by Secretary of State Seward (author's collection)

When Seward showed the draft to Lincoln, the President circled that language and wrote: "Leave out." And when the document was ultimately finalized, Lincoln directed that the American minister to England not read or show the document to his British counterpart or to anyone else. Seward dutifully followed that directive, but added to the dispatch: "You will keep back nothing when the time arrives for its being said with dignity propriety and effect."

Then, in November 1861, another crisis arose when the Union navy stopped a British ship and seized two Confederate diplomats (John Slidell and James Mason) en route to London. When England vehemently protested this violation of international law, Lincoln openly worried about having "two wars on his hands at a time."

To a divided Cabinet, the President asked Seward to present a legal brief as to why Slidell and Mason had to be released; upon that presentation, the cabinet unanimously agreed (albeit reluctantly) to the Confederates' release.

Recognizing that public opinion in the North had cheered the seizure and would be greatly agitated by the diplomats' release, Seward accompanied that action with a public note to the British government in which he argued that the U.S. Navy's action had been justified, while also expressing thanks to the British for finally acknowledging that their acts of impressment during and before the War of 1812 had been wrong. One observer of this high-wire performance wrote: "Seward is not only right, but sublime."

In 1862, as the War was going poorly for the North, it looked increasingly like England and France would recognize the South. Seward and Lincoln fought on various diplomatic fronts to forestall those actions, including a direct appeal to the Russian tsar.

By the summer of 1862, Lincoln became convinced that emancipation of the slaves had become "absolutely essential for the salvation of the Union." Issuing an emancipation proclamation would not only change the focus of the Civil War away from merely restoring the status quo ante of the Union, it would also likely deter the European nations from taking any formal action to assist the South, since slavery was extraordinarily unpopular among the European citizenry.

The President's cabinet was, again, of disparate minds on Lincoln's proposal. Seward was himself dubious of the efficacy of proclamations "without bayonets to enforce them"; he nonetheless suppressed those skeptical thoughts and supported the President.

At the same time, however, Seward told Lincoln (and the cabinet) that he "question[ed] the expediency of its issue at this juncture.

The depression of the public mind, consequent upon our repeated reverses, is so great that I fear it may be viewed as the last measure of an exhausted government, a cry for help ... our last shriek, on the retreat." Better to wait, Seward counseled Lincoln (and the cabinet), until the North wins a battle, and then "hang your proclamation about his neck."

Seward's advice, which Lincoln acknowledged he had "entirely overlooked, ... struck [the President] with very great force." In September of 1862, Antietam was deemed enough of a Northern victory for Lincoln to issue the proclamation (in draft form). And with that went the likelihood of European recognition of the Confederacy, which in tum constituted the effective end of the South's last, best chance to "win" the Civil War.

Friends

As their professional relationship grew, so did Lincoln and Seward's personal relationship. Each man, in the words of Lincoln's greatest biographer, began to "court" the other. Lincoln, for example, began a pattern of strolling across Lafayette Park to visit Seward's house; once ensconced, the President would put his boots up and swap stories with his Secretary of State.

And Seward, who liked to be driven in a carriage around Washington at the end of the business day, frequently got the President to join him; and together they often traveled to the forts encircling the Capitol, where they could meet with soldiers.

Even more telling was Seward's gift to Lincoln's sons of several kittens; not only did the boys love their pets, but kittens climbing all over a bemused President became a common sight.

More important were Seward's public and nonpublic disavowals of any interest in succeeding Lincoln, either in 1864 or 1868. Once Seward made clear to Lincoln that he was not a political threat to the President, this allowed the two men to move to a greater level of personal intimacy. They discovered that they had similar senses of humor, and they took turns making the other laugh. On one of their carriage rides, the coachman was cursing at the horses so intensely that the following exchange took place:

> *Lincoln*: "Driver, my friend, are you an Episcopalian?"
> *Coachman*: "No, Mr. President, I ain't much of anything; but if I go to church at all, I go to the Methodist Church."
> *Lincoln*: "Oh, excuse me. I thought you must be an Episcopalian for you swear just like Secretary Seward, and he's a church-warden."

Seward was "vastly amused" by Lincoln's teasing exchange.

As the Civil War ground on, Lincoln's burdens grew, as did his dependence on Seward. By 1864, the Secretary of the Navy, Gideon Welles, wrote in his diary that Lincoln's "confidence in Seward is great," and that on matters "of the gravest importance [Seward was Lincoln's] only confidant and adviser."

Thus, it was Seward alone who accompanied Lincoln aboard the *River Queen* in February 1865 to meet with three Confederate representatives to discuss a possible settlement. Lincoln and Seward both emphasized a liberal reconstruction, but only upon a complete and unconditional return of the Southern States to the Union. After the negotiations broke down, Seward sent a freedman out in a rowboat to deliver a basket of champagne to the departing Confederate dignitaries. As the Southerners were gratefully acknowledging the gift, Seward replied via a boatsman's trumpet: "Keep the champagne, but return the negro."

Less than three months later, the Civil War was almost over. While Lincoln was visiting captured Richmond, Seward was thrown from his carriage and suffered numerous injuries, including a fractured jaw. Upon returning to Washington, Lincoln went straight to Seward's house, where he found his friend in bed with a metal head brace, wrapped like a mummy in bandages, and in great pain.

Barely able to whisper, Seward spoke first: "You are back from Richmond?" Lincoln replied: "Yes, and I think we are near the end, at last." Then Lincoln lay down on the bed next to Seward and for the next half hour told him about his trip and of Grant's progress. After Seward finally fell asleep, the President left his friend's bedside.

The two men never saw each other again. But they are linked in history by the assassination conspiracy. Lincoln, of course, was fatally shot. Seward was simultaneously assaulted with a large bowie knife, which missed inflicting a fatal wound by a millimeter. Seward's doctors did not tell him of Lincoln's assassination for fear of its impact on his recovery.

A few days later, however, Seward looked out of his window and saw a half-mast flag at the War Department. "The President is dead," he said to his attendant. Refusing to acknowledge any denials, Seward added, with "great tears coursing down his gashed cheeks": "If he had been alive he would have been the first to call on me; but he has not been here, nor has he sent to know how I am, and there's the flag at half-mast."

Postscript

The starting points for reading more about Lincoln and Seward must be David Donald's *Lincoln* (Simon & Schuster 1995), Glyndon Van Deusen's *William Henry Seward* (Oxford University Press 1967), and Walter Stahr's *Seward: Lincoln's Indispensable Man* (Simmon & Schuster 2012). Doris Goodwin's *Team of Rivals* (Simon & Schuster 2005) is also an excellent resource for the inner workings of Lincoln's cabinet.

We have Seward and Lincoln to thank for our current Thanksgiving holiday. Prior to the Civil War, Thanksgiving was celebrated at different times, according to the individual preferences of each state's governor. In October 1863, Seward met with Lincoln and there was the following exchange:

> *Seward*: "They say, Mr. President, that we are stealing away the rights of the States. So I have come today to advise

you that there is another State right I think we ought to steal."

Lincoln: "Well, Governor, what do you want to steal now?"
Seward: "The right to name Thanksgiving Day."

Seward then presented Lincoln with a proclamation, asking God "to heal the wounds of the nation" and establishing the last Thursday in November as Thanksgiving Day "in every part of the United States." Lincoln agreed without hesitation, opining that a President "had as good a right to thank God as a Governor."

Mary Lincoln was very jealous of the time her husband spent with Seward. Calling him a "dirty abolitionist sneak," she also told the President: "It makes me mad to see you sit still and let that hypocrite, Seward, twine you around his finger as if you were a skein of thread." She took her irrational hatred even further, explicitly snubbing Mrs. Seward when she paid a social call on the First Lady at the White House.

The Secretary of State accompanied the President to Gettysburg, and gave his own speech on that sacred ground—although no one remembers Seward's words today. Seward promised the assemblage that the Civil War would end not only with the abolition of slavery, but also with a restored Union "having only one hope, one ambition, and one destiny."

CHAPTER XXVIII

George Patton and Military Law

Just as General George S. Patton Jr. was completing what General Dwight D. Eisenhower wrote would be studied as "a model of swift conquest by future classes in the War College in Leavenworth"—leading the Seventh Army to victory in Sicily, liberating Palermo, and beating Bernard Montgomery into Messina—Patton self-destructed, not once, but twice; and it almost ended his military career.

On August 3, 1943, Patton visited the 15th Evacuation Hospital, near Nicosia, Sicily. There, among many wounded men, who were "brave and cheerful," sat Private Charles H. Kuhl, who had no visible wounds. When Patton asked Kuhl what he was doing in the hospital, the solider stammered: "I guess I can't take it." Patton called Kuhl a coward and ordered him out of the hospital tent, but when Kuhl sat frozen in fear, Patton became even more irate and slapped his face with a glove and pushed him out of the tent with a "kick in the rear." In his diary that night, Patton wrote that Kuhl was "the only arrant coward I have seen in the Army," and that such men "should be tried for cowardice and shot."

Ten days later Patton visited the 83rd Evacuation Hospital. Greeting one wounded man after another, Patton came upon Private Paul G. Bennett, who was shivering on a cot. Responding to the General's question as to what he was suffering, Bennett choked out: "It's my nerves. I can't take the shelling anymore." Patton, who did not believe in "combat fatigue," thundered: "Your nerves. Hell, you are just a goddamned coward, you yellow son of a bitch. Shut up that goddamned crying. I won't have these brave men here who have been shot seeing a yellow bastard sitting here crying.... You're a disgrace to the Army and you're going back to the front to fight although that's too good for you. You ought to be lined up against a wall and shot. In fact, I ought to shoot you myself right now, God damn you!"

Patton then pulled out one of his revolvers and waved it in front of the terrified soldier. Ordering the hospital commander to banish Bennett ("I won't have these brave boys seeing such a bastard babied."), Patton then slapped Bennett twice, the second time knocking the private's helmet liner to the ground.

After leaving the hospital, Patton encountered his deputy commander, General Omar Bradley. He told Bradley that he had just come from a hospital where he had slapped a malingerer "to make him mad and put some fight back in him." The next day, Bradley received a report from the hospital staff about Patton's visit. And while Bradley put the report in his safe, a second copy found its way to Eisenhower's chief surgeon, who presented the report to Ike.

The matter did not stay there. The American press corps covering Sicily got wind of the "slapping incidents" and turned them into a cause célèbre. One reporter presented a written report to Eisenhower's chief of staff, General Walter Bedell Smith, and his naval aide, Captain Harry C. Butcher, stating ("if I am correctly informed") that Patton had committed a court-martial offense by striking an enlisted man. The press corps, which had grown to dislike Patton wholly independent of the "slapping incidents"—they believed that there were "at least 50,000 American soldiers on Sicily who would shoot Patton if they had the slightest chance"—actually tried to go further and force Eisenhower to can Patton.

What Was the Legal Case Against "Old Blood and Guts"?

The war correspondents' assumption (which has widely been adopted by histories and biographies since) was perhaps not well grounded. *A Manual for Courts Martial U.S. Army* applicable to that period did not list as a specific offense an officer striking an enlisted man (although Article 64 does specifically provide that it was an offense to assault a superior officer). The closest hook for bringing on a case against Patton would appear to have been Article 65 ("Conduct Unbecoming an Officer and a Gentleman"), which lists as one of the sanctionable indicia the "cruel treatment of soldiers." But even if that had been an appropriate legal basis for proceeding against Patton, there would have been a significant procedural hurdle to such a court-martial: there was not a sufficient number of ranking generals in the European Theatre to try Patton.

More telling perhaps is that none of the key individuals—George Marshall (the Army's Chief of Staff), Eisenhower, Patton, or Bradley—ever wrote of the slappings as a court-martial offense. When this was first brought to Eisenhower's attention by his chief surgeon, Ike's only reaction was that he would have "to give George Patton a jacking up." Upon further reflection, Eisenhower knew the real danger was a media/political maelstrom: "If this thing ever gets out, they'll be howling for Patton's scalp, and that will be the end of Georgie's service in this war." Accordingly, Eisenhower devised a two-pronged strategy for dealing with the problem as he now understood it: first, he had to save Patton from himself by scaring him to death; and, second, he had to use all of his political skills to co-opt the press.

Eisenhower's Political Brilliance

As to the former, Ike dispatched a letter to his oldest and closest friend in the Army (encaptioned "Dear General Patton"), enclosing the report and "strongly advis[ing]" that Patton apologize to the "individuals concerned"; he also demanded a written response "sent to me personally and secretly." Informing Patton that the report had made Eisenhower "seriously question your good judgment and your self-discipline, as to raise serious doubt in my mind as to your future usefulness," Ike ended with: "No letter that I have been called upon

General Patton in 1942
(author's collection)

to write in my military career has caused me the mental anguish of this one, not only because of my long and deep personal friendship for you but because of my admiration for your military qualities; but I assure you that conduct such as described in the accompanying report will not be tolerated in this theatre no matter who the offender may be." A deeply chastened Patton not only apologized to the soldiers and the hospital staffs, he also "apologized" to every division in the Seventh Army.

With respect to the second prong, Eisenhower invited the press into his office, let them rant and vent against Patton, and then, while giving them the famous Ike grin, said: "You men have got yourselves good stories, and as you know, there's no question of censorship involved." Having opened the trap door, Eisenhower then told them that if they did publish their stories, Patton—who was "indispensible to the war effort. One of the guarantors of victory"—would be destroyed. At that point, the correspondents blinked; not wanting to damage the war effort, they pledged not to break the story. One correspondent even went so far as to say they "were not only going to kill the story but deny it if any of the correspondents broke it."

Was Patton Really Outside the Mainstream?

As inexcusable as Patton's behavior seems today, in the crucible of a life-and-death struggle is there a different way to consider Patton's behavior? Interestingly, in Eisenhower's eyes the answer seems to have been "yes."

While he was pondering what to do about his Patton problem, Eisenhower unburdened himself to his naval aide, Captain Butcher. Two excerpts from Butcher's diary are revealing; and these comments have to be understood as coming from a commander who had suffered a humiliating rout in the U.S. Army's first encounter with the Germans at Kasserine Pass in Tunisia (which Ike thought might have caused him to be cashiered by General Marshall). In the first excerpt, Ike told Butcher: "Ike makes a point that in any army one-third of the soldiers are natural fighters and brave; two-thirds inherently are cowards and skulkers. By making the two-thirds fear the possible public upbraiding as Patton gave during the campaign, the skulkers are forced to fight. Ike said Patton's method was deplorable but his result was excellent."

In Butcher's second excerpt, he recorded: "To me Ike cited history to show that great military leaders had practically gone crazy on battlefields in their zeal to win the fight. Patton is like this ... [T]he truth is that soldiers love and respect a successful leader. Nothing breeds confidence like success, Ike said.... The United Nations have not developed another battle leader as successful as Patton, Ike thinks."

Slapping Redux

Unfortunately for Patton (and Eisenhower), although Ike's deal with the war correspondents did not crack, somehow Drew Pearson of the *Washington Post* got hold of the story and it became national news. Now it was Secretary of War Henry Stimson (*see* Chapter XXIX) and General Marshall who stood by Eisenhower's decision to keep Patton. Stimson, in fact, publicly challenged a Senate committee looking into the matter, declaring that Patton would be needed for his "aggressive, winning leadership in the bitter battles which are to come before final victory." Privately, Stimson, a long-time Patton friend and mentor, rebuked Georgie, expressing his "disappointment that so brilliant an officer should so far have offended against his own traditions"; at the same time, however, the Secretary of War told Patton that Mrs. Patton's "wonderful tact and devotion ... did much to forward the favorable result." The "favorable result" was that the Pearson publicity blew over and did not change public opinion (80 percent of those polled by Gallup believed Patton should remain on active duty); Patton would not have to go home in disgrace.

Postscript

Patton went on to command the Third Army in Europe, leading that army on a historic charge through France, Belgium, Luxembourg, Germany, and Czechoslovakia. In perhaps his most famous campaign, Patton broke the back of the German offensive in the Ardennes (the Battle of the Bulge) by relieving the surrounded American forces in Bastogne.

Patton's "apologies" to the Seventh Army's divisions met with varied responses. Some groups sat in silence. One division would not even let Patton speak, chanting "Georgie," "Georgie," until "Old Blood and Guts" started crying and left. In front of another division, Patton started off with: "I just thought I'd stand up here and let you soldiers see if I am as big of a son of a bitch as you think I am." As recorded by Captain Butcher: "The GIs practically raised the roof with their cheers. You can't keep a fellow like that down."

Besides Stimson's critical intervention, support for Patton at various points in his turbulent career came from other New York lawyers, as well. John J. McCloy, for example, who was the Assistant Secretary of War during World War II, backed up Eisenhower's decision to save Patton, citing "Lincoln's remark when they got after Grant comes to mind when I think of Patton—"I can't spare this man—he fights." Even more important support came from FDR, who called Patton "our greatest fighting general, and sheer joy."

Patton's battlefield skill was not only admired by Hitler ("that crazy cowboy general"; "the most dangerous man [the Allies] have") and Stalin but also by his German counterparts: Oberstleutnant Horst Frieheer von Wagenheim ("General Patton is the most feared general on all fronts. [His] tactics are daring and unpredictable.... He is the most modem general and the best commander of [combined] army and infantry forces."); General der Infanterie Gunther Blumentritt ("We regarded Patton ... as the most aggressive Panzer-General of the Allies. A man of incredible initiative and lightning-like action."); Field Marshall Gerd von Rundstedt ("Patton, he is your best."). When General Alfred Jodi, Chief of Staff for the German Armed Forces (Oberkommando der Wehrmacht) heard reports during the war that Patton might be cashiered because he had slapped two enlisted men, he believed that it was merely Allied disinformation—the Allies would never take out of operation their most effective battle commander.

The "slapping incidents" played a role in one of John Wayne's most famous movies: *Sands of Iwo Jima*. In the film, Wayne's character—Sergeant Stryker—gets into a fistfight in boot camp with one of his troops (played by Forrest Tucker). The U.S. Marine Corps objected to the scene, but relented when another scene was added in which Stryker teaches fighting footwork to another soldier by dancing with him. (This is the only movie in which the "Duke" danced with another man.)

After the "slapping incidents," Patton was on double secret probation (à la *Animal House*), unsure of whether he would play any role in the battles to come in Northwest Europe. President Roosevelt, stopping over in Sicily on his return from the Tehran Conference, made a specific point of reaching out to his favorite "fighting general" and telling him: "General Patton, you will have an army command in the great Normandy operation." Patton thereupon stepped into an empty room and burst into tears.

The best biography of George Patton is Carlo D'Este's *Patton: A Genius for War* (Harper Collins 1995). Patton's diaries are wonderfully edited by Martin Blumenson: *The Patton Papers* (Houghton Mifflin, Vol. I 1972; Vol. II 1974).

CHAPTER XXIX

The Serendipity of History: Henry Stimson and the Saving of Kyoto

Henry L. Stimson was certainly one of the great Americans of the twentieth century. Successor to Elihu Root as the leading member of the New York City Bar, Stimson was a founding partner of Winthrop, Stimson, Putnam & Roberts (now Pillsbury Winthrop Shaw Pittman), U.S. Attorney for the Southern District of New York, Governor-General of the Philippines, Secretary of War for William Howard Taft, Secretary of State for Herbert Hoover, and Secretary of War once again for Franklin Roosevelt and Harry Truman.

During World War I, the 50-year-old Stimson joined the army and was commissioned as a colonel in the 77th Regiment. Stimson revered his army service; he took great pride in being addressed as Colonel Stimson for the remainder of his life.

And while Stimson was at the heart of many of the twentieth century's historic events, it is a serendipitous trip he took in the summer of 1926 as a private citizen, which is the focus of this chapter.

As part of a "second honeymoon" tour of the Orient with his wife, Stimson visited Kyoto, the ancient capital of Japan.[1] Kyoto was (and is) the cultural and historical center of Japan. Unlike the rest of that nation, Kyoto had resisted aping the Western world and had retained its pre-Matthew Perry look and feel.

---

[1] In the award-winning movie *Oppenheimer,* it is mistakenly cited as Stimson's "original" honeymoon.

The city impressed the Stimsons as a place of great physical beauty, and they were moved by its fascinating art, its gardens, and the ancient religious structures they witnessed. (Three years later, in his capacity as Secretary of State, Stimson again visited Kyoto.)

War Passion and Hysteria

Fast forward two decades to the spring and summer of 1945: Franklin Roosevelt has died; the war in Europe is over; the war in the Pacific is still raging; and an old (77) and tired Secretary of War is the neophyte president's principal advisor on, among other things, the development and deployment of S-1 (the atomic bomb).

Stimson, in attempting to counsel Truman on that unprecedented situation, recognized that he was faced with overcoming "the feeling of war passion and hysteria which seizes hold of a nation like ours in the prosecution of such a bitter war."

One particular sore point for Stimson was the military's wide-scale targeting of enemy civilians for air force bombing sorties. Universally thought to be immoral and contrary to the laws of war prior to 1940, this practice by 1945 seemed to bother very few people (in or out of the government). Stimson was one, however, and he had extracted a promise from a key aide, Robert Lovett (the Assistant Secretary of War for Air), that "there would be only precision bombing in Japan."

Notwithstanding Lovett's personal rectitude, that promise did not stand for much in the face of General Curtis LeMay's 20th Bomber Command, which in 1945 was engaged in the massive fire-bombing of Japanese cities.

On March 9, LeMay's bombers perfected this tactic of war, virtually incinerating 16 square miles of Tokyo and killing approximately 100,000 people (more than the number that would die at either Hiroshima or Nagasaki); a little more than two months later, on May 25, LeMay's planes returned to Tokyo and destroyed another 19 square miles of the city.

Just two weeks before the second attack on Tokyo, the government's Target Committee (in charge of picking out sites for the atomic bomb(s)) met. As reflected in the minutes of meetings on May 10 and 11, the Committee resolved that the *primary* target would be Kyoto—a site that Stimson had lobbied the head of the Army Air Force, Hap Arnold, to be spared from LeMay's bombers. The Committee's rationale for selecting Kyoto was as follows:

> This target is an urban industrial area with a population of 1,000,000. It is the former capital of Japan and many people and industries are now being moved there as other areas are being destroyed. From the psychological point of view there is the advantage that Kyoto is an intellectual center for Japan and the people there are more apt to appreciate the significance of such a weapon as the gadget.

And just so this latter point was not lost on anyone, the minutes later reiterated the Committee's consensus that "Kyoto has the advantage of the people being more highly intelligent and hence better able to appreciate the significance of the weapon."

After the Target Committee reaffirmed on May 25 that Kyoto would be the primary target, Stimson called for General Leslie Groves, who was the military's man in charge of the S-1 project (and the overseer of the Target Committee).

In a direct confrontation between the two men, Groves defended the selection on the ground that Kyoto was "large enough in area for us to gain complete knowledge of the effects of the bomb. Hiroshima [the Committee's second choice] was not nearly so satisfactory in this respect."

Stimson, however, overruled Groves, uncharacteristically barking: "On this matter, I am the kingpin." Labeling it akin to the Japanese targeting the Lincoln Memorial, Stimson demanded that Kyoto be taken off the list altogether.

Stimson Was No "Dove"

Having saved Japan's cultural hub (or so he thought) did not mean that Stimson was squeamish about using the atomic weapon.

In fact, on May 31, at a meeting of the Interim Committee (the president's group of senior advisors on the S-1, chaired by Stimson), "the Secretary [of War] expressed the conclusion, on which there was general agreement, that we could not give the Japanese any warning; that we could not concentrate on a civilian area; but that we should seek to make a profound impression on as many of the inhabitants as possible.

"At the suggestion of Dr. Conant the Secretary [of War] agreed that the most desirable target would be a vital war plant employing a large number of workers and closely surrounded by workers' houses."

On June 6, Stimson met with Truman at the White House to brief him on several matters. When the subject turned to S-l, Stimson later wrote that he told the President: "I was a little fearful that before we could get ready the Air Force might have Japan so thoroughly bombed out that the new weapon would not have a fair background to show its strength. He laughed and said he understood."

Kyoto Redux

Notwithstanding Stimson's unequivocal order vis-à-vis Kyoto, General Groves did not give up so easily. On July 21, while Stimson was at the Potsdam Conference, he received a detailed report from Groves on the successful testing of the S-1. Stimson read the report in its entirety to Truman and Secretary of State James Byrnes. According to Stimson, the president "was tremendously pepped up" by the report, telling Stimson that "it gave him an entirely new feeling of confidence" (a confidence reflected in his subsequent dealings with Stalin).

Later that same day, Stimson received two cables on S-1 from an aide in Washington, one of which reflected Groves's request to reverse Stimson's decision to strike Kyoto as the primary target. Angered by

Groves's action, Stimson cabled back: "[I] saw no new factors for reversing myself but on the contrary the new factors seemed to confirm it." [Exactly what "new factors" "confirm[ed]" Stimson's decision are unclear. They may well have been the deciphered Japanese cables reflecting that Japan was seeking a way out of the war via Soviet mediation, as well as Stalin's commitment at Potsdam to enter the Pacific War by mid-August.]

The next day, Stimson revisited this issue with the President, and reported on his cable back to Washington; Stimson later wrote in his diary: "As to the matter of the special target [Kyoto] which I refused to permit, [Truman] strongly confirmed my view and said he felt the same way." Running into Hap Arnold later that day, Stimson replayed the matter to the Army Air Force chief, who told Stimson "he agreed with me about the target which I had struck off the program."

On July 24, Stimson met with Truman to go over a host of pressing issues (e.g., the text of the Potsdam Declaration). Stimson later wrote that toward the end of the meeting:

> We had a few words more about the S-1 program, and I gave him my reasons for eliminating one of the proposed targets [Kyoto]. He again reiterated with the utmost emphasis his own concurring belief on that subject, and he was particularly emphatic in agreeing with my suggestion that if elimination was not done, the bitterness which would be caused by such a wanton act might make it impossible during the long post-war period to reconcile the Japanese to us in that area rather than to the Russians. It might thus, I pointed out, be the means of preventing what our policy demanded, namely a sympathetic Japan to the United States in case there should be any aggression by Russia in Manchuria.

And on July 25, Truman recorded in his own diary:

> This weapon is to be used against Japan between now and August 10th. I have told the Sec. of War, Mr. Stimson, to

> use it so that military objectives and soldiers and sailors are the target and not women and children. Even if the Japs are savages, ruthless and fanatic, we as the leader of the world for the common welfare cannot drop this terrible bomb on the old capital [Kyoto] or the new [Tokyo].

Conclusion

Because of Stimson's persistence, Kyoto was saved. Hiroshima thus became the target for the first nuclear weapon ("Little Boy") on August 6, 1945. Serendipity of a different sort played a role in the dropping of the second bomb ("Fat Man"): Because the weather was too cloudy over Kokura on August 9, Nagasaki became the target.

Postscript

Stimson was very much a product of the elite, Victorian society into which he was born and raised. Two of his quotations illustrate this well. The first is: "The only way to make a man trustworthy is to trust him." The other comes from when, as Secretary of State, he shut down that department's cryptoanalytic office, justifying the action: "Gentlemen do not read each other's mail."

The starting point for further reading on Stimson is *On Active Service in Peace and War,* a memoir he wrote with McGeorge Bundy (Harper & Brothers 1948); most historians have cautioned that the memoir's depiction of the decision making vis-à-vis the dropping of the atomic weapons on Japan is not a complete one. A book by Sean Malloy (*Atomic Tragedy: Henry L. Stimson and the Decision to Use the Bomb Against Japan,* Cornell University Press 2008) presents the current historiography on this important subject. *See also* J. Samuel Walker, "Recent Literature on Truman's Atomic Bomb Decision: A Search for Middle Ground" (*Diplomatic History,* April 2005), and Evan Thomas's *Road to Surrender* (Penguin House 2023). Books that put the atomic decision making within in greater context of the end of World War II include Max Hasting's *Retribution: The Battle for Japan, 1944-45* (Knopf 2008) and Tsuyoshi Hasegawa's *Racing the Enemy: Stalin, Truman, and the Surrender of Japan* (Harvard University Press 2005).

Stimson was an important mentor to many future leaders and left a lasting impression on many he never met. That influence is well captured in Walter Isaacson and Evan Thomas's *The Wise Men* (Simon & Schuster 1986). Two examples of Stimson's influence should suffice. First, Robert Lovett, who would later serve as Undersecretary of State and Secretary of Defense in the Truman administration, was summoned by President John F. Kennedy to the White House at the height of the Cuban Missile Crisis (Kennedy had previously offered Lovett his choice of Secretary of State, Treasury, or Defense; he declined them all). Upon his arrival, Lovett went to the office of McGeorge Bundy, JFK's National Security Adviser. As recorded in *The Wise Men*:

> On a small table near Bundy's desk Lovett noticed a photograph of Henry Stimson. "All during the conversation," Lovett recalled, "the old Colonel seemed to be staring me straight in the face." Lovett invoked their mutual icon: "Mac, I think the best service we can perform for the President is try to approach this as Colonel Stimson would." Bundy agreed; Stimson would be their "benchmark."

Second, Stimson, an Andover graduate and Chairman of the Board of Trustees, addressed the graduates of the class in the spring of 1940, against the backdrop of France's collapse and Great Britain gearing up to stand alone against a possible German invasion. As World War II looked to engulf the United States, the colonel sought to inspire the entire prep school audience:

> [A]s I look into your faces and realize your responsibilities, I am filled, not only with pity for what you are facing, but with a desire to congratulate you on your great opportunity.

> I envy you that opportunity. I would to God that I were young enough to face it with you.

In the audience was an idealistic under former named George Herbert Walker Bush. After Pearl Harbor, Bush vowed to heed Stimson's call to service and join the Naval aviation program once he graduated. In the spring of 1942, Stimson again gave the graduation address. This time, however, he told the graduating seniors (including Bush) to go to college first and then serve their country. After the ceremony, Bush's father confronted his son: "Well, George, did the Secretary say anything to change your mind?" "No, sir," answered the forty-first President, "I'm going in."

CHAPTER XXX

The Court-Martial of Captain Charles McVay

Doug Stanton's book, *In Harm's Way,* tells a harrowing tale of the sinking of the *USS Indianapolis* in the last days of World War II. Already assigned a bit part in history because of its role in delivering to the island of Tinian the necessary parts of the atomic weapon later dropped on Hiroshima, the battle cruiser was torpedoed by a Japanese submarine in the dead of night, as it headed for its next assignment at Leyte in the Philippines.

The Sinking

The ship sank in 12 minutes. Some 300 men died in the immediate explosions and sinking; approximately 900 survivors jumped or fell into the oil-drenched Pacific Ocean, hundreds of miles from land in any direction. Bereft of any meaningful supplies, the men drifted in packs for four-plus days, with increasing numbers dying, drowning, giving into temptation to drink salt water, being subject to escalating physical and mental breakdowns, and (perhaps most frightening) being attacked regularly by roving bands of sharks.

The Navy, because of a series of errors and miscues, failed to notice that the *Indianapolis* had not reached Leyte in a timely fashion. It was only after an American plane, a PV-1 Ventura hunting for Japanese submarines, spotted men floating in the ocean that frantic rescue efforts began. Three hundred twenty-one (living) men were pulled from the water, with 317 ultimately surviving (four died in military hospitals). The ordeal was not over for one man, however—the Captain of the *Indianapolis,* Charles McVay.

Court of Inquiry

Ten days after Captain McVay was plucked from the Pacific Ocean (and one day before Japan surrendered on August 14), a court of inquiry was conducted on Guam. The court considered various aspects of the disaster. For example, there was testimony and evidence regarding the intelligence report (enemy submarines were known to be on the route McVay was ordered to undertake, but that was not disclosed in the report because it had been uncovered by the top secret ULTRA program); McVay thus believed the route was free from ominous danger(s). The intelligence officer who briefed McVay prior to the *Indianapolis*'s departure testified that he believed a Japanese submarine attack had been "practically negligible."

After 43 witnesses had given testimony, the court recommended that McVay be court-martialed. That finding was based on two articulated grounds. The first was the failure to transmit a distress signal. On this point, there was disputed testimony. McVay averred that he did not think a message had been sent out in the 12-minute period. The ship's radioman, however, testified that an SOS had been transmitted; and, in fact, it was received by various personnel at Leyte, but not effectively acted upon for a series of reasons, some unfathomable.

The second basis for the court's recommendation was the Captain's order to cease "zigzagging" on the night the ship was torpedoed. McVay's orders had been to zigzag during the day; at night, he was to do so, at his discretion, during periods of good visibility. On the fateful night, McVay had ordered the zigzagging to cease. The sea was quite rough and the sky had only occasional glimpses of a thin strip of moon in and among a heavy cloud cover. In the words of Stanton: "At times, it was so dark that men on the bridge had to announce themselves by name." Nonetheless, the court cited to "good [conditions] with intermittent moonlight" in support of its recommendation.

Court-Martial

Although Admirals Chester Nimitz and Raymond Spruance counseled against a court-martial, Admiral Ernest King (the head of Naval operations) and James Forrestal (the Secretary of the Navy) believed one was warranted. At that point, however, the Navy's judge advocate general had not finalized what charges to bring against McVay!

Charge I was set—the failure to zigzag. As to other charges, it was decided to drop the matter of whether a distress signal had been sent. But if they stopped there, a trial was deemed to be unnecessary because it was indisputable that the ship had not been zigzagging when hit by the torpedoes. The Navy brass believed that the case was "of vital interest not only to the families of those who lost their lives, but also to the public at large," so a second charge was coopered up. Charge II became "failure to abandon ship in a timely manner." Proving such a charge would be problematic, at best; but that was of little or no importance.

The court-martial trial was set for Washington, D.C., on December 3, 1945. McVay learned of the proceeding five days beforehand. His request for a short delay to accommodate the schedule of his chosen attorney was refused; as such, he was left with inexperienced counsel with just days to prepare a defense—a defense for the first captain in American history to be court-martialed for losing his ship to enemy action in wartime.

Testimony by *Indianapolis* survivors cut against the government's case. To a man, they all averred that visibility on the night of the attack was poor. The government's rebuttal to the court was that it was at least clear enough for the Japanese submarine to see and torpedo the ship. And, in furtherance of that point, the Navy flew the submarine commander in from Japan to testify about "what he saw, what he did, and how he did it."

Unusual Strategy

That unusual strategy, just four months after the war's conclusion, brought howls of protest in Congress and in the media. More interesting perhaps for trial lawyers was the poor job of horseshedding that was done with Japanese Commander Mochitsura Hashimoto. In his direct testimony, he explained to the court that zigzagging would have had absolutely no effect upon what he did on the fateful night—that the *Indianapolis* would have been sunk regardless of her orders. And, if that were not enough, another key witness—this time one of America's leading submarine commanders—testified that zigzagging was not an effective defensive mechanism against submarine attack.

Notwithstanding that devastating testimony, as well as the fact that Admiral King had recently been given a report detailing the intelligence failures that put the *Indianapolis* on a course that ensured its meeting with the Japanese submarine (a report that McVay's lawyer was, of course, unaware, just as he was unaware of the intelligence failure and the reasons therefore—the ULTRA secret being years away from being declassified), McVay was ultimately convicted under Charge I. Charge II was, not surprisingly, dismissed. And while his sentence was remitted on the recommendations of Admirals King and Nimitz, McVay's active naval career was over; he officially retired a few years later and became an insurance salesman.

Aftermath

Almost right after he returned to the states, Captain McVay started receiving ugly hate mail, purportedly coming from family members of lost crewmen and blaming him for their deaths. But the survivors of the *Indianapolis* did not blame him. Rather, they revered him, honoring their captain at a survivors' reunion in 1960. They also began an effort to clear his Naval record.

Before their efforts bore any fruit, however, McVay's inner torment (and the weight of the hate mail) got the better of him. He committed suicide.

Years later, spurred in part by the declassification of intelligence reports that demonstrated that the *Indianapolis* had been sent (unbeknownst to McVay and his crew) into harm's way, as well as by the efforts of a Florida teenager whose history project caught the attention of the media (and thereafter some politicians), Congress enacted a resolution in 2000: (1) citing McVay's "lack of culpability for the tragic loss of the *USS Indianapolis*," and (2) stating that because "certain exculpatory information was not available to the court-martial board ... Captain McVay's military record should now reflect that he is exonerated." Notwithstanding that action, the Navy has not expunged the 1945 conviction because "internal and external reviews have supported the fairness and legality of the court-martial proceedings ...." In the words of a Navy officer who has examined the proceedings: "The lesson here is that a decision can be legally correct and still be unjust."

CHAPTER XXXI

William Evarts: The Man to See (In the Nineteenth Century)

Before Elihu Root or Henry Stimson—preeminent leaders of the New York Bar and national and international statesmen (*see* Chapters XXIX and XXXII)—there was William M. Evarts. Today, virtually no one even knows his name, let alone what he accomplished over his long and prodigious career.

Evarts was the first president of the New York City Bar Association (his portrait still hangs at 44th Street), a political protégé of William Henry Seward (he put Seward's name in nomination at the 1860 Republican National Convention, and later moved to make Abraham Lincoln's nomination unanimous after the third ballot), an agent of the Secretary of State to England and France during the Civil War (working to ensure that those nations stayed neutral and did not provide ships to the Confederacy), U.S. Attorney General (under Andrew Johnson), counsel for the Republican Party before the 1876 Electoral Commission (which resolved the disputed electoral votes of Florida, Louisiana, and South Carolina), Secretary of State (under President Rutherford B. Hayes), and U.S. Senator from New York.

Rather than focus on those parts of his career, however, this chapter will look at two episodes in which his legal talents shone brightest.

International Arbitration in Geneva: United States Versus England

During the Civil War, a number of ships flying the Confederate flag were built and/or equipped in England; some were even manned by English sailors. Those ships (e.g., the *Alabama*, the *Florida*) caused a great deal of damage to American ships and to the Northern war effort generally. As a result, there was considerable bitterness on the part of most (Northern) Americans directed at England.

Secretary of State Seward tried to reach a diplomatic accord to have the matter arbitrated, but was unsuccessful. His successor, Hamilton Fish, was finally able to broker the Treaty of Washington in 1871. By that pact, an international tribunal of five arbitrators was created to adjudicate what became known as the "Alabama claims"; this experiment in resolving international disputes was empaneled in Geneva, Switzerland.

There was some political pushback from Radical Republicans to naming Evarts (because of his being part of the Johnson administration as attorney general); nonetheless, he joined Caleb Cushing (attorney general under Franklin Pierce) and Morrison Waite (who one day would be named Chief Justice of the United States) as counsel representing the United States before the arbitrators (five men from Italy, Brazil, Switzerland, England, and the United States).

The two arbitrating nations also appointed agents to actually prosecute their individual positions; the Americans appointed J.C. Bancroft Davis, Fish's Assistant Secretary of State.

Unfortunately, Davis prepared the American case in a blunderbuss style (without Evarts's input), seeking payment of a huge, gross sum in money damages—most problematic was the fact that America sought recovery for "indirect" claims and damages—an approach contrary to international precedent (and with dangerous overtones to the United States in the future). Both Fish and Evarts were less than enthused about Davis's work product. Fish's last instruction to Evarts before he left for Europe was to say as little as possible about the indirect claims theory; laughingly, he suggested that Evarts might use them in oral argument "as bars on which the spread eagle might perch."

England's initial legal position was very different. It denied factual responsibility for any Confederate ships, except for the *Alabama* and the *Florida*; and as to those two ships, England asserted that it had tried to prevent their sailing. When America's indirect claims theory was made public, the British government and media went into an uproar. Evarts, upon his arrival in England, was met with a firestorm of criticism of such ferocity that it appeared the British would pull out of the arbitration. One member of Parliament exclaimed to Evarts: "How can we [participate] when we are determined not to pay an award on them?"

As the British teetered on the edge (and they were not bluffing), Evarts (along with Charles Francis Adams, the U.S.' arbitrator) brokered a compromise with Evarts's English counterparts whereby the arbitrators would simply decline jurisdiction over indirect claims. (Davis was opposed to the United States withdrawing the claims; the British wanted, among other things, to have a stipulation by the governments that the arbitrators did not have the power to award damages on such claims.) By this diplomatic coup, Evarts (and the American legal team) were then able to turn to the legal merits of the case.

The direct claims centered on rules set forth in the Treaty of Washington for evaluating violations of neutrality, principally: (1) what constitutes a neutral government's "due diligence" to prevent the arming (etc.) of a vessel "which it has reasonable grounds to believe, is intended to ... carry on war"; and (2) whether a neutral government has allowed a belligerent to make use of its waters or ports (or failed in its "due diligence" obligations to prevent said use).

The Swiss arbitrator, over England's objections, suggested that the case of each ship be considered individually. The case of the *Florida* was first drawn. After three days, the arbitrators were ready to move on. The British protested, however, and the panel agreed to allow further argument by both sides (orally or in writing) on a few, specific points.

The British did not limit themselves, but instead put in a comprehensive brief, in which they attacked the entire American case, arguing that British municipal law was the only governing law that could be applied to the conduct at issue.

In reply, Evarts made an oral presentation to the tribunal. Curiously, he addressed the arbitrators in English—a language in which three of the arbitrators were not conversant. Perhaps his intent (because this is what happened) is that he hoped to engage the English arbitrator in a Socratic dialogue, and use that rhetorical mechanism to prove the overall American case.

During the course of his two-day oration, Evarts gave a masterly dissertation on the principles of international law. He demonstrated that British municipal law did not (and could not) trump international law and that the British had failed to meet its "due diligence" obligations under the Treaty of Washington, regardless of when or where it had outfitted a ship (i.e., within or just outside territorial waters)—especially a ship flying under the flag of a nonrecognized, belligerent nation.

Ultimately, the arbitrators (with some dissents with respect to specific ships) ruled in favor of the American position. The panel next ruled that damages be assessed at $15.5 million (an obvious compromise number). This experiment in international dispute resolution was then concluded with hopeful expressions of future peace between nations and an artillery salvo. As for Evarts, Joseph Choate (a prominent lawyer and future Ambassador to the Court of St. James) proclaimed that his work was "the most notable professional achievement that ever fell to the lot of an American advocate."

Defending the Presidency of Andrew Johnson

The hostility between President Andrew Johnson and Congress grew to a white-hot intensity as Reconstruction progressed (or failed to progress). That led to Congress enacting the Tenure of Office Act, which purported to strip from the President the ability to discharge cabinet officers without the explicit consent of the Senate.

Johnson thereafter removed his irksome Secretary of War, Edwin Stanton (not once, but twice). And when he did it the second time, the House of Representatives went into impeachment mode.

Ultimately, the House drew up 11 articles of impeachment, virtually all of which related to Johnson's removal of Stanton (the tenth article was that the President's "inflammatory and scandalous harangues" had brought Congress into dispute; the eleventh was an omnibus article, incorporating the first 10 and charging that Johnson had denied and intended to deny valid Congressional legislation).

The House Managers (led by Benjamin Butler, who by dint of his administration of New Orleans during the Civil War had been tagged "Beast Butler") promptly went before the Senate. Chief Justice Salmon Chase declared that he would officiate, and that the Senate's deliberations over the President's fate would be conducted like a trial. That second pronouncement would prove to be far off the mark.

Johnson's Cabinet met and unanimously agreed that Henry Stanbery, the Attorney General, should step down and act as the President's lead counsel. Others selected included Benjamin Curtis, a retired Supreme Court Justice (he dissented in the *Dred Scott* case). Evarts was the last member of the team chosen; his selection was due to Seward's influence (and notwithstanding a public address Evarts had given at the Cooper Union in October of 1867, at which he described Johnson as a "President without a party").

The Senate "trial" got off to a rocky start when the defense team asked for a 40-day postponement to allow them to prepare adequately. Butler leaped to his feet, emoting: "Forty days! As long as it took God to destroy the world by a flood." The defense was ultimately (and grudgingly) granted 10 days by the Senate.

On March 23, 1868, the "trial" began in earnest. Stanbery and Curtis addressed the first nine articles; Evarts, who had sole responsibility for drafting answers to articles 10 and 11, addressed those last two (Johnson did not like Evarts's answer to the omnibus article—11).

Butler's opening statement came a week later. In it, he denied the Senate was a court and that the proceeding was a trial. Instead, he declared that the Senate was conducting an "inquest" into whether Johnson had committed an act "subversive of some fundamental or essential principle of government, or highly prejudicial to the public interest" (any one of which would, be an impeachable offense). Then, just to show how low he could and would go, Butler linked Johnson to Lincoln's murder ("the election of an assassin").

As the witnesses began to be called, Evarts tried to make the proceeding more like a trial and interposed that the Chief Justice should rule on questions relating to the admissibility of evidence. The Senators, however, rejected that notion, reserving such authority to themselves. This was a key procedural Rubicon because it led to the Senate overruling Chase at critical points throughout the case.

For example, General William Sherman's testimony was restricted by the Senators; a Cleveland editor's hearsay testimony was allowed by the Senators; and most importantly, Gideon Welles (the Secretary of the Navy) was prevented by the Senators from testifying as to Cabinet discussions on and the Cabinet's advice to the President regarding compliance with the Tenure of Office Act.

Evarts argued that this testimony was critical on the issue of the President's intent: "the bearing of all circumstances of intent and of deliberation and inquiry and pursuit of duty, on the part of the great official to arrive at and determine what is his official duty, under an apparent conflict between the Constitution and the law, forms a part of the general issue of impeachment and defense."

Chase himself commented that he "could conceive of no evidence more proper to be received." But by a 29-to-20 vote, the Senate precluded any and all such testimony. This vote had two further consequences: It scrapped the testimony of other Cabinet members (Seward, Browning, and McCulloch), and it engendered support for Johnson from some wavering Senate Republicans who thought this deprived the President of a fair hearing.

As the "trial" progressed, Evarts evolved into the defense team's lead counsel. This led to some notable confrontations with the volcanic Butler. On April 16, for example, Evarts told Chase that "we have reached a point at which it will be convenient to us that we should not be required to produce more evidence today."

Butler's intemperate objection included the following: "We are asked 'Why stand ye idle here?' by every true man in the country.... While we are being courteous, the true Union men of the South are being murdered, and on our heads and on our shirts is their blood if we remain any longer idle."

At the conclusion of Butler's histrionics, Evarts remarked: "I have never heard such a harangue before a court of Justice, but I cannot say that I may not hear it again in this Court." Incredibly, one Senator then challenged whether Evarts's use of the word "harangue" was in order!

On April 18, after the Senate's shutting down of Cabinet officer testimony, Evarts announced that the defense would call no more witnesses.

At that point, the Radical Republicans thought the President's conviction was in the bag. Evarts, however, wrote that he believed Johnson would not be convicted for two reasons: "The first is the weakness of the case on the evidence, and the second, the preference of certain politicians for the present situation to the change proposed [i.e., exchanging Johnson for the Senate's President Pro Tern, Ohio Senator Benjamin Wade]." Evarts also had another reason that had nothing to do with the legal merits of his client's case.

While the "trial" was ongoing, Evarts decided that he needed to level the political playing field a bit. With the support of several Republican Senators, Evarts went to the President and proposed that he nominate General John Schofield as Secretary of War. He told Johnson that appointing the popular Schofield would convince a number of Senators that the President's final year in office would be (at least) tolerable; thus assuaged, they would likely vote based on the evidence, as opposed to their visceral hatred of Johnson.

Authorized by the President, Evarts met with Schofield on April 21 at the Willard Hotel. Schofield was wary of the offer, saying that he wanted to vet the issue with General Grant. Grant was equally wary (he believed Johnson would be convicted; undoubtedly, he was also not sure about how these events might impact his becoming president); but Grant nonetheless told Schofield he should take the post for the good of the country. When the nomination was sent to the Senate on April 24, it appeared to have the desired impact upon the intended audience; one Senate observer wrote that "impeachment has gone rapidly astern."

Having protected his (and the President's) political flank, Evarts turned to his closing statement. By the Senate's procedure, each side's lawyers were permitted to make an oration (first the prosecution, next the defense, next the prosecution, etc.). By the time this process yielded to Evarts, passions had been re-inflamed and there was an anticipation that the President's future would rise or fall on his advocacy.

As the Senate galleries fell into a "dead hush," Evarts began. He first spoke not only to the unprecedented nature of what was being contemplated, but to the Senators who did not like their colleague, Benjamin Wade—warning of the dangers (current and future) of having a president chosen by the Senate, as opposed to by the people.

Evarts then reviewed the gravamen of the case against Johnson—that he stood accused not of treason or bribery, but rather of transgressing a law that Congress had passed for the first time, which not only sought to change how Presidents could deal with their Cabinets but also contemplated that noncompliance therewith would constitute a "high misdemeanor"—an impeachable offense.

Evarts concluded his first day's remarks by rebutting Butler's attempt to have the proceeding not be a trial and the Senate not be a court: "The Constitution makes this a court; it makes its proceedings a trial.... [I]t is a court and nothing but a court ... if this is not an altar of justice which we stand about ... it is an altar of sacrifice ... to the divinity of party hate and party rage. If this is not a court, it is a scaffold."

Prior to starting up the second day, Evarts's mentor, William Seward, called upon Evarts at the Willard Hotel and praised him on his prior day's work: "Ah, Mr. Evarts, the country is safe." But Evarts had a lot more to do and say. Instead of picking up on the solemn note on which he had previously closed, Evarts switched oratorical gears and chose to have some fun at the expense of the House Managers.

His main target was Massachusetts Congressman George Boutwell. Boutwell's over-the-top closing statement had contemplated that Johnson's true punishment (beyond removal from office) would be a hole in the sky near the Southern Cross into which the disgraced President would be heaved.

Confessing that he belonged to a profession that "sharpens and does not enlarge the mind," Evarts stated that this extra-constitutional punishment was unknown to him, but he admired the fact that Boutwell "had discovered an untenanted and unappropriated region in the skies, reserved, he would have us think, in the final councils of the Almighty, as a place of punishment for convicted and deposed American Presidents." Since Boutwell alone knew of this punishment, however, he would have to take responsibility for executing on the judgment:

> When the President made fast to his broad and strong shoulders, and, having essayed the flight by imagination, better prepared than anybody else to execute it in form, taking advantage of the ladders as far as ladders will go to the top of this great Capitol, and spuming then with his foot the crest Liberty, let him set out on his flight, while the two houses of Congress and all the people of the United State hill shout *Sic utur ad, astra*. But here a distressing doubt strikes me: how will the Manager get back? He will have gone beyond the reach of gravitation to restore him, and so ambitious a wing as his could never stoop to a downward flight.

The senatorial gallery roared with laughter at this surgical and witty dissection of Boutwell. As Chase smilingly rapped his gavel for order, Boutwell was described as "almost suffocated."

On the third day of Evarts's closing statement, he addressed various arguments put forward by the other House Managers. As to the contention that Johnson had made contemptible speeches, for example, Evarts quoted back the Managers' own bombastic rhetoric during the impeachment proceedings.

The *New York Herald* wrote that by "slowly and deliberately applying the fatal fuse, he set the whole superstructure of the Radical Managers in a blaze … the flames hissing and crackling with alarming effect." Evarts's systematic and relentless style led Secretary of the Navy Welles to observe that "the radical cause is growing weaker, and indications [are] that the radical leaders have apprehensions."

On the fourth (!) and last day of his closing, Evarts put aside humor and relied on a careful review of the law (along with an appeal to the heartstrings). He laid out the legislative history of the Tenure of Office Act and demonstrated that a number of Senators were explicit in their views that the legislation was not meant to apply to Cabinet members held over from the Lincoln administration.

Evarts then turned to an impassioned defense of Johnson, one of the few political leaders of the South who had stood by the Union in its time of crisis:

> Bred in a school of Tennessee democratic politics, he had always learned to believe that the Constitution must and should be preserved; … he loved the Constitution more than he loved his section, and the glories that were promised by the evil spirit of rebellion. He is no rhetorician and no philosopher. The Constitution is to him the only book he reads. The Constitution is to him the only authority that he obeys…. For it and under it he served the state from boyhood up—labored for and loved it. For it he has stood in arms against rebellious forces of the enemy; and to it he has bowed three times a day with more than eastern devotion.

When he finally concluded, Senators from both sides rushed to congratulate Evarts. And the press (both pro and con) highly praised his efforts. Not surprisingly, Butler and his fellow Managers were not part of the admiring throng; Butler called Evarts a "pseudo-Republican who had stolen the livery of Heaven in which to serve the devil."

Johnson's fate now lay in the hands of the Senate—36 votes were needed for conviction, 19 for acquittal. Ultimately, 7 Republicans stood with 12 Democrats, and the President survived by 1 vote. It truly was a political "profile in courage," because not one of the 7 Republicans was ever returned to Congress.

Postscript

President Andrew Johnson, who must have been a difficult client, was particularly disturbed by Evarts's handling of his case during the Senate "trial." With respect to Butler's "bloody shirt" outburst, Johnson commented: "All Mr. Evarts had to say was that it was a harangue, and 1 believe he thinks he did a most smart and dreadful thing.... There was the chance to have administered a rebuke that would not only have told upon the Senate but upon the whole country.... The Managers alluded to me as a 'criminal.' Why has that not been replied to by my counsel?"

Although Johnson did not feel fully comfortable with Evarts during the Senate "trial," afterward he certainly had no complaints. And when the Senate refused to confirm Henry Stanbery back to his prior position, the President (at Seward's urging) nominated Evarts to become attorney general. Evarts was confirmed, and spent the last nine months of the President's term in the Cabinet.

As a precursor to Watergate, Butler employed spies to break into Evarts's room at the Willard Hotel to search for damaging materials. Incredibly, Butler later publicly bragged about this (unsuccessful) burglary.

Evarts, the grandson of Declaration of Independence signer Roger Sherman, was the grandfather of famed literary editor Maxwell Perkins ("Editor of Genius") and great-grandfather of Watergate prosecutor Archibald Cox.

CHAPTER XXXII

Elihu Root: Legal Icon, American Statesman, and Fierce "TR" Partisan

There can be little doubt that Elihu Root was a great man. One of New York's preeminent lawyers (U.S. Attorney for the Southern District of New York (1883-85)), he started a great law firm: Root Clark—later known as Dewey Ballentine; his clients included William "Boss" Tweed, Jay Gould, and E.H. Harriman. He served as Presidents William McKinley and Theodore ("TR") Roosevelt's Secretary of War (1899-1904), as well as President Roosevelt's Secretary of State (1905-1909); in 1912, Root received the Nobel Peace Prize for his efforts in furtherance of international peace. After Root left the Roosevelt administration, the New York State Legislature elected him to the U.S. Senate. He declined to serve a second term; he also declined the 1916 Republican nomination for president. Thereafter, as an "elder" statesman, Root undertook a number of important diplomatic assignments (e.g., a 1917 mission to Russia; a delegate to the 1921-1922 Washington Naval Conference), and worked to fulfill the promise of the Permanent Court of International Justice. An amazing career!

Republican Roots

Root's first national political mentor was Chester Alan Arthur, who, as president, named him U.S. Attorney. But two years prior to that, Root cut his political teeth on a race for the New York State Legislature by an impetuous newcomer, Theodore Roosevelt. Later that same decade, Root played an important managerial role in TR's unsuccessful campaign to become New York City's mayor.

But Root really proved himself to Roosevelt when TR, flush with his Spanish-American War heroics, put his hat into the ring for the 1898 New York governor's race. On September 24, 1898—three days before the Republican nominating convention—Roosevelt's principal rival leaked to the media that Roosevelt was not a New York State citizen. This charge was based on a tax representation that Roosevelt had been a legal resident of Washington, D.C., since October 1, 1897. While this had saved TR $50,000 in New York State taxes (a lot of money back then), it appeared to disqualify his candidacy as a matter of law.

The Meanings of "Resident"

Root and Joseph Choate were called in by the party bosses to deal with this "legal" issue. The evidence did not seem all that helpful—TR, for example, had previously also declared himself a resident of New York City to escape taxes on his home at Oyster Bay. Choate, likely because of the evidentiary record, proved a bit squeamish about putting his name "on record," but that did not stop Root. Perhaps anticipating a future president who would frame a legal defense around varying definitions that could be attributed to the verb "is," Root prepared a legal defense based on the different meanings of "resident." That, plus Root's willingness to stand up at the nominating convention and use a lot of "ballyhoo" to obfuscate the issue (and thus satisfy the delegates), carried the day. And like the work that Abe Fortas did to save Lyndon B. Johnson in the 1948 Texas Senate race (*see The Worst Supreme Court Decisions, Ever! (And Related Tales)* (Twelve Tables Press 2024)), Roosevelt knew that Root had rescued his political career and never forgot it.

TR and Hearst

It would be fair to say that Roosevelt and William Randolph Hearst really detested one another. Hearst, for one, viewed Roosevelt through a complex prism, which combined envy, contempt, class warfare, and unadulterated political ambition. And it further galled Hearst that the principal beneficiary of the Spanish-American War—a war he had fomented—was TR; Roosevelt, moreover, was merely a spoiled Harvard aristocrat who wore pink shirts and a tasseled silk sash instead of a vest (as reported by Hearst's *New York Journal-American*). Contemplating his own political career (leading to the White House he hoped), Hearst authorized his cartoonists and editorial writers to defeat Roosevelt's 1898 gubernatorial campaign by any and all means. For example, TR was regularly depicted in cartoons as an overgrown child, playing in a military uniform; he was called "a humbug" and labeled "a prideless office seeker."

"Influence for Evil"

Roosevelt, for his part, believed that Hearst was "the most potent single influence for evil we have in our life." TR termed Hearst's private life as "disreputable," and found his "sensational, scandal-mongering newspapers" to be "entire[ly] unscrupulous." Hearst, by Roosevelt's reckoning, "preach[ed] the gospel of envy, hatred and unrest . . . , car[ing] nothing for the nation, nor any citizens in it."

This mutual dislike would one day draw in Elihu Root, and in a fascinating way.

The Election of 1906

By 1906, Roosevelt had been president for five years (since President William McKinley's assassination in 1901). And although he had pledged not to seek another term in 1908, TR was still a highly charged political animal; moreover, he wanted to ensure a smooth path for his chosen successor.

The main obstacle to that plan was William Randolph Hearst. By that point, Hearst was a congressman from New York, and he had amassed a great deal of power in the Democratic Party, thanks to his vast wealth and octopus-like media empire. Hearst's plan for the future was a simple one: run for and be elected New York's governor in 1906, and then run for and be elected president in 1908 (or 1912).

Roosevelt, contemplating such a scenario, thought that while Hearst would represent a "lower level than we have ever sunk as President," he "would be more dangerous" as New York's governor. As such, he took several steps to check Hearst's ambitions. First, he engineered the Republican nomination for Charles Evans Hughes, a well-known anti-boss crusader (who would one day become Chief Justice of the U.S. Supreme Court). But even with a formidable candidate, TR worried about Hearst's "enormous popularity among ignorant and unthinking people," and pledged himself to "a savage and aggressive fight."

Hearst meanwhile was engaged in a full-court press, campaigning all over the state in a tireless manner. Years before Al Jolson "sang" in *The Jazz Singer*, Hearst blanketed the state with himself as the star of "talking pictures" (which were, in turn, advertised in the various Hearst publications). The blitz appeared to be working, and Hearst's victory seemed imminent. This led TR to pull off the gloves and turn to more drastic measures.

The McKinley Assassination

While William McKinley was in office, Hearst was a partisan opponent, using all of his media to attack the President on an ongoing basis. In February of 1900, when the Governor-Elect of Kentucky, William Goebel, was killed, Ambrose Bierce (the famous journalist who was on Hearst's payroll) wrote in the *Journal*: "The bullet that pierced Goebel's breast cannot be found in all the West. Good reason, it is speeding here to stretch McKinley in his bier."

The Killing

And if that were not enough, Arthur Brisbane wrote a *Journal* editorial just a month after McKinley's second inauguration in 1901, which ended with the following sentiment: "If bad institutions and bad men can be got rid of only by killing, then the killing must be done."

When the foregoing was written, Hearst was severely criticized. After the President was assassinated in September of 1901, however, he was accused by many of having caused McKinley's death, or being a coconspirator with the assassin (or worse). Hearst was burned in effigy, was the target of numerous death threats, and took to keeping a gun handy (as well as burying unknown boxes he received for fear they carried bombs).

Five years later (an eternity in American politics), most people had pushed this matter back into the deep recesses; not Roosevelt. Rather than taking on Hearst directly, however, TR enlisted the services of his Secretary of State, Elihu Root.

Some Republican leaders debated the wisdom of having Root be an administration attack dog—not because of the questionable idea of dragging the Secretary of State into the middle of New York State politics, but rather because they worried that Root's corporate background could be exploited by the "populist" Hearst. Roosevelt and others (notably, James Sherman, chair of the Republican Congressional Campaign Committee) overrode that objection and sent Root into the fray.

Root the Partisan

Just days before the election, Root held forth at a large Republican rally in upstate New York. With advance warning as to the importance of Root's speech, every newspaper was represented to hear Root attack Hearst. At first, the attack was political in nature:

> I say to you, with the President's authority, that he regards Mr. Hearst to be wholly unfit to be Governor, as an insincere, self-seeking demagogue, who is trying to deceive the working men of New York by false statements and false promises. I say to you, with the President's authority, that

> he considers Mr. Hearst's election would be an injury and a discredit alike to all honest labor and to honest capital, and a serious injury to the work in which he is engaged of enforcing just and equal laws against corporate wrong-doing.

"By the President's Authority"

But thereafter, Root went for the jugular, accusing Hearst ("by the President's authority") of complicity in McKinley's death:

> In President Roosevelt's first message to Congress, in speaking of the assassin of McKinley, he spoke of him as inflamed 'by the reckless utterances of those who, on the stump and in the public press, appeal to the dark and evil spirits of malice and greed, envy and sullen hatred.' ... I say, by the President's authority, that in penning these words, with the horror of President's McKinley's murder fresh before him, he had Mr. Hearst specifically in mind. And I say, by the President's authority, that what he thought of Mr. Hearst then he thinks of Mr. Hearst now.

Needless to say, that accusation was front-page news everywhere. And while the Hearst media dubbed "Root, the Rat," the damage was immense and (as TR had planned it) virtually impossible to counteract in the few days before the election.

Hearst's Career Ends

On election day, it was evident that Root's brutal attack had worked. Out of approximately 1.5 million votes, Hughes squeaked to victory by approximately 60,000. Hearst's career in electoral politics was over.

Postscript

Although his career in politics was ended by Root's speech, Hearst remained a considerable power behind the scenes in

Democratic politics. His last prominent role was in securing the presidential nomination for Franklin Delano Roosevelt at the 1932 convention (with the able assistance of Joseph P. Kennedy).

In the movie *Citizen Kane*, the political career of Charles Foster Kane (the thinly veiled Hearst) is ended when he crosses the Party Boss (played by Ray Collins, who would later gain fame as Lt. Tragg in *Perry Mason*); the Boss leaks to the media that Kane is having an extramarital affair, and that news kills Kane's chances of being elected governor of New York.

One of Root's most famous statements (at least pertaining to the law) was: "About half of the practice of a decent lawyer is telling would-be clients that they are damned fools and should stop."

CHAPTER XXXIII

John McCloy: The "Wise Man"

During his lifetime, John J. McCloy was one of the most famous lawyers in the world. Assistant Secretary of War during World War II, U.S. High Commissioner for Germany in the aftermath of the war, president of the World Bank, chairman of Chase Manhattan Bank, chairman of the Council on Foreign Relations, member of the Warren Commission, advisor to numerous presidents (one of "The Wise Men"), McCloy was frequently dubbed the "Chairman of the American Establishment" by the media. In addition to the foregoing, McCloy was also a name partner in Milbank, Tweed, Hadley & McCloy.

But before McCloy took on any of these formidable roles, as a young lawyer in New York he made all that possible by his dogged pursuit of a fascinating matter: the Black Tom explosion.

Espionage in World War I

In 1914, Count Johann Von Bernstorff arrived in the United States; he was Germany's ambassador. His principal mission was not diplomacy, however. Rather, Von Bernstorff and his staff were here to assist Germany in its efforts to win the Great War (later known as World War I); and to do so by whatever means necessary.

Well-endowed by the German government with millions of dollars, Von Bernstorff undertook numerous nefarious tasks. Where he was most successful (it would appear) was in interfering with the manufacture of explosives and in the sinking of ships filled with cargo to help the Allies. And it is at the intersection of those efforts that led to the Black Tom explosion.

Black Tom Island was a small spit of land in New York Harbor, close to the Statue of Liberty. On the night of July 30, 1916, the Island was a major munitions dump, chockablock full of many tons of TNT, as well as 69 railroad cars with thousands of tons of ammunition; all of this material was to be shipped to England and France. At 2:08 a.m., an explosion the equivalent of a 5.5 Richter scale earthquake occurred. That explosion (and those that followed) were felt 90 miles in every direction. Bullets, shells, and metal fragments were sent flying across the Hudson River; most people were rocked out of their beds; immigrants on neighboring Ellis Island had to be evacuated; windows in Manhattan and Brooklyn were shattered; and the Statue of Liberty sustained serious structural damage (the interior of Lady Liberty's torch has been closed to visitors since the explosion). The total property damage was estimated to be $20 million ($427 million in 2012 dollars); miraculously, only seven people died as a direct result of the explosions. It quickly became apparent that this was no accident. Initially, it was thought that railroad employees were at fault; then, suspicion centered on guards at the pier who had lit smudge pots to ward off mosquitoes. But the official investigations at the time came to naught. Most people believed it was foul play (especially with other, similar incidents later in World War I), but there was no proof. In fact, it was the first major terrorist attack on American soil directed by a foreign sovereign power (not counting the torching the British did to Washington during the War of 1812).

The Mixed Claims Commission

After World War I ended, the German-American Mixed Claims Commission was established to resolve war-related claims of German and American companies. This process proved to be difficult, because of the large number of disputes put before the Commission, daunting evidentiary issues, and obvious geopolitical considerations in the postwar era. As such, matters like the Black Tom explosion went unresolved for quite some time.

In September of 1930, the new head of Cravath, Henderson & de Gersdorff's Paris office, John McCloy, received a cable from New York, directing him to go to The Hague; one of Cravath's clients, Bethlehem Steel, was litigating a claim before the Commission that German agents were responsible for the Black Tom explosion and Bethlehem's millions of dollars of damages. Cravath and McCloy had been brought in to assist because the lawyer of record for a group of companies seeking compensation (including Bethlehem), Amos Peaslee, was hopelessly out of his depth. And after just a few days of attending the hearing, McCloy came to share that view (Peaslee did not have his "ducks all lined up in a row"). Ultimately, Peaslee's case—although he had some pretty damning evidence from confessed German agents (as well as an official German cable authorizing sabotage "in every kind of [U.S.] factory for supplying munitions of war")—proved not to be bulletproof. On November 15, 1930, the commissioners unanimously rejected the claims for damages, with both the German and American commissioners specifically finding that the German agents were "liars, not presumptive, but proven."

McCloy's Obsession

At that point, McCloy took over. Filing an appeal, McCloy went all over Europe in search of evidence, meeting "shady kinds of characters in dives, the worst kind of bars, even houses of ill-repute." Some of those efforts were for naught; others, however, bore fruit. Back in America, a recently discovered message in lemon juice (readable only after the document had been warmed by a steam iron) seemed particularly promising because it tied specific individuals to the Black Tom explosion. McCloy's new evidence moved the bar slightly—his appeal lost, but the Commission's December 3, 1932, ruling was now not unanimous (McCloy got the vote of the American commissioner). And so on he went, even as his law partners began to despair of McCloy's growing obsession.

In 1933, McCloy's doggedness paid off: he discovered (and was able to prove) that Germans (1) had bribed one of McCloy's own handwriting experts on the lemon juice document, and (2) had bribed other witnesses. On the basis of those developments, the Commission reopened the case on December 15, 1933. That then prompted McCloy to dig further.

In Ireland, he was able to get a very helpful affidavit from James Larkin, a radical Irish labor organizer who detailed German sabotage efforts in the United States. In Austria, he smuggled a historian into a military archive to find documents evidencing the German terror campaign. In Germany, he hired detectives to trail suspected individuals and he had telephone calls traced.

By 1936, the German government (spearheaded by Herman Goering and Rudolph Hess) indicated that it would consider settling the matter. In early July, McCloy, and a team of lawyers were in Munich negotiating in a "terrifying" environment ("All those goose-stepping soldiers ... I knew then that they were a bunch of thugs."). And while it appeared that a deal had been struck, ultimately it came undone because some of the American companies in the case believed they would be disadvantaged by the settlement (e.g., Chase National Bank) and surreptitiously killed the deal.

So, back went McCloy to litigating the dispute before the Commission. Further digging uncovered a damning document by a German American who tied "pencil bombs"—cigar-sized cases filled with acid in copper chambers; after the acid melted the copper, intense flames would be created (used to ignite the Black Tom explosion)—to the German bad guys. With this last piece of evidence, McCloy had now lined up his ducks "in a row."

Oral argument based on all that McCloy had put together took place before the Commission in late 1938. By early 1939, when it was clear that the Commission was going to rule in favor of the claimants, the German commissioner "retired." The remaining commissioners then awarded approximately $50 million in damages. Certain of the claimants (again, led by Chase) sought to contest the ruling in federal court. In 1941, the U.S. Supreme Court rejected that challenge. McCloy's decade-long crusade had been justified.

Postscript

Amos Peaslee received $4.4 million as a result of the Commission's ruling. McCloy's partnership income was substantially increased in 1941 to $94,105.

McCloy's Black Tom crusade made him, in Secretary of War Henry Stimson's eyes, the perfect man to help him, first as a consultant on intelligence matters and soon thereafter as Assistant Secretary of War. In that latter position, McCloy was at the heart of many of World War II's most controversial events (e.g., the internment of Japanese Americans, the decision not to bomb the Nazi death camps, saving General George S. Patton's career, the dropping of the atomic bomb on Japan).

McCloy's father died when he was six. Because he left no insurance, McCloy's mother was forced to go to work as a hairdresser. Through force of will, she ensured that her son got a first-rate education (Amherst, Harvard Law School). Among the odd jobs he took on to make ends meet, McCloy taught John D. Rockefeller Jr.'s children how to sail in Seal Harbor, Maine. After completing law school, McCloy returned to his home city, Philadelphia, and sought out an old friend of his father's, who was also the undisputed dean of the Philadelphia Bar: George Wharton Pepper. Pepper gave it to the ambitious, young McCloy straight:

> [I] am not wrong about this. I know Philadelphians. It is a city of blood ties. You have good grades, but they don't mean anything here. Family ties do.... [T]hey'll never take you seriously in this town. In New York, however, your grades will count for something.

And so McCloy accepted a job offer at Cadwalader, Wickersham & Taft. A few years later he joined Cravath, where he subsequently made partner. After the war, McCloy was unable to come to terms with Robert Swaine, Cravath's managing partner, and joined Milbank instead, adding his name to the masthead.

The starting point for John McCloy is Kai Bird's definitive biography *The Chairman: John J. McCloy, The Making of the American Establishment* (Simon & Schuster 1992). Also not to be missed is Walter Isaacson and Evan Thomas's *The Wise Men: Six Friends and the World They Made* (Simon & Schuster 1986). An excellent work on the Black Tom explosion is Jules Witcover's *Sabotage at Black Tom* (Chapel Hill Press 1989).

CHAPTER XXXIV

Tom Dewey's Brilliant Legal Career

For most lawyers active today in the Second Circuit, Thomas E. Dewey is a faint memory. He was, of course, almost president of the United States (twice nominated by the Republicans, first in 1944 and then in 1948), a three-term governor of New York (1943-54), instrumental in making Dwight D. Eisenhower president in 1952 (and Richard M. Nixon his vice president), mentor of many of the twentieth century's most famous lawyers (e.g., John A. Wells, Frank Hogan, J. Edward Lumbard, Charles Breitel, Lawrence Walsh, William Rogers), recipient of the Federal Bar Council's Emory Buckner Medal (in 1968), and senior partner of the prominent law firm Dewey, Ballentine, Bushby, Palmer & Wood. The focus of this chapter, however, is on his pre-political career in the law, which, because of his success and prominence, catapulted him into the public spotlight, where he remained for decades.

Dewey's Legal Education

Born in 1902 in Owosso, Michigan, Dewey began his higher education at the University of Michigan. Besides his studies, his main focus was on his promising singing career, in which his voice was praised for its "velvety texture." After winning a statewide competition in his senior year (and, thereafter, finishing third in the national finals), Dewey decided to enroll in Michigan Law School, while continuing his vocal training.

Whether it was because of his divided focus or not, Dewey found his first-year studies little more than "scrivener's work." Upon completion of his 1L, Dewey shipped off to Chicago that summer for more singing training. This, in turn, led him to bigger and better things in New York City; with that came Dewey's transfer to Columbia Law School. While at Columbia, Dewey augmented his income by singing in churches and synagogues. A bad performance at a public recital (caused by laryngitis), however, caused him to rethink his future plans.

Focusing more on his legal studies, Dewey's grades, class rank, and standing among his classmates and peers (e.g., William O. Douglas) began to soar. When it came time to apply to Wall Street law firms, Dewey visited many of the usual suspects, but found the experience less than dazzling (at White and Case, for example, he was told, "Of course, you ... realize that we regard a young man as nothing but a pair of legs the first two years.") Ultimately, he received three offers (the going rate: $35 per week); he decided to accept the one proffered by Larkin, Rathbone and Perry, a 36-lawyer firm that focused mainly on corporate leasing work.

Law Practice

For Dewey, who wanted to try cases, the work was tedious and unstimulating. To make matters worse, he soon found himself at odds with one of the firm's senior partners. After one year, his services were terminated.

Fortunately, Dewey was able to find a job at the small firm of McNamara & Seymour, even though Stuart McNamara worried that Dewey might be "a little too bumptious." Dewey's prickly temperament did cause some problems for him in such a small office but his undeniable talent and thoroughness also were recognized—so much so that McNamara assigned Dewey to handle an important customer lawsuit against one of the firm's largest clients, Empire Trust Company. As the case got closer to picking a jury, Dewey was prevailed on to "second chair" the matter in deference to a very experienced trial lawyer, George Z. Medalie.

This "in the trenches" experience proved to be a career-altering event for the young attorney. Not only did Dewey impress his mentor (who soon was calling Dewey a "legal prodigy"), but when Medalie was nominated to become the U.S. Attorney in January 1931, he made a point of telling Dewey he wanted him to join his staff. Dewey went a step further: He convinced his boss to appoint him as the U.S. Attorney's chief assistant.

The U.S. Attorney's Office

Dewey's track record in that job was a bit mixed at the beginning. Everyone was aware of and appreciated his intelligence, attention to detail, and quest for perfection. At the same time, however, many considered him arrogant and difficult to deal with, especially given that the chief assistant was exercising authority over a number of vastly more experienced lawyers. Fortunately for Dewey, he was able to shift his focus to actual trial work. In the first case in which he acted as "first chair," Dewey prevailed in a criminal prosecution against James Quinliven, a corrupt member of New York City's Vice Squad.

A particular focus of the U.S. Attorney was the pervasive grip of organized crime over the city. He tasked Dewey to head up a squad to go after those gangsters who might have exposure to income tax evasion charges. One such target was Joseph Castaldo, who, because of his efforts to illegally corner the market on artichokes in New York City, became known as the "Artichoke King." After one day's evidence at trial, the King threw in the towel and pled guilty.

In the midst of Dewey's attempt to systematically assemble evidence and begin to prosecute numerous bad guys in New York City, Medalie took a leave of absence from his post to run for the U.S. Senate in 1932. That left Dewey in de facto charge of the office. Besides his political efforts to help Medalie in a decidedly un-Republican year, Dewey chose to go after Waxey Gordon. Gordon was a street urchin turned major league bootlegger. He had earned multiple millions with barely a nod to the Internal Revenue Service (in 1930, for example, Gordon paid the IRS $10.76). Because Gordon had hidden his wealth in more than 200 bank accounts, none of which bore his moniker, it took a Herculean effort to put all the paper pieces together. While Dewey and his staff were engaged in that effort, various members of Gordon's gang were found dead on the eve of their grand jury appearances. Two days into Gordon's trial in November 1933, Medalie resigned his post. President Franklin D. Roosevelt, who had been inaugurated in March, had yet to name a new U.S. Attorney; as such, the judges of the Southern District (invoking an 1894 precedent) acted quickly and unanimously named Dewey the interim U.S. Attorney. Dewey left the courtroom to be sworn in and then returned to continue the prosecution.

A critical witness for the prosecution was Helen Denbeck, a short-order waitress at a restaurant near a garage owned by Gordon. She described in great detail the comings and goings of Gordon's beer trucks. How did she know they carried beer? "I smelled the beer." How did she know what beer smelled like? "I drink lots of beer. I know how it smells, too." Denbeck then identified a number of Gordon's key henchmen when shown pictures: "Frankie the Chauffeur," "Joe the Fleabag," etc.

Exasperated by the level of detail she provided, Gordon's lawyer blew himself up on cross: "You know everybody.... Next you'll be telling us you know an Oscar!" Denbeck's answer? "Sure, Oscar Brockert. He was Waxey's brewmaster."

The jury deliberated for under an hour. Gordon was sentenced to 10 years and received an $80,000 fine. The trial judge was effusive in his praise of Dewey and his trial team. Dewey, in turn, issued a public warning to Gordon and his colleagues not to harm any witnesses who had testified at the trial.

The case made newspaper headlines across the country and Dewey not only made a national radio address broadcast thereafter, he also was prominently featured in news segments in movie theaters. Five weeks later, President Roosevelt named a Democrat to succeed Dewey. Dewey exited public life, determined one day to head up a leading Wall Street law firm and "make a hell of a lot of money."

Next Steps: The Special Prosecutor

Dewey went back to private practice, opening up his own law offices at 120 Broadway. Not only did his practice flourish, but his ability to remain in the public eye continued. For example, he was retained by the New York State Bar Association to bring proceedings against Municipal Judge Harold L. Kuntsler, who somehow had deposited $166,000 into his bank account over a fairly short period of time. On Dewey's cross, Kuntsler's explanations for the 107 separate deposit slips consisted of "I don't know" and "I can't remember." Before the trial concluded, Kuntsler resigned on the grounds that "his usefulness had been impaired" by all the brouhaha. A week later, Kuntsler skipped town with an ex-prostitute, who later accused him of stealing her jewels.

In 1935, a newly appointed grand jury, constituted to investigate the "numbers racket" (aka the "policy racket"—the pervasive corruption that permeated all of New York City), would change Dewey's trajectory. The duly elected District Attorney for Manhattan, William C. Dodge, was a Tammany Hall creature (the Democratic Boss, Jimmy Hines, called him "stupid, respectable, and my man"). The grand jury not only excluded Dodge from its deliberation, but went even further: It demanded a new prosecutor. After much politicking (including, it would appear, William O. Douglas, then the head of the Securities and Exchange Commission, who vouched for his old law school classmate to President Roosevelt), Governor Herbert Lehman announced that because all of his other choices had turned him down he was amenable to Thomas A. Dewey being appointed

Special Prosecutor to address New York's rackets (costing the taxpayers upward of $100 million per year). On July 1, 1935, Dewey, after demanding (and getting) complete independence from Dodge, agreed to the appointment.

Initially, he was a general without an army. Dewey, however, quickly and skillfully moved to consolidate political heft behind his new office, enlisting the support of Mayor Fiorello La Guardia, Secretary of the Treasury Henry Morgenthau, U.S. Attorney General Homer Cummings, FBI Director J. Edgar Hoover, U.S. Attorney for the Southern District Frank Adams, Arthur Sulzberger of the *New York Times*, and Governor Lehman. With that support, he was able to get the city's Board of Estimate to give his office a five-month budget of $121,000. But, he still needed troops. To that end, Dewey was besieged by thousands of lawyers, hundreds of accountants, investigators, and secretaries, as well as scores of others (e.g., dentists, bricklayers, ex-baseball players) who just wanted to make a difference. Eventually, Dewey hired a staff of more than 60 individuals, a group that included a number of old hands from the U.S. Attorney's office (e.g., Murray Gurfein), as well as a number of young, unknown attorneys (e.g., Charles Breitel, Stanley Fuld, Frank Hogan). Dewey was very stern with his chosen group, advising them not to fall prey to any kind of inducements that might be waved in their direction: "If you want to have a good time, go to New Jersey!" To the people of New York, he promised to "prosecute every crime which is part of an organized racket ... every crime in the book, from conspiracies and malicious mischief to assault in the first degree, from extortion to perjury, from income tax violation all the way to murder."

The first order of business was to figure out who was who and what was what in New York City's rackets. With incredible diligence, Dewey's staff assembled a comprehensive chart, listing 25,000 names and covering every conceivable racket. The Dewey team then proceeded to track down each lead and every tip, following up on each wiretap 'and every surveillance. Soon, the office had a mountain of evidence, and its first target was Dutch Schultz (aka Arthur Flegenheimer), New York's most flamboyant gangster.

Schultz's reaction to Dewey's focus was to the point: He decided to assassinate the Special Prosecutor. Unfortunately for Schultz, he offered the hit to Albert Anastasia, who promptly told Lucky Luciano (aka Salvatore Lucania), the de facto head of the Mafia in New York. Luciano hated publicity and had not been happy with the negative media hullabaloo that Schultz's violent tactics had engendered. When he conferred with his fellow Mafia chieftains, to a man they agreed that Schultz's assassination plot against Dewey could not be countenanced, with one demurrer, they agreed that it would be best for Schultz to be hit instead. (Meyer Lansky dissented, offering prescient advice to Luciano: "Right now, Schultz is your cover. If Dutch is eliminated, you're gonna stand out like a naked guy who just lost his clothes.") With the contract thus assigned, Schultz and a number of his gang met their end on October 23, 1935, at the Palace Chop House and Tavern in Newark, New Jersey. That eliminated one problem, but Lansky proved correct: with Schultz gone, Dewey turned his focus on Luciano.

Dewey's means of getting to Luciano? A full-court press against the extensive prostitution operation that was overseen (ultimately) by Luciano. Luciano's initial reaction was one of indignation: "I may not be the most moral and upright man that lives, but I have not stooped so low as to become involved in aiding prostitution." After a Rube Goldberg–like extradition from Arkansas, Luciano was arraigned back in New York City, with $250,000 in bail imposed, and a trial set for May 1936.

To the jury, Dewey explained the difficult row he had to hoe: "Frankly, my witnesses are prostitutes, madams, heels, pimps, and ex-convicts.... We can't get bishops to testify in a case involving prostitution.... We have to use the testimony of bad men to convict other bad men." Dewey's other challenge was to tie Luciano directly to the acts of others far below him in the underworld's food chain.

Prostitute after prostitute testified to the degrading lifestyle in which they worked. Crucial to Dewey's case, however, was Cokey Flo Brown, who not only knew Luciano but also was able to testify about his direct involvement (including putting madams on salaries).

Equally important, she held up under a withering cross-examination by defense counsel—an ordeal made more difficult by the fact that she was in the midst of withdrawal from addiction to heroin. Luciano then testified in his own behalf, avowing on direct examination that he knew none of the prostitutes who had testified and had no involvement in such an unsavory racket. On cross-examination, Dewey tried to skewer Luciano's reputation for truthfulness by going through his litany of run-ins with the law and his track record for veracity. As compelling as it was, there was no Perry Mason moment, and certainly no admission of guilt by Luciano. Indeed, in his closing Dewey had to acknowledge that "he hadn't proved that Luciano was himself putting women into houses of prostitution." But Dewey had proven Luciano to be "the greatest gangster in America," and he pleaded with the jury to "[c]onvict him, in the name of the safety of the people of this city." And convict him the jury did.

Having brought down Luciano, Dewey did not rest on his laurels; he continued to press on against the multiple rackets operating throughout the city. But he was bone-weary, and his personal finances were down to $300. As a result, when John Foster Dulles offered Dewey a partnership at Sullivan & Cromwell in 1937 worth $150,000 per year, Dewey quickly agreed. Shortly thereafter, however, in response to Republican overtures and implorings, Dewey also agreed to take on the party's nomination for Manhattan District Attorney. (Dewey went back to Dulles, who quickly concurred with this change of plans: Dewey "had to do it.")

Politics and the Law

Dewey jumped into politics with both feet, addressing up to ten audiences a night. Extremely well-financed by the Republican establishment, his formidable campaign organization helped the new politician become familiar with the ethno-cultural, tribal nature of the city's electorate. Dewey soon found that he enjoyed the game and he proved effective at retail politics; ultimately, he outpolled the Tammany Hall candidate by over 100,000 votes.

Shifting his prosecutors and staff just a few blocks to the Manhattan District Attorney's office, Dewey hit the ground running, first cleaning up the mess at the Tombs and instituting innovations to ensure effective defense counsel to those in need. Then he turned for another big scalp; this time, however, it was one who wore a white collar.

Richard Whitney, one of Wall Street's most prominent financiers (and former head of the New York Stock Exchange), was not only in dire straits financially but he also had engaged in wrongdoing to try to stay one step ahead of his creditors. On March 9, 1938, Dewey announced Whitney's indictment for stealing over $100,000 from his wife's trust fund. When Securities and Exchange Commission Chairman William O. Douglas reported the news to President Roosevelt (an old friend of Whitney's; both had gone to Groton and Harvard), his anguished response was, "No. Not Dickie Whitney! . . . I can't believe it." The trust fund turned out not to be Whitney's only theft; ultimately, he spent several years in Sing Sing.

Dewey next took aim at James J. Hines, the legendary head of Tammany Hall. Indicted on conspiracy charges involving an illegal lottery and corrupt judges, Hines retained prominent attorney Lloyd Paul Stryker. Dewey versus Stryker promised to be what the tabloids called "The Battle of the Century." And Hines himself was no Luciano-style defendant (famed corruption fighter Samuel Seabury had said, "Jimmy Hines is the most likeable rogue I know.").

Once the trial began, Dewey encountered another opponent: Judge Ferdinand Pecora. The judge hoped for the Democratic nomination for governor in 1938 (which would be open, if Governor Lehman opted to run for the Senate), and was led to believe by White House operatives that President Roosevelt would favor him if he ran roughshod over Dewey (thus, perhaps derailing Dewey's ambitions for higher political office). As such, the district attorney often found himself on the losing end of many rulings during the trial.

But all the pyrotechnics among Dewey, Stryker, and Pecora could not obfuscate the mounting evidence of Hines's financial arrangements with Dutch Schultz and other mobsters that came in before the jury. Hines's former lawyer Dixie Davis ("Kid Mouthpiece") was a key witness against Hines. Notwithstanding, Pecora declared a mistrial based on one fairly innocuous question Dewey asked a Stryker witness on cross. The judge's ruling was on shaky ground (to say the least), but, as Dewey acknowledged, "unfortunately, ... the People of the State of New York have no appeal from this or any other of the decisions in this case." To his troops, Dewey was not cowed, declaring, "Let's get to work. There'll be another trial. And we'll win it."

The setback did not seem to impact Dewey's public profile; in September 1938, New York Republicans fell all over themselves to nominate him to run for governor. Dewey embraced the new role, telling his mother, "I can do so much more for all of the things I believe in and have fought for if I am Governor than if I am merely the District Attorney of one of 62 counties of New York." Dewey ran a compelling race against the formidable incumbent, Herbert Lehman (who had been persuaded not to run for the Senate). Perhaps if President Roosevelt had not interjected himself late into the campaign, contending that the Republicans were waging an anti-Semitic campaign against Lehman, Dewey might have won. As it was, he lost by only 64,000 votes (carrying every county outside of New York City except one). This was widely viewed as a victorious defeat; indeed, it set the stage for Dewey's ambitions at the national level. While balancing his growing national fame (and calls for him to run for president in 1940), Dewey realized he still had to produce in his day job. Dewey next took on corruption in the subway system, as well as in the oversight of the city's taxicabs. Then, in January 1939, he was back in court to prosecute Hines. One piece of good news was that Judge Pecora would not preside. On the negative side: A key prosecution witness had committed suicide. Dewey's team solved that problem, however, by reading into the record at the second trial his testimony from the first trial. All the other evidence from the first trial also was brought before the jury.

Putting his predecessor William C. Dodge through the wringer on the stand, Dewey asked him whether he had a mother-son relationship with Hines. Dodge retorted, "I've never been a mother. I can't say." That bought guffaws from those in the courtroom, but

Dodge had been set up because Dewey then produced prior Dodge testimony where he had in fact described his relationship with the Tammany leader in precisely those terms. As things went south, Stryker took a gamble and decided not to put his client on the stand. Presumably, that did not sit well with the jury, which quickly convicted Hines on February 24, 1939.

The national headlines for this latest victory now made Dewey a favorite in the 1940 presidential race (even out-polling President Roosevelt). With a lot of Republican establishment support, he decided to make a run for the party's nomination. Dewey did well on the hustings (and in the primaries), but the growing war in Europe was probably too much of a hurdle for a "38-year-old kid" with no foreign policy experience—and there also was the Wendell Wilkie phenomenon, which swept the Republican convention in Philadelphia.

Even though not nominated, Dewey was clearly a political comer. He was active across the country in speaking against a third term for President Roosevelt. Thereafter, he decided he would not run for reelection as district attorney, but instead would retire to private practice and then try for the New York governorship again in 1942. To ensure a smooth transition, Dewey cut a deal with Tammany Hall whereby his able assistant Frank Hogan would be the Democratic candidate to succeed him. Dewey's last day in office was December 31, 1941, and he transitioned to private practice at 20 Exchange Place (Charles Breitel came with him). His return to the law was a mere holding pattern, however, as Dewey focused like a laser on getting the gubernatorial nomination (which came to him at least as enthusiastically as had the 1938 nod). Running against an uninspiring John J. Bennett (the state's Democratic attorney general), Dewey won by an overwhelming 647,000 vote margin.

Dewey, Ballentine, Bushby, Palmer & Wood

It would be 12 years until Dewey would return to his original goals of running a prominent law firm and "mak[ing] a hell of a lot of money." After two unsuccessful tries for the presidency in 1944 and 1948, he finished his third term as governor at the end of 1954. Not interested in any formal role thereafter in public life, Dewey was recruited to be the savior of the Root Clark firm (*see* Chapter XXXV), which, with the death of Emory Buckner and the departure of a number of key partners to start Cleary, Friendly, Gottlieb & Steen, was in serious decline. Recast as Dewey, Ballentine, Bushby, Palmer & Wood, effective January 1, 1955, the firm took off like a rocket, with Dewey becoming a rainmaker of the first rank. He never became President, but at least he did achieve his first two goals.

Postscript

The best Dewey biography is by Richard Norton Smith, *Thomas E. Dewey and His Times* (Simon & Schuster 1982). Other helpful materials on Dewey's career include Stanley Walker's *Dewey: An American of This Century* (McGraw Hill 1944); Mary Stulberg's *Fighting Organized Crime: Politics, Justice and the Legacy of Thomas E. Dewey* (Northeastern University Press 1995); and Richard Hammer's "Playboy's Illustrated History of Organized Crime" (Playboy 1975).

Dewey's showdown with Luciano quickly went Hollywood with Warner Brothers releasing *Marked Woman* in 1937. Betty Davis starred as Mary Dwight (in the Cokey Flo Brown role); Mary's "job" was sanitized a bit insofar as Davis portrayed a "hostess" in the nightclub of vice czar Johnny Vanning (Lucky Luciano), who was played by Eduardo Cianelli. Humphrey Bogart co-starred in the Dewey role as crusading District Attorney David Graham. One of the other "hostesses" was played by Mayo Methot, Bogart's third wife, who he would later divorce in order to marry Lauren Bacall.

Alice Roosevelt Longworth (Teddy's daughter) was widely credited in 1944 with calling Dewey "the little man on the wedding cake." In fact, Democratic apparatchiks Isabel Kinnear Griffin and Helen Essary Murphy originated those damning words, and then attributed them to Longworth to help publicize them; Longworth never disabused people as to their actual source. Regardless of origin, the image created was one that hurt Dewey with many voters, and he was never able to live it down.

Dewey appointed his mentor, George Medalie, to the New York Court of Appeals on September 28, 1945, where he served until his death on March 6, 1946. Gladys Heldman, the prominent tennis promoter (and founder of *World Tennis* magazine), was Medalie's daughter. Julie Heldman, who was once a highly ranked tennis professional (at one point No. 5 in the world), is Medalie's granddaughter.

Upon joining his new firm in 1955, Dewey insisted not only that his name lead the masthead but that at no time in the future, for whatever reason, could that status ever be changed. Thus, when Dewey Ballentine merged with LeBoeuf Lamb, the firm was re-cast as Dewey & LeBoeuf. With the merged firm's messy collapse in 2012 and certain of its leadership under criminal indictment and imminent trial, those unfamiliar with Tom Dewey's imposing career and legacy now only know his name in the media under the most unfortunate of circumstances.

CHAPTER XXXV

The Man Who Mentored Lawyers

History teaches us that even great law firms are fragile institutions (*see* Chapter I). That lesson was brought home again more recently with the demise of Dewey LeBoeuf. This chapter will not focus on that event. Rather, it will recall a giant who helped to create and sustain the antecedent Dewey firm; a lawyer to whom many famous lawyers owe their careers and who is little remembered today: Emory Buckner.

Emory Buckner was one of the leading members of the New York Bar in the first half of the twentieth century. Not only was he one of America's most illustrious prosecutors, he was one of the founders of Root, Clark, Buckner & Howland; that firm later became Dewey, Ballentine, Busby, Palmer & Wood (and ultimately Dewey LeBoeuf).

A Poor Boy from Nebraska

Born to a Nebraska minister who had very little money, Buckner attended the University of Nebraska. Even though he was married during college and compelled to work in his spare time to make ends meet, Buckner nonetheless was one of a select group to be elected to Phi Beta Kappa in 1904. Interested in attending law school, Buckner contacted Roscoe Pound, who was then the Dean of the Nebraska Law School. Pound "steered" Buckner to attend the Harvard Law School (and helped to raise money locally to pay for tuition). At

Harvard, Buckner excelled (after his first year he was in the top six out of a starting class of 288); invited to join the *Harvard Law Review*, he declined on the ground that he could not afford to (he was making ends meet as a stenographer, mostly to law professors).

Buckner was a popular student; friends included future partners Elihu Root Jr., Grenville Clark, Silas Howland, and Arthur Ballentine. Importantly, another Harvard student, Felix Frankfurter, became an intellectual alter ego and lifelong friend. When he learned years later that he had graduated third in his class, Buckner wrote Frankfurter:

> I was honestly and frankly surprised. Had I supposed I stood any such chance as that I would have cut a few dozen less lectures and done a few hours more work—with all my troubles I could have done it easily enough.... Well, how unimportant it all seems, now that we look back on it, except for biographical reasons.

Buckner's Early Career

Based on his stellar law school record and the lure of $1,000 per annum, Buckner was offered and he accepted a position as a law clerk at Cravath, Henderson & deGessdorff in 1907. At that point, Cravath's system did not permit young lawyers to do too much ("Cravath men are not thrown into deep water and told to swim; rather, they are thrown into shallow water and carefully taught strokes."); as such, Buckner did not handle many important assignments. In the first case, he got to say something in court (Municipal Court), Buckner's opponent did not show up. As the judge grew somewhat frustrated, it took another lawyer to prompt him: "Ask to have it dismissed." With that sotto voce help, Buckner intoned: "Would your Honor dismiss the case?" Persuaded by the power of such advocacy, the judge replied: "Why, of course." Upon such a foundation was Buckner's brilliant career at the bar built.

After a brief tenure at Cravath, Buckner was asked by U.S. Attorney Henry Stimson (*see* Chapter XXIX) to join the Southern District of New York office. Stimson—with the help of President Theodore Roosevelt—had revolutionized how the U.S. Attorney's office was run: making it a top-flight, full-time job, with a non-partisan staff of the brightest young lawyers available (most of them recruited by Frankfurter, Stimson's chief assistant). Buckner's experience with Stimson was pivotal in his career, not only with respect to his professional development and the associations he formed with his colleagues, but also in forming his views about public service and the responsibilities prosecutors had with respect to their duties and the public. Those views would be instrumental in informing how he ran the U.S. Attorney's office—two decade later.

After Charles Whitman was elected Manhattan district attorney in the fall of 1909, he asked Buckner to join his team. While this meant an exponential increase in compensation and also led to Buckner getting a lot of first-chair litigation experience (his most important/notorious trial was the case of "the shooting showgirls"—one he lost), Buckner found Whitman's politicization of his office troubling. Using it as a platform to run for governor, Whitman constantly played to the media. One example of this was his demand for an indictment in the *Triangle Fire* case of 1911—before the office had completed its investigation ("You go and get an indictment. We can always *nol pros* it if we can't maintain it."). Whitman's motivation? To appease William Randolph Hearst's media empire, which was yelling for scalps.

Private Practice

Ultimately, Buckner decided "to take the plunge into private practice." First trying unsuccessfully to persuade Frankfurter to join him, Buckner was able to convince one of his law school friends, Silas Howland, to establish a partnership with him in 1912. A year later, two more law school friends—Elihu Root Jr. and Grenville Clark—convinced Buckner and Howland to join forces with them; and on September 1, 1913, Root, Clark, Buckner & Howland opened for business at 31 Nassau Street.

The firm was not only loaded with legal talent, it was extremely well-connected; Root's father, Elihu Root, was the most famous lawyer in America (*see* Chapter XXXII), and he joined the firm as "of counsel." Soon the firm was very busy with a wide array of work from an eclectic group of clients. And while Buckner's talents as a trial lawyer became more and more well-known (and a draw for clients), his contributions to the firm were more in two other essential areas.

The first related to how the firm was organized and structured. Almost consciously rejecting the Cravath "system," Buckner changed the concept of young lawyers: instead of "law clerks," they now became known as "associates," and the young associates were expected to take on significant responsibilities right off the bat. Furthermore, he instituted systems for keeping account of lawyers' time, how files were to be kept (in a "file room"), how matters were to be tracked on a calendar, requiring associates to read advance sheets, etc. Perhaps infamously, he established an annual luncheon with lead partners at other firms to set the "going rate" for new lawyers (a blatant price-fixing conspiracy); at the same time, Buckner chose to keep secret that young lawyers at Root Clark also received a year-end bonus, which meant that his firm kept ahead of the "going rate."

More important was Buckner's role in hiring new lawyers. With quality as the only attribute, Root Clark became the first "white shoe" firm to hire not just White Anglo-Saxon Protestants. A nonexhaustive list of young lawyers recruited to the firm included: Leo Gottlieb, Hugh Cox, Leslie Arps, Herbert Brownell (a future Attorney General), John M. Harlan (who not only became Buckner's chief assistant at the firm and later at the U.S. Attorney's office, but ultimately a Justice on the U.S. Supreme Court), and Henry J. Friendly (who ultimately became the legendary judge on the Court of Appeals for the Second Circuit). Interestingly, the hiring of Friendly came only after a bitter battle between Frankfurter and Buckner over the brilliant young man's future. Frankfurter was furious that he did not prevail. Friendly's subsequent verdict: "There's never been a lawyer before or since who made such an effort to help young lawyers."

The U.S. Attorney's Office

In the aftermath of the Harding administration's scandals, President Calvin Coolidge wanted to clean house and he started with the Justice Department, bringing in Harlan F. Stone (dean of the Columbia Law School) as attorney general. Stone, among other initiatives, recruited Buckner to head up the U.S. Attorney's office in New York in 1925. Buckner's first order of business was to signal that his office would vigorously enforce prohibition. In order to show his commitment, Buckner publicly did away with his large cellar of bootleg liquor (and he required all of his Assistant U.S. Attorneys to forswear liquor). He also changed enforcement tactics, targeting not individual violators (75,000 a year), but instead "padlocking" prominent establishments that were serving liquor. Although his "padlocking" efforts clearly had an impact (and drew prominent media), by mid-1926 Buckner realized that he could never plug enough holes in the dyke to keep New York "dry," and at that point he turned his focus to the other pressing priorities of his office.

Buckner's second order of business at the outset of his tenure was to replicate the recruiting efforts he had instituted at his law firm. Besides bringing Harlan with him as his chief assistant, Buckner hired a veritable "who's who" of the future leaders of the bar, including J. Edward Lumbard, David Peck, Bethuel Webster, Frederic Coudert, George Leisure, Carl Newton, and Frank Reavis. And, as he did at his law firm, Buckner gave his young lieutenants a lot of responsibility, very quickly. Bethuel Webster, having been sent into court to deliver his first summation to a jury, turned around after he had finished and saw an unannounced Buckner sitting behind the prosecutor's table. Clapping Webster on the back, Buckner congratulated him on a job well done. Webster, 40 years later, remembered that moment with great clarity: "That's *leadership*!" Buckner similarly celebrated in a public fashion the trial victories of Leisure, Newton, and others; not surprisingly, this avuncular support and praise from Buckner drew his colleagues into an ever-increasingly close "band of brothers."

The most significant case brought during Buckner's tenure was a criminal prosecution against former Attorney General Harry Daugherty and two of his cronies for a conspiracy to deprive the government of honest services. The case stemmed from some blatant influence-peddling to ensure a $7 million payment for securities seized in 1918 by the Alien Property Custodian, pursuant to the Trading with the Enemy Act. Of particular importance at trial was the fact that Daugherty—formerly the government's preeminent lawyer—had burned critical documents in the case. After three days and nights, the jury came back with an inconclusive verdict: 7-5 for conviction of Daugherty, 10-2 for conviction of his remaining alleged coconspirator, Thomas Miller (the former Alien Property Custodian). (Daugherty's other indicted, alleged co-conspirator died before trial.)

After sounding out the opinions of those he trusted and respected (Frankfurter and various Root Clark partners), Buckner announced that he would retry the defendants. Jury selection may well have influenced the outcome of the second trial: one prospective juror, during voir dire, said he had known politicians at their best and their worst; despite misgivings, Buckner accepted him on the panel. At trial, Buckner put on an impressive and thorough presentation of the evidence. Convinced that "the case [had come in] better than before," he nonetheless knew that it was a complicated matter, made more challenging by the fact that "[t]he jury appears to be unintelligent, uninterested and wholly uninformed by the evidence. Even the burning of the records appear[s] to arouse no interest on their part."

Miller's counsel rested without putting on any defense. Daugherty's counsel put on some current and former Justice Department officials, one of whom was now a senator from West Virginia (Guy Goff); the transcript of Buckner's cross-examination of Senator Goff makes for painful reading—Goff was shredded by use of his prior grand jury testimony.

The closings were a bit odd insofar as (1) Daugherty's counsel accused Buckner of bringing the case to further his political ambitions to become governor of New York, and (2) Buckner, in reply, announced his resignation as U.S. Attorney "within two months." He then spent the next nine-plus hours reviewing the evidence put before the jury. Once the jury got the case, it again took three days and nights to deliberate. Miller was found guilty in one hour. And although the jury ultimately voted 11 to 1 to convict Daugherty, juror No. 7—the man who had known all kinds of politicians—refused to budge.

Under pressure from the trial judge, Buckner agreed to drop the indictment against Daugherty. Buckner was condemned by some in the press for having brought on a "vicious and irresponsible prosecution." Senator Goff lost no time in firing off a telegram to Buckner in which he said, among other things: "[Y]ou are a liar and a coward." Others thanked Buckner for prosecuting "with a thoroughness and vigor that must have challenged the admiration of every man and woman in the United States who loves justice and honesty in the public service." It would appear that Buckner never second guessed his controversial prosecution of the former Attorney General; years later he wrote that "Harry Daugherty is … doubtless hugging his wrongs when he should be hugging juror No. 7."

Back to Private Practice

Even before Buckner had technically left the U.S. Attorney's position, Root Clark was in such desperate need of its leading trial lawyer that the firm got a special dispensation from the Attorney General so Buckner could start consulting on firm business just four days after the Daugherty-Miller verdict. And when he officially rejoined the firm on April 7, 1927, old and new clients beat a hasty path to his comer office. In one matter, Buckner was up on appeal to the Second Circuit. John Harlan, back with Buckner at Root Clark, had written a 150-page brief in support of the client's position. At oral argument Buckner's old friend Learned Hand pointed at the massive brief, scowled, and asked him: "Is this your brief?!" Buckner responded: "Yes, your Honor." Hand: "Well, I'm not going to read it. It's too long." Buckner: "Well it will be your loss, your Honor. It's a very good brief. My assistant wrote it, and I put my name on it." Hand then threw the brief over the bench and on to the counsel table, where it landed with a loud bang. (Not surprisingly, Harlan was devastated. After the case was decided, Hand called Harlan into chambers and said: "Just wanted to say it was a very good brief.")

Buckner took on any and all matters—from will contests to stockholder suits to antitrust actions. In one antitrust case in which he represented German potash interests, Buckner settled the matter with the government on a train from New Mexico to Chicago in which he and the head of the Antitrust Division (William "Wild Bill" Donovan) were clad only in their underwear.

Buckner was now at the apex of his profession, charging clients huge fees and being exceptionally well compensated for his efforts. But then his health gave way. In 1932, he suffered a "light stroke." And then came serious gallbladder surgery on February 24, 1933. In September of 1936, Buckner suffered a stroke that left him partially paralyzed on his left side. But even as his health continued to decline, Buckner was determined to keep his hand in at the firm, not just to assist clients, but especially to help young lawyers in whatever way possible. He lived long enough to see Frankfurter's appointment to the Supreme Court in 1939, and took great interest in reading his friend's opinions. On March 11, 1941, Buckner suffered another stroke and died at the age of 63.

Postscript

For those wishing greater detail into Buckner's life, I commend Martin Mayer's *Emory Buckner* (Harper & Row 1968). *See also* David Dorsen's *Henry Friendly: Greatest Judge of His Era* (Harvard University Press 2012).

Grenville Clark started his legal career as a law clerk at Carter, Ledyard & Milburn. One day while sitting in the firm's "bullpen," he listened in astonishment to a fellow clerk muse about his planned political career: New York State legislature, Assistant Secretary of the Navy, Governor of New York, President of the United States. Clark's fellow clerk? Franklin Delano Roosevelt.

After some of the best and the brightest decided to leave Root, Clark in 1945 to form Cleary, Gottlieb, Friendly & Cox, the future of Buckner's old firm looked dim. A decade later, on January 1, 1955, the firm brought on a new senior partner, Thomas E. Dewey, and the firm became known as Dewey, Ballentine, Busby, Palmer & Wood. Dewey's legal prowess, not to mention his political connections, ensured the firm's success for future decades.

After Buckner's death in 1941, Felix Frankfurter published a tribute to his long-standing, close friend. It included this observation, which has timeless application:

> [W]hat is much more important is that in all these prosecutorial offices Buckner realized that he who wields the instruments of justice wields the most terrible instruments of government. In order to assure their just and compassionate use, a prosecutor must have an almost priest-like attitude toward his duties. Buckner practiced this attitude without deviation.

The Federal Bar Council has long awarded the Emory Buckner Award for "Outstanding Public Service." In one man's opinion, the best acceptance speech was given by Mary Jo White in 2001. In accepting the award, the former U.S. Attorney (for both the Southern District of New York and the Eastern District of New York) recognized that the first recipient of the Award had been J. Edgar Hoover in 1962. White then told the assembled audience of New York's leading lawyers that she shared two important characteristics with the long-serving FBI Director: "We are both short, and we both like to wear dresses." No one saw that coming!

CHAPTER XXXVI

Simon Rifkind and the Lawyer's Role and Responsibility

Horace Greeley, editor (and founder) of the *New York Tribune,* once famously remarked: "Fame is a vapor, popularity an accident, and riches take wings. Only one thing endures and that is character." The truth of Greeley's words can be proven many ways; this chapter will focus on one. In the twentieth century, Simon H. Rifkind was one of this country's legal giants. Yet, to the law students I teach every year, his name draws blank stares. In 1975, Judge Rifkind wrote a seminal article in the New York City Bar Association's publication, *The Record,* entitled "The Lawyer's Role and Responsibility in Modern Society." Each semester I start off class by having the students read this wonderful essay, to help them understand what those roles and responsibilities were in 1975 and what they are today.

The Adversary System

Rifkind's overall focus was on the workings of the adversary system, and by that focus he stressed at least eight important concepts to his readers. The first concept concerned his response to the frequent question: "How could you represent so-and-so?" To explain his answer he used the example of law students publicly picketing Washington lawyer Lloyd Cutler concerning his representation of General Motors; more specifically, the law students were upset that Cutler was helping GM "obstruct" proposed safety regulations for cars. Rifkind's response: "Had they [the law students] mastered the meaning of the adversary system they would have know their conduct was subversive of the central tenet of the profession they were about to enter." Rifkind's disdain for the clueless law students was striking in the after math of the 1960s and the Vietnam War, the term "subversive" had a particular charge to it. One other interesting note is that one of the "safety" features at issue at the time turned out to be anything but safe: airbags for babies and small children (and one of the government's leading "safety" proponents in fact knew them to be unsafe).[1]

The next concept Rifkind tackled was what to do about the "inequality of resources between contestants [and] the disparity of talent" between opposing counsel. Without a perfect answer to those facts of life, Rifkind fell back on the "sage words" of Oliver Wendell Holmes (the "Yankee from Olympus"): "The life of the law has not been logic; it has been experience." The point being that our jurisprudential system, while not perfect, has worked well over a long period of time in resolving controversies to the general satisfaction of the public. I also use Rifkind's answer to tell students that, when backed into a corner and without anything else to cite or say, they (like Rifkind) can always pull out this old chestnut from the Yankee from Olympus (it is certainly better than using a "cf" cite!).

Rifkind's third point was to respond to those who say a lawyer has conflicting duties to the client and to society. To Rifkind, such a contention was completely wrong. Not only do lawyers owe no duties to society, but lawyers are not to judge their clients or the wisdom of the argument or arguments they make on their behalf. To illustrate this point, Rifkind relied on the famous interchange between Samuel Johnson and James Boswell:

> *Boswell*: "But what do you think of supporting a cause which you know to be bad?"

---

[1] Incredibly, years later (in 2020) this same law student protest took place, but this time at Rifkind's law firm over its representation of Exxon Mobil.

> *Johnson*: "Sir, you do not know it to be good or bad till the judge determines it.... An argument which does not convince yourself may convince the judge to whom you urge it; and if it does convince him, why then, sir; you are wrong and he is right. It is his business to judge; and you are not to be confident in your opinion that a cause is bad, but to say all you can for your client, and then hear the court's opinion."

Rifkind called this espousal "radical doctrine today." But as we will see shortly, it is far more "radical" today.

Rifkind next took on the "body of lawyers who call themselves public interest lawyers." He called such lawyering "unctuous" (even if you do not know what that word means, it sure sounds bad!), and then went on to observe: "[T]he most baffling problem of substance is how to locate the public interest." Is the landlord always wrong, the tenant always right? "Oh, if only life were that simple!"

The fifth point addressed was whether a lawyer is merely a "hired gun" (or a "menial servant"). Acknowledging that the client may give appropriate instructions, Rifkind opined that in all other respects "the lawyer is in command." Of all of Rifkind's guideposts, this one seems perhaps the most out-of-date given the undeniable transformation of the legal profession over the past five decades. Maybe in Rifkind's time he could follow Elihu Root's famous maxim ("about half of the practice of a decent lawyer is telling would-be clients they are damned fools and should stop"), but anyone telling this to a would-be client today (as opposed to 1975 or 1905) would most likely be turning that would-be client into a client for an eager competitor across the street.

Rifkind's sixth point was to stress the lawyer's duty of zealous advocacy, subject only to the applicable rules of ethics. To Rifkind, this dearly was part of what made lawyering great fun; it allowed the lawyer to engage in the "muscular stretch" of being an "inventor and innovator." Contrast that to today where a number of states, when enacting ethics "reforms," take seeming pride in announcing that the word—indeed, the very concept of—"zealousness" has been purposefully banished from any trace of their code of professional responsibility.

A Stool Pigeon?

Rifkind's seventh concern was the solution proposed by some for the ethical problems faced by lawyers: "[T]he attempt to convert the lawyers routinely into an informant against his client." This "solution" brought on Rifkind's strongest condemnation: "The merest suggestion that the lawyer become a stool pigeon against his client fills us with abhorrence.... [O]ur revulsion is instantaneous, if not instinctive." He went on to opine that such a result would threaten our "free society and a democratic government," both of which depend on an "uncensored and uninhibited" relationship between attorneys and their clients. Of course, today, with one of the Securities and Exchange Commission's Sarbanes-Oxley "reforms" targeting capital markets attorneys to disclose client confidences, and with many states having multiple grounds for allowing for permissive disclosure of client confidences (and some states having circumstances in which mandatory disclosure is required), query what Rifkind would say about the current state of our "free society" and "democratic government."

Rifkind's final point was to disabuse those who believe trials are a search for metaphysical truth. Hogwash! For Rifkind, a trial was instead a "game," with rules (e.g., procedure, evidence) to filter out all sorts of information from being considered. And the point of the game was not to determine "absolute truth," but rather to resolve "controversy by the principled application of the rules of the game." This final point is, of course, as true today as when Rifkind wrote it five decades ago. To my law students, at first blush, it sounds very cynical; it is my hope that over the course of the semester they come to embrace this insight, as well as Rifkind's other timeless pieces of wisdom.

CHAPTER XXXVII

Simon Rifkind and the Case of the Maligned Author

Having explored Simon Rifkind's views on the lawyer's role and responsibility in the previous chapter, the focus of this chapter will be on Mr. Rifkind's most famous client, Jacqueline "Jackie" (Bouvier) Kennedy Onassis, and the turmoil over her attempts (legal and otherwise) to scuttle the publication of *The Death of a President* (Harper & Collins 1967), authored by William Manchester.

An Authorized History

Within weeks of John F. Kennedy's assassination, and mindful that many would be vying for the chance to write the definitive book on the events surrounding that tragedy, Jackie Kennedy ultimately picked Manchester for the job. Her first choice, Theodore White (her collaborator in starting the "Camelot" legend—*after* the assassination), declined. Manchester had written a highly admiring (some believed fawning) book on JFK during his lifetime (*Portrait of a President* (Little, Brown 1962); moreover, he had given the President control over that book's galleys. Those two facts may have tipped the scales in his favor. And although he was quite busy on other projects, Manchester did not feel he could say no to the martyred President's widow.

The next step for Manchester was to meet with the Attorney General, Robert F. Kennedy. At his first meeting with RFK, the author was "shocked by his appearance. I have never seen a man with less resilience. Much of the time he seemed to be in a trance, staring off into space, his face a study in grief." RFK notwithstanding made it clear he had his sister-in-law's authority over the project. And to that end, he told Manchester the book would be issued by Harper & Row and edited by Evan Thomas (who had performed similar work for the Kennedys on *Profiles in Courage* and *The Enemy Within*); that Manchester was contractually obligated to another publisher was a minor technicality. Ultimately, a memorandum of understanding was crafted and signed to cover the book project, with its points including:

- The book would come out after the November 1968 election (unless it was finished earlier).
- The final manuscript would not be published "unless and until approved" by both RFK and Mrs. Kennedy.
- Manchester's compensation would be a flat $36,000 (without expenses); he would also be entitled to royalties from (1) foreign sales (if any), and (2) magazine serialization(s) (if any).

The Attorney General's office then announced the book project to the public, stating that "these arrangements have been made with Mr. Manchester in the interest of historical accuracy and to prevent distortion and sensationalism."

A Work in Progress

Manchester immediately terminated all other endeavors, moved to Washington, and started to work. Besides extensive research and visits to every site to be described in the book, Manchester also met Mrs. Kennedy for two five-hour interviews. The sessions were taped and, as Manchester's later wrote: "Future historians may be puzzled by odd clinking noises on the tapes. They were ice cubes. The only way we could get through those long evenings was with the aid of great containers of daiquiris.... There are also frequent sounds of matches being struck.... Before [the first interview] I hadn't smoked for two years ...; eight years would pass before I quit again."

Manchester worked around the clock. Within a short period, he had lost 20 pounds and his clothes fit him so poorly that Ethel Kennedy told him he needed a new tailor. On March 26, 1965, Manchester checked himself into a Connecticut hospital with "nervous exhaustion." Out after ten days, he drove himself on and by March 1966 he had produced a first draft entitled "The Death of Lancer" (JFK's Secret Service name). Evan Thomas then informed him that RFK and Mrs. Kennedy would not be reviewing the manuscript; instead, in addition to reviews by Thomas and Manchester's literary agent (Don Congdon), two RFK aides/friends (Ed Guthman and John Seigenthaler) were being delegated the task of protecting the Kennedy family's legacy (and Camelot). The group of reviewers expanded quickly to include the chairman of Harper's (Cass Canfield), Ethel Kennedy, Arthur Schlesinger, and Dick Goodwin (former speechwriter for JFK and later LBJ).

The Early Reviews

Over the course of the spring of 1966, Manchester started getting feedback. Thomas, for example, wrote: "This is the finest book I've read in 20 years here." Canfield weighed in with: "A work of unusual distinction and great power." Schlesinger wrote: "I think this is a remarkable and potentially great book. The research, the feeling, the narrative power, the evocation of personality and atmosphere, much of the writing—all are superb.... I hope you can stop them from editing too much history out of the manuscript." And Goodwin called it "a masterful achievement."

At the same time, the reviewers had over 100 suggested changes, virtually all of which were non-substantive (e.g., Guthman—"Page 10—First line. Question the use of the word ... 'ignorant.' I think this should be checked. Largely unfamiliar or unacquainted might be better." "Page 686—Reference to Angel's four mighty Boeing engines. The plane is a Boeing but the engines are Pratt-Whitney."; "Page 1177—wrong identification for Carmine Bellino. He is a certified public accountant."). Of Goodwin's few comments, the most significant was to recommend the title be changed to *The Death of a President*. Manchester responded affirmatively to this round of comments, believing "virtually all [the proposed changes] improved the manuscript."

The Next Set of Reviews

The euphoria of the first read-through was quickly diminished as a result of reviewers' second and third read-throughs. Of the people closest to RFK, the principal concern was the often unflattering portrayal of JFK's successor, Lyndon B. Johnson, and the potential political fallout this Kennedy-authorized work could have on RFK's difficult relationship with LBJ, as well as on RFK's political future. A 36-hour session with Thomas in a Manhattan apartment was designed to eliminate any and all negative LBJ references (e.g., Manchester had described LBJ as a practitioner of political tergiversation. Thomas asked: "What does tergiversation mean?" Manchester: "Evasiveness, equivocation—running a broken field." Thomas: "That goes.") Manchester left the meeting with Thomas believing that all of the political objections had been addressed. He was wrong.

Two lengthy sessions going over additional revisions were required in June and July of 1966. After the second one, Seigenthaler, speaking for RFK and Mrs. Kennedy, declared that the manuscript was approved for possible serialization and publication. Thomas and Manchester, however, believed they needed some affirmation directly from RFK; after a bit of pestering, RFK sent Manchester a telegram stating: "While I have not read William Manchester's account of the death of President Kennedy, members of the Kennedy family will place no obstacle in the way of publication of his work."

This telegram allowed Harper to proceed with targeting the book to be released in January 1967. It also allowed for Congdon to conduct a bidding war for magazine serialization—a war ultimately won by *Look* magazine for $665,000. Manchester thereupon called RFK in Hyannis Port. RFK's reaction?: "Great! Isn't that a record? [It was.] *Look* has been so nice to the family and Henry Luce [publisher of *Life*] has been such a bastard."

Enter Jackie

Manchester was pleased (he would suddenly be rich), and RFK certainly seemed okay where things stood; but one person was not: JFK's widow. Mrs. Kennedy, who had been upset with Arthur Schlesinger when his Pulitzer Prize–winning book on JFK had been serialized, was even more upset now. From Evan Thomas, Manchester learned that Mrs. Kennedy was objecting to the serialization money not going to the JFK library; but what ultimately became clear to Manchester was that "she didn't really want any book, that at most she would accept only a dull, obscure volume." ("I thought," she would tell Manchester in September, "that it would be bound in black and put away on dark library shelves.") RFK, under immense pressure from his sister-in-law, now made that clear to Thomas, wiring him: "Under the present circumstances, with the situation as difficult as it is, I feel the book on President Kennedy's death should neither be published nor serialized." This led to a stormy meeting in August of 1966 in RFK's Senate office (he had been elected in 1964), in which Thomas, Seigenthaler, RFK, and Manchester "conferred, fumed, shouted, and glared—and settled nothing." According to Manchester, "Bobby was at his most abrasive; at various times he threatened to take *Look* to court, insisted that [Manchester] give more money to the library, and demanded that I stop the serialization, all the while assuring [Thomas] that he wanted the book to be published."

At the same time, Seigenthaler was submitting over 100 new changes—which Manchester viewed as "frank distortion." And a new editor was introduced: Mrs. Kennedy's secretary, Pam Turnure (also one of JFK's many alleged paramours). Turnure issued 77 changes, most of which were directed to dealing with personal items about the former First Lady about which the public knew nothing (e.g., the fact that Mrs. Kennedy regularly smoked cigarettes).

Also in August was a meeting of *Look* executives with RFK, Mrs. Kennedy, and her lawyer, Simon Rifkind. In response to a variety of threats, *Look* agreed to reduce the number of installments from seven to four. This was a substantial monetary hit to the magazine, but it did little to appease the Kennedys.

Mrs. Kennedy then tried a new approach: she invited Manchester and Goodwin to Hyannis Port to resolve things. The Kennedy plane, the *Caroline*, flew the two men to the Cape, where Mrs. Kennedy met them on the tarmac, "wearing sunglasses and a green miniskirt; she looked stunning." After some sporting events, the three got down to business. Unfortunately, the session was chaotic, with wild emotional swings and no real progress at getting to a rational compromise. What was clear to Manchester was that Mrs. Kennedy was determined to fight and to win; memorably she said: "Anybody who is against me will look like a rat unless I run off with Eddie Fisher." (Fischer had entered tabloid hell in the 1950s when he had left his wife, Debbie Reynolds, for Elizabeth Taylor.)

With Harper's now lawyering up, bringing in Harriet Pilpel of Greenbaum, Wolf & Ernst, *Look* was also exploring how to protect itself—not just from the Kennedys, but also from Manchester; the author, now totally frazzled, had suggested that he might seek an injunction to block the magazine. *Look*'s response?: it would sue him for "at least several hundred thousand dollars."

As if that were not enough, Goodwin now weighed in again, seeking the deletion of thousands of words from the four *Look* installments. RFK then invited Manchester to Hickory Hill (his Virginia estate), where, *inter alia*, he expressed concern that what Manchester had written "will injure both Johnson and me" (even while admitting he still had not read a single word written by the author).

Trying to escape the pressure cooker, Manchester booked passage for England aboard the *Queen Mary*. The night before it left, the author, at a Manhattan hotel under an assumed name, was surprised in the lobby by Thomas, who bore 30 more demanded changes from Seigenthaler and Turnure. The following morning, at breakfast he was confronted by Goodwin and Burke Marshall (a key aide under RFK at the Justice Department) with nine new demands. Shaken, he retreated up to his hotel room; within minutes, RFK was pounding on the door, yelling: "Bill, Bill, I know you're in there!"

Manchester somehow avoided a mano a mano confrontation with RFK and made his cruise. In his absence, Mrs. Kennedy shifted her anger to Harper's and, more particularly, to Evan Thomas. Blaming him for the entire *Look* imbroglio (as well as other sins), she leaned over at the end of a meeting and whispered to Thomas: "I'm going to ruin you."

While in England, Manchester continued to receive a battery of suggested changes from Goodwin, many of which the author agreed to. Harper's then weighed in, demanding more changes or it would not publish the book. This latter piece of news made JFK's widow very happy; it also caused Manchester to make 28 more changes to the manuscript. With that, Harper's green-lighted the book. And Mrs. Kennedy went nuclear.

Rifkind in Motion

Issuing a statement (written by Ted Sorenson) that the book was "tasteless and distorted" and that Manchester and his publishers had disregarded "accepted standards of propriety and good faith" and had violated "the dignity and privacy of [her] children," Mrs. Kennedy authorized Rifkind to go to New York State Supreme Court on December 16, 1966, to enjoin both Harper's and *Look*. Manchester, on board the *Queen Mary*, returning to America, now recalled her words at Hyannis Port and realized he was being cast as Eddie Fischer (i.e., the "rat").

But on closer inspection, the papers supporting Rifkind's submission had some serious flaws. First and foremost was Mrs.

Kennedy's affidavit. Notwithstanding the Sorenson-drafted statement, she averred that she had "never seen Manchester's manuscript"; she further averred neither Harper's nor *Look* had allowed her to see it. That second representation was not accurate. Moreover, given the voluminous paper record of RFK representing her interests in the project and the numerous Kennedy representatives' involvement in the back and forth on the manuscript, a full detailing of all that in court would be telling (and not in her favor).

Even more problematic was RFK's affidavit, in which he "categorically state[d] that at no time did I ever give my approval or consent to the text of the manuscript, to any publication thereof, or to any time of publication; nor did I ever say or do anything from which the defendants could reasonably have believed that I did.... The fact is that no one who read the manuscript had authority to approve it on behalf of Mrs. Kennedy or me." As Manchester later wrote, these bold statements opened up RFK to possible perjury, since "[t]here were at least twenty witnesses who could testify that this simply was not so."

Indeed, upon review of the Kennedy legal papers, *Look*'s general counsel offered to quit if he did not win such a slam-dunk case. That said, the public relations war was at an all-time high and it was a poker game with a lot at stake—if *Look* had to postpone one issue, it could cost millions; RFK's reputation for ruthlessness was being revived; the uproar was increasing the public's interest in the book (the opposite of what Mrs. Kennedy wanted); Mrs. Kennedy's poll numbers were in decline (for the first time), among other things. Simon Rifkind also weighed in extrajudicially: "I don't know about literary integrity, nor the matter of history. But I believe strongly in a man keeping his word, particularly when it is in a written memorandum of understanding."

On January 16, 1967, the trial was set to start, with RFK scheduled as the first witness. Hours before this rendezvous with destiny, the parties settled. In exchange for some further, non-substantive edits (e.g., substituting "vanished" for "disappeared")—a total of seven pages of a 710-page book was cut—a consent decree was ordered by a New York State judge that allowed the "revised" manuscript to be published. By the term of the decree, Mrs. Kennedy could seek injunctive relief against anyone publishing a form of the book inconsistent with the "revised" manuscript (*Stern* magazine in Germany promptly announced it would do just that); the decree also, *inter alia,* ordered destruction of the "original" manuscript (except for four copies), and the delivery of Manchester's tapes with Mrs. Kennedy to the John F. Kennedy Presidential Library (under seal). Judge Rifkind was quoted in the *New York Post*: "I never like to speak in terms of victory or defeat in a law case. I'll just say we are satisfied."

Postscript

Manchester quickly patched up his relationship with a number of Kennedy loyalists, and later campaigned for RFK during his presidential run in 1968.

By 1970, royalties for *The Death of a President* totaled $1,057,247.64, all of which were donated to the JFK Library. When the first check for $750,000 reached the library, Mrs. Kennedy contacted Manchester and also issued a "gracious statement" to the press: "I think it is so beautiful what Mr. Manchester did."

Evan Thomas, who Manchester felt had let him down in the face of the Kennedys' pressure, ultimately left Harper's for another firm. More importantly, having gotten multiple sclerosis in the 1950s, Thomas's disease had gone into remission (for the most part) thereafter. Unfortunately, the stress of this drama brought the disease back to the fore and stayed with him until his death in 1998. Perhaps ironically, his son (also Evan Thomas) would later write the best, extant biography of RFK: *Robert Kennedy: His Life* (Simon & Schuster 2006).

Someday, if the Kennedys allow it, a great book will be written tracing the provenance of the various edits to the manuscript as it was tinkered with by so many people with different agendas (historical, political, and other).

The historical record is unclear of exactly when it happened. But at some point, Mrs. Kennedy sat down in her apartment at 1040 Fifth Avenue and finally read Manchester's book cover-to-cover. When she finished it, it is reported that she said only one word: "fascinating."

CHAPTER XXXVIII

Theresienstadt: My Exposure to Nazi "Justice"

After a three-week bench trial in federal court in Washington, D.C., and then (immediately thereafter) a two-week arbitration in Singapore, I was ready for a vacation. And so my wife and I flew to Europe, first to Vienna and then to Prague—two cities to which I had never been. The Prague visit looked to be particularly fun because we had been invited to have dinner with the American Ambassador to the Czech Republic, my former partner, Norman Eisen.

At dinner at the Ambassador's residence—the Petschek Palace (which became the U.S. Embassy as a result of World War II reparations)—Norm asked me how many days we were planning to stay in Prague and what was on our list to see and do. Hearing my answer, he told me we really needed to devote a day to visiting Theresienstadt. And so we did, hiring a local driver to spend the day with us exploring the site.

Theresienstadt

Theresienstadt is a walled garrison town about an hour's drive north from Prague. It was founded in 1784 by Emperor Joseph II of Austria in honor of his mother, Empress Maria Theresa. Originally a holiday resort for Czech nobility, it was later converted into a military base (the "Main Fortress"), with the "Small Fortress" across the river converted into a prison. After the Nazis took over Czechoslovakia, the Gestapo in 1941 turned the town into a Jewish ghetto and concentration camp.

Initially, the town was intended to house Jews from Czechoslovakia; over time Jews from Germany, Austria, the Netherlands, and Denmark were deported there as well. During World War II more than 144,000 Jews were sent to Theresienstadt. Although it was technically not an extermination camp, approximately 33,000 people died there. About 88,000 others were transported to Auschwitz, Treblinka, and other extermination camps (of that number, it is estimated that 3,500 people survived the war).

Because of inquiries made by the Danish government about its citizens "housed" at Theresienstadt, the Nazis authorized representatives of the Danish Red Cross and the International Committee of the Red Cross (from Switzerland) to visit the town in 1944. Prior to the visit the Nazis initiated "Operation Embellishment"—an attempt to present the town as an example of enlightened stewardship: the area was cleaned up, gardens were planted, fake shops and cafes were built, many inmates were moved to nicer living quarters (especially the Danish Jews), and 7,503 people (the sick, elderly, or disabled) were shipped to Auschwitz. On June 23, 1944, the inspection took place under the supervision of Adolf Eichmann. The Red Cross representatives were taken on a carefully choreographed tour of the town, a tour that included a children's soccer game and a performance of Verdi's *Requiem,* conducted by Czech composer Rafael Schächter and sung by an adult chorus of 150 Jews. Eichmann was later quoted as saying: "Those crazy Jews—singing their own requiem." (Schächter was sent to Auschwitz on October 16, 1944; he was executed the following day.) Incredibly (and unfortunately), the Red Cross representatives were fooled by the ruse and later issued a benign report to the world about the conditions at Theresienstadt (that, as the Nazis had claimed, the ghetto was essentially a self-governing Jewish settlement).

Based on that experience, the Nazis then determined to make a propaganda film about their "model" internment camp. Starting

Entrance to the Small Fortress
(author's collection)

on September 1, 1944, Kurt Gerron—a Jewish prisoner who was an experienced actor and director—oversaw 11 days of moviemaking. After the filming was completed, most of the cast and Gerron were sent to Auschwitz (he was executed on October 28, 1944). The film was entitled *Theresienstadt. Ein Dokumentarfilm aus dem jüdischen Siedlungsgebiet* (*Terezin: A Documentary Film from the Jewish Settlement Area*). Because of the imminence of the end of World War II, the film was never distributed publicly, although a few screenings were held and excerpts were included in a German newsreel.

General Dwight D. Eisenhower ordered General George S. Patton not to advance into Czechoslovakia farther than Pilsen, and so it was the Soviet army which liberated Theresienstadt on May 8, 1945. Because of a typhoid epidemic, the Russians imposed a quarantine over the area (ultimately 1,500 prisoners and 43 Soviet medical personnel died). After the quarantine was lifted, the thousands of

Theresienstadt cemetery
(author's collection)

remaining inhabitants of the camp were repatriated to their original countries of origin.

In October of 1991 (after the Velvet Revolution), the Theresienstadt Ghetto Museum was inaugurated. It is estimated that 250,000 people visit the town every year.

Our Visit to the Camp

Driving into Theresienstadt is an eerie experience, in and of itself. Like Dealey Plaza in Dallas (which will forever be frozen in time in November 1963), both the town (called its Czech name, Terezin, with a population of about 3,000 people) and the camp seem frozen in 1944. Everything looks just as it must have when the Red Cross was duped by the Nazis. And while the buildings and grounds are intact and in 1944 condition, the "feel" of it all seems much like a ghost town, devoid of lively noise and everyday activity.

Above the gate leading into the Small Fortress is the infamous "Arbeit Macht Frei" ("Work Sets You Free"). Once inside, we toured the rooms where prisoners were onboarded to the camp, then we went through the "barracks" where the inmates were housed. Outside, we saw the wall against which people were lined up and shot, as well as the area where prisoners were hung by piano wire. Not far from those gruesome spots is the crematorium, which suffered some flood damage in 2002. In the town itself, we saw the commandant's house, with the swimming pool built nearby by prisoners.

Moving inside to the Ghetto Museum, things took a very different turn. Many educated Jews were interned at Theresienstadt; there were numerous scholars, philosophers, scientists, artists, and musicians (some, like Schächter, internationally known). As a result (and unlike other Nazi camps), the ghetto enjoyed a rich cultural life, especially in 1943-1944 (as Eichmann et al. were planning the Red Cross visit).

Vibrant artwork created in those years (by both adult artists and children) is prominently displayed. Also extensively documented are the musicals performed and the compositions written for those performances (musicians had been allowed to bring their instruments); I still have a vivid memory of the costumes used for a production of *Carousel*. Newspapers and magazines were also produced on a regular basis; and there was a library that, at its peak, housed over 100,000 books. Finally, although formal education was barred by the Nazis, children were secretly taught, among other things: Czech, German, Hebrew, history, geography, and mathematics; evidence of this pedagogy is prominently on display.

My wife and I came away from seeing all of these materials inspired by the grit and determination of the Theresienstadt prisoners to create full and meaningful lives for themselves in the midst of this absolute horror. It was only later that I learned that Viktor Ullman, who composed over 20 works of music while imprisoned at Theresienstadt, felt the same way. He believed that the cultural life created in the camp constituted a spiritual resistance to the imprisonment (a "spark of humanity"): "By no means did we sit weeping by the rivers of Babylon; our endeavors in the arts were commensurate with our will to live."

At the conclusion of our day, we came to a small (for lack of a better word) "souvenir" shop. I have two distinct memories of that shop. The first is numerous pictures of children, taken during the Red Cross visit, with plaques below as to the dates they died in Auschwitz. (I remember one boy playing soccer, who was sent to Auschwitz on August 4, 1944, and was killed on August 6.) My other memory is the cache of very large and very numerous books in that room in which the Nazis kept the most detailed records of all the people who came to Theresienstadt and their ultimate fates. Holocaust deniers do not seem to understand that the Nazis were very meticulous in wanting to document the "Final Solution."

A Return to New York City

The week after we got back to New York City, I was having lunch with a good friend I had known for more than 40 years (Charlie Temel, who was in the class behind me at Cornell). Not surprisingly, I was interested in relating to him our visit to Theresienstadt. Charlie listened very carefully, and in silence, to my recounting of the experience. After I had finished, he very quietly said to me: "Do you know that my mother and grandmother were at Theresienstadt?" With my jaw agape, all I could say was: "How did they survive?" Charlie answered: "Well, after Theresienstadt they were shipped off to the death camps, first to Riga, then to Kaiserwald, and then to Stutthof." Again, all I could say was: "How did they survive?" Again, very quietly, he asked me: "Have you seen *Sophie's Choice*?" "Yes," I replied. "Well, on the second day at Riga they were in a line of people [two by two] being onboarded, with a fellow inmate behind a cardboard table keeping a record for the Germans. Once the two got to the table, one person would go right, and the other would go left—and the person going right would never be seen again. As my mother was about to go right, my grandmother grabbed her and said: 'You're coming with me.' The record-keeping inmate did not report this obvious, important rule infraction to the Germans [an infraction for which she could be killed]. Later that week in the camp, my grandmother ran into her fellow inmate, who asked whether she was from a small town in Eastern Europe. After my grandmother replied 'yes,' the woman said: 'I thought so. When I was a small girl in that town, I went into your father's store and picked out the most delicious piece of food I could find. I went up to your father and said: 'I am so hungry, but I have no money.' And your father said to me: 'That's all right!'"

Listening to that amazing story—in which the father's small act of kindness had saved his entire family—filled my eyes with tears (and even today, when I tell people this story, it still does). A few months after our lunch, I met my friend's mother for the first time. All I could say to that amazing woman was: "Your son just recently told me how you survived World War II. I don't know what to say other than, can I give you a hug?"

Postscript

Charlie's mother survived the two subsequent camps for two reasons: (1) she was tall for her age and her mother passed her off as a near adult, and (2) the Russian troops were advancing rapidly toward the camps, which were very far east.

At the Ghetto Museum shop, I purchased two books documenting the history of the walled garrison town and its use by the Nazis as a concentration camp. The best book on the camp, however, is by Czech writer and historian H.G. Adler: *Theresienstadt 1941-45: The Face of a Coerced Community* (originally published in German in 1955; published in English by Cambridge University Press in 2017). Adler and his family were deported to Theresienstadt in February 1942; they were later sent to Auschwitz in October 1944. He ultimately survived that death camp, but his wife (who also could have lived) refused to abandon her mother and died with her in the gas chamber.

Adler believed that the Nazis' use of Theresienstadt as a propaganda tool to demonstrate to the world that Jews were being treated in a humane fashion was "the most gruesome ghost dance in the history of Hitler's persecution of the Jews." Even more ominously he wrote: "Theresienstadt is still possible. It can be imposed on a massive scale, and, in the future, the Jews—who in mankind's overall history of suffering so often have had to serve as harbingers and as those most especially at others' mercy—might not be the only victims. Theresienstadt stands not only as an experiment but as the writing on the wall, and it is more alluring than our disgust at the horror is yet willing to admit."

Other important works on Theresienstadt include Helga Hoskova-Weissova's *Helga's Diary: A Young Girl's Account of Life in a Concentration Camp* (W.W. Norton 2013) and Zuzana Justman's "My Terezin Diary: And What I Did Not Write About," *The New Yorker* (September 16, 2019).

Norm Eisen has written a fascinating account of the history of the Petschek Palace: *The Last Palace: Europe's Turbulent Century in Five Lives and One Legendary House* (Crown 2018).

CHAPTER XXXIX

Making Up Her Own Mind

In September 1879, Jessie Mary Boulton, Class of 1883, left her home in Oil City, Pennsylvania, and traveled to Ithaca by train. For the next four years, she wrote letters to her family. Her mother copied each one into a notebook that now resides in Cornell's Rare and Manuscript Collections.

At the start of classes Jessie wrote of being "discouraged to note how much the professors know." She did not stay discouraged for long. On September 26, she wrote that her algebra professor "entirely ignored the girls till I put up my hand once and he gave the question to me." She worked hard: four hours of study a day and "on most days," four hours of recitations. She admitted to "two or three hours a day idling." By October 4, she reported that she felt "as if I had been a student here for a long time," and wrote, "the boys are quite rude here and they seem to be very fond of applauding. Yesterday I was about ten minutes late at a lecture in rhetoric and when I came in I went up front and took a seat. Immediately they interrupted the speaker by applauding me."

When she dropped her Latin course, she wrote that she had only one regret: "I hated to have those boys think I was unable to keep up."

Life was not all work, though. Just before Christmas break, Jessie wrote that "after coming home from church Mr. W. and I went over to one of the falls, 'Triphammer' by name, and viewed it by moonlight. It was one of the prettiest sights I have ever seen." The identity of Mr. W. remains a mystery.

Returning to school in January, Jessie was out of sorts because her eating table at Sage had become dominated by males. "I believe in coeducation but I get tired of coeating." And like generations of Cornellians to follow, she complained about the weather. To her father: "It is raining steady today. It is very disagreeable here." To her mother. "It is so disagreeable to go from one building to another in the rain." She quoted Longfellow: "The day is cold and dark and dreary. It rains and the wind is never weary."

Despite good first semester grades, Jessie confessed that "the people know so much around here that I get discouraged. I hear so many things mentioned and I don't know what half of them mean. Maybe I might know something at some future time but l guess that time is very far distant."

In March, Jessie wrote that all students, male and female, had been canvassed for their choices in the upcoming presidential race: "I did not care much whom I voted for but I gave Blaine 1st and Sherman 2nd. It may be the only time that I will have an opportunity to vote for the nomination of President and I thought I might as well embrace it." Jessie's other political observation was to report on whether Rutherford B. Hayes's son—a Cornell student—was "handsome or not. He is neither handsome or ugly, just medium."

Anticipating her financial needs for the spring, Jessie wrote to her father: "I think you had better send me $150. There will be 11 weeks' board to pay amounting to $55, tuition $25, private lessons in Latin and my new dress and sack besides other little things." She heard that a good friend from home, Charley Thorp 1884, would be matriculating in the fall.

By the time Jessie returned for sophomore year she felt like a veteran on campus. Academic life was not as intimidating—having "lost its power over one individual at least." She joined the first choir at Cornell, took up the new sport of lawn tennis ("I cannot send the ball very far and it has not gone where it ought to more than once or twice"), and initiated discussions with some female classmates about establishing a chapter of the Kappa Alpha Theta society at Cornell.

She wrote to her mother: "Of course Mamma if you do not wish me to do this, I will not, but I should like very much to. I can see no objections to it save that it will cause a little talk at first, and there may be some fun made of it, but that will soon blow over and I think we would really be doing some good; as fraternities certainly do make a bond of union between persons which does not otherwise exist. I do not see why we should not have fraternities as the boys have them." By winter, the group had established Cornell's first sorority and Jessie began wearing her pin.

Jessie was trying to convince her sister, Sadie, to come to Cornell. Before the end of the school year, Jessie wrote, "Charley says to tell you that he wants you to come next year and if you do he will call once every two weeks if that will be any inducement."

The inducements worked. On September 12, 1881, the two Boulton girls arrived at the "classic halls of Sage," with the elder Boulton having made the "transition between Sophomore boastfulness and Junior dignity." That same month, Cornell's first president, A.D. White returned to campus. Although his German course made her "tremble," his modern history course was widely perceived to be easy. Jessie's letters began to mention a Mr. Kent, who was "quite an addition to our table."

Her schedule for winter term was formidable: Latin, French, history, political economy, moral philosophy, physics, and chemical laboratory. (She seems to have particularly enjoyed the latter, noting that it was taught by a "certain young unmarried Professor.") While she attributed her growing independence to "reading on women's rights," her academic successes may have been equally important. She reported that one of her professors praised her oration as "one of the best deliveries ever seen in a girl," and that "Mr. Kent told the boys down at the Theta Delt block that Miss Boulton's oration was the best that was delivered that morning." She added that she was "not puffed up in the least."

On March 5, 1882, the day after her twentieth birthday, Jessie wrote about a cousin's marriage, adding, "I come next after Charlie

[Boulton] so you had better look out. I promise you, however, to wait until I get out of College."

That spring Jessie was appointed an editor of the *Cornell Daily Sun* for her senior year (nominated by Mr. Kent). She did not tell her father of the appointment to the board of the one-year-old paper until after she had accepted, "for I wanted to make up my own mind." She also wrote that Cornell was establishing a chapter of Phi Beta Kappa: "I am anxious to learn whether it will be restricted to gentlemen or not. I am very much afraid it will be. My present ambitions are centered on that object and I even went so far as to remark that I wished I was a boy—a wish which was repented as soon as spoken. But I would like very much to belong and if girls are admitted at all, I think I might stand a very good chance."

Jessie mused to her mother, wondering whether "my College education is paying, but when I think it is but a matter of $500 or less besides my board, I think that it is certainly worth it. It is not so much what we actually learn as it is what we get started in." She expressed shock that Charley Thorp "is so utterly devoid of ambition. If I were a boy with his chances I should at least imagine that I was going to do something great. I have always been so ambitious that to me it seems very strange."

The returned to Sage in the fall of 1882 "feeling her Senior dignity very much." She disagreed with President White's ban on dancing on Saturday night "except for a very few minutes just after supper. Verily things are becoming narrow. I expect very soon to hear that only occasional callers are allowed and those not without the President's permission." She also wrote of her electioneering for senior class essayist. She ran on each of the two tickets in the field ("I have had little difficulty in polling votes").

Senior year, Jessie's major focus was on her thesis: "American Colonization Society and Its Bearing on Slavery." Less than 20 years had passed since the Civil War when she wrote: "It is hard to realize that the slaves were treated so cruelly; one could hardly blame Harriet Beecher Stowe for exaggerating slave trials after reading this

Jessie Boutlon Thorp, holding the author's father (circa 1919)
(author's collection)

record." Jessie also wrote to her father about the abolitionist William Lloyd Garrison: he was "very much opposed to the Society and very fiery." Jessie's thesis was 31 pages long, on "good sized paper," and she felt it was "certainly the best thing [she] ever wrote." Ambivalent about letting her parents see it, for fear they would not "agree with my view of the matter," Jessie did give them a glimpse of her analysis: "I do not laud abolitionists to the skies as I should do—however, I guess I shall let you judge for yourselves."

With commencement looming, Jessie found that her junior year's dream had been realized. "I have an appointment to Phi Beta

Kappa and I am so happy. Someday I hope that you will think I have not altogether wasted my opportunities."

Jessie's last letter went to her mother June 10, 1883, just before her parents' departure for Ithaca and commencement. With all of her belongings, not to mention having "no less than 80 books," she advised them to "bring a trunk."

Despite Jessie's doubts, Charley Thorp did amount to something. Admitted to the Pennsylvania Bar in 1886, he later established one of Pittsburgh's leading law firms, and practiced law until his death in December 1942. Jessie Mary Boulton and Charles Monroe Thorp were married May 22, 1888. Four of their children, five grandchildren, and three great-grandchildren (including the author of this book) followed them to Cornell. And three generations of lawyers followed Charles Thorp, including my father, Charles Thorp Stewart, one of the most distinguished attorneys of his generation.

Founded 1880
Incorporated 1905
Member of The
A.P. and UPI

The Cornell Daily Sun

"Ithaca's Only Morning Newspaper"

WEATHER
Partly Cloudy
Chance of Showers
High: 58

VOL. XCI — 33 ITHACA, NEW YORK, SATURDAY, FEBRUARY 14, 1998 12 PAGES—10¢

STEWART TURNS 80!

University To Change Its Name: From Now On It's "Stewart U"

Rawlings Reveals That School Motto Will Also Change

Ithaca - In keeping with the Board of Trustees' decision to change *Cornell's* name, President Hunter Rawlings reported today that the original founder's motto will also be altered. "From now on, the University's shield will read: 'I would found an institution where anyone can get a liberal arts education, go on to law school (preferably *Yale*), and then head for *Wall Street* to defend the interests of corporate America.' " Asked whether this would have any impact upon the University's "need-blind" admissions policy, Rawlings said that he viewed this change as a real plus "because students will undoubtedly be able to pay off their loans much faster." Don Randel also supported the move, saying

Continued on page 3

Secret Nixon Diary Uncovered

Yorba Linda - Former President Richard M. Nixon kept a secret diary, the contents of which were revealed yesterday by lawyers for his estate. The most amazing revelation is that Nixon's first choice for Vice President in 1968 was former New York Young Republican Chairman, Charles T. Stewart. At the Miami convention, Nixon wrote: "I wanted to name Chuck, but Rockefeller blocked it because he feared that Chuck's charisma would eclipse Rocky in New York." Stewart, whose advice Nixon rejected on how to handle the White House tapes, expressed no regrets at not getting the nod.

Continued on page 4

Chairman of the Board of Trustees Executive Committee Charles T. Stewart '40, and Chairman of the Board Robert W. Purcell '32 announcing in 1974 that student trustee Gordon Chang has mysteriously disappeared.

Tanner Announces Decision To Stunned Student Activists

Ithaca - Harold Tanner, Chairman of Cornell's Board of Trustees, made public today what had been rumored for months: that Cornell's name would be changed. "I am very pleased to announce that the Board has unanimously voted to amend the university's charter to rename itself after one of its favorite sons, Chuck Stewart." Charles T. Stewart '40, former Chairman of the Board of Trustees' Executive Committee and Vice Chairman of the Board, received the news with equanimity. "At my age, this kind of thing is nice. But frankly, my major focus is on getting ready to join the Senior PGA tour." Stewart's wife, Patricia Carry Stewart '50, also a former Vice Chair of the Board, stated that she thought it was "well-deserved," adding that "maybe now this will spur them to get that pumpkin down!" At press time, the pumpkin was unavailable for comment. Student activists, however, were quick to jump on Chairman Tanner's announcement, demanding separate housing for pre-law students, as well as the right to pre-approve all law school recommendations.

Continued on page 2

Stewart To Join Senior PGA

Augusta - The *PGA* announced yesterday that Charles T. Stewart had finally agreed to join its prestigious senior tour. Speaking to reporters from Augusta, Jack Nicklaus could hardly supress his glee: "We've been trying to get Chuck out with us for years. Although his length from the tee is awesome, we're all more worried about his short game. From now on, we'll just be playing for second place." Arnold Palmer, Stewart's old rival, also welcomed him to the tour, vowing that "nobody beats me ten times in a row !"

Continued on page 12

Left: Stewart and Palmer after a round at St. Andrew's.

Cornell Daily Sun, February 14, 1998

CHAPTER XL

Juris Imprudence

Focus On:

Judge Leonard Sand

By Eve B. Burton

(Eve Burton is in-house counsel for the Daily News and a former law clerk to Judge Sand.)

During his almost 20 years on the bench, Judge Leonard Sand has handled some of the Southern District's most complex and high profile cases. For example, two of his decisions have had a particularly lasting impact on the protection of individual rights.

In *Corliss Lamont v. The United States Department of State*, Judge Sand found that federal funding of religious programs overseas violated the Establishment Clause of the First Amendment.

And in *United States Department of Justice v. The City of Yonkers*, he found in favor of the federal government, which charged that the City of Yonkers had for half a century systematically discriminated against people of color in its publicly funded housing and educational programs.

Case Manager

Judge Sand, in his management of these and other civil and criminal cases, still acknowledges the contributions of fellow Judge Charles Brieant and the late Judge Irving Kaufman to his judicial management style. As were both of these judges, Judge Sand is a firm case manager.

Promptly after cases are filed, his chambers requests that the parties attend a pre-trial conference. At that conference Judge Sand begins to learn about the case, but makes no attempt to give "advice or insight" as to how he may rule since at that stage he "never knows enough about the case."

While a case is pending, Judge Sand does not "micro-manage" discovery. Rather, he micro-manages his docket, being certain that there is a specific date on the calendar for every case that marks the next milestone, such as motion practice or a trial date. Judge Sand adopted this practice from "Judge Charlie Brieant who had a safety net for each case." As Judge Sand says, "When a lawyer gets a call from chambers and realizes that the court cares about the case," the lawyer cares more about the case.

Federal Bar Council News (author's collection)

APPENDIX

Selected Correspondence from a 47-Plus-Year Legal Career

Donovan Leisure Letters

Law Offices of

Donovan Leisure Newton & Irvine

30 Rockefeller Plaza

New York, N.Y. 10020

TELEPHONE: 212 489-4100

CABLE ADDRESS: DONLARD, N. Y.

TELEX: 127429

WILLIAM J. DONOVAN
1929-1959

GEORGE S. LEISURE
CARL ELBRIDGE NEWTON
RALSTONE R. IRVINE
THOMAS J. McFADDEN
OTTO C. DOERING, JR.
DAVID TEITELBAUM
JAMES R. WITHROW, JR.
MALCOLM FOOSHEE
JAMES V. HAYES
THEODORE S. HOPE, JR.
RICHARD Y. HOLCOMB
GEORGE S. LEISURE, JR.
A. VERNON CARNAHAN
MAHLON F. PERKINS, JR.
JOHN E. TOBIN
SAMUEL W. MURPHY, JR.
JOHN DOAR
WALTER L. STRATTON
STUART B. PEERCE
DOUGLAS V. LEWIS
JULIUS P. FOUTS
HELMUT F. FURTH
JOHN COOLEY BAITY
ROGER V. PUGH, JR.
ENNETH N. HART
. LAUCK WALTON
J. TRUMAN BIDWELL, JR.
ROBERT S. OGDEN, JR.

1666 K STREET, N. W.
WASHINGTON, D. C. 20006
TELEPHONE: 202-785-8900
TELEX: 892687

130, RUE DU FAUBOURG SAINT HONORÉ
PARIS 75008 FRANCE
TELEPHONES: 225-47-10 / 225-46-20
TELEX: 290907

16/17 PALL MALL
LONDON SW1Y 5LU, ENGLAND
TELEPHONE: 839-3551
TELEX: 919363

GORDON CONDIE OSMOND
SANFORD M. LITVACK
ANDREW J. KILCARR*
JOHN J. McCANN
ROGER W. KAPP
LOUIS C. LUSTENBERGER, JR.
VERNON EDWARD VIG
REGINALD S. KOEHLER III
THOMAS O. ROSE*
JAMES R. WIENER
JOHN H. WILKINSON
JAMES A. MAGEE
JAMES E. DANIELS
FRANK S. IOPPOLO
JOHN J. McGRATH, JR.
WILLIAM J. T. BROWN
HERBERT L. CAMP
PAUL A. CROTTY
J. PETER COLL, JR.
THOMAS R. TROWBRIDGE III
RICHARD H. SAYLER

*ADMITTED TO DISTRICT OF COLUMBIA BAR ONLY

OWEN McGIVERN
ROBERT M. ESTES
COUNSEL

September 13, 1976

Mr. C. Evan Stewart
304 1/2 Elmwood Ave.
Ithaca, New York 14850

Dear Evan:

This letter will confirm what we have already told you - how delighted we were to have you with us during this summer and how much we are looking forward to your returning to us as a permanent associate after your graduation from law school. You demonstrated the high capabilities and qualities which are essential to success in meeting the challenge of a practice which we believe is unsurpassed in this country.

As you likely know, we have just increased the salary for starting associates from $22,500 to $25,000. We would hope you would plan to take the New York bar examination prior to joining us next year. We will pay in advance the expenses of your bar review course. In recognition of the time spent, we will pay, upon your starting with us, the equivalent of two weeks salary, provided you take the bar exam prior to commencing work. In addition, we will pay the expense of your personal travel to start work in New York and will pay reasonable expenses of shipping your belongings here if you will submit an estimate of this expense to us in advance.

Mr. C. Evan Stewart 2.

It is understandable that you will want to take some time in considering this important career choice. We very much hope, however, that you will respond to our offer as soon as you reasonably can. We look to our summer program to provide the central core of our new associates and, until we hear from that group, it is difficult for us to make decisions with respect to offers to others. I am sure you will take this into proper account in keeping us posted on your thoughts and letting us know of your decision as promptly as possible.

I would like to extend an invitation to have you telephone me or any other members of the firm collect about any questions you may have concerning our offer or the firm in general. Again, I would like to stress what an outstanding impression you made on all of us here at Donovan Leisure who worked with you and how very much we hope that you will be joining us.

Best regards for a fine school year.

Sincerely,

Reg

Reginald S. Koehler III

4/21

Office of the General Counsel

SHEARSON LEHMAN BROTHERS
An American Express company

Good luck, Evan. Sounds like a great spot - and you'll bring real distinction to it. Had a nice visit with Steve Friedman last week.

All the best (from Fla.)

Sam

(212) 528-0548

April 12, 1988

Samuel W. Murphy, Jr., Esq.
Davis, Markel & Edwards
100 Park Avenue
New York, New York 10017

Dear Sam:

Effective May 9, 1988, I will have a new moniker and address:

General Counsel
The Nikko Securities Co. International, Inc.
One World Financial Center
200 Liberty Street
New York, New York 10281

Sincerely yours,

Evan

C. Evan Stewart

CES:MW-D

GEORGE LEISURE
P.O. BOX 30221
SEA ISLAND, GA 31561
Tel: (912) 638-0102
Fax: (912) 638-0106

April 10, 1997

Dear Evan:

Thanks so much for sending me the materials on your ethics course. I am afraid I would have flunked your exam (but hopefully not if I had take your course). Thank you also for the interesting articles you have written. I recognize many of the citations.

In your course and in your articles you are dealing with many of the problems that have in the past, and still are, plaguing many lawyers. Even when a decision comes down that seems to resolve old problems (eg - Upjohn), they still seem to persist.

Congratulations on the important work you are doing, and I hope that we will see each other again on your next visit to Sea Island.

Best regards.

Sincerely,

George

George Leisure

Law Offices of

Donovan Leisure Newton & Irvine

89 MAY 25 AM 9:54

30 Rockefeller Plaza

New York, N.Y. 10112

1950 K STREET, N.W.
WASHINGTON, D.C. 20006
TELEPHONE: 202 862-4700
TELEX: 6974839 - DONLARD
TELECOPIER: 202-785-1058

333 SOUTH GRAND AVENUE
LOS ANGELES, CALIFORNIA 90071
TELEPHONE: 213-253-4000
TELEX: 194418
TELECOPIER: 213-617-2368

TELEPHONE: 212 632-3000
W. U. TELEX: 127429
ITT TELEX: 424102
CABLE ADDRESS: DONLARD, N.Y.
TELECOPIER: 212-632-3315

130 RUE DU FAUBOURG SAINT-HONORÉ
75008 PARIS
TELEPHONE: 1-42-25-47-10
TELEX: 290907
TELECOPIER: 1-42-56-08-06

WRITER'S DIRECT DIAL NUMBER:
212-632 3010

May 23, 1989

C. Evan Stewart, Esq.
General Counsel
The Nikko Securities Co.
Int'l., Inc.
One World Financial Center, Tower A
200 Liberty Street
New York, New York 10281

Dear Evan:

I return your copy of the materials you put together several years ago about some "highpoints" and "lowpoints" of the proceedings in 1980-83 in the Pinney and Litton cases upon the occasion of Bob Siverd's departure for Penn Central. I truly enjoyed reading this again; on numerous of the items I found myself seized by uncontrollable laughter, and on occasion tears rolled down my cheeks. Those close to me in the office and on the train when I was re-reading the "motion papers", surely must have thought that I was an escapee from the funny farm.

At least to those of us who went through battles in 1980-83 with Velvel et al., the years have enriched and improved the humor content of the activities recorded. The passage of time has the effect of enabling one to put things in perspective better. The main remembrance of all of this is that we were fortunate indeed to have gone through these experiences (seemingly difficult and even impossible, at the time) with such good colleagues as Bob, Curtis and you who were able to keep their good humor at all times. Thanks for the memories!!

Best regards.

Kenneth N. Hart

Enclosure

KENNETH N. HART
187 WESTCOTE DRIVE
WAKEFIELD, R.I. 02879

January 6, 2006

Dear Evan:

I enjoyed hearing from you and receiving your pack of informative materials touching on some of your exploits and accomplishments this past year. The result (an acquittal on criminal charges) you helped obtain for your client Theodore Sihpol III is surely deserving of highest laurels. I'd love to hear more on how the proceedings went. I congratulate you, and wish you well, on becoming a member of the Zuckerman Spaeder firm. It would seem to be a great professional opportunity. I am, as always, very proud of you, Evan, and the manner in which you have pursued your professional career, and the considerable accomplishments you have attained along the way.

I always enjoy reading copies of the interesting and informative pieces you have authored. The Federal Bar piece on the ill-fated Clement Haynsworth nomination in 1969 was particularly informative and timely.

I still look forward to our getting together some time next spring for lunch (or dinner) at some spot between Madison and Wakefield. It would be great to see you in living color and catch up on things.

All the best,

Ken

Kenneth N. Hart
187 Westcote Drive
Wakefield, R.I. 02879

May 28, 2008

C.Evan Stewart, Esq.
1070 Park Avenue, Apt. #3C
New York, New York 10128

Dear Evan:

Thanks for the copy of the laudatory obit that the New York Times saw fit to publish about "Dick Netzer…Municipal Finance Expert". I recall very well his shameful performance on the witness stand in the *Yeshiva v NEEI* Case where he cooked up outrageously fanciful numbers about the damages he projected that Yeshiva suffered by reason of mental health professionals being deceived by Dr. Guerrett's promotional materials about his competitive programs on the Cape. Judge Sands surely made no bones about the fact that he and his court were offended by Dr. Netzer's unprofessional rantings. And, of course, the jurors told us after their verdict that a major reason for their verdict was the comparison of Yeshiva's "experts" with our good Dr. Jay Schulman.

I regret that you were not able to get away to attend the DLN&I reunion at the River Club on May 22nd.It was a most interesting and enjoyable evening. About 180 alums attended the event. Being at the River Club, it brought back memories of Mr. Newton's magic tricks and the humorous skits put on by the associates.

Hopefully, there is still a good chance that we can get together for a yummy lunch some time soon. I would love to see you.

With Fond Remembrances,

NIKKO

The Nikko Securities Co.
International, Inc.

One World Financial Center
200 Liberty Street, New York, N.Y. 10281-1092

Telephone: (212) 416-5441
Facsimile: (212) 416-5687

C. Evan Stewart
Executive Vice President
General Counsel

September 24, 1996

Sanford M. Litvack, Esq.
Senior Executive Vice President
& Chief of Corporate Operations
The Walt Disney Company
500 South Buena Vista Street
Burbank, CA 91521

Dear Sandy:

Going through some files this morning I uncovered the song I adapted from "Grease" for the December 1979(!) Donovan Leisure Christmas dinner (and which we later reprised at your "goodbye" party). I thought you and Judy might enjoy this "oldie but goodie"!

Please pass on my regards to Joe Santaniello and Val Cohen.

Very truly yours,

Evan

C. Evan Stewart

Enclosure

SANDY

EJL L 1: Standin' at the gas pump
RJS L 2: Without Mobil fuel
L 3: What will they say
1/2/3: In the steno pool

ENTER GREASER:

SANDY

Can't you see
I'm in misery
You gave me my start
Now we're apart
There's nothing left for me

CHORUS:

You have flown
Off to Jimmy
I sit and wonder
why (chorus - ei ei)
why, you left me
my Sandy

Oh Sandy
Maybe, someday
When IBM is through
somehow, some way
there'll be none left to sue
then you'll come back to Donlard
and never will you stray
oh please say you'll stay
my Sandy (Cindy)

-15-

Speaking: (AAC)

Sandy, my partner,

You know it's true, you've hurt me real bad

and Sandy

You've got to believe me when I say,

I just can't litigate without you

Chorus:

You have flown

off to Jimmy

I sit and wonder why (ei ei)

Oh why (~~cut music~~)

You left me

my Sandy

WHITE & CASE

1747 Pennsylvania Avenue, N.W.
Washington, D.C.
125 Worth Avenue, Palm Beach
20 Place Vendôme, Paris

1155 Avenue of the Americas
New York, New York 10036
(212) 819-8200
Telex: 126201

66 Gresham Street, London
15 Queen's Road Central, Hong Kong
50 Raffles Place, Singapore
Grev Turegatan 2, Stockholm

JTB:MAG

October 10, 1984

C. Evan Stewart, Esq.
Donovan Leisure Newton & Irvine
30 Rockefeller Plaza
New York, New York 10112

Dear Evan:

Thanks for your thoughtful note of October 1, 1984. I reciprocate your kind thoughts, and I, too, have always been proud of our association. It is people such as yourself who give me great confidence that Donovan Leisure will survive and thrive. I wish you well, as I do all of the Firm, and look forward to watching as you continue to grow both personally and professionally. I am sure that when I am old and gray that you will be one of the luminaries both at the Firm and at the Bar, in general.

Again, my thanks.

Sincerely,

Truman

J. Truman Bidwell, Jr.

Donovan Leisure Newton & Irvine

October 1, 1984

J. Truman Bidwell, Jr., Esq.
White & Case
1155 Avenue of the Americas
New York, New York 10036

Dear Truman:

I am sorry not to have had the chance to say goodbye to you in person last Thursday. Although we never had occasion to work together, I did want you to know that, dating back to my days in law school, I have appreciated your kindness toward me and was always proud to be associated with you. I wish you the best of success and happiness at White & Case.

Best regards.

Sincerely,

C. Evan Stewart

David S. Versfelt 6/24/99

To: EVAN STEWART

I return to you herewith the supporting "evidence" that confirms your prescience. Yet another instance of what your friends have seen you display time & time again!

D

TTAN LAWYER ■ AUG. 29, 1989 – SEPT. 11, 1989

COMMENTARY

)issenting Voice of Securities Arbitration

the Current Dispute-Resolution Process Is N

By C. Evan Stewart

:e the facts are not in ably true that arbitra- ore informal and less :ter of any complexity putes between securi- e the facts are at issue, :ngthy and expensive :o a court case. In fact, l or evidentiary rules sessions, arbitration time-consuming than

s are not bound by ap-

appealing arbitration awards, the process provides finality.

• Arbitrators, having backgrounds in and knowledge of the industry, are able to rule more quickly and easily on the parties' competing positions.

ILLUSORY VIRTUES

The trumpeted benefits appear substantial. Unfortunately, they are largely illusory. Even worse, in the near future the arbitration process will likely come to resemble the cumbersome, costly civil litigation system it was designed to replace.

Here's how the "virtues" look in today's environment:

• In the run-of-the-mill broker/cus-

C. Evan Stewart is general counsel of the Nikko Securities Company International Inc.

my view, not good. el they should reach a Solomonic award, regardless of the merits or how courts have ruled on similar cases. Justice Oliver Wendell Holmes was right: Individuals and institutions have a right to understand what is acceptable conduct — commercial or otherwise — and to be sure that such conduct will be protected.

• I also do not see the benefit of according finality to an arbitration award that may have no real relationship to the evidence presented or applicable law. Whether the award is, in fact, in tune with the evidence or law may well be unknowable since arbitrators are under no obligation to write an opinion or state their reasoning.

• There is a clear advantage to having people with securities experience hear these disputes. Because of charges of bias from customers and consumer advocates, however, the Securities and Exchange Commission and industry self-regulatory organizations are cutting back opportunities for people to serve as arbitrators if they have any connection with the securities industry. While this is politically understandable, lengthier and costlier proceedings will certainly result.

COURTLIKE PROCEEDINGS

On May 10, a few days before *Rodriguez* was decided, the SEC approved significant amendments to the arbitration rules of the New York Stock Exchange, the American Stock Exchange and the National Association of Securities Dealers. As a result of these changes, together with court decisions on the nature and scope of arbitration, securities arbitration faces a brave new world, indeed.

• Under the new rules, there will be formal, courtlike discovery, with sanctioning power given to arbitrators to enforce compliance with discovery obligations.

• To resolve discovery disputes and other procedural and evidentiary questions, pre-arbitration conferences will become common.

• There will be greater utilization of the rules and procedures (evidentiary and otherwise) of the civil litigation system.

• Individual cases against a common broker or set of brokers will be consolidated into one arbitration — not unlike a class action.

• There will which the arbitr set forth. New Y Exchange and Ch change arbitratio made available t maries have start obvious corollary sions will take on

• Although m forbid recovery o torney fees in ar changing — m increased empha tion. That tre strengthen. Inde dividual states' award form just York Stock Exc plays areas for a damage claims.

• There will vent all "indu from serving on make the proce the civil judge-a

Perhaps the c as well as those If there is to be in arbitration, i be confident th ducted on an e current change completely resh praise arbitratio that those same ing. We seem t resolution syst away importan significant othe

often feel they should reach a Solomonic gardless of the merits or how courts have n similar cases. Justice Oliver Wendell s right: Individuals and institutions have understand what is acceptable conduct sure that such conduct will be protected.

Footnote

1. Yes, Aristot 1, Chapter 13, a agree to arbitratio umpire in an arbit the juryman sees

Perkins Coie

1201 Third Avenue, Suite 4800
Seattle, WA 98101-3099
PHONE: 206.359.8000
FAX: 206.359.9000
www.perkinscoie.com

Reginald S. Koehler III
PHONE: 206.359.8632
FAX: 206.359.9632
EMAIL: RKoehler@perkinscoie.com

October 12, 2004

C. Evan Stewart
Goldman, Sachs & Co.
One New York Plaza
New York, NY 10004

Dear Evan:

This will belatedly thank you for the good letter and enclosed articles that you sent to me last month. I enjoyed reading all of them and will be on the lookout for some of the Italian wines that you recommended.

I and all our family members had a splendid time at the cocktail party that you and your mother kindly hosted during our visit to Kennebunkport. I would like to keep in touch and find an easy way to do so is by email. My email address is RKoehler@perkinscoie.com. When you have a second, please drop me an email with your address.

Warm regards.

Sincerely,

Reg

Reginald S. Koehler III

RSK:gck

UNITED STATES DISTRICT COURT
SOUTHERN DISTRICT OF NEW YORK
UNITED STATES COURTHOUSE
500 PEARL STREET
NEW YORK, NEW YORK 10007

CHAMBERS OF
PAUL A. CROTTY
UNITED STATES DISTRICT JUDGE

(212) 805-6309
FAX: (212) 805-6304
PAUL_A_CROTTY@NYSD.USCOURTS.GOV

July 29, 2014

C. Evan Stewart, Esq.
Cohen & Gresser, LLP
800 Third Avenue
New York, New York 10022

Dear Evan:

Thanks for your note of June 18—and thanks for the clippings you enclosed. I finished reading them this weekend.

We were most fortunate to have started our careers with Donovan Leisure. I never met the General, but I met all the other named partners in the firm, as well as luminaries like Walter Mansfield, Jim Withrow, Sam Murphy, John Tobin, George Leisure, Jr., and the list goes on and on. They were all great men, and great lawyers. Working for them and with them have to be high points in our careers.

I am enclosing a eulogy for Kevin Walsh who worked with us and who appreciated what it meant to be a Donovan Leisure lawyer.

Hope to see you soon.

Sincerely yours,

Paul Crotty

Paul A. Crotty
United States District Judge

PAC:cp
Enc.

Judicial Letters

UNITED STATES DISTRICT COURT
UNITED STATES COURTHOUSE
500 PEARL STREET
NEW YORK, NY 10007

CHAMBERS OF
PETER K. LEISURE
SENIOR DISTRICT JUDGE

1/1/05

Dear Mr. Stewart:

I was most impressed with your scholarly, thorough article in the Federal Bar Council News, entitled "Alger Hiss in the Second Circuit (Redux)" The painstaking care with which you review the background and draw your conclusions probably tells us the kind of person that you are.

I was pleased to see from Martindale Hubbell that you were at Donovan Leisure and served as a special assistant district attorney. Although my father suffered a severe stroke in 1978 at age 89, and was never himself while you were at the firm, you will be surprised that he never could bring himself to believe that Hiss was guilty. He thought that a man with his experience and abilities could never be a spy, and that he might be covering for his wife, as a supreme sacrifice and act of Honor. Of course, he did not live long enough to hear of the revelations from Soviet intelligence. Also the defections of the Philby Cambridge comrades, were of similar significance, and consideration.

When it came before me, I decided to release all the significant Hiss grand jury transcripts, in an unusual ruling (because of the precedent protecting grand jury secrecy). I thought it worthwhile to put to rest speculation by Hiss followers that the proceedings were tainted and unfair. U.S. Attorney Mary Jo White decided not to appeal my decision, although I never felt that I was on firm ground because of the time-honored concepts of grand jury secrecy. But I hope I achieved my goal.

Hope to see you in Madison.

Sincerely,

Peter K. Leisure

UNITED STATES DISTRICT COURT
FOR THE
EASTERN DISTRICT OF VIRGINIA
ALEXANDRIA, VIRGINIA 22314

LEONIE M. BRINKEMA
DISTRICT JUDGE

October 3, 1996

To Evan, the cartoonist lawyer,
who sent to his judge-friend Dee Dee
some smile-causing sketches
'bout lawyers and kvetches,
a warm hearted thanks from me.

Dee Dee

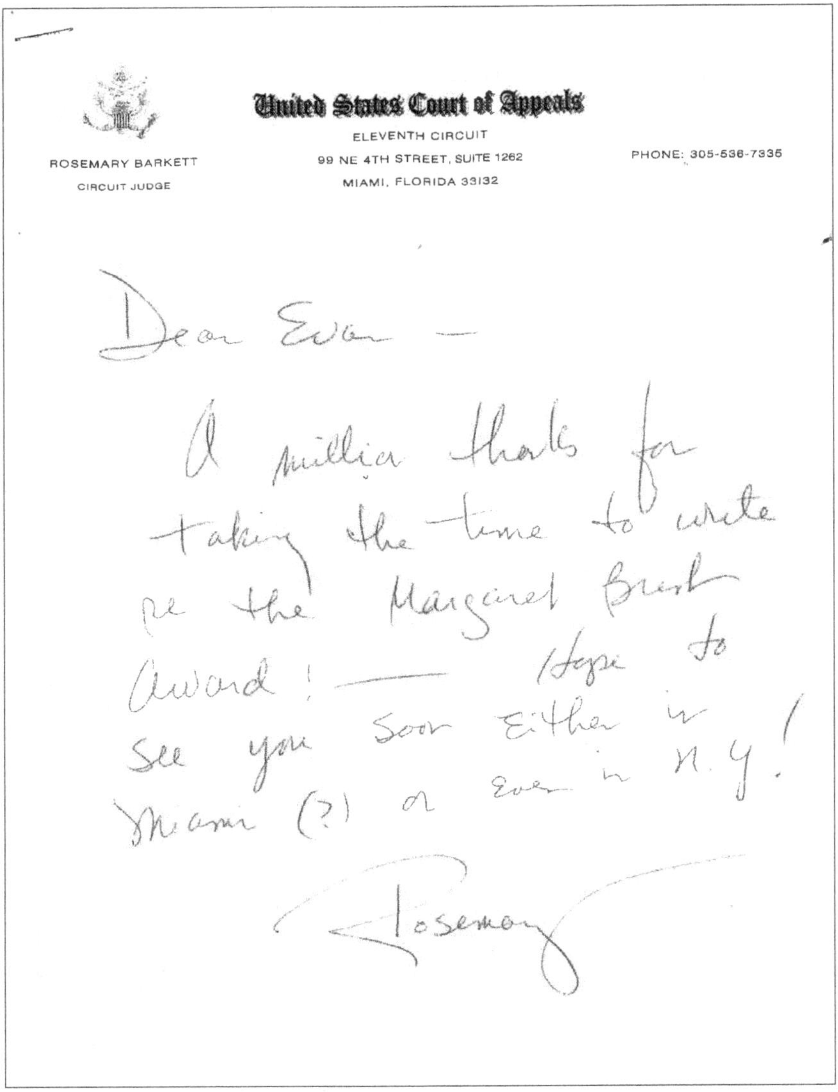

United States Court of Appeals
ELEVENTH CIRCUIT
99 NE 4TH STREET, SUITE 1262
MIAMI, FLORIDA 33132

ROSEMARY BARKETT
CIRCUIT JUDGE

PHONE: 305-536-7335

Dear Evan —

A million thanks for taking the time to write re the Margaret Brent Award! — Hope to see you soon either in Miami (?) or even in N.Y.!

Rosemary

NIKKO

The Nikko Securities Co. International, Inc.

One World Financial Center
200 Liberty Street, New York, N.Y. 10281-1092

C. Evan Stewart
Executive Vice President
General Counsel

Telephone: (212) 416-5441
Facsimile: (212) 416-5687

October 7, 1996

The Honorable Rosemary Barkett
U. S. Court of Appeals, 11th Circuit
Federal Justice Building
99 North East Fourth Street, Suite 1223
Miami, FL 33132

Dear Rosemary:

I was very pleased to read of your being awarded the 1996 Margaret Brent Women Lawyers of Acheivement award. Obviously it is well deserved!

Best regards.

Sincerely,

Evan

C. Evan Stewart

UNITED STATES COURT OF APPEALS
DISTRICT OF COLUMBIA CIRCUIT
333 CONSTITUTION AVENUE, N.W.
WASHINGTON, D.C. 20001-2866

JUDITH W. ROGERS
UNITED STATES CIRCUIT JUDGE

May 16, 1997

C. Evan Stewart, Esquire
Executive Vice President
and General Counsel
The Nikko Securities Company
One World Financial Center
200 Liberty Street
New York, NY 10281-1092

Dear Evan:

Thank you for your nice letter. It's good to know how "the real world" reacts to an opinion.

We all missed seeing you on March 1. Please give my regards to Trisha and Charlotte.

Best regards,

Judy

Judith W. Rogers

NIKKO

The Nikko Securities Co. International, Inc.

One World Financial Center
200 Liberty Street, New York, N.Y. 10281-1092

Telephone: (212) 416-5441
Facsimile: (212) 416-5687

C. Evan Stewart
Executive Vice President
General Counsel

May 13, 1997

The Honorable Judith W. Rogers
U. S. Court of Appeals
District of Columbia Circuit
333 Constitution Avenue, N.E.
Washington, DC 20001-2866

Dear Judy:

I read with great interest the BNA report of your decision in the Lavin case. From my perspective you hit all the right buttons in what was a complex circumstance!

Trisha and Charlotte join me in extending our best regards and wishes to you.

Respectfully,

Evan

C. Evan Stewart

C. Evan Stewart, Esq.

UNITED STATES DISTRICT COURT
EASTERN DISTRICT OF NEW YORK
BROOKLYN, NEW YORK 11201

CHAMBERS OF
JACK B. WEINSTEIN
SENIOR JUDGE

3/30/15

Dear Mr Stewart,

I very much enjoyed your "Tom Dewey in the Second Circuit" in the Dec/Jan/Feb 2015 Fed. Bar Council Q. As a clerk for Stanley Fuld in the NY Ct A I got to know some of Dewey's extraordinary staff: Gurfein, Breitel, Hogan and Fuld, head of his appeals bureau — many from Columbia L.S. They were a powerful group. I was anti-Dewey because I felt he held up the overseas voting bill, preventing me from voting when I was overseas in WWII.

Sincerely yrs
Jack Weinstein

CHAMBERS OF
JACK B. WEINSTEIN
SENIOR JUDGE
UNITED STATES DISTRICT COURT
BROOKLYN, NEW YORK 11201

Mailed From 11201
US POSTAGE

RECEIVED
APR 02 2015

C. Evan Stewart, Esq.
Cohen & Gresser LLP
800 Third Avenue
New York, New York 10022

Jan. 6. 2003 3:10PM No.6497 P. 2

UNITED STATES COURT OF APPEALS
SECOND CIRCUIT

CHAMBERS OF
JAMES L. OAKES
SENIOR CIRCUIT JUDGE
P.O. BOX 696
BRATTLEBORO, VERMONT 05302-0696

TELEPHONE 802-254-5000
FACSIMILE 802-257-1922

January 2, 2003

RECEIVED JAN - 6 2003

C. Evan Stewart, Esq.
Federal Bar Council
370 Lexington Avenue
New York, NY 10017

Dear Mr. Stewart:

I really enjoyed reading your piece in the recent Federal Bar Council News on the law firm of "Wild Bill" Donovan. There was one significant omission, however, and that was reference to Walter R. Mansfield, my great friend and colleague on the Court of Appeals from 1970 until his death in 1987.

Walter, who was a member of the firm, was the only OSS person dropped behind the lines in both the European Theater (Yugoslavia) and in the Asian Theater (Mongolia), and, as such, he organized guerillas and performed many other notable exploits. He was for many years President of the former OSS Veterans.

He also was a great judge and a great human being, to whom the Federal Bar Council dedicated a tree from the John Jay Estate -- the tree has now been removed to the foreground of the Court of International Trade -- with all due ceremony.

I was delighted to know him as a man and was always impressed by his abilities as a judge.

But thank you for your nice piece.

Sincerely,

James L. Oakes

mfr

C. Evan Stewart

From:	Robert_Katzmann@ca2.uscourts.gov
Sent:	Wednesday, August 1, 2012 5:06 PM
To:	Stewart, Evan
Subject:	Many thanks

Dear Evan (if I may),
Just a note of thanks for sending me your writings. I had read some of them, for example, your excellent Myron Taylor piece in the Federal Bar Council News. Please keep me you on your mailing list so that I can keep learning from you. All my best, Bob K.

Richard C. Wesley
United States Circuit Judge

18 August 2008
Geneseo NY

Dearest Evan,

I enjoyed talking with the summer law class. I agree we should do it again next year. Owen looks terrific. I'll watch for his application this fall.

Dick

Richard C. Wesley
United States Circuit Judge
Livingston County Government
6 Court Street
Geneseo, New York 14454-10?

United States Postage
$ 00.42
0004804783
Mailed from Zipcode 10007

C. Evan Stewart, Esq.
Zukerman, Spaeder, LLP
1540 Broadway, Suite 1604
New York, New York 10036

C. Evan Stewart

From:	Elizabeth_Stong@nyeb.uscourts.gov
Sent:	Thursday, May 1, 2014 7:16 PM
To:	C. Evan Stewart
Cc:	Stewart, Evan (Evan.Stewart@gs.com)
Subject:	Re: FW: "Positively 4th Street*: Lawyers and the "Scripting" of Witnesses"
Attachments:	00150531.DOCX

This is terrific - I just sent it to my law clerks to read. Thanks again.
--ess

Hon. Elizabeth S. Stong
U.S. Bankruptcy Court
Eastern District of New York
271 Cadman Plaza East
Brooklyn, NY 11201
(347) 394-1862 telephone
(347) 394-1865 fax
Elizabeth_Stong@nyeb.uscourts.gov

From: "C. Evan Stewart" <EStewart@CohenGresser.com>
To: "'Elizabeth_Stong@nyeb.uscourts.gov'" <Elizabeth_Stong@nyeb.uscourts.gov>
Cc: "Stewart, Evan (Evan.Stewart@gs.com)" <Evan.Stewart@gs.com>
Date: 05/01/2014 02:58 PM
Subject:FW: "Positively 4th Street*: Lawyers and the "Scripting" of Witnesses"

Elizabeth: many thanks for your very nice note, and special thanks for signing up to take another intern this summer! Sounds like you had a great time in Europe! Herewith, for your in-box reading materials, is my latest (pre-publication). Best regards. evan

From: Angela Olverson
Sent: Wednesday, April 09, 2014 11:21 AM
To: C. Evan Stewart; evan.stewart@gs.com
Subject: "Positively 4th Street*: Lawyers and the "Scripting" of Witnesses"

(See attached file: 00150531.DOCX)

C. Evan Stewart

From: P Castel <PKevin_Castel@nysd.uscourts.gov>
Sent: Tuesday, January 18, 2022 9:31 PM
To: C. Evan Stewart
Subject: Re: A few days ago there was a piece . . . .

Thanks, Evan. All is well on my end.

Get Outlook for iOS

From: C. Evan Stewart <EStewart@CohenGresser.com>
Sent: Tuesday, January 18, 2022 6:13:11 PM
To: P Castel <PKevin_Castel@nysd.uscourts.gov>
Subject: RE: A few days ago there was a piece . . . .

CAUTION - EXTERNAL:

Thank you very much! So nice to hear from you. I hope your New Year is off to a great start, and that you and your family are well. Best regards.

From: P Castel <PKevin_Castel@nysd.uscourts.gov>
Sent: Tuesday, January 18, 2022 6:07 PM
To: C. Evan Stewart <EStewart@CohenGresser.com>
Subject: A few days ago there was a piece . . . .

Evan

A few days ago there was a piece about a 22 year old US soldier station in Germany who mailed a letter home on Dec 6, 1945. It was just delivered by the US Postal Service.

In that vein I am writing to complement you on an excellent piece in the FBCQ in the Dec/Jan/Feb 2020 issue, nearly two years ago. I only read it today when I found it in a stack of papers. It was an excellent summary of Bush v Gore, some of which I never knew and some that I had forgotten. It is extremely difficult to synthesize a complex matter in such a concise and effective manner. I now plan to save your article.

Belated congratulations.

Kevin Castel

C. Evan Stewart

From: Raymond_Dearie@nyed.uscourts.gov
Sent: Monday, April 6, 2015 9:22 AM
To: C. Evan Stewart
Subject: Re: Tom Dewey

Don't you dare. Just wanted you to know that your very enjoyable article unlocked a very pleasant memory. Thanks again.

Sent from my iPhone

On Apr 6, 2015, at 9:17 AM, C. Evan Stewart <EStewart@CohenGresser.com>
wrote:

Judge Dearie: many thanks for you very nice note! When I re-publish the piece I promise to correct my oversight! Best regards. Evan Stewart

Sent from my iPad

> On Apr 5, 2015, at 4:09 PM, "Raymond_Dearie@nyed.uscourts.gov"
<Raymond_Dearie@nyed.uscourts.gov> wrote:
>
>
> Dear Mr. Stewart,
>
> I thoroughly enjoyed your article in the FBC Quarterly. I forgive you
for
> omitting one significant event in Mr. Dewey's career. On December 17,
> 1969, he was the guest speaker at my induction in the Second Department.
> My Dad was a great admirer of Dewey and after he spoke briefly at the
start
> of the program, my father followed him out the door and approached him
> as he was about to get into his limousine. The two spoke at the curb
> on Monroe Place for almost 20 minutes, long enough for my Dad to miss
> the
meat
> of the program and his son's swearing in as a lawyer. "Small price to
> pay," he would often remark.
>
> Thanks again for the piece. Best wishes.
>
> Ray Dearie
>
> Sent from my iPhone
>

ZUCKERMAN SPAEDER LLP

1540 BROADWAY SUITE 1604
NEW YORK, NY 10036-4039
212.704.9600 212.704.4256 fax www.zuckerman.com

C. Evan Stewart
Partner
(212) 704-4348
estewart@zuckerman.com

March 7, 2011

The Honorable Shira A. Scheindlin
United States District Judge
Southern District of New York
United States Courthouse
500 Pearl Street, Room 1620
New York, NY 10007

Dear Shira:

I very much appreciate your extremely thoughtful e-mail.

Herewith enclosed are the two articles that were referenced at Saturday's meeting, along with a few others you may find of interest. I do hope you will enjoy the piece on Myron Taylor.

Thank you for your exemplary public service, as well as your work for Cornell.

Best regards.

Sincerely,

Evan

C. Evan Stewart

3078517.1

WASHINGTON DC NEW YORK TAMPA BALTIMORE WILMINGTON, DE

Page 1 of 1

Stewart, Evan

From: Shira_A_Scheindlin@nysd.uscourts.gov
Sent: Monday, March 07, 2011 10:13 AM
To: Stewart, Evan
Subject: Articles

Dear Evan,

It was so thoughtful of you to give me the two articles at the Advisory Meeting. But I was not so thoughtful. I was sure I popped them in my briefcase and was looking forward to reading them over the weekend. When I got to Chambers I searched over and over but apparently left them at the meeting. I felt terrible. Would you be so kind as to send them again . . . either as a pdf to an email reply or by regular mail. I apologize for the inconvenience. Good to see you over the weekend and again congratulations on "our" victory. Best regards,

Shira A. Scheindlin
500 Pearl St. Rm 1620
New York, New York 10007
(212) 805-0246 (phone)
(212) 805-7920 (fax)

CHAMBERS OF
SIDNEY H. STEIN
UNITED STATES DISTRICT JUDGE
UNITED STATES COURTHOUSE
500 PEARL STREET
NEW YORK, NEW YORK 10007-1312

3/20/99

Dear Evan

Thank you for sending me your recent piece on arbitration. I find I'm taking another plane out West later this week; somehow it's appropriate that I take the articles to read on the flight.

I enjoyed seeing you in Hawaii.

Sincerely,

Sidney

NIKKO

The Nikko Securities Co.
International, Inc.

One World Financial Center
200 Liberty Street, New York, N.Y. 10281-1092

C. Evan Stewart
Executive Vice President
General Counsel

Telephone: (212) 416-5441
Facsimile: (212) 416-5687

February 25, 1999

The Honorable Sidney H. Stein
U. S. District Judge
U. S. Courthouse
500 Pearl Street, Room 1010
New York, NY 10007

Dear Judge Stein:

It was very nice to have several chances to get reacquainted in Hawaii this week. I hope the rest of the week was great fun.

Herewith, as "promised," are some recent pieces on arbitration (Judge Gertner's decision was affirmed by the 1st Circuit insofar as the plaintiff was allowed to litigate the discrimination claims in court, based upon facts unique to the case; the Court of Appeals specifically dis-endorsed her broader views as to (i) barring per se the arbitration of such claims, and (ii) the "structural bias" of the SRO process). Also enclosed is my monograph on the 1995 and 1998 "reforms" (if nothing else, perhaps you will find of interest fns. 4 & 34!).

Respectfully,

Evan

C. Evan Stewart

Enclosures

Lawyer Letters

EMERY CELLI BRINCKERHOFF & ABADY LLP

ATTORNEYS AT LAW
600 FIFTH AVENUE AT ROCKEFELLER CENTER
10TH FLOOR
NEW YORK, NEW YORK 10020

RICHARD D. EMERY
ANDREW G. CELLI, JR.
MATTHEW D. BRINCKERHOFF
JONATHAN S. ABADY
EARL S. WARD
ILANN M. MAAZEL
HAL R. LIEBERMAN
DANIEL J. KORNSTEIN
O. ANDREW F. WILSON
ELIZABETH S. SAYLOR
DEBRA L. GREENBERGER
ZOE SALZMAN
SAM SHAPIRO
ALISON FRICK
DAVID LEBOWITZ
DOUGLAS E. LIEB
ALANNA KAUFMAN
JESSICA CLARKE
EMMA L. FREEMAN
DAVID BERMAN
ASHOK CHANDRAN

TELEPHONE
(212) 763-5000
FACSIMILE
(212) 763-5001
WEB ADDRESS
www.ecbalaw.com

CHARLES J. OGLETREE, JR.
DIANE L. HOUK

October 16, 2017

C. Evan Stewart, Esq.
Cohen & Gresser
800 Third Avenue
New York, NY 10022

Dear Evan:

I read all of your articles with interest, but especially enjoyed your article on Griswold in the October 2017 issue of the NYSBA Journal. I was most struck by your excellent and important discussion of "Bad" and "Good" Substantive Due Process, a topic that has bothered me and has never gotten the attention it deserves. I touched on it briefly at pp. 145-46 in the enclosed book, and more generally in the pages leading up to that, but found your treatment more explicit. Good work.

As chair of the NYC Bar Association Committee on Legal History, I was wondering if (and hoping) you would like to come to one of our monthly meetings to present your views on "Good" and "Bad" Substantive Due Process. Let me know if you are interested, and I will send you our meeting schedule. Thanks.

Regards,

Daniel J. Kornstein

Enc.

C. Evan Stewart

From: George Yankwitt <george@georgeyankwitt.com>
Sent: Saturday, June 09, 2018 11:07 AM
To: C. Evan Stewart
Subject: RE: Re:

I was having dinner recently with an old friend who happens to be a US DJ SDNY. He/she asked if I had read the recent article by Evan Stewart concerning whether Justice Rehnquist lied about a memo he wrote as a law clerk. I became immediately defensive and said that I read everything that Evan writes but had not yet read that article. (I now have.) He/she responded by saying that Evan Steward might be the best lawyer/journalist in our times.

I think he/she is right. Terrific article.

From: C. Evan Stewart [mailto:EStewart@CohenGresser.com]
Sent: Monday, September 26, 2016 12:30 PM
To: George Yankwitt
Subject: Re:

George: many thanks and best regards! Evan

Sent from my iPad

On Sep 26, 2016, at 10:37 AM, George Yankwitt <george@georgeyankwitt.com> wrote:

> Every time I read a piece by you in the FBC News, I want to write to you to tell you how much I enjoyed it; how well done I thought it was. I just read your piece on Bork, a subject which I had thought I remembered well (to the extent that I remember anything well at this point). It was excellent. Thanks.
>
> Hope you are well.

C. Evan Stewart

From: Harper, Gerard E <gharper@paulweiss.com>
Sent: Saturday, October 7, 2017 8:43 PM
To: C. Evan Stewart
Subject: Simon Rifkind

In connection with writing a book which I hope to complete before I die (I started it ten years ago), I just came across your article in a 2013 issue of the *Federal Bar Quarterly* about Judge Rifkind which, to my embarrassment, I had not previously seen. It is a wonderful piece.

I had the great good fortune to work closely with Rifkind almost immediately upon my arrival at Paul, Weiss in 1979 until shortly before his death in 1995. Pure luck on my part – just a baby associate plucked from a list to work on a case in which he was the senior partner – and then, through no evil acts of my own, when my more senior associates on the case left the firm for other pastures, I suddenly became, at a frightfully tender age, the lead associate. The first dispositive motion I ever argued – I think I was a second-year associate – was a summary judgment motion in a multi-million case in which the only other PW lawyer there, acting as my "second chair" in a North Carolina federal court, was Simon Rifkind, who insisted I argue it. Alas, such opportunities do not occur anymore.

We worked together on a variety of cases thereafter, and he often welcomed me to his office for simple chats. As an adjunct, I, too, used his essays to provoke discussions on the adversary system. He was an extraordinary man. I wrote the History section on our firm's website, but this captures only a tiny excerpt from a career the likes of which we are unlikely to see again.

Anyway, I much appreciated reading your piece. All the best,

Gerry Harper
Paul, Weiss, Rifkind, Wharton & Garrison LLP
1285 Avenue of the Americas | New York, NY 10019-6064
+1 212 373 3263 (Direct Phone) | +1 212 492 0263 (Direct Fax)
gharper@paulweiss.com | www.paulweiss.com

Stewart, Evan

From: Kroenlein, David
Sent: Thursday, October 17, 2002 8:19 PM
To: Stewart, Evan
Subject: FW: Evan Stewart

I never thought of you as inspirational but now I have new insight! Jayne is one of the senior faculty members at William & Mary (Marshall-Wythe) Law School.

-----Original Message-----
From: Jayne Barnard [mailto:jwbarn@wm.edu]
Sent: Thursday, October 17, 2002 7:00 PM
To: Kroenlein, David
Subject: Evan Stewart

David -- Please congratulate your partner on his productivity. I'm familiar with his writings in BNA. He seems to be a remarkable scholar on the side of his "real" work. Here's a story you might want to pass along -- about a year ago, I sent a colleague of mine in her first year of teaching to one of his articles in BNA -- it formed the basis for her first law review article, which will be published later this year in the Georgetown Journal of Legal Ethics. She cites Stewart and me as her inspirations.

Stewart, Evan

From:	Robert Rifkind <RRifkind@cravath.com>
Sent:	Saturday, May 18, 2013 12:42 PM
To:	Stewart, Evan
Subject:	Fw: Homework
Attachments:	Scanned Doc.pdf

Dear Evan:

I have now done my homework and, as I should have guessed, I very much enjoyed it. The pieces on Cravath alumni were especially fun to read. Your evocations of my father were touching. I am delighted that the principles he believed in and which I imbibed at the dinner table still have an articulate spokesman. I am always surprised to find that those ideas do not inevitably command the respect of many of our colleagues -- so I hope you will go on preaching.

The issue you raise in "Mad Dogs" is one I keep confronting in the context of transnational arbitrations. Sitting as an arbitrator with lawyers from the UK and the Continent has dramatized for me the very different attitudes we bring to weighing evidence. It only slightly overstates it to say that the civil lawyers have sometimes seemed willing to believe anything that was written and nothing that was oral. For your entertainment (a rather poor quid pro quo) I attach a paper I gave at an ICC Conference in Paris some years ago. I fear that the audience emerged only more convinced that American trial lawyers are knaves or worse.

I greatly enjoyed our lunch, and I hope we can get together again without waiting for the book-party on the publication of your Taylor biography.

All best.

Bob

EPSTEIN BECKER & GREEN, P.C.

ATTORNEYS AT LAW
TWO GATEWAY CENTER
12TH FLOOR
NEWARK, NJ 07102-5003
973.642.1900
FAX: 973.642.0099
EBGLAW.COM

HERVÉ GOURAIGE
TEL: 973.639.8536
FAX: 973.642.0099
HGOURAIGE@EBGLAW.COM

September 21, 2009

C. Evan Stewart, Esq.
Zuckerman Spaeder LLP
1540 Broadway, Suite 1604
New York, New York 10036

Dear Mr. Stewart:

I enjoy very much reading your recent article in the June/July/August 2009 Federal Bar Council Quarterly, Vol. XVI, No. 4 regarding Judge Benjamin Cardozo and the Palsgraf case. I write to bring a point to your attention.

You state: "The more basic reason for Cardozo's declaration that proximate cause had nothing to do with the case is that, at an October 1927 meeting of the American Law Institute, the great judge had articulated a new theory that there should be no tort duty to an unforeseeable plaintiff." As you are aware, there remains a great deal of controversy and perhaps mystery surrounding this ALI advisers meeting and Judge Cardozo's role, if any, at the meeting. Abrahamson, "Refreshing Institutional Memories: Wisconsin and the American Law Institute," 1995 Wisc. L. Rev. 1, 25-27. One adviser to both Restatements of Torts (Professor Laurence H. Eldredge) takes the position that the meeting never occurred—at least not in 1927. According to this adviser, the first time that the ALI advisers took up the Palsgraf issue was in June 1928, after the New York Court of Appeals decision in the case on May 29, 1928. According to Dean Prosser, Judge Cardozo was present at the advisers' meeting and took no part in the discussion.

In view of the controversy and incomplete historical accounts of this meeting, it may be putting the case a bit stronger than warranted to conclude that Judge Cardozo "articulated a new theory." But perhaps you are aware of other evidence of which I am unaware to support this stronger version.

Best regards.

Sincerely,

Hervé Gouraige

HG:rr

ATLANTA • CHICAGO • DALLAS • HOUSTON • LOS ANGELES • MIAMI
NEWARK • NEW YORK • SAN FRANCISCO • STAMFORD • WASHINGTON, D.C.

EPSTEIN BECKER GREEN WICKLIFF & HALL, P.C. IN TEXAS ONLY

NE:3146932v1

Village of Westbury

Village Justice Court
235 Lincoln Place, Westbury, New York 11590-3295
516-334-1700 FAX 516-334-7563

THOMAS F. LIOTTI
VILLAGE JUSTICE

ELIZABETH D. PESSALA
ACTING VILLAGE JUSTICE

December 16, 2016

C. Evan Stewart, Esq.
Cohen & Gresser, LLP
800 Third Avenue
New York, NY 10022

Dear Mr. Stewart:

I have been reading your articles in the Federal Bar Council Quarterly. Congratulations and thank you for writing them.

Each year my Village Court sponsors programs for the community on Law Day and Constitution Day. Our 2017 Law Day program will occur on May 1, 2017 at & 7:00 p.m.. The title for the program taken from the American Bar Association is: "The 14th Amendment: Transforming American Democracy." We will have other speakers but I would very much like to have you as a principal speaker. Please R.S.V.P. as soon as possible. Thank you.

Sincerely,

Tom

Thomas F. Liotti

TFL: re

Stewart, Evan

From: Daugherty, Patrick D. [PDaugherty@foleylaw.com]
Sent: Tuesday, November 12, 2002 3:00 PM
To: Edward H. Fleischman (E-mail)
Cc: Stewart, Evan
Subject: FW: One if by land...

Ed -- C. Evan Stewart, Esq., now at Winston & Strawn/NYC, was previously GC of (if I recall correctly) Nomura Securities and before that he was a partner in an old-line NYC law firm. He is a firebrand in the tradition of George Bermant who pens columns with titles like "10 New Laws We Do NOT Need Because of 'Enron.'" In brief, a kindred spirit. Possibly I exceeded my authority by inviting him into your conspiratorial den of zealous advocates for malefactors of great wealth. Maybe; maybe not. The Patriots did not employ cumbersome vetting techniques. They just got the job done. Trust me on this one. -- Pat

-----Original Message-----
From: Stewart, Evan [mailto:Estewart@winston.com]
Sent: Tuesday, November 12, 2002 2:51 PM
To: Daugherty, Patrick D.
Subject: RE: One if by land...

many thanks for your kind words. perhaps ed will want to peruse my piece before inviting me to join?!

-----Original Message-----
From: Daugherty, Patrick D. [mailto:PDaugherty@foleylaw.com]
Sent: Tuesday, November 12, 2002 2:24 PM
To: Stewart, Evan
Cc: Edward H. Fleischman (E-mail)
Subject: FW: One if by land...

Evan,

I just read your latest column in BNA's Corporate Counsel Weekly ("Holding Lawyers Accountable"). Excellent analysis and critique. Seems to me you are probably the sort of lawyer who would want to (literally) sign on to Ed Fleischman's initiative. (See below.) If so, why don't you send him an e-note with your permission. Just an idea.

Sincerely,
Pat Daugherty
Cornell L.S. '81

Foley & Lardner
150 West Jefferson Avenue

1

DEBEVOISE & PLIMPTON

875 THIRD AVENUE
NEW YORK, NY 10022
(212) 909-6000

555 13TH STREET, N.W.
WASHINGTON, DC 20004
TELEPHONE (202) 383-8000
TELECOPIER (202) 383-8118

21 AVENUE GEORGE V
75008 PARIS
TELEPHONE (33-1) 40 73 12 12
TELECOPIER (33-1) 47 20 50 82

13/F ENTERTAINMENT BUILDING
30 QUEEN'S ROAD CENTRAL
HONG KONG
TELEPHONE (852) 2810 7918
TELECOPIER (852) 2810 9828

TELECOPIER: (212) 909-6836

601 SOUTH FIGUEROA STREET
LOS ANGELES, CA 90017
TELEPHONE (213) 680-8000
TELECOPIER (213) 680-8100

1 CREED COURT, 5 LUDGATE HILL
LONDON EC4M 7AA
TELEPHONE (44-171) 329 0779
TELECOPIER (44-171) 329 0860

1065 BUDAPEST
RÉVAY KÖZ 2 III./ 2
TELEPHONE (36-1) 131 0845
TELECOPIER (36-1) 132 7995

November 20, 1995

Mr. C. Evan Stewart
Executive Vice President & General Counsel
The Nikko Securities Co. International Inc.
One World Financial Center
200 Liberty Street
New York, NY 10281

Dear Evan:

Your *Law Journal* piece on derivatives is terrific! And "testosterone-bloated blusterings of Master of the Universe Wannabees" is a line for the ages.

I had one thought about the tapes. I wonder if it is really necessary to keep them for more than a few weeks? Even if there is a forward settlement, I assume that confirmations are sent out promptly.

With best regards.

Sincerely yours,

Stephen J. Friedman

WP{WP}.BK6

Salomon Inc

Co.

Seven World Trade Center, New York, New York 10048 212 783 7508

Robert H. Mundheim
Executive Vice President and
General Counsel

December 6, 1996

C. Evan Stewart, Esq.
Executive Vice President
General Counsel
The Nikko Securities Co. International, Inc.
One World Financial Center
200 Liberty Street
New York, New York 10281-1092

Dear Evan:

Thank you for noticing the piece in CCM.

I never knew Frank Coker, but Bill Cary always talked about him with great admiration. Bill relied on him extensively in the Investment Company Act area.

With all best wishes to you and your family for a happy holiday season.

Sincerely,

Bob

RHM/las

NIKKO

The Nikko Securities Co.
International, Inc.

One World Financial Center
200 Liberty Street, New York, N.Y. 10281-1092

Telephone: (212) 416-5441
Facsimile: (212) 416-5687

C. Evan Stewart
Executive Vice President
General Counsel

December 3, 1996

Robert H. Mundheim, Esq.
Executive Vice President
& General Counsel
Salomon Inc.
Seven World Trade Center, 39th Floor
New York, NY 10048

Dear Bob:

Congratulations on the very nice piece in CCM. From my personal experience and vantage point, it all is true! I had not realized that your past history included Hamburg.

With respect to your early work at the Commission, did you ever run into my godfather, Frank Coker--he was a Yale Law School professor, who was doing a fair amount of consulting for the SEC in those years (in fact, he died of a heart attack on June 28, 1962, right after having made a presentation to the Commission)?

Again, kudos on not only having done such a wonderful job, but also getting recognition for it.

Best wishes to you and Guna for a joyous holiday season.

Sincerely,

Evan

C. Evan Stewart

Law Offices of
Donovan Leisure Newton & Irvine
30 Rockefeller Plaza
New York, N.Y. 10112

TELEPHONE 212 307-4100
W U TELEX 127429
ITT TELEX 424102
CABLE ADDRESS DONLARD, N Y
TELECOPIER: 212-307-4836

1850 K STREET, N W
WASHINGTON, D C 20006
TELEPHONE: 202 862-4700
TELEX: 6974539-DONLARD
TELECOPIER: 202-785-1058

333 SOUTH GRAND AVENUE
LOS ANGELES, CALIFORNIA 90071
TELEPHONE: 213-253-4000
TELEX: 194418
TELECOPIER 213-617-2368

130 RUE DU FAUBOURG SAINT-HONORÉ
75008 PARIS
TELEPHONE: 1-42-25-47-10
TELEX 290907
TELECOPIER: 1-42-56-08-06

WRITER'S DIRECT DIAL NUMBER
212-307 4359

December 24, 1986

Martin Flumenbaum, Esq.
Paul, Weiss, Rifkind, Wharton & Garrison
1285 Avenue of the Americas
New York, New York 10019

Dear Mr. Flumenbaum:

I read with great interest the article appearing under your name in today's New York Law Journal. Drawing upon the spirit of Charles Caleb Colton ("imitation is the highest form of flattery"), I thank you (see my enclosed article in the December 1, 1986 edition of The National Law Journal).

Most sincerely yours,

C. Evan Stewart

C. Evan Stewart

Enclosure

PAUL, WEISS, RIFKIND, WHARTON & GARRISON

1285 AVENUE OF THE AMERICAS
NEW YORK, NEW YORK 10019

TELEPHONE (212) 373-3000
TELECOPIER (212) 757-3990
TELEX WUI 666-843

RANDOLPH E. PAUL (1946-1956)
LOUIS S. WEISS (1927-1950)
JOHN F. WHARTON (1927-1977)

ADRIAN W. DeWIND
LLOYD K. GARRISON
JOSEPH S. ISEMAN
JAMES B. LEWIS
PAUL J. NEWLON
MORDECAI ROCHLIN
HOWARD A. SEITZ
SAMUEL J. SILVERMAN
JOHN C. TAYLOR, 3RD
COUNSEL

DOMINIQUE FARGUE**
SAMUEL MYERS
EUROPEAN COUNSEL

WRITER'S DIRECT DIAL NUMBER

1615 L STREET, N. W.
WASHINGTON, D. C. 20036
TELEPHONE (202) 223-7300
TELECOPIER (202) 223-7420
TELEX 248237 PWA UR

199, BOULEVARD SAINT GERMAIN
75007 PARIS, FRANCE
TELEPHONE (33-1) 45.49.33.85
TELECOPIER (33-1) 42.22.64.38
TELEX 203178F

2008 TWO EXCHANGE SQUARE
8 CONNAUGHT PLACE, CENTRAL
HONG KONG
TELEPHONE (852) 5-220041
TELECOPIER (852) 123-4286
TELEX HX66208

MORRIS B. ABRAM
NEALE M. ALBERT
MARK H. ALCOTT
DANIEL J. BELLER
MARK A. BELNICK
ALLAN BLUMSTEIN
RICHARD S. BORISOFF
JOHN F. BREGLIO
DAVID C. BRODHEAD
RICHARD J. BRONSTEIN
JOSEPH E. BROWDY
CAMERON CLARK
LEWIS R. CLAYTON
JEROME ALAN COHEN
EDWARD N. COSTIKYAN
JAMES M. DUBIN
RICHARD A. ENGELMAN
LESLIE GORDON FAGEN
PETER L. FELCHER
GEORGE P. FELLEMAN
BERNARD FINKELSTEIN
MITCHELL S. FISHMAN
ROBERT C. FLEDER
MARTIN FLUMENBAUM
TERENCE J. FORTUNE*
MAX GITTER
RICHARD D. GOLDSTEIN
BERNARD H. GREENE
JAY GREENFIELD
PETER R. HAJE
ALBERT P. HAND
GERARD E. HARPER
SEYMOUR HERTZ
ROBERT M. HIRSH
JAMIE P. HORSLEY*
ARTHUR KALISH
LEWIS A. KAPLAN
ANTHONY B. KUKLIN
JEROME KURTZ
STEVEN E. LANDERS
ROBERT L. LAUFER

WALTER F. LEINHARDT
ARTHUR L. LIMAN
MARTIN LONDON
BAYLESS MANNING
JOHN E. MASSENGALE
JOHN P. McENROE
COLLEEN McMAHON
ROBERT E. MONTGOMERY, JR
ROBERT H. MONTGOMERY, JR
DONALD F. MOORE
TOBY S. MYERSON
MATTHEW NIMETZ
KEVIN J. O'BRIEN
LIONEL H. OLMER*
JOHN J. O'NEIL
STUART I. ORAN
MARC E. PERLMUTTER
JAMES L. PURCELL
LEONARD V. QUIGLEY
CARL L. REISNER
SIMON H. RIFKIND
STUART ROBINOWITZ
SIDNEY S. ROSDEITCHER
RICHARD A. ROSEN
STEVEN B. ROSENFELD
PETER J. ROTHENBERG
ERNEST RUBENSTEIN
JOHN A. SILBERMAN
MOSES SILVERMAN
EILEEN S. SILVERS
STEVEN SIMKIN
ROBERT S. SMITH
MARILYN SOBEL
THEODORE C. SORENSEN
GERALD D. STERN
ALLEN L. THOMAS
JUDITH R. THOYER
JAY TOPKIS
JOSE E. TRIAS
DAVID T. WASHBURN
ALFRED D. YOUNGWOOD
NORMAN ZELENKO

*NOT ADMITTED TO NEW YORK BAR
**CONSEIL JURIDIQUE IN FRANCE ONLY

(212) 373-3191

December 24, 1986

C. Evan Stewart, Esq.
Donovan Leisure Newton & Irvine
30 Rockefeller Plaza
New York, New York 10112

Dear Mr. Stewart:

Thank you for your note.

I had planned and started my column on summary judgment approximately two months ago and almost decided to pull it after seeing your excellent column in <u>The National Law Journal</u>. Since my focus was more on the Second Circuit Court of Appeals, and the two papers do have different readerships, I decided that the overlap was insignificant.

If we choose the same topic again, however, we may have to investigate for leaks. Have a happy holiday.

Sincerely,

Marty

Martin Flumenbaum

MF:km

<u>BY HAND</u>

22 THE NATIONAL LAW JOURNAL Monday, December 1, 1986

CIVIL PROCEDURE

By C. Evan Stewart

Rulings Make Summary Judgment Possible in Complex Litigation

OVERSHADOWED perhaps by the glare of cases involving issues of high political intensity, three decisions were handed down last term by the U.S. Supreme Court that will have a profound impact on litigation in the federal courts.

While the cases addressed a seemingly technical aspect of the law — the procedural bases for granting summary judgment — there is no doubt there will be widespread application of those decisions in a host of significant substantive areas.

Their impact ultimately may be to give true meaning to the overall purpose of the Federal Rules themselves: "To secure the just, speedy and inexpensive determination of every action."[1]

Rule 56(c) OF the Federal Rules of Civil Procedure provides that summary judgment should be entered when "pleadings, depositions, answers to interrogatories, and admissions on file, together with the affidavits, if any, show that there is no genuine issue as to any material fact and that the moving party is entitled to a judgment as a matter of law."

RULE 56'S procedures thus are designed to obviate the need for a trial where no fact issues exist. Conversely, where there are disputes with respect to material facts, summary judgment is not warranted. Rule 56 has been widely hailed since its original adoption in 1938 as improving the federal judicial system by, among other things, protecting the courts from vexatious litigation and promoting the expeditious resolution of cases.[2] Nonetheless, in practice, it has fallen short of the panacea that had been envisioned.

Why? The Supreme Court's 1962 decision in *Poller v. Columbia Broadcasting System Inc.*[3] is the principal answer.

In *Poller*, a plaintiff alleged that CBS and others had engaged in an antitrust conspiracy to restrain and monopolize trade in the TV broadcasting business, with the result of driving him out of that business. The defendants, after discovery, moved for summary judgment and the motion was granted. The Supreme Court reversed that judgment based on the rationale that Rule 56 did not have a significant role to play in complex litigation:

> We believe that summary procedures should be used sparingly in complex antitrust litigation where motive and intent play leading roles, the proof is largely in the hands of the alleged conspirators, and hostile witnesses thicken the plot. It is only where the witnesses are present and subject to cross-examination that their credibility and the weight to be given their testimony can be appraised. Trial by affidavit is no substitute for trial by jury which so long has been the hallmark of 'even-handed justice.'"[4]

While the Supreme Court arguably toned down that sweeping rule somewhat six years later in *First National Bank of Arizona v. Cities Service Co.*,[5] district courts and courts of appeals have been extremely reluctant to grant summary judgment because of *Poller* and the court's reasoning therein. Thus, for example in the 6th U.S. Circuit Court of Appeals, the well-established policy in complex, antitrust litigation has been that "summary judgment is particularly disfavored and the standard for granting summary judgment is strict."[6]

ALL THIS WAS changed dramatically last term by the Supreme Court's rulings in *Matsushita Electric Industry Co. Ltd. v. Zenith Radio Corp.*,[7] *Anderson v. Liberty Lobby Inc.*[8] and *Celotex Corp. v. Catrett*.[9]

In *Matsushita*, the court reviewed the granting of summary judgment in a complex antitrust suit, where massive volumes of record evidence had been submitted by the parties and analyzed by the lower courts. Rejecting the notion that "metaphysical doubt as to the material facts" could defeat a Rule 56 motion, the court stressed that the issue of fact must be "genuine": "The non-moving party must come forward with 'specific facts showing that there is *genuine issue for trial*.'"[10]

With respect to that burden, it was ruled to be greater where, as in that case, the moving party would have no "plausible" or "rational economic motive" to engage in the alleged anti-competitive conduct. The court, based on these standards, held that evidence submitted on the conduct at issue was not sufficient to create a genuine issue for trial.

Rule 56's procedures are designed to do away with the need for a trial where no fact issues are present. However, where there are disputes with respect to material facts, summary judgement is not warranted.

In *Anderson*, the appropriateness of summary judgment in the context of a libel action was addressed. Besides making clear that for purposes of "materiality" under Rule 56 "it is the substantive law's identification of which facts are critical and which facts are irrelevant that governs,"[11] the court ruled that the standard for granting summary judgment "mirrors the standard for a directed verdict under Federal Rule of Civil Procedure 50(a), which is that the trial judge must direct a verdict if, under the governing law, there can be but one reasonable conclusion as to the verdict."[12] In remanding the case so that the correct standard under Rule 56 could be applied, the court directed:

> ...[T]he judge must ask himself not whether he thinks the evidence unmistakably favors one side or the other but whether a fair-minded jury could return a verdict for the plaintiff on the evidence presented. The mere existence of a scintilla of evidence in support of the plaintiff's position will be insufficient; there must be evidence on which the jury could reasonably find for the plaintiff. The judge's inquiry, therefore, unavoidably asks whether reasonable jurors could find by a preponderance of the evidence that the plaintiff is entitled to a verdict — 'whether there is [evidence] upon which a jury can properly proceed to find a verdict for the party producing it, upon whom the *onus* of proof is imposed.'"[13]

In *Catrett*, the court addressed the question of the burden of production of evidence placed by Rule 56 on moving and non-moving parties. Rejecting the contention that because the moving party had not used affidavit evidence the non-moving party's failure to adduce material evidence to defeat the motion should be excused, the court held that a non-moving party to a summary judgment motion is required to "designate 'specific facts showing that there is genuine issue for trial.'"[14] The rationale for that determination was straightforward:

> In our view, the plain language of Rule 56(c) mandates the entry of summary judgment, after adequate time for discovery and upon motion, against a party who fails to make a showing sufficient to establish the existence of an element essential to that party's case, and on which that party will bear the burden of proof at trial. In such a situation, there can be 'no genuine issue as to any material fact,' since a complete failure of proof concerning an essential element of the non-moving party's case necessarily renders all other facts immaterial. The moving party is 'entitled to judgment as a matter of law' because the non-moving party has failed to make a sufficient showing an essential element of her case with respect to which she has the burden of proof."[15]

To ensure that no one missed the message, the Supreme Court did not cite the Poller decision in *Matsushita*, the first of the three cases; and, as if to further demonstrate the rejection of *Poller*, the dissent in *Matsushita* did not cite it either. The final nail in *Poller*'s coffin was hammered by the court in *Anderson*, when it specifically rejected plaintiffs' reliance on *Poller*.[16]

LITIGANTS AND the courts have rapidly adapted to the "new" Rule 56. For example, federal judges in the Southern District of New York recently granted summary judgment in three complex cases.

In *Apex Oil Co. v. Dimauro*,[17] an antitrust action, Judge John M. Walker Jr. utilized each of the court's decisions. Initially citing *Matsushita* as "demand[ing] that the district court, in considering summary judgment, give searching scrutiny to the inferences available from the typically ambiguous mass of evidence,"[18] the court noted that the teachings of *Anderson* were that "[t]he question is not whether there is *any* evidence supporting the non-movant but whether 'there is sufficient evidence favoring the non-moving party for a jury to return a verdict for that party.'"[19]

The court then went on to review the requirements detailed in *Catrett* — specifically, whether the non-moving party had met its burden to designate specific facts demonstrating a genuine issue — and concluded that that burden had not been met.

In *Rizzuto v. Nexxus Products Co.*,[20] Judge Edward Weinfeld dismissed a libel action on a summary judgment motion. Relying on *Anderson*, the court posited the issue as whether in response to the motion the plaintiffs had produced evidence "such that a reasonable jury could find malice with convincing clarity.'"[21] Because the plaintiffs had not offered "an iota of evidence" from which a jury could find actual malice by "clear and convincing evidence,"[22] Judge Weinfeld granted the Rule 56 motion.

Finally, in *Spannaus v. Federal Election Commission*,[23] Judge Louis L. Stanton dismissed an injunctive action brought against the FEC. The gravamen of the plaintiffs' complaint was that the commission's investigative and enforcement actions were motivated by bad faith and were infringing on the plaintiffs' First Amendment rights. Because plaintiffs had failed to make "even a preliminary showing" in support of those contentions, however, the court, relying on *Catrett*, granted the FEC's summary judgment motion.[24]

* * *

The above-mentioned cases are merely illustrative of the tremendous impact of the Supreme Court's trilogy of Rule 56 decisions.[25] It is clear, moreover, that *Matsushita*, *Anderson* and *Catrett* will be of growing significance as their teachings are applied by the federal courts across the wide spectrum of substantive legal areas.

Counsel must therefore be prepared to adjust their litigation strategy accordingly; no longer can they blithely assume that summary judgment will not be a significant obstacle to the right to a jury trial.[26]

Mr. Stewart practices with the New York law firm of Donovan Leisure Newton & Irvine.

(1) Fed. R. Civ. P. 1.
(2) See, e.g., Clark, Code Pleading Sec. 88 (2d ed. 1947); Washington Post Co. v. Keogh, 365 F.2d 965, 968 (D.C. Cir.), cert. denied, 385 U.S. 1011 (1966); Louis, Federal Summary Judgment Doctrine: A Critical Analysis, 83 Yale L.J. 745 (1974); Schwarzer, Summary Judgment Under the Federal Rules: Defining Genuine Issues of Material Fact, 99 F.R.D. 465 (1984).
(3) 368 U.S. 464 (1962).
(4) 368 U.S. at 473.
(5) 391 U.S. 253, 290 (1968) (summary judgment proper, even in seemingly complex antitrust cases, "in the absence of any significant probative evidence" tending to support claims asserted in a complaint).
(6) Hand v. Central Transport Inc., 779 F.2d 8, 10 (6th Cir. 1985). Notwithstanding that policy, on rare occasion a district court in the 6th Circuit has granted summary judgment in a complex case. E.g., Pinney Dock & Transport Co. v. Penn Central Corp., 1982-83 Trade Cas. (CCH) para 65,054 (N.D. Ohio 1982), appeal pending, 86-3226 (6th Cir 1986).
(7) 106 S. Ct. 1348 (1986).
(8) 106 S. Ct. 2505 (1986).
(9) 106 S. Ct. 2548 (1986).
(10) 106 S. Ct. at 1356 (emphasis in original) (quoting Fed. R. Civ. P. 56(e)).
(11) 106 S. Ct. at 2510.
(12) Id. at 2511. The governing law in Anderson was the actual malice standard (and the quality and quantum of proof required to meet that standard) under the New York Times doctrine. New York Times Co. v. Sullivan, 376 U.S. 254 (1964).
(13) Id. at 2512, citing Improvemment Co. v. Munson, 14 Wall. 442, 448 (1872) (emphasis original).
(14) 106 S. Ct. at 2553.
(15) Id. at 2552-53.
(16) 106 S. Ct. at 1514.
(17) 82 Civ. 1796 (S.D.N.Y. Aug. 8, 1986).
(18) Id., slip op. at 20.
(19) Id., slip op. at 27.
(20) 84 Civ. 7878 (S.D.N.Y., Aug. 4, 1986).
(21) Id., slip op. at 11.
(22) Id., slip op. at 13.
(23) 80 Civ. 9404 (S.D.N.Y. Aug. 25, 1986).
(24) Id., slip op. at 32.
(25) Indeed, shortly before the three decisions the 2d Circuit Judicial Conference released a report that was directed "to dispel the prevalent misconception that summary judgments are disfavored in this Circuit" and to "encourage more frequent disposition of cases by summary judgment." 2d Circuit Committee on the Pretrial Phase of Civil Litigation 5, 17-18 (June 11, 1984); accord Knight v. U.S. Fire Insurance Co., 86-739, slip. op. (2d Cir. Oct. 23, 1986) (Feinberg, C.J.) (affirming grant of summary judgment, while urging that litigants not be deterred from submitting "justifiable" Rule 56 motions); see also Argus Inc. v. Eastman Kodak Co., 1986-2 Trade Cas. (CCH) para. 67,324 (2d Cir. 1986), aff'g 612 F. Supp. 904 (S.D.N.Y. 1985) (applying Matsushita in complex antitrust case). These decisions and pronouncements represent a 180-degree shift from the 2d Circuit's prior view of summary judgment. See Heyman v. Commerce and Industry Insurance Co., 524 F.2d 1317, 1320 (2d Cir. 1975).
(26) Of course the flip side is also true. Under the new standards, if a plaintiff can defeat a defendant's Rule 56 motion before trial it would be most unusual for him not to defeat a Rule 50(a) motion at the conclusion of his case, and thereby reach the jury.

New York La

SERVING THE BENCH AND BAR

.UME 196.—NO. 121

NEW YORK, WEDNESDAY, DE(

Seconu Circuit Review

By Martin Flumenbaum

3 Rulings On Summary Judgment

Last term, the U.S. Supreme Court handed down three decisions revitalizing the summary judgment process under Rule 56 of the Federal Rules of Civil Procedure. Although relatively unheralded at the time, these decisions already have had a profound effect on litigation in the Second Circuit. This month's column will discuss these Supreme Court cases and also will review a number of recent summary judgment rulings by the Court of Appeals for the Second Circuit, which has explicitly encouraged litigants to make greater use of the summary judgment procedure.

•

Rule 56

Rule 56 of the Federal Rules of Civil Procedure provides that a motion for summary judgment shall be granted where the "pleadings, depositions,

Continued on page 2, column 1

Court to Weigh Beekman Place Rezoning Plan

It's usually the other way around: neighbors enthusiastically supporting a rezoning proposal that prohibits "overconstruction" by reducing the density ratio for new buildings in an effort to maintain the neighborhood's residential characteristics.

But in an era when there appears to be no limit on prices paid for prime Manhattan real estate, some owners of Beekman Place cooperative apartments apparently have joined the "looking out for No. 1" club. This occurred when they sued in State Supreme Court for a declaratory judgment to void the Board of Estimate's approval of a zoning resolution that significantly discourages developers from purchasing their building and the adjacent air rights to make way for a new and larger building.

The decision is on page 11, column 1.

The cooperative apartment owners succeeded temporarily when Justice Wallace R. Cotton ruled, in *1 Beekman Place Inc. v. City of New York*, that more information was required before he could resolve the conflicting claims by the residents and the City over whether the rezoning was valid.

Underlying the action is the claim that the proposal is discriminatory because it applies only to 1 Beekman Place, a sixteen-story, forty-unit cooperative, and the air rights over its adjacent one-story garage, not to two larger buildings on the block, 2 Beekman Place and 10 Mitchell Place.

Beekman Place is a two-block stretch between Forty-ninth and Fifty-first Streets overlooking the FDR Drive and the East River. The rezon-

Award Cut in Shareholder's A(

Federal Judge De Defendant Agreed

By Alan Kohn

A federal judge has awarded counsel in a shareholder's derivative action a fee of $59,699.50 even though the defendant, in settling the claims, had agreed to pay $100,000.

In limiting the fee award to hours worked times hourly rates for non-contingent cases, Judge William C. Conner cited the "slight" benefit achieved in the suit, which challenged the advisory fee for the manager of a mutual fund.

The judge pointed out that the "only concession" the plaintiff had obtained was a "slight and gradual scaling down" of the manager's advisory fee if the fund's net assets rose.

Claim Against Adviser

The judge's decision in *Weissman v. Alliance Capital Management Corporation*, 84-8904, Dec. 19, involved a claim by a shareholder of Alliance Capital Reserves, a money-market mutual fund, against its investment adviser, Alliance Capital Management Corporation.

The judge's thirteen-page opinion on the fee request by plaintiff Susan J. Weissman's law firm, Milberg Weiss Bershad Specthrie & Lerach, was handed down in the U.S. District Court for the Southern District of New York.

At issı tween th set an a cent of r ment p payment settleme Conner down th reached percent lion of a further

The a adviser counsel of $7,500 fees was $7,500, e expense:

Judge ment on counsel which, hours of of paral customa hourly t

In den raising t

Conti

Co-Op Sponsor De To Acquire Inside

By Martin Fox

Finance.
Nelson Seitel—Secretary.
James J. Hurd—Production Manager.

Published daily except Saturdays, Sundays and legal holidays.

SUBSCRIPTION RATES

One year (in advance)	$290.00
Six months (in advance)	$175.00
Three months (in advance)	$110.00
One month (in advance)	$38.00

The New York Law Journal (ISSN 0028-7326) (USPS 383000) is published daily except Saturdays, Sundays and legal holidays by The New York Law Publishing Co., 111 Eighth Avenue, New York, N.Y. 10011. Second class postage paid at New York, N.Y. and additional mailing offices. POSTMASTER: Send address changes to The New York Law Journal, 111 Eighth Avenue, New York, N.Y. 10011. Available on microfilm and microfiche. Rates on request.

Telephone 212-741-8300
Bronx telephone 212-863-3400
Brooklyn telephone 718-522-7070
Queens telephone 718-658-5391
Nassau telephone 516-741-8737

MEMBER AUDIT BUREAU OF CIRCULATIONS

New York's Medical Malpractice Insurance Crises — A New Direction for Reform.

Published quarterly. Subscription: $15 annually, $5 per issue. Office: 140 West Sixty-second Street, NYC 10023.

Pace Law Review
Volume 6, Number 3

Articles

Must the American Criminal Justice System Be Impotent? By Ernest van den Haag.

Racketeer Influenced and Corrupt Organizations (RICO) — Securities and Commercial Fraud as Racketeering Crime After *Sedima*: What Is a "Pattern of Racketeering Activity"? By Barbara Black.

Notes & Comments

Who Gets the Signal? — Unauthorized Interception and § 605, Now § 705, of the Communications Act.

Behind Closed Doors: The Confidentiality of Psychotherapeutic Records in Medicaid Fraud Investigations.

Oregon v. Elstad: The Supreme Court Puts the Cat Back in the Bag.

Published four times a year. Subscription: $15 annually ($17 foreign), $4.00 an issue. Office: 78 North Broadway, White Plains, NY 10603.

The Catholic Lawyer
Volume 30, Number 3

Articles

Confidentiality of Ecclesiastical Records. By Rev. Edward Dillon.

Discovery and Use of Church Records by Civil Authorities. By David J. Young and Steven W. Tigges.

The Supreme Court and the Religion Clauses: 1982 and 1984 Terms. By Donald H.J. Herman.

Update on Tax Developments: Exempt Organizations. By Milton Cerny.

Property and Contracts in Church Law. By Rev. Jordan Hite.

The Work of the Court of Appeals for the Federal Circuit: An Unseen Influence. By Howard T. Markey.

Bequests and Gifts to the Church Under the Code of Canon Law. By Rev. Daniel J. Ward.

Regional Meetings of Diocesan Attorneys. By Joseph J. Brandlin and James A. Serritella.

Business Meeting & Report of the General Counsel. By Wilfred R. Caron.

Published quarterly. Subscription: $5 annual, $1.50 per copy. Office: Fromkes Hall, Grand Central & Utopia Parkways, Jamaica, NY 11439.

departed active com
appellate wars ever
the applicant, to eac
members of the Bench
they had separately le
dence: that now retire
ment Clerk Joseph
genuinely interested i
Chief Clerk of the Co
before now Chief A
Judge Joseph Bellaco
fully vied for that p
three years ago.

They each separat
than traveled togethe
courthouse for anothe
entered the Clerk's of
none other than the as

Second Circuit Review

Continued from page 1, column 1

answers to interrogatories, and admissions on file, together with the affidavits, if any, show that there is no *genuine* issue as to any *material* fact and that the moving party is entitled to a judgment as a matter of law."

Rule 56 was designed to protect the federal judiciary from vexatious litigation and to promote the expeditious resolution of disputes. In practice, however, Rule 56 has failed to satisfy these twin objectives. As stated by U.S. District Judge William W. Shwarzer (N.D. Calif.):

"Summary judgment is plagued by confusion and uncertainty. It suffers from misuse by those lawyers who insist on making a motion in the face of obvious fact issues; from neglect by others who, fearful of judicial hostility to the procedure, refrain from moving even where summary judgment would be appropriate; and from the failure of trial and appellate courts to define clearly what is a genuine issue of material fact."

•

Summary Judgment in the Supreme Court.

Last term, the Supreme Court handed down three decisions which reversed lower-court rulings that had denied motions for summary judgment. In the process, the Court removed all doubts as to the perceived judicial hostility to the summary judgment procedure and indicated that summary judgment should be utilized even in complex litigation.

Matsushita v. Zenith.

In *Matsushita Electric Industry Co., Ltd. v. Zenith Radio Corp.*, the Supreme Court, in an opinion written by Justice Powell, reversed the Third Circuit's denial of a motion for summary judgment in a remarkably complex antitrust suit.

In *Matsushita*, the petitioners were twenty-one Japanese corporations that manufactured and/or sold consumer electronic products (principally, television sets). The respondents were American corporations that manufactured and/or sold television sets. In 1974, respondents brought an action in the U.S. District Court for the Eastern District of Pennsylvania alleging that, over a twenty-year period, petitioners had conspired illegally to drive American firms from the American television market by engaging in a scheme to fix and maintain artificially high prices for television sets sold by petitioners in Japan and, at the same time, to fix and maintain low prices for television sets exported to and sold in the United States.

After four years of extensive discovery, petitioners filed motions for summary judgment on all claims brought against them. The district court found that the admissible evidence did not raise a genuine issue of material fact as to the existence of the alleged conspiracy. The Third Circuit reversed, concluding that a reasonable factfinder could find a conspiracy to depress prices in the American market designed to drive out American competitors. According to the Third Circuit, a reasonable factfinder could also find that such a conspiracy was funded by excess profits obtained in the Japanese market.

The Supreme Court granted *certiorari* to determine whether the Third Circuit applied the proper standard in reviewing the district court's decision to grant petitioners' motion for a summary judgment. The Court held that it did not and reversed.

'Genuine-Fact Issue' Required

"To survive petitioners' motion for summary judgment," noted Justice Powell, "respondents must establish that there is a genuine issue of material fact as to whether petitioners entered into an illegal conspiracy that caused respondents to suffer a cognizable injury." To establish that an issue of fact is "genuine," respondents must "do more than simply show that there is some metaphysical doubt as to the material facts." Respondents must, as the language of Rule 56 provides, come forward with "specific facts showing that there is a genuine issue for trial." If the factual context renders respondents' claim economically implausible, then respondents must "come forward with more persuasive evidence to support their claim than would otherwise be necessary."

After describing the nature of the alleged conspiracy and detailing the practical — and substantial — obstacles to its implementation, the Court concluded that petitioners had no rational economic motive to conspire and that the alleged predatory pricing scheme makes no practical sense. The Court then delved into economic theory: pedatory pricing schemes require conspirators to suffer substantial losses in order eventually to realize illegal gains. The gains depend on a host of economic uncertainties, making such schemes more likely to fail than to succeed. In this case, observed Justice Powell, the alleged scheme calls for petitioners to "destroy companies far larger and better established than themselves" and offers no explanation as to how "they could recover the losses they would need to sustain along the way."

Economic Theory Applied

By piercing the pleadings and applying prevailing economic theory, the Court concluded that the extensive evidence submitted by respondents to support their allegations of anticompetitive conduct was insufficient to create a genuine issue of material fact and remanded the case to the Third Circuit for further proceedings consistent with its opinion.

Justice White (joined by Justices Blackmun, Brennan and Stevens) dissented on the grounds that the majority decision relies on assumptions that invade the factfinder's province and muddies the standards for considering motions for summary judgment. Justice White also urged that the majority decision, by instructing the district judge to consider the relative plausibility of the parties' positions, undermines the doctrine that courts deciding motions for summary judgment must view the evidence in the light most favorable to the nonmoving party.

Anderson v. Liberty Lobby.

In *Anderson v. Liberty Lobby, Inc.*, the Supreme Court, in an opinion written by Justice White, ruled that the standard for granting summary judgment "mirrors the standard for a directed verdict under Federal Rule of Civil Procedure 50(a)" and that "the substantive law identifies which facts are material."

Liberty Lobby, Inc., a nonprofit corporation, filed a libel action in the U.S. District Court for the District of Columbia alleging that certain statements in a series of articles written by Charles Bermant and published by defendant Jack Anderson were published with actual malice. To satisfy the requirements of *New York Times v. Sullivan*, Liberty Lobby had the burden of proving with "convincing clarity" that the defendant published the articles with knowledge that the defamatory statements were false or with reckless disregard of whether or not they were false.

Following discovery, Anderson moved for summary judgment, asserting that, as a matter of law, actual malice was absent in view of an affidavit by Bermant stating that the articles in question had been thoroughly researched and the facts therein had been obtained from a wide variety of trustworthy sources. Opposing the motion, Liberty Lobby claimed that an issue of actual malice was presented since several of the sources relied on were patently unreliable and Anderson had failed adequately to verify the information prior to publication.

Convincing-Clarity Standard

The district court applied the substantive "convincing clarity" standard to its analysis of the record and granted Anderson's motion for summary judgment. The Court of Appeals for the District of Columbia Circuit reversed as to nine of the allegedly defamatory statements. The Court, in an opinion written by Judge (now Supreme Court Justice) Antonin Scalia, held that, for purposes of summary judgment, actual malice need only be proved by a preponderance of the evidence — rather than by clear and convincing evidence. The Court of Appeals concluded that summary judgment had been improperly granted because a jury could reasonably find that certain of the statements at issue were published with actual malice.

The Supreme Court granted *certiorari* to consider whether the Court of Appeals erred in holding that the heightened evidentiary requirements that apply to proof of actual malice may be dispensed with for purposes of considering a motion for summary judgment. The Supreme Court began its discussion by noting that the standard for granting summary judgment mirrors the standard for directing a verdict — that is "whether the evidence presents a sufficient disagreement to require submission to a jury or whether it is so one-sided that one party must prevail as a matter of law."

Justice White then addressed the pivotal question presented by this appeal. "We are convinced that the inquiry involved in ruling on a motion for summary judgment or for a directed verdict necessarily implicates the substantive evidentiary standard of proof that would apply at the trial on the merits." In other words, if a defendant in a civil case moves for summary judgment based on the lack of proof of a material fact, the judge must ask whether a fair-minded jury could return a verdict for the plaintiff based on the evidence presented. The mere existence of a scintilla of evidence in support of the plaintiff's position would be insufficient; there must be evidence on which the jury could reasonably find for the plaintiff.

Quantum, Quality of Proof

Applying these principles to the facts of *Liberty Lobby*, the Court noted that the "convincing clarity" standard should be applied in ruling on Anderson's motion for summary judgment. "When determining if a genuine factual issue as to actual malice exists in a libel suit brought by a public figure, a trial judge must bear in mind the actual quantum and quality of proof necessary to support liability under *New York Times*." According to Justice White, "the judge must view the evidence presented through the prism of the substantive evidentiary burden."

Accordingly, where the factual dispute concerns actual malice, the trial judge must determine whether the evidence in the record could support a reasonable jury finding either that the plaintiff has shown actual malice by clear and convincing evidence or that the plaintiff has not. Because the Court of Appeals did not apply the correct standard in reviewing the district court's grant of summary judgment, the Supreme Court vacated its decision and remanded for further proceedings consistent with its opinion.

Justices Brennan and Rehnquist dissented in separate opinions on the ground that a trial judge's application of the substantive standard of proof in deciding summary judgment motions involves weighing the evidence and will, by necessity, invade the province of the jury by depriving it of the opportunity to assess the credibility of witnesses or to draw inferences from documentary evidence.

Celotex v. Catrett.

In *Celotex Corp. v. Catrett*, the Supreme Court, in an opinion written by Justice (now Chief Justice) Rehnquist, addressed the burden of production of evidence placed on moving and non-moving parties by Rule 56.

In September, 1980, administratrix Catrett filed a wrongful-death action against Celotex Corp. (Celotex) in the U.S. District Court for the District of Columbia, alleging that her husband's death resulted from exposure to asbestos products manufactured by Celotex. In September, 1981, Celotex filed a motion for summary

Continued on page 3, column 1

On Puniti

To the Editor:

Mr. Hogan's letter
(Dec. 10) accuses r
punitive damages (D
ing from false premis
to "false conclusion
what he claims "has
strong deterrent to th
and sale of unsafe
rhetoric appears to fit
For example, how,
whom has his claim
terrent" actually bee

The writer creat
premises and conclus
sarily consistent with
For example, on th
claims that without
ages "the costs of wil
conduct would be m
then cites statistic
show the relatively n
of punitive awards
volved in only a tin
tort cases. He cann
ways.

Similarly, Mr. Ho
with the fear of pu
"products will be sa
the toll of . . . [inju
will be reduced." Y
age doctrine has
around for quite a
writer's alleged "
theory really held t
now exist in a relat
free environment —
obviously will not

The writer uses
average payments
ucts injury claima
"such small levels
that adequate com
terrence of miscor
vided. Yet such av
torts the actual f
says in *How to Li*
28 (W.W. Norton &
trick commonly u
wishing to influen
sell advertising s
simply, assume
five students. Fou
one is aged sixty.
of each student
does not accurat
dent nor does it e
tent "ballpark" d
So, too, with Mr. H
real impact of
settlements occu
levels at a frequ
to trial lawyers
personnel to obs

The second h
polemic against
forms, appears t
sonal view of
down to the err
"only a few sta
characterizes
damages as an
to do reform's
judge-made co
punitive dam
appropriate m
change. Well b
United States
served that p
"windfall reco
is "unpredicta
stantial." *Elec*
442 U.S. 42, 50

Nothing offe
ter "proves"
jected by the
contexts and
injury claims,
is certainly e
belief but not
or "proof."

Aides said Governor Cuomo revealed his plans during a meeting Monday night of the Legislature's four leaders, who were trying to reach an agreement on funding the Metropolitan Transportation Authority.

Cuomo's proposed commission, "so nothing's changed."

At the same time, though, aides to the Governor said it has not been determined whether the commission Mr. Cuomo has in mind would have to seek funds from the Legislature.

corruption would have the opposite result. Anyone with the most superficial experience knows that all these different agencies and officials working in the same general area with similar objectives would get in each other's way and hinder, rather than aid, the ultimate objective. As it is there have already been some difficulties in this regard and adding another commission would inexorably lead to similar difficulties.

Seabury Investigation

It has been suggested that the proposed commission is needed, as was the Joint Legislative Investigation Committee with Samuel Seabury as counsel in the early 1930's and the Knapp Commission in 1970. But the analogy is false. When the Seabury investigation was proceeding there were no other agencies in the State or City which were engaged in investigating corruption. As a matter of fact, in those days the state district attorneys did nothing to cooperate with Judge Seabury's investigation. (They even went to the extent of in-

has been suggested in order to accomplish its objective.

While I have negative views about the value of such a commission, I certainly respect the views of the distinguished panel for making the proposal and the views of some of the media which have given support for the recommendation. Should the Governor decide to implement the recommendation, I trust he will appoint commission members alert to the civil-liberties requirements to avoid leaks to the press, which all too frequently tarnish the reputation of innocent persons.

Victor J. Herwitz, a Manhattan attorney, has had the following experience as an investigator and prosecutor: 1931-1932 — law clerk investigator on the staff of Samuel Seabury in the Joint Legislative investigation of the affairs of the City of New York; 1935-1942 — Assistant District Attorney, New York County, under Thomas E. Dewey assigned to the investigation of labor racketeering and official corruption including the investigation of Federal District Court Judge Martin T. Manton; 1951-1955 — Assistant Corporation Counsel of the City of New York; Chief of the Division of General Litigation and Special Counsel to the New York City Police Department in the departmental prosecution of over seventy-five members of the Police Department involved in the Harry Gross gambling conspiracy.

Second Circuit Review

Continued from page 2, column 4

judgment, asserting that Catrett had failed during discovery to produce any evidence to support her allegation that the decedent had been exposed to products manufactured by Celotex. In response, Catrett produced documents allegedly demonstrating the existence of a genuine issue of material fact as to whether the decedent had ever been exposed to Celotex asbestos products. Celotex urged that these documents were inadmissible hearsay and could not be considered in opposition to its summary judgment motion.

In July, 1982 the district court granted Celotex's motion for summary judgment, ruling that Catrett failed to establish that the decedent had been exposed to Celotex asbestos products. The Court of Appeals for the District of Columbia Circuit reversed, finding that Celotex's motion for summary judgment was "fatally defective" by virtue of the fact that Celotex "made no effort to adduce any evidence, in the form of affidavits or otherwise, to support its motion."[a] According to the Court of Appeals, the party opposing a motion for summary judgment bears the burden of responding only after the moving party has met its burden of coming forward with proof of the absence of any genuine issues of material fact — i.e., affirmative proof tending to negate exposure.

Supreme Court Disagrees

The Supreme Court disagreed. According to Justice Rehnquist, "we find no express or implied requirement in Rule 56 that the moving party support its motion with affidavits or other similar materials negating the opponent's claim."[a] Indeed, Rules 56(a) and (b) expressly provide that parties may move for summary judgment "with or without supporting affidavits."

In cases where the non-moving party bears the burden of proof at trial on a dispositive issue, a party may move for summary judgment relying solely on the "pleadings, depositions, answers to interrogatories, and admissions on file." The non-moving party thus would be required under Rule 56(e) to go beyond the pleadings and designate — through affidavits, depositions, answers to interrogatories or admissions on file — specific facts showing that there is a genuine issue for trial.

The Supreme Court concluded its opinion with a ringing endorsement of the summary judgment procedure: "The Federal Rules of Civil Procedure have for more than fifty years authorized motions for summary judgment upon proper showings of the lack of a genuine, triable issue of material fact. Summary judgment procedure is properly regarded not as a disfavored procedural shortcut, but rather as an integral part of the Federal Rules as a whole, which are designed to secure the just, speedy and inexpensive determination of every action .... Rule 56 must be construed with due regard not only for the rights of persons asserting claims and defenses that are adequately based in fact to have those claims and defenses tried to a jury, but also for the rights of persons opposing such claims and defenses to demonstrate in the manner provided by the Rule, prior to trial, that the claims and defenses have no factual basis."[a]

•

Summary Judgment in the Second Circuit.

As a result of the Supreme Court's revitalization of Rule 56, the Second Circuit Court of Appeals has also encouraged the expanded use of the summary judgment procedure. In recent months, the Second Circuit has upheld grants of summary judgment in libel actions, in cases brought under Title VII of the Civil Rights Act of 1964" and in cases brought under the Clayton and Sherman Antitrust Acts." The Second Circuit has also taken the extraordinary step of encouraging litigants to make greater use of the summary judgment procedure.

Meiri v. Dacon.

In *Meiri v. Dacon*," the Second Circuit, in an opinion written by Judge Irving R. Kaufman, upheld the district court's grant of summary judgment in favor of the Immigration and Naturalization Service (INS) and against Miriam Meiri, who alleged she was discharged from her clerk-stenographer position at the INS because of her religion.

The Second Circuit said it believed summary jdugment was appropriate in this case despite the welter of state of mind/intent issues that characterize discrimination suits brought under Title VII. According to Judge Kaufman, "The summary judgment rule would be rendered sterile if the mere incantation of intent or state of mind would operate as a talisman to defeat an otherwise valid motion. Indeed, the salutary purposes of summary judgment — avoiding protracted, expensive and harassing trials — apply no less to discrimination cases than to commercial or other areas of litigation."[a]

The Court added, "To allow a party to defeat a motion for summary judgment by offering purely conclusory allegations of discrimination, absent any concrete particulars, would necessitate a trial in all Title VII cases. Given the ease with which these suits may be brought and the energy and expense required to defend such actions, we believe the trial judge properly granted summary judgment."[a]

Guccione v. Hustler Magazine.

In *Guccione v. Hustler Magazine, Inc.*," the Second Circuit, in an opinion written by Judge Jon O. Newman, reversed a judgment of the district court awarding Robert Guccione, the publisher of *Penthouse* magazine, $1 in nominal damages and $1.6 million in punitive damages for an allegedly libelous statement appearing in *Hustler* magazine.

Based on the substantial truth of the alleged libelous statement and Guccione's "libel-proof" status as to adultery at the time the article appeared, the Second Circuit granted summary judgment in favor of *Hustler* magazine. In so ruling, the Court cited *Liberty Lobby* and demonstrated its willingness to dispose of libel claims brought by public figure plaintiffs on summary judgment.

Argus v. Eastman Kodak.

In *Argus Inc. v. Eastman Kodak Co.*," the Second Circuit, in an opinion written by Judge Ralph K. Winter, relied on *Matsushita* to uphold the district court's grant of summary judgment in a case where plaintiffs could not prove a causal nexus between their alleged economic injury and defendant's alleged anticompetitive activity.

Argus, a licensor of the trademark "Argus" for use on camera equipment, and Interphoto Corporation (Interphoto), a wholesale distributor of cameras and camera equipment, sued Eastman Kodak Corporation (Kodak) in the U.S. District Court for the Southern District of New York in August, 1979. The complaint alleged that Kodak's secret development between 1972 and 1975 of the "flipflash" device and compatible Kodak cameras prevented Interphoto from offering a flipflash camera as a "lead line" until after the 1975 Christmas selling season. As a result, Interphoto allegedly sustained a significant decline in sales of its entire range of products and in 1980 was forced into liquidation. Argus claimed that the damage to Interphoto's sales of Ar-

Continued on page 7, column 1

Rezoning Proposal

Continued from page 1, column 2

mental nature" of the area concerning whether, as the plaintiffs contended, "high-rise construction predominates," or if rezoning from an R10 district to a lower-density R8-B designation "can reasonably be related to the end sought to be achieved, maintaining the character and scale of the neighborhood."

• Whether the rezoning conflicted with existing waterfront development policy which the complaint maintains "permits high-density development." Moreover, both sides offered "a distinctly different view" of waterfront development policy.

• Is 1 Beekman Place "better situated in terms of access of light, air" and a public park than 2 Beekman Place and 10 Mitchell Place? If so, then a basis might exist for the claim of denial of equal protection to prohibit redevelopment of the plaintiffs' site while excluding the two neighboring structures.

• Did the rezoning reflect the City's "implementation of contextual zoning in Manhattan and, as such, was in accordance with a comprehensive plan to promote the general welfare"?

Triable Issues

Justice Cotton decided the best approach at this stage of the litigation was to deny a declaratory judgment to either side because of the number of triable issues that exist.

He applied the same rationale to the plaintiffs' assertion that the rezoning was "arbitrary ... discriminatory and violates the doctrine of Equal Protection."

"What the conditions are at these three properties and how they related to valid zoning considerations cannot be adequately determined on the papers," the court concluded. "Thus, the parties should have an opportunity to fully present the matter ... Moreover, the issues of fact ... as to arbitrariness, contextual zoning and waterfront policy all have implications on whether this rezoning as applied to 1 Beekman Place was a denial of equal protection."

AAA Reports 24% Increase In Commercial Arbitrations

A 24 percent increase in filings of commercial cases for the year ended Oct. 31 has been reported by the American Arbitration Association. During the period, 10,248 cases were filed for arbitration before the AAA, Robert E. Meade, its vice president of program development, reported.

The total dollar amount of commercial claims and counterclaims for the first ten months of calendar 1988 was $1.5 billion, he stated, with the average amount of a claim being $150,000. The AAA administers arbitrations in fifty-seven commercial categories, Mr. Meade noted. Construction, computer and franchising disputes are among the most active categories, he stated.

NEW YORK LAW JOURNAL—

Second Circuit Review

Continued from page 3, column 2

gus-brand photo equipment deprived it of trademark royalties that it had expected to earn.

After canvassing the record, the Second Circuit concluded that "there is no genuine issue of fact with regard to whether the flipflash confidentiality agreement caused Interphoto's and Argus's commercial demise."[29] Based on evidence indicating that the present theories advanced by Interphoto and Argus are mere litigation afterthoughts and are inconsistent with uncontroverted contemporaneous documents, the fact that Interphoto and Argus were mired in financial straits at the time the flipflash announcement was made, and the fact that the introduction of the flipflash reduced — rather than increased — Kodak's share of the amateur still camera market, the Second Circuit, citing *Matsushita*, ruled that "Argus's and Interphoto's causality claims are thoroughly implausible and cannot survive a motion for summary judgment absent persuasive evidence rebutting the [foregoing] facts."[30] According to the Court, the testimony submitted by plaintiff's officers and employees was patently inadequate to create a genuine issue of fact in light of the volumes of evidence to the contrary. Accordingly, the Second Circuit affirmed the district court's grant of summary judgment.

Knight v. United States Fire Insurance Co.

In *Knight v. United States Fire Insurance Company*,[31] the Second Circuit, in an opinion written by Chief Judge Wilfred Feinberg, extolled the virtues of the summary judgment procedure and urged practitioners in the Second Circuit to make greater use of the procedure.

After quoting from the Supreme Court's opinion in *Celotex* and observing that the summary judgment procedure — where used properly — enables a court to streamline the process for terminating frivolous claims and to concentrate its resources on meritorious litigation, Chief Judge Feinberg stated, "It appears that in this circuit some litigants are reluctant to make full use of the summary judgment process because of their perception that this court is unsympathetic to such motions and frequently reverses grants of summary judgment. Whatever may have been the accuracy of this view in years gone by, it is decidedly inaccurate at the present time …"[32]

In so concluding, Judge Feinberg relied upon a recent study by the Second Circuit Committee on the Pretrial Phase of Civil Litigation, headed by Professor Maurice Rosenberg, which analyzed the published and unpublished decisions of the Second Circuit for the period from July 1, 1983 to June 30, 1985 and found that the affirmance rate on appeals from orders granting summary judgment was 79 percent. Judge Feinberg thus observed "that grants of summary judgment are upheld on appeal in most cases. [The 79 percent] figure is comparable to this circuit's 84 percent affirmance rate for appeals in civil cases generally. The widespread misperception regarding the disposition of appeals of summary judgment may be due to the fact that reversals are much more likely to be reported in published opinions than affirmances, which frequently are disposed of by unpublished orders under our Local Rule §0.23. We hope that the Committee's study dispels the misperception so that litigants will not be deterred from making justifiable motions for summary judgment."[33]

•

Summary Judgment in the District Courts.

The impact of the recent summary judgment rulings has been quite pronounced in the district courts within the Second Circuit.

During the past five months, there have been twenty-nine district court decisions granting summary judgment and citing *Matsushita*, *Liberty Lobby* and *Celotex*.[34] Significantly, these decisions involve a host of substantive areas in which courts traditionally (pre-*Matsushita*, *Liberty Lobby*, *Celotex*) declined to grant the burden to plaintiff under Fed. R. Civ. P. 56(e). Thus, to survive defendants' motion for summary judgment, Apex must establish that there is a genuine issue of material fact as to whether defendants entered into a conspiracy. To make such a showing, Apex must offer significant probative evidence which tends to exclude the possibility the alleged conspirators acted independently."[26]

This decision underscores the intersection between the obligation of district judges to evaluate evidence under the standards of *Matsushita* and the practical effect of the burden-shifting authorized by *Celotex*. The net result is — and will continue to be — an increased willingness on the part of courts in the Second Circuit to grant motions for summary judgment.

•

Brad S. Karp, an associate at Paul, Weiss, Rifkind, Wharton & Garrison, assisted in the preparation of this column.

---

(1) Fed. R. Civ. P. 56(c) (emphasis added).
(2) Schwarzer, "Summary Judgment under the Federal Rules," 99 F.R.D. 465 (1984).
(3) *Matsushita Electric Industry Co., Ltd. v. Zenith Radio Corp.*, 106 S.Ct. 1348 (1986).
(4) The opinion of the district court filled 217 printed pages; the opinion for the Third Circuit, 69 pages. In addition, the parties filed in the Supreme Court a forty-volume appendix containing the evidence relied on by the district court and the court of appeals. Not surprisingly, the Supreme Court observed at the outset of its opinion: "Stating the facts of this case is a daunting task." 106 S.Ct. at 1351.
(5) *Id.* at 1355-56.
(6) *Id.* at 1356.
(7) *Id.*
(8) *Id.* at 1362.
(9) Last week, the Third Circuit affirmed the district court's grant of summary judgment against all defendants. *In re Japanese Electronic Products Antitrust Litigation*, Nos. 80-2080, 81-2331, 81-2332, 81-2333, Slip op. (3d Cir. Dec. 12, 1986).
(10) *Anderson v. Liberty Lobby, Inc.*, 106 S.Ct. 2505 (1986).
(11) *Id.* at 2511.
(12) *Id.* at 2510.
(13) *New York Times v. Sullivan*, 376 U.S. 254 (1964).
(14) *Anderson*, supra, 106 S.Ct. at 2512.
(15) *Id.*
(16) *Id.* at 2513.
(17) *Id.*
(18) *Celotex Corp. v. Catrett*, 106 S.Ct. 2548 (1986).
(19) *Catrett v. Celotex Corp.*, 756 F. 2d 181, 184 (D.C. Cir. 1985).
(20) *Celotex*, supra, 106 S.Ct. at 2553.
(21) *Id.* at 2555.
(22) 42 USC §1000e *et. seq.* (1982).
(23) 15 USC §1, 15(a) (1982).
(24) *Mriri v. Dacon*, 759 F. 2d 989 (2d Cir. 1985).
(25) *Id.* at 995.
(26) *Id.*
(27) *Guccione v. Hustler Magazine, Inc.*, 800 F. 2d 298 (2d Cir. 1986). This decision was discussed previously in this column on Sept. 24, 1986.
(28) *Argus Inc. v. Eastman Kodak Co.*, 801 F. 2d 38 (2d Cir. 1986).
(29) *Id.* at 42.
(30) *Id.* at 46.
(31) *Knight v. United States Fire Insurance Company*, No. 86-7294, slip op. (2d Cir. Oct. 22, 1986).
(32) *Id.* at 186-87.
(33) *Id.* at 186-87.
(34) *Baum v. Phillips, Appel & Walden, et al.*, No. 81 Civ. 5512 (PKL), Slip op. (SDNY Dec. 8, 1986) (federal securities law, RICO violations); *Board of Education v. CNA Insurance Co., et al.*, No. 85 Civ. 6830 (CLB), Slip op. (SDNY Nov. 19, 1986) (insurance law); *Slavenburg Corp. v. Cohen, et al.*, No. 86 Civ. 3476 (MGC), Slip op. (SDNY Nov. 20, 1986) (validity of personal guarantees on corporate debts); *Jensen v. Times-Mirror, et al.*, Civ. No. B-82-588 (PCD) Slip op. (D. Conn. Nov. 19, 1986) (libel law); *Aldon Industries, Inc. v. Brown, et al.*, No. 84 Civ. 2285 (PKL), Slip op. (SDNY Nov. 24, 1986) (contract law); *Margrave v. British Airways*, No. 83 Civ. 4070 (PKL), Slip op. (SDNY Sept. 12, 1986) (personal injury law); *United States v. Anthony, et al.*, No. 84 Civ. 7119 (PKL), Slip op. (SDNY Sept. 4, 1986) (mortgage law); *Spannaus, et al. v. Federal Election Commission*, No. 85 Civ. 0404 (LLS), 641 F. Supp. 1520 (SDNY 1986) (First Amendment law re campaign activities); *Carto, et al. v. Buckley, et al.*, No. 84 Civ. 1817 (RJW), Slip op. (SDNY Nov. 25, 1986) (libel law); *Bliss Wholesale Drug v. Eli Lilly and Co.*, No. 85 Civ. 4422, Slip op. (EDNY Dec. 1, 1986) (breach of contract); *Diamond v. Arend, et al.*, No. 84 Civ. 0731 (SWK), Slip op. (SDNY Nov. 25, 1986) (securities law violations, breach of fiduciary duty); *United States v. DeFilippo*, No. 85 Civ. 1623 (RWS), Slip op. (SDNY Nov. 12, 1986) (mortgage law); *Martin v. H.R.A.*, No. 83 Civ. 6278 (PKL), Slip op. (SDNY Nov. 10, 1986) (civil rights law, Title VII sex discrimination); *Gannett Co., Inc. et al. v. MCP, Inc., et al.*, No. 86 (contract law); *Cook v. Pan American World Airways, Inc., et al.*, No. 84 Civ. 1651 (RWS), Slip op. (SDNY Nov. 12, 1986) (Title VII age discrimination); *Daniel Foster v. Turner Broadcasting Inc.*, No. 85 Civ. 1974 (JFK), Slip op. (SDNY Oct. 22, 1986) (defamation); *Stanford v. Kuwait Airways Corp.*, No. 85 Civ. 477 (SWK), Slip op. (SDNY Oct. 21, 1986) (breach of contract); *Alfaro Motors, Inc. v. Ward*, No. 85 Civ. 1939 (JFK), Slip op. (SDNY Nov. 3, 1986) (civil rights law); *United States v. All Funds and Other Property Contained in Account Number 011-837368 in the Name of Rogelio Cespedes, et al.*, Nos. 83 Civ. 554, 965, 372, 373, 375, 5033 (RLC), Slip op. (SDNY Oct. 31, 1986) (civil forfeiture); *Landa v. Birchie Finger Print Laboratories, Inc.*, No. 85 Civ. 8033 (RWS), Slip op. (SDNY Oct. 17, 1986) (breach of contract); *Deere*

LIS PENDENS

NEW YORK COUNTY

December 18, 1986

Block 64; Lot 9; N.Y. State Chamber of Commerce and Industry, Inc., v. Wall Street Building, Ltd., The People of the State of N.Y., et al.; attorneys: Brill and Meisel, 532 Madison Ave., New York City 10022.

Block 867; Lot 62; Kamco Supply Corp. v. Evergreen Drywall Corp., et al.; attorneys: Pinks Brooks Stern and Arbeit, 1383-26 Veterans Memorial Highway, Hauppauge, N.Y. 11787.

Block 968; Lot 1213; The Dime Savings Bank of N.Y. v. Robert K. Marceca, Sr. and Robert K. Marceca, et al.; attorney: Billie C. Johnson, 1325 Franklin Ave., Suite 255, Garden City, N.Y. 11530.

December 19, 1986

Block 1330; Lot 7; TCF National Properties, Inc., v. Sped Associates, Jump Associates, et al.; attorneys: Debevoise & Plimpton, 875 Third Ave., New York, N.Y. 10022.

Block 1331, Lot 17; Same v. Same; Same attorneys.

Block 1445, Lot 7; Same v. Same; Same attorneys.

BRONX COUNTY

December 18, 1986

Block 2547, Lot 69; Dept. of Housing Preservation v. 1315 Merriam Avenue Corp., et al. (order to correct violations); attorney: Bruce Kramer, 125 Church St., N.Y.

Block 3211, Section 11, Lot 30; Capital Resources Corp. v. Sandra Fraser, et al.; attorney: James A. Kridel, Jr., 510 Broad Hollow Road, Melville, N.Y.

December 19, 1986

Block 2526, Section 9, Lot 83; Citi Equity Group, Inc., and Gary W. Lefkowitz v. Hugh Pike, et al. (judgment granting specific performance); attorneys: Fischer, Kagan, Ascione & Zaretsky, 10 East 40th St., N.Y.

Block 4033, Lot 1; Same v. Hugh Pike, et al. (impress a lien); Same attorney.

Block 3748, Section 14; The New York Guardian Mortgagee Corp. v. Juan Torres, et al.; attorneys: Deutsch & Schneider, 3450 Fulton, St., Brooklyn.

MECHANICS' LIENS

NEW YORK COUNTY

December 18, 1986

Block 1579; Lot 49; Arrow Restaurant, Inc., v. 300 East 83rd Sreet Corp., owner and contractor; $13,090.

Block 839, Lot 34; CMA Enterprises, Ltd., v. 37th Street Association Corp., owner; Time Equity, Inc., contractor; $715.

Block 1302, Lot 43; Micon Construction Development v. Townan Realty Corp., owner; Indo-U.S. Investment Corp., Ltd., contractor; $5,370.

Block 1302; Lot 43 and Block 899; Lot 1; Haff Enterprises, Inc., v. 205 Third Ave., Inc., owner; Same contractor; $492,310.

December 18, 1986

Block 1710; Lot 24; Fort Clea Roofing and General Construction, Inc., v. 455 East 116th Street Realty Corp., owner; Reymond Staggers, contractor; $1,845.

Block 1725; Lots 71 and 72; Same v. Same owner and Same contractor.

Block 1403, Lot 33; Korbl & Son Plumbing & Heating, Inc., v. Robert Rosen, owner; Bakit Industries, Inc., contractor; $4,000.

Block 1431, Lot 104; Bernard A. Marson v. 205 East 76th Associates, owner; New-Lux Association, contractor; $14,890.

BRONX COUNTY

December 19, 1986

Block 2763, Section 10, Lot 123; Mystic Transportation v. 1315 Lafayette Avenue Corp., owner and contractor; $614.

Ruling on Co-Op

Continued from page 1, column 4

the Filippons and handed over or assigned to Conversion Equities Inc.," he held. Moreover, the justice said, in correspondence between the parties, "no mention is made of a designee, but rather it is Conversion Equities that claims an interest in the apartment."

On a final point in deciding to dismiss the complaint, the claim of tortious interference with a contract was not established, the court explained, because there must be a showing the acts were "intentional" and "malicious." The sponsor was found to be entitled under the offering plan to make a "buy-out" offer to the Filippons because the same offer was made to all tenants.

The plaintiffs were represented by Jaspan, Ginsberg, Ehrlich, Reich & Levin of Garden City; the sponsor and other defendants by Stuart F. Gruskin of Fischbein Olivieri Rozenholc & Badillo.

[illegible] was patently inadequate to create a genuine issue of fact in light of the volumes of evidence to the contrary. Accordingly, the Second Circuit affirmed the district court's grant of summary judgment.

Knight v. United States Fire Insurance Co.

In *Knight v. United States Fire Insurance Company*,[31] the Second Circuit, in an opinion written by Chief Judge Wilfred Feinberg, extolled the virtues of the summary judgment procedure and urged practitioners in the Second Circuit to make greater use of the procedure.

After quoting from the Supreme Court's opinion in *Celotex* and observing that the summary judgment procedure — where used properly — enables a court to streamline the process for terminating frivolous claims and to concentrate its resources on meritorious litigation, Chief Judge Feinberg stated, "It appears that in this circuit some litigants are reluctant to make full use of the summary judgment process because of their perception that this court is unsympathetic to such motions and frequently reverses grants of summary judgment. Whatever may have been the accuracy of this view in years gone by, it is decidedly inaccurate at the present time ..."[32]

In so concluding, Judge Feinberg relied upon a recent study by the Second Circuit Committee on the Pretrial Phase of Civil Litigation, headed by Professor Maurice Rosenberg, which analyzed the published and unpublished decisions of the Second Circuit for the period from July 1, 1983 to June 30, 1985 and found that the affirmance rate on appeals from orders granting summary judgment was 79 percent. Judge Feinberg thus observed "that grants of summary judgment are upheld on appeal in most cases. [The 79 percent] figure is comparable to this circuit's 84 percent affirmance rate for appeals in civil cases generally. The widespread misperception regarding the disposition of appeals of summary judgment may be due to the fact that reversals are much more likely to be reported in published opinions than affirmances, which frequently are disposed of by unpublished orders under our Local Rule §0.23. We hope that the Committee's study dispels the misperception so that litigants will not be deterred from making justifiable motions for summary judgment."[33]

•

Summary Judgment in the District Courts.

The impact of the recent summary judgment rulings has been quite pronounced in the district courts within the Second Circuit.

During the past five months, there have been twenty-nine district court decisions granting summary judgment and citing *Matsushita*, *Liberty Lobby* and *Celotex*.[34] Significantly, these decisions involve a host of substantive areas in which courts traditionally (pre-*Matsushita*, *Liberty Lobby*, *Celotex*) declined to grant summary judgment. That no longer appears to be true. District judges, apparently comforted by the Supreme Court and Second Circuit's resuscitation of the summary judgment procedure, now appear willing — if not eager — to use that procedure to dispose of all varieties of complex civil actions.

For example, in *Apex Oil Co. v. DiMauro*, Judge John M. Walker, of the Southern District of New York, granted defendants' motion for summary judgment in a case involving, *inter alia*, claims of antitrust conspiracy and commodities manipulation. Citing *Matsushita* and *Celotex*, Judge Walker observed:

"In *Matsushita*, the Supreme Court made it clear that in an antitrust conspiracy case ambiguous evidence is to be treated skeptically on a motion for summary judgment, since an inference of unlawful conduct which arises only from ambiguous evidence will be of no use to the plaintiff at trial ... The test enunciated in *Matsushita* dictates that ambiguous evidence, because it is by definition incapable of a dominant inference, will not alone defeat a motion for summary judgment.

"In this case, defendants' sworn denials are more than sufficient to shift

Zenith Radio Corp., 106 S.Ct. 1348 (1986).

(4) The opinion of the district court filled 217 printed pages; the opinion for the Third Circuit, 69 pages. In addition, the parties filed in the Supreme Court a forty-volume appendix containing the evidence relied on by the district court and the court of appeals. Not surprisingly, the Supreme Court observed at the outset of its opinion: "Stating the facts of this case is a daunting task." 106 S.Ct. at 1358.

(5) *Id.* at 1355-56.

(6) *Id.* at 1356.

(7) *Id.*

(8) *Id.* at 1362.

(9) Last week, the Third Circuit affirmed the district court's grant of summary judgment against all defendants. *In re Japanese Electronic Products Antitrust Litigation*, Nos. 80-2080, 81-2331, 81-2332, 81-2333, Slip op. (3d Cir. Dec. 12, 1986).

(10) *Anderson v. Liberty Lobby, Inc.*, 106 S.Ct. 2505 (1986).

(11) *Id.* at 2511.

(12) *Id.* at 2510.

(13) *New York Times v. Sullivan*, 376 U.S. 254 (1964).

(14) *Anderson*, supra, 106 S.Ct. at 2512.

(15) *Id.*

(16) *Id.* at 2515.

(17) *Id.*

(18) *Celotex Corp. v. Catrett*, 106 S.Ct. 2548 (1986).

(19) *Catrett v. Celotex Corp.*, 756 F. 2d 181, 184 (D.C. Cir. 1985).

(20) *Celotex*, supra, 106 S.Ct. at 2553.

(21) *Id.* at 2555.

(22) 42 USC §1000e et. seq. (1982).

(23) 15 USC §1, 15(a) (1982).

(24) *Meiri v. Dacon*, 759 F. 2d 989 (2d Cir. 1985).

(25) *Id.* at 998.

(26) *Id.*

(27) *Guccione v. Hustler Magazine, Inc.*, 800 F. 2d 298 (2d Cir. 1986). This decision was discussed previously in this column on Sept. 24, 1986.

(28) *Argus Inc. v. Eastman Kodak Co.*, 801 F. 2d 38 (2d Cir. 1986).

(29) *Id.* at [illegible]

(30) *Id.* at 45.

(31) *Knight v. United States Fire Insurance Company*, No. 86-7296 slip op. (2d Cir. Oct. 22, 1986).

(32) Id. at 186-87.

(33) *Id.* at 186-87.

(34) *Baum v. Phillips, Appel & Walden, et al.*, No. 81 Civ. 5912 (PKL), Slip op. (SDNY Dec. 8, 1986) (federal securities law, RICO violations); *Board of Education v. CNA Insurance Co., et al.*, No. 85 Civ. 5239 (CLB), Slip op. (SDNY Nov. 19, 1986) (insurance law); *Slavenburg Corp. v. Cohen, et al.*, No. 86 Civ. 3470 (MGC), Slip op. (SDNY Nov. 20, 1986) (validity of personal guarantees on corporate debts); *Jensen v. Times-Mirror, et al.*, Civ. No. B-82-365 (PCD) Slip op. (D. Conn. Nov. 19, 1986) (libel law); *Aldon Industries, Inc. v. Brown, et al.*, No. 84 Civ. 2265 (PKL), Slip op. (SDNY Nov. 24, 1986) (contract law); *Margrave v. British Airways*, No. 85 Civ. 4070 (PKL), Slip op. (SDNY Sept. 12, 1986) (personal injury law); *United States v. Anthony, et al.*, No. 84 Civ. 7119 (PKL), Slip op. (SDNY Sept. 4, 1986) (mortgage law); *Spannaus, et al. v. Federal Election Commission*, No. 85 Civ. 0404 (LLS), 641 F. Supp. 1520 (SDNY 1986) (First Amendment law re campaign activities); *Carto, et al. v. Buckley, et al.*, No. 84 Civ. 1812 (RJW), Slip op. (SDNY Nov. 28, 1986) (libel law); *Bliss Wholesale Drug v. Eli Lilly and Co.*, No. 85 Civ. 4422, Slip op. (EDNY Dec. 3, 1986) (breach of contract); *Diamond v. Arend, et al.*, No. 84 Civ. 0781 (SWK), Slip op. (SDNY Nov. 28, 1986) (securities law violations, breach of fiduciary duty); *United States v. DeFilippo*, No. 85 Civ. 7023 (RWS), Slip op. (SDNY Nov. 12, 1986) (mortgage law); *Martin v. H.R.A.*, No. 85 Civ. 6278 (PKL), Slip op. (SDNY Nov. 10, 1986) (civil rights law, Title VII sex discrimination); *Gannett Co., Inc. et al. v. MCP, Inc., et al.*, No. 86 (contract law); *Cook v. Pan American World Airways, Inc., et al.*, No. 84 Civ. 1651 (RWS), Slip op. (SDNY Nov. 12, 1986) (Title VII age discrimination); *Daniel Foster v. Turner Broadcasting Inc.*, No. 85 Civ. 1914 (JFK), Slip op. (SDNY Oct. 22, 1986) (defamation); *Stanford v. Kuwait Airways Corp.*, No. 85 Civ. 477 (SWK), Slip op. (SDNY Oct. 21, 1986) (breach of contract); *Alfaro Motors, Inc. v. Ward*, No. 85 Civ. 1039 (JFK), Slip op. (SDNY Nov. 3, 1986) (civil rights law); *United States v. All Funds and Other Property Contained in Account Number 031-217368 in the Name of Rogelio Cespedes, et al.*, Nos. 85 Civ. 351, 352, 372, 373, 376, 3020 (RLC), Slip op. (SDNY Oct. 21, 1986) (civil forfeiture); *Landr v. Sirchie Finger Print Laboratories, Inc.*, No. 85 Civ. 4038 (RWS), Slip op. (SDNY Oct. 17, 1986) (breach of contract); *Desco Shoe Corp. v. Naturalizer of Pittsburgh, Inc.*, No. 84 Civ. 8085 (MGC), Slip op. (SDNY Oct. 9, 1986) (liability on promissory notes); *Arnell, et al. v. Pan American World Airways, Inc.*, No. 84 Civ. 385 (LLS), Slip op. (SDNY Oct. 7, 1986) (Title VII age discrimination); *Wing Hing (Tong) Fabrics Manufacturing Co., Ltd. v. Rafaella Sportswear*, No. 84 Civ. 9024 (JFK), Slip op. (SDNY Aug. 25, 1986) (breach of contract); *Adler v. Conde Nast Publications, Inc.*, 643 F. Supp. 1558 (SDNY 1986) (WK) (libel); *Boracci v. Malloy, et al.*, 643 F. Supp. 1013 (SDNY 1986) (JES) (civil rights law); *New York State Energy Research and Development Authority v. Nuclear Fuel Services, Inc.*, 640 F. Supp. 1555 (WDNY 1986) (Elfvin, J.) (breach of contract); *McGriff v. Coughlin*, 640 F. Supp. 877 (SDNY 1986) (PNL) (civil rights law); *Apex Oil Co. v. DiMauro*, 641 F. Supp. 1246 (SDNY 1986) (JMW) (antitrust, federal securities law violations); *Pocrill v. Nassau County Police Dept.*, 639 F. Supp. 1382 (EDNY 1986) (Wexler, J.) (civil rights law).

(35) *Apex Oil Co. v. DiMauro*, 641 F. Supp. 1246, 1257 (SDNY 1986) (JMW).

Martin Flumenbaum, a member of Paul, Weiss, Rifkind, Wharton & Garrison, specializes in civil and criminal litigation. He is a former Assistant U.S. Attorney for the Southern District of New York.

Daily columns on page 1 of the *Law Journal* give readers an opportunity to rely on experts to keep them abreast of developments in many areas of practice.

N.Y.

Block 3211, Section 11, Lot 30; Capital Resources Corp. v. Sandra Fraser, et al.; attorney: James A. Kridel, Jr., 510 Broad Hollow Road, Melville, N.Y.

December 19, 1986

Block 2526, Section 9, Lot 82; Citi Equity Group, Inc., and Gary W. Lefkowitz v. Hugh Pike, et al. (judgment granting specific performance); attorneys: Fischer, Kagan, Ascione & Zaretsky, 10 East 40th St., N.Y.

Block 4632, Lot 1; Same v. Hugh Pike, et al. (impress a lien); Same attorney.

Block 3748, Section 14; The New York Guardian Mortgagee Corp. v. Juan Torres, et al.; attorneys: Deutsch & Schneider, 3450 Fulton, St., Brooklyn.

MECHANICS' LIENS

NEW YORK COUNTY

December 18, 1986

Block 1578; Lot 48; Arrow Restaurant, Inc., v. 500 East 83rd Street Corp., owner and contractor; $13,090.

Block 839, Lot 34; CMA Enterprises, Ltd., v. 37th Street Association Corp., owner; Time Equity, Inc., contractor; $715.

Block 1302, Lot 43; Micon Construction Development v. Townan Realty Corp., owner; Indo-U.S. Investment Corp., Ltd., contractor; $5,370.

Block 1302; Lot 43 and Block 899; Lot 1; Half Enterprises, Inc., v. 205 Third Ave., Inc., owner; Same contractor; $492,310.

December 19, 1986

Block 1710; Lot 24; Fort Cica Roofing and General Construction, Inc., v. 455 East 116th Street Realty Corp., owner; Raymond Staggers, contractor; $1,648.

Block 1722; Lots 71 and 72; Same v. Same owner and Same contractor.

Block 1403, Lot 33; Korbl & Son Plumbing & Heating, Inc., v. Robert Rosen, owner; Bakit Industries, Inc., contractor; $4,000.

Block 1431, Lot 104; Bernard A. Marson v. 205 East 76th Associates, owner; New-Lux Association, contractor; $14,990.

BRONX COUNTY

December 19, 1986

Block 2763, Section 10, Lot 123; Mystic Transportation v. 1815 Lafayette Avenue Corp., owner and contractor; $814.

Ruling on Co-Op

Continued from page 1, column 4

the Filippons and handed over or assigned to Conversion Equities Inc.," he held. Moreover, the justice said, in correspondence between the parties, "no mention is made of a designee, but rather it is Conversion Equities that claims an interest in the apartment."

On a final point in deciding to dismiss the complaint, the claim of tortious interference with a contract was not established, the court explained, because there must be a showing the acts were "intentional" and "malicious." The sponsor was found to be entitled under the offering plan to make a "buy-out" offer to the Filippons because the same offer was made to all tenants.

The plaintiffs were represented by Jaspan, Ginsberg, Ehrlich, Reich & Levin of Garden City; the sponsor and other defendants by Stuart F. Gruskin of Fischbein Olivieri Rozenholc & Badillo.

Firm's Fee Reduced

Continued from page 1, column 4

pointed out the fund's assets had risen beyond the $1.25 billion breakdown for a reduction in the advisory fee but the savings will amount to $1,600 annually, against a $6.33 million annual advisory fee.

Even if the fund's assets should increase by 20 percent to $1.5 billion, the judge stated, the annual saving in fees would amount to "only" $25,000, as against an advisory fee of $7.5 million.

In exchange for the "trifling fee concession," Judge Conner commented, the plaintiff dropped her claims for past overcharges, that the composition of the fund's board of directors made the agreements unenforceable and gave the defendants future immunity from such claims.

The settlement, the judge commented, was a "remarkably cheap premium to pay for such insurance."

Ms. Weissman was represented on the fee application by Richard M. Meyer, of Milberg Weiss. Defense lawyers included Anthony R. Mansfield, of Seward & Kissel, and Otto G. Obermaier, of Obermaier, Morvillo & Abramowitz.

Miscellaneous Letters

F&E R&I *Franklin & Eleanor* ROOSEVELT INSTITUTE

711 Fifth Avenue, Suite 900
New York, New York 10022
Phone 212-339-2579 ▪ Fax 212-339-2657

William J. vanden Heuvel
Founder & Chair Emeritus

June 17, 2008

Mr. C. Evan Stewart
Zuckerman Spaeder LLP
1540 Broadway, Suite 1604
New York, NY 10036-4039

Dear Evan:

What a pleasure to have lunch with a fellow "historian." As Arthur Schlesinger once wrote, "History is to the nation what memory is to the individual…" It is so important that those who would lead us should have a sense of the history of the time and events that have made our country so great. Thank you also for sending me some representation of your work. I attended the second trial of Alger Hiss with Roger Baldwin, so it was most interesting to read your analysis and history of its long, painful process. Also fascinating was George Leisure's attitude – an attitude shared by many of his generation. I once lived in Garrison, New York – I believe Williams Evarts came from that area, or at least many of his direct descendents lived there – and as to the Schecter case, I am a great advocate of FDR's court reform plan as a means of saving the New Deal. Owen Roberts fateful change of opinion was the event that reflected once more how political the processes of the Supreme Court truly are. We need to look only at Gore vs. Bush in the year 2000 to see the political nature of the Court. I look forward to our further discussion of that crucial problem. Recently I had the opportunity to dine with Justices O'Connor and Breyer – a marvelous opportunity to review FDR's thinking and the subsequent history of the Court.

I look forward to your biography of Myron Taylor with great interest. The history of the law firm is an important story – and an interesting insight into Herbert Hoover. The General was not designed to be a politician. He was an extraordinary leader but the compromise and manipulation and expediency that politics involves were not the way he wanted to live.

As soon as I have a copy of "On His Own," I will send it to you – and then in the weeks ahead we can get together again to continue a very interesting dialogue.

Warmest regards,

Sincerely,

William J. vanden Heuvel

WINSTON & STRAWN

35 WEST WACKER DRIVE
CHICAGO, ILLINOIS 60601-9703

43 RUE DU RHONE
1204 GENEVA, SWITZERLAND

444 SOUTH FLOWER STREET
LOS ANGELES, CALIFORNIA 90071-2911

200 PARK AVENUE
NEW YORK, NEW YORK 10166-4193

(212) 294-6700

FACSIMILE (212) 294-4700

www.winston.com

21 AVENUE VICTOR HUGO
75116 PARIS, FRANCE

1400 L STREET, N.W.
WASHINGTON, D.C. 20005-3502

C. EVAN STEWART
(212) 294-4781
estewart@winston.com

May 30, 2000

Mr. William F. Buckley
Founder & Editor at Large
National Review
215 Lexington Avenue, 4th Floor
New York, NY 10016

Dear Mr. Buckley:

I very much enjoyed speaking with you on the way to the tarmac on Sunday, after your exceptional baccalaureate address. Herewith enclosed are the snippets from David Acheson's book, about which I mentioned. Also enclosed is the brief article I wrote on the Hiss trials (you will most enjoy the picture of Ed Jones, who did not want his face immortalized along with that of Hiss's!).

Best regards.

Sincerely,

C. Evan Stewart

C. Evan Stewart

Enclosures

NATIONAL REVIEW **215 Lexington Ave., New York, New York 10016**
Tel. (212) 679-7330

WILLIAM F. BUCKLEY, JR.

June 26, 2000

Dear Mr. Stewart:

Am just back from my long trip and had an enormous kick out of both documents you sent me. I hadn't known until you told me that Dean Acheson was the principal entrepreneur in getting the presidency for Whit Griswold--a neat way of handling it, to dangle Robert Hutchins over the corporation! And what a choice piece on the whole Alger Hiss scene. I'm going to send it on to Sam Tanenhaus. The episodes you single out are wonderful and wonderfully handled.

With cordial regards,

Bill

Wm. F. Buckley Jr.

Mr. C. Evan Stewart
Winston & Strawn
200 Park Avenue
New York, NY 10166-4193

NIKKO

The Nikko Securities Co.
International, Inc.

One World Financial Center
200 Liberty Street, New York, N.Y. 10281-1092

C. Evan Stewart
Executive Vice President
General Counsel

Telephone: (212) 416-5441
Facsimile: (212) 416-5687

July 18, 1996

Ms. Maureen Dowd
The New York Times Company
229 West 43rd Street
New York, NY 10036-3959

Dear Ms. Dowd:

I am devastated. For months I have been carefully explaining to friends and colleagues why you **had** to be the author of "Primary Colors." My comprehensive six point analysis had been honed to (what I thought was) perfection: 1) it had to be someone who is in the aging baby boomer group (only those of us old enough to have watched the Andy Devine show in the '50s would know of and be able to use the phrase "pluck your magic twanger, froggy"!) (we are the same age); 2) it had to be someone in the world of journalism, who had impeccable political sources, etc. (who better than you?); 3) it had to be someone who had time to write it (you had recently stepped down as White House correspondent); 4) it had to be someone knowledgeable about both Washington and New York City; 5) it had to be someone who not only writes well, but also has a great sense of humor (your column on Hillary having to step down as First Lady, to be replaced by Gore, is a classic); and 6) the reason for the anonymity was because the author would be writing in the future about political events involving, among others, the people caricatured in the book and would not want to have her/his objectivity, etc. challenged (witness the flak Klein is now getting). The recent article in the Times's Sunday Book Review seemed only to be further confirmation (having been written, so it seemed, by a woman).

Just to show you that I had the courage of my convictions, I went public with my conclusion (see footnote 2). Oh well, you can't win 'em all (as Dick Nixon was once overheard to say). In the meantime, I remain a devoted reader, and I look forward to your book--whenever (as Bob Dole would say).

Most sincerely,

C Evan Stewart
C. Evan Stewart

Enclosure

The New York Times

Liberties

Mr Stewart —
You & I both!
I'd like that
$6 million!
— M

MAUREEN DOWD

The New York Times
WASHINGTON BUREAU
1627 I STREET NW • SUITE 700
WASHINGTON, DC 20006-4085

C. Evan Stewart / NIKKO
One World Financial Center
200 Liberty St.
New York, NY
10281-1092

LAW OFFICES
WILLIAMS & CONNOLLY LLP
725 TWELFTH STREET, N.W.
WASHINGTON, D. C. 20005-5901
(202) 434-5000
FAX (202) 434-5029

EDWARD BENNETT WILLIAMS (1920-1988)
PAUL R. CONNOLLY (1922-1978)

July 27, 2000

C. Evan Stewart, Esq.
Winston & Strawn
200 Park Avenue
New York, N.Y. 10166

Re: Federal Bar Council Article

Dear Evan:

Thank you for the wonderful article on Ed. I am sharing it with Brendan Sullivan and my other partners. I have to say that I wish you had written the Williams biography instead of Evan Thomas – Evan is really not interested in what made Ed a great lawyer, and it's simply missing from his book. Anyway, thanks for thinking of me.

Sincerely,

Gerson A. Zweifach

THEODORE B. OLSON
SUITE 900
1050 CONNECTICUT AVENUE N. W.
WASHINGTON, D. C. 20036
(202) 955-8668

March 3, 1999

(202) 955-8668

Mr. C. Evan Stewart
The Nikko Securities Co.
International, Inc.
One World Financial Center
200 Liberty Street
New York, NY 10281-1092

Dear Mr. Stewart:

Thank you for your gracious letter of February 25.

I certainly hope Beth comes out of this quagmire sometime soon. She certainly deserves better treatment than she has received.

Very truly yours,

Theodore B. Olson

TBO/egm

WA990610.156/1+

NIKKO

**The Nikko Securities Co.
International, Inc.**

One World Financial Center
200 Liberty Street, New York, N.Y. 10281-1092

C. Evan Stewart
Executive Vice President
General Counsel

Telephone: (212) 416-5441
Facsimile: (212) 416-5687

February 25, 1999

Theodore B. Olson, Esq.
Gibson, Dunn & Crutcher
1050 Connecticut Avenue, N.W.
Washington, DC 20036-5306

Dear Mr. Olson:

Kudos to you on your splendid column in yesterday's *Journal*. Perhaps I am somewhat biased because it expressed my views *en toto*, but I was most pleased to see it articulated so well and to a broad audience (although, it is unfortunate that many people--especially here in NYC--refuse even to glance at the *Journal's* editorial page!).

As a life-long friend of Beth Nolan, I also write to thank you for your steadfast support of her. While it seems she will never be able to remove the "acting" title, I hope that history will not sweep her into the larger morass of the problems at the Clinton DoJ. As a fellow contributor to *Briefly*, I much enjoyed your monograph on punitive damages. Finally, please pass on my felicitations to my old colleague, Joe Warin.

Very truly yours,

C Evan Stewart

C. Evan Stewart

Wiley, Rein & Fielding

1776 K Street, N.W.
Washington, D.C. 20006
(202) 719-7000

Clifford M. Sloan
(202) 719-7307
csloan@wrf.com

Fax: (202) 719-7049
www.wrf.com

March 23, 1999

C. Evan Stewart
The Nikko Securities Co. International, Inc.
One World Financial Center
200 Liberty Street
New York, NY 10281-1092

Dear Mr. Stewart:

Thank you very much for your letter and for the enclosed column. I read it with interest, and greatly enjoyed your insights. It was a pleasure reviewing your National Legal Center report – not only because of the analysis, but also because of your lively writing style (which is not, shall we say, necessarily typical in legal writing!)

All the best.

Sincerely yours,

Cliff Sloan

Clifford M. Sloan

March 1999 The Metropolitan Corporate Counsel Page 43

Book Review

While Rome Burns: Fiddling With Reforming Securities Reform

By C. Evan Stewart

Reviewed by Clifford M. Sloan

The Private Securities Litigation Reform Act ("PSLRA") was enacted with great fanfare in 1995.[1] A bipartisan group of supporters in Congress had supported the legislation, and it was adopted over the President's veto. For those in the business community, and particularly in the often-volatile high-tech sector, the Act promised relief from what frequently seemed to be abusive class action securities lawsuits.

More than three years later, many questions loom about both the effects and the efficacy of this legislation. In an incisive new study for the National Legal Center for the Public Interest, C. Evan Stewart, the Executive Vice President and General Counsel of the Nikko Securities Co. International, Inc. analyzes the legislation and the current context. He addresses three fundamental questions - (1) whether the PSLRA has delivered on its promise; (2) whether additional "reform" legislation is necessary to deal with any perceived shortcomings in the PSLRA; and (3) whether an emphasis on securities litigation reform is obscuring even more important issues for the securities industry. Stewart's analysis of these critical issues is thoughtful and provocative. His study should produce its desired effect – stimulating serious thought about the most important questions facing the securities industry.

The PSLRA has numerous notable provisions. Among the most important, it addresses the standard for pleading scienter in securities fraud litigation. To survive a motion to dismiss, a plaintiff now must specify each misleading or false statement, describe how it is false or misleading, and state facts regarding state of mind with particularity. The Act also provides for an automatic stay of discovery and other proceedings while a motion to dismiss is pending. Significantly, it affords a safe harbor from liability for public companies that issue forward-looking statements, unless such statements are false and knowledge of falsity can be established. Other provisions include a procedure for the investor with the largest losses to select lead counsel, a mechanism designed to ensure that those with the most serious losses, rather than nominal plaintiffs, drive the litigation. Numerous other substantive and procedural provisions also are included.

With regard to the effect of the PSLRA, Stewart provides interesting insights. The law of unintended consequences is in full bloom. Courts have splintered on the meaning of the new pleading standard. The additional requirements for federal actions, moreover, are driving more plaintiffs to state law suits. And, far from having a significant impact, the counsel designation provision does not appear to be having a measurable effect on the dynamic of class action securities litigation.

On the second point - the prospects of further reform - Stewart advises caution. Just as the first legislation led to unintended consequences, so too current reform proposals may lead to unanticipated consequences, and may represent, at most, improvements "around the edges." Notably, in the same month that Stewart's analysis was published, Congress in fact enacted subsequent reform legislation. As has been explained in these pages,[2] Congress recently adopted the Securities Litigation Uniform Standards Act of 1998, Pub. L. No. 105-353, 112 Stat. 3227 (1998). The statute pre-empts many state-based securities class actions, but permits limited class actions, which concern matters of corporate governance, based on the state law of the issuer's incorporation. The new statute also allows federal courts to stay proceedings in parallel state court actions, a provision that likely will lead to interesting legal challenges. Whether the new legislation has a significant, desired effect – or whether, as Stewart fears, it may lead to unanticipated consequences and, at most, marginal improvements – remains to be seen.

It is on the third issue - the possibility that an emphasis on securities class action reform is obscuring even more important issues – that Stewart is especially interesting. He argues that the "Sturm and Drang" over securities litigation reform "is distracting practitioners and policy makers from quite significant recent developments affecting the securities industry." Stewart points to five developments that, in his view, are receiving inadequate attention: (1) the imposition of attorney liability under Section 10(b); (2) the impact of a recent Supreme Court decision limiting the duration of consolidation in complex, multi-district litigation;[3] (3) the SEC's aggressive position in various enforcement matters, which has led to judicial decisions rejecting SEC positions;[4] (4) the possibility of punitive damages in securities arbitrations; and (5) serious threats to the viability of the securities industry's mandatory arbitration system. On all these issues, Stewart sounds a call to arms. He maintains that the extensive intellectual and legal activity focused on securities litigation reform, and on "reforming reform," now should be directed to a wide array of pressing matters.

C. Evan Stewart has provided a timely and exceptionally thoughtful analysis of issues facing the securities industry. His effort to broaden the vistas of the current debate - from a focus on fine-tuning "reform" legislation to engagement on fundamental questions such as the scope of the SEC's enforcement authority and the viability of mandatory arbitration— is a persuasive call for a redeployment of energy. With the PSLRA and its successor legislation now on the books, it is an appropriate time to reassess the securities landscape and the challenges that lie ahead.

---

*The reviewer, **Clifford M. Sloan**, is a Partner at Wiley, Rein & Fielding in Washington, DC. He serves on the Legal Advisory Council of the National Legal Center for the Public Interest. The publication was published in November, 1998 by the National Legal Center for the Public Interest.*

---

[1] *Private Securities Litigation Reform Act of 1995, Pub. L. No. 104-67, 109 Stat. 737 (1995).*

[2] See, *E. Stong*, Reforming the Reform Act: Congress Takes Aim At State Court Securities Class Actions. *THE METROPOLITAN CORPORATE COUNSEL, Feb. 1999, p. 10.*

[3] See, Lexecon Inc. v. Milberg Weiss Bershad Hynes & Lerach, *118 S. Ct. 956 (1998).*

[4] See, e.g., Checkosky v. SEC, *139 F.3d 221 (D.C. Cir. 1998)*; Johnson v. SEC, *87 F.3d 484 (D.C. Cir. 1996).*

NIKKO

The Nikko Securities Co. International, Inc.

One World Trade Center, 79th Floor
New York, New York 10048

Telephone: 212-466-2529
Facsimile: 212-466-2544
email: stewart_evan@nikko.com

C. Evan Stewart
Executive Vice President
General Counsel

July 12, 1999

Mr. Bernard L. Madoff
Chairman
Bernard L. Madoff Investment Securities
885 Third Avenue
New York, NY 10022

Dear Bernie:

Herewith is where I can now be found (for a while, at least). Thanks again for your help on that lead (regardless of the outcome)!

Best regards.

Sincerely,

Evan

C. Evan Stewart

Stewart, Evan

From: charles.temel@ubs.com
Sent: Friday, October 30, 2009 1:29 PM
To: Stewart, Evan
Subject: wow
Attachments: Legal Disclaimer.txt

Evan

You were the hit of morning TV on CNBC.
What aplomb, what grace under pressure, is Oprah next?

You were great and even if you thought you could sneak by - we saw it.

Charlie

Charles S. Temel, CIMA
Senior Vice President - Investments
UBS Financial Services Inc.
212-821-2030 & 800-317-3002
212-821-2870 (fax)
charles.temel@ubs.com

We have moved to new offices at:

299 Park Avenue -26th floor
New York, NY 10171

My new phone numbers are:

(212) 821-2030
(800) 317-3002 - Toll Free
(212) 821-2870 - FAX

E-Mail remains the same

Our Mission:

- Listening and taking a comprehensive view of the client's needs.
- Focusing on the client's risk tolerance and objectives.
- Working to preserve capital while growing the value of the assets.
- Providing excellent service and clear communication.

10/30/2009

DAVIS POLK & WARDWELL

I CHASE MANHATTAN PLAZA
NEW YORK, N.Y. 10005
212-530-4000
TELEX: ITT-421341
TELECOPIER: 212-530-4800

499 PARK AVENUE
NEW YORK, N.Y. 10022

1575 I STREET, N.W.
WASHINGTON, D.C. 20005

4, PLACE DE LA CONCORDE
75008 PARIS

I FREDERICK'S PLACE
LONDON EC2R 8AB

ROBERT B. FISKE, JR.
212-530-4090

July 18, 1989

PERSONAL

C. Evan Stewart, Esq.
General Counsel
The Nikko Securities Co.
International, Inc.
One World Financial Center
200 Liberty Street
New York, New York 10281

Dear Evan:

Thanks very much for your letter, which I appreciate a great deal.

It was obviously a disappointment for me not to become the Deputy Attorney General - particularly when the allegations concerning my chairmanship of the ABA Judiciary Committee had been demonstrated to be so totally baseless. I must say, it is a result that I never contemplated as even a remote possibility when I first got started in this process.

It was very good to hear from you and so many of my other friends. I hope we will see each other soon.

With best regards.

Sincerely yours,

Bob

Robert B. Fiske, Jr.

NIKKO

The Nikko Securities Co. International, Inc.

One World Financial Center
200 Liberty Street, New York, N.Y. 10281

Telephone: (212) 416-5441

C. Evan Stewart
General Counsel

July 7, 1989

Robert B. Fiske, Jr., Esq.
Davis Polk & Wardwell
One Chase Manhattan Plaza
New York, New York 10005

Dear Bob:

I was distressed to see the news regarding your withdrawal from consideration for the Deputy Attorney General position. Not only are you superbly qualified and deserving, but the events surrounding this unhappy episode will promote widespread cynicism about the desirability of public service.

My thoughts are with you and your family at this difficult time.

Sincerely,

Evan

C. Evan Stewart

NATIONAL BASKETBALL ASSOCIATION

OLYMPIC TOWER · 645 FIFTH AVENUE · NEW YORK, N. Y. 10022 · 212-826-7000

GARY B. BETTMAN
SENIOR VICE PRESIDENT &
GENERAL COUNSEL

December 28, 1992

C. Evan Stewart, Esq.
General Counsel
The Nikko Securities Co.
International, Inc.
One World Financial Center
200 Liberty Street
New York, NY 10281-1092

Dear Evan:

Many, many thanks for the warm wishes. As you can imagine, I am extremely excited about the challenges ahead. I look forward to seeing you in the near future.

Best wishes for a healthy and happy New Year.

Sincerely,

Gary

GBB/dw

NIKKO

**The Nikko Securities Co.
International, Inc.**

One World Financial Center
200 Liberty Street, New York, N.Y. 10281-1092

Telephone: (212) 416-5441
Facsimile: (212) 416-5687

C. Evan Stewart
General Counsel

December 14, 1992

Gary B. Bettman, Esq.
5 Dunmore Road
New City, NY 10956

Dear Gary:

Let me be the next to last to congratulate you on your being named the first commissioner of the National Hockey League. Not only is it a well deserved honor to you personally, but it is also yet another example of how special the food was up in Ithaca during our undergraduate years! Hopefully, for our Twentieth Reunion (June 1994), we can highlight your achievements and talents in some way. In the meantime, best of luck as you undertake what promises to be a truly facinating job.

Warmest regards.

Sincerely,

Evan

C. Evan Stewart

The New Republic
1220 - 19th Street NW
Washington, DC 20036
January 29, 1993

Mr. C. Evan Stewart
Nikko Securities International
One World Financial Center
200 Liberty Street
New York NY 10281-1092

Dear Mr. Stewart:

Thanks for your letter, for the compliments, and for your law review article. Perhaps Walsh's statements were abusive, but the outrage of Republican politicians about it was highly selective.

Congratulations, by the way, on getting a cartoon into a law review.

Yours sincerely,

Michael Kinsley

NIKKO

The Nikko Securities Co. International, Inc.
One World Financial Center
200 Liberty Street, New York, N.Y. 10281-1092
Telephone: (212) 416-5441
Facsimile: (212) 416-5687

C. Evan Stewart
General Counsel

December 31, 1992

Mr. Michael Kinsley
Senior Editor
The New Republic
1220 19th Street, N.W.
Washington, DC 20036

Dear Mr. Kinsley:

Although I do not always agree with the conclusions you reach, I am a big fan of the clarity of your logic and prose. I also admire your ability to go mano-a-mano night after night with the likes of Messrs. Buchanan, Sununu, etc.

Compliments aside, I write with respect to your recent column: "The Criminals Lobby." I feel compelled to raise a technical point or two. In arabic paragraph (4), and under the ethical guidelines to which you referred, the publicly reported comments of the Independent Counsel would (i) violate the guidelines, and (ii) go well beyond what have been termed "speaking indictments." Finally, putting to one side the political efficacy of President Bush's comments vis-a-vis Mr. Noriega, he is not a lawyer and thus not subject to the same guidelines as the Independent Counsel.

Keep up the good work in 1993!

Very truly yours,

C Evan Stewart

C. Evan Stewart

P. S. The enclosed reprint may be of some interest on the guidelines issue (see, for example, fns. 13 & 21). In any event, I hope you will like the cartoon!

NIKKO

The Nikko Securities Co. International, Inc.
One World Financial Center
200 Liberty Street, New York, N.Y. 10281-1092
Telephone: (212) 416-5441
Facsimile: (212) 416-5687

C. Evan Stewart
General Counsel

March 4, 1993

Mr. Garry Wills
Henry R. Luce Professor
of American Culture and Public Policy
Northwestern University
2674 Sheridan Road
Evanston, Illinois 60208

Dear Mr. Wills:

Congratulations on your National Book Award. I am a big fan, and it is certainly well deserved.

I was re-reading another book of yours last evening ("Lead Time"), and I was particularly interested in the piece on Murat Halstead. Since there is no bibliography in the book, would you happen to know whether his works on the 1856 and 1860 conventions are publicly available today?

Many thanks for any help you can spare.

Most sincerely,

C Evan Stewart

C. Evan Stewart

Yes, in a book called *Three Against Lincoln*. Out of print, but good libraries have it.
Best, GW

CBS
NEWS

A Division of CBS Inc.
524 West 57 Street
New York, New York 10019
(212) 975 4321

C. Evan Stewart
The Nikko Securities co.
One World Financial Center
200 Liberty Street
New York, NY 10281-1092

Dear Mr. Stewart, February 27, 1998

Although you would not conclude so from the time it has taken me to thank you for your letter, for Paul Fussell's essay and for your version of "The Speech", I was very much interested in reading all of them.

I'd like it if we got to know each other well enough to exchange Evans and Andys and will look for you at future Century events to try and accomplish that.

Sincerely,

Andrew A. Rooney

NIKKO

The Nikko Securities Co.
International, Inc.

One World Financial Center
200 Liberty Street, New York, N.Y. 10281-1092

C. Evan Stewart
Executive Vice President
General Counsel

Telephone: (212) 416-5441
Facsimile: (212) 416-5687

October 31, 1997

PERSONAL

Mr. Andy Rooney
CBS, Inc.
"60 Minutes"
555 West 57th Street
New York, NY 10019

Dear Mr. Rooney:

I very much enjoyed meeting you last evening, and appreciate the opportunity to talk a bit about some subjects of mutual interest.

As promised, I am sending on the Hand and Hiss articles (as well as two other legal "history" pieces on Nixon and Brandeis).

With respect to Patton, I did pull the D'Este book off the shelf when I got home and was pleased to refresh my memory as to your exchange with Patton's daughter (p. 813). FYI, I am enclosing Paul Fussell's essay on the movie vs. real life; the book from which it is taken--"Past Imperfect, History According to the Movies"--is very well done and you might well enjoy it. I am also taking the liberty of sending on my own version of "The Speech."

Keep up your wonderful work, and I hope our paths will cross at the dinner next year.

Very truly yours,

C. Evan Stewart

C. Evan Stewart

Enclosures

Page 1 of 1

Stewart, Evan

From: Diana B. Henriques [dianah@nytimes.com]

Sent: Tuesday, October 06, 2009 12:43 PM

To: Stewart, Evan

Subject: A pleasure to "meet" you today

I wouldn't be much of a financial writer if I couldn't quickly identify someone of your stature in the securities law bar, so I was a bit amused by your coy refusal to introduce yourself in Judge Lifland's court today. Goldman Sachs's interest in the Chais matter is transparent to anyone who looked at the papers on file, so I felt sure it had someone on watch today -- it took but a moment to learn that it was you.
My real regret is that, by not introducing yourself, you denied me the opportunity to tell you how much I enjoyed your columns in the New York Law Journal over the years.
Best regards,
Diana

Diana B. Henriques
Senior Financial Writer
The New York Times
620 Eighth Avenue, 2nd Floor
New York, N.Y. 10018-1405
212.556.4397 (o)
201.214.2050 (c)
dianah@nytimes.com

10/6/2009

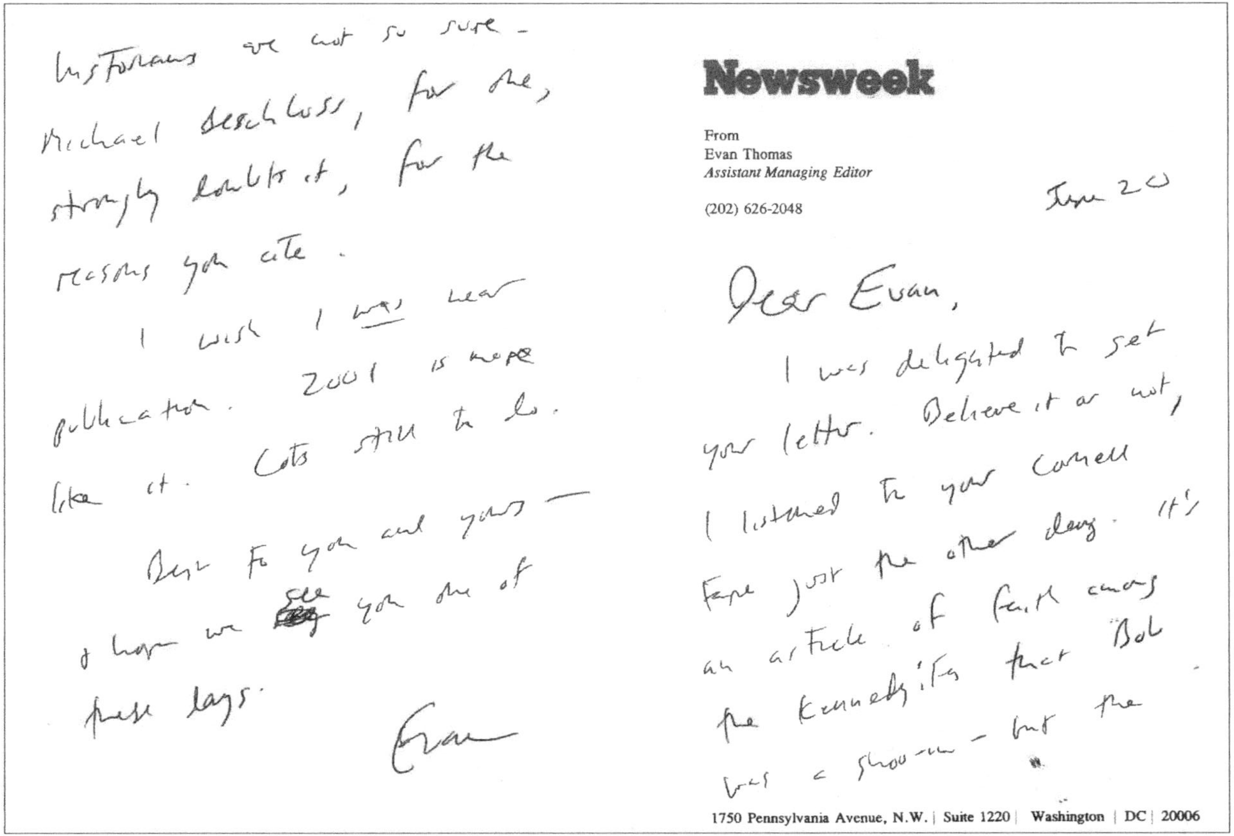

Newsweek

From
Evan Thomas
Assistant Managing Editor

(202) 626-2048

June 20

Dear Evan,

I was delighted to get your letter. Believe it or not, I listened to your Cornell tape just the other day. It's an article of faith among the Kennedyites that Bob was a shoo-in — but the historians are not so sure — Michael Beschloss, for one, strongly doubts it, for the reasons you cite.

I wish I was near publication. 2001 is more like it. Lots still to do.

Best to you and yours — I hope we see you one of these days.

Evan

1750 Pennsylvania Avenue, N.W. | Suite 1220 | Washington | DC | 20006

NIKKO

The Nikko Securities Co. International, Inc.

One World Financial Center
200 Liberty Street, New York, N.Y. 10281-1092

C. Evan Stewart
Executive Vice President
General Counsel

Telephone: (212) 416-5441
Facsimile: (212) 416-5687

June 17, 1998

Mr. Evan Thomas
Assistant Managing Editor
Newsweek Magazine
1750 Pennsylvania Avenue, NW
Washington, DC 20006

Dear Evan:

I just saw your article on RFK, which hopefully means that you are close to publication. I was relieved to see you include the Dutton quote. So many Kennedy hagiographers (e.g., the Schlesinger article that followed yours) proclaim with certainty that RFK would undoubtedly have won the nomination in Chicago. As your research no doubt has shown (and as you remember firsthand), RFK was way behind in the delegate count, the initial buoyancy of California was based upon a 49% projection--rather than the actual 46%, he had a tough primary fight ahead in NY, and the "bosses" still ran the nominating process (witness LBJ controlling the Vietnam part of the plank). Given your track record, I am looking forward to a detailed and balanced look into a truly unique American politician--it will be a great read and allow you to retire on the residuals!

Warmest and best regards to you, Oscie and the girls.

Most sincerely,

Evan

C. Evan Stewart

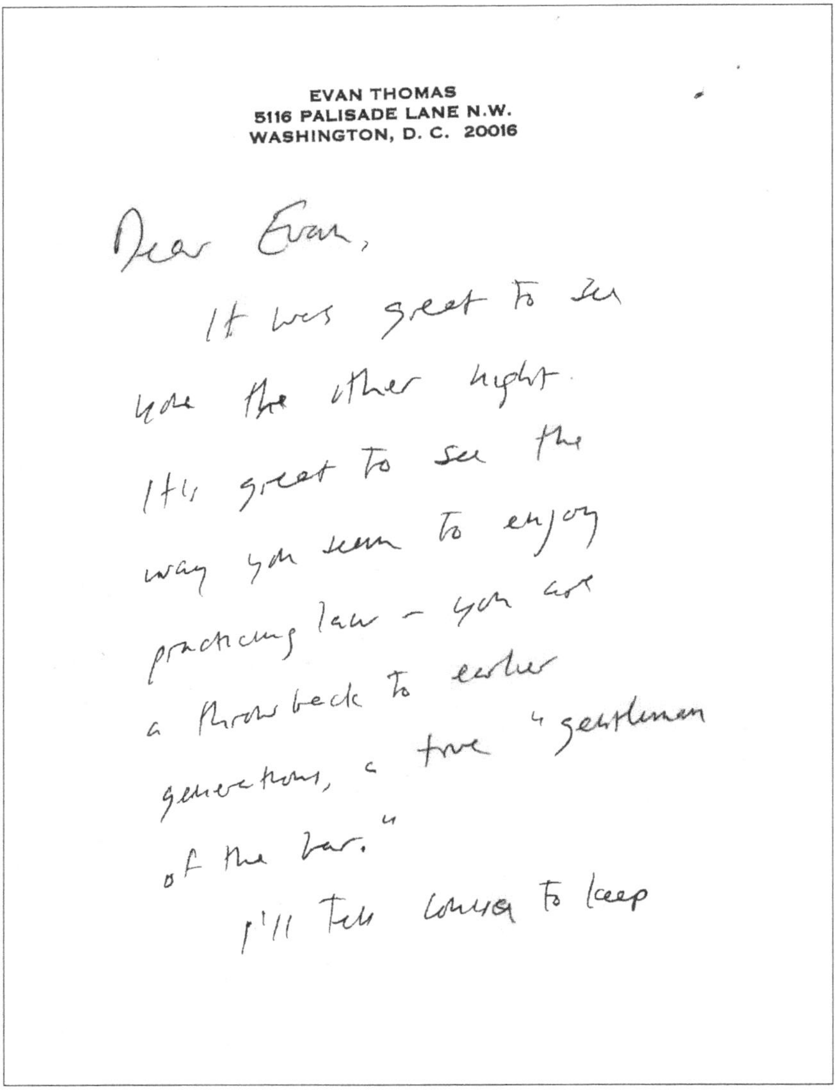

EVAN THOMAS
5116 PALISADE LANE N.W.
WASHINGTON, D. C. 20016

Dear Evan,

It was great to see you the other night. It's great to see the way you seem to enjoy practicing law – you are a throwback to earlier generations, a true "gentleman of the bar."

I'll tell Louisa to keep

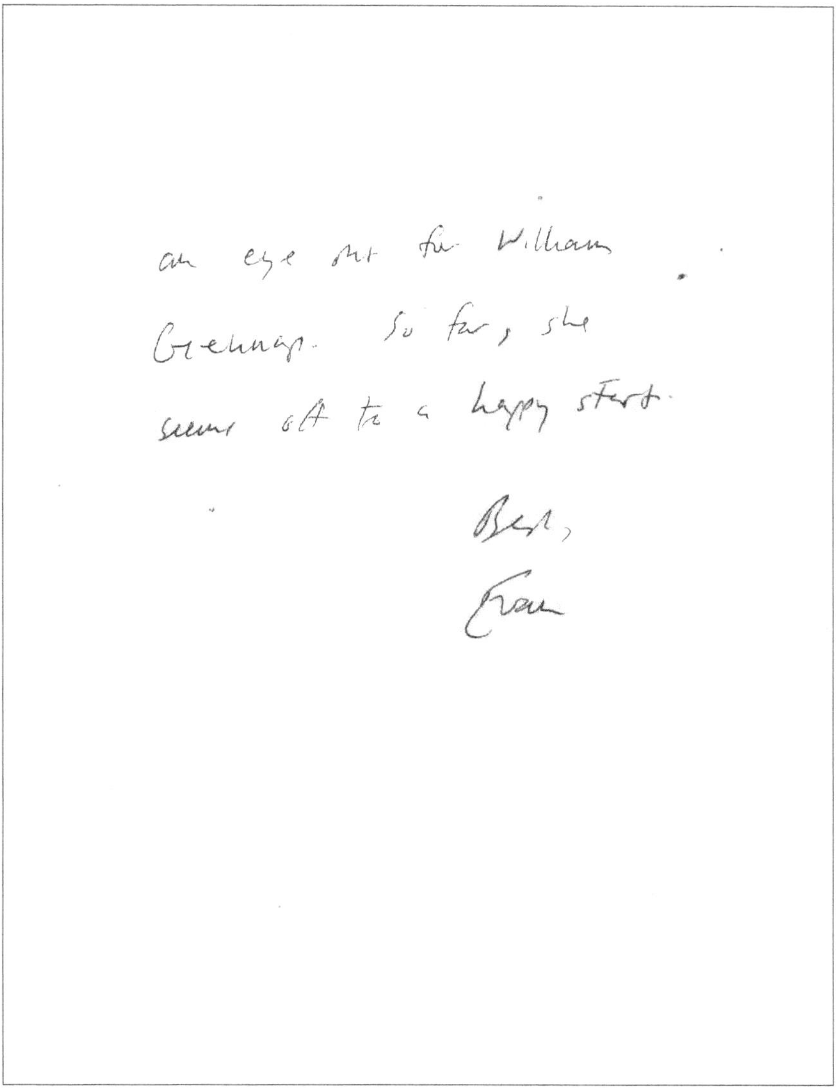

an eye out for William
Greenings. So far, she
seems off to a happy start.

Best,
Evan

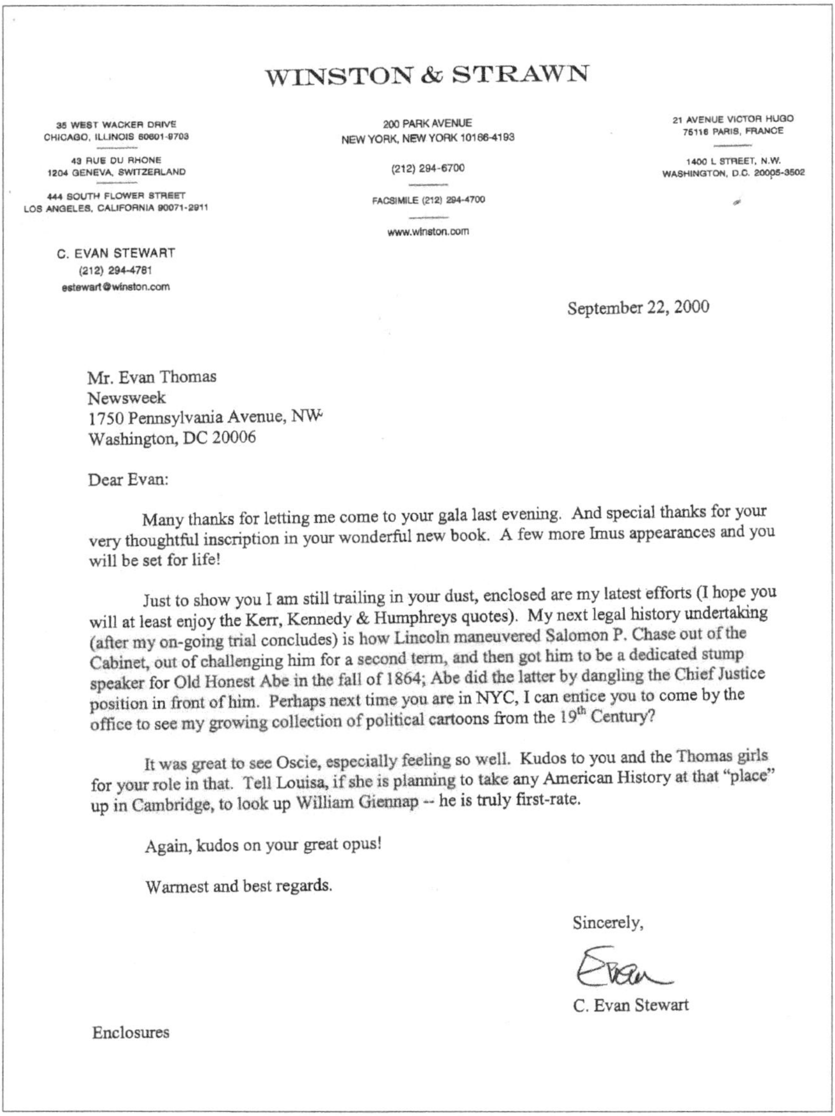

WINSTON & STRAWN

35 WEST WACKER DRIVE
CHICAGO, ILLINOIS 60601-9703

43 RUE DU RHONE
1204 GENEVA, SWITZERLAND

444 SOUTH FLOWER STREET
LOS ANGELES, CALIFORNIA 90071-2911

200 PARK AVENUE
NEW YORK, NEW YORK 10166-4193

(212) 294-6700

FACSIMILE (212) 294-4700

www.winston.com

21 AVENUE VICTOR HUGO
75116 PARIS, FRANCE

1400 L STREET, N.W.
WASHINGTON, D.C. 20005-3502

C. EVAN STEWART
(212) 294-4781
estewart@winston.com

September 22, 2000

Mr. Evan Thomas
Newsweek
1750 Pennsylvania Avenue, NW
Washington, DC 20006

Dear Evan:

Many thanks for letting me come to your gala last evening. And special thanks for your very thoughtful inscription in your wonderful new book. A few more Imus appearances and you will be set for life!

Just to show you I am still trailing in your dust, enclosed are my latest efforts (I hope you will at least enjoy the Kerr, Kennedy & Humphreys quotes). My next legal history undertaking (after my on-going trial concludes) is how Lincoln maneuvered Salomon P. Chase out of the Cabinet, out of challenging him for a second term, and then got him to be a dedicated stump speaker for Old Honest Abe in the fall of 1864; Abe did the latter by dangling the Chief Justice position in front of him. Perhaps next time you are in NYC, I can entice you to come by the office to see my growing collection of political cartoons from the 19th Century?

It was great to see Oscie, especially feeling so well. Kudos to you and the Thomas girls for your role in that. Tell Louisa, if she is planning to take any American History at that "place" up in Cambridge, to look up William Giennap -- he is truly first-rate.

Again, kudos on your great opus!

Warmest and best regards.

Sincerely,

Evan

C. Evan Stewart

Enclosures

LEONARD GARMENT
2101 L STREET, N. W.
WASHINGTON, D. C. 20037

May 30, 1989

Dear Mr. Stewart,

Thanks for taking the time to say nice things about the Hill case article. Writing is a bloody business, but a few words like yours helps redeem it.

Best,

Leonard Garment

C. Evan Stewart, Esq.
The Nikko Securities Co.
International, Inc.
One World Financial Center
200 Liberty Street
New York, New York 10281

May 2, 1989

Leonard Garment, Esq.
Dickstein, Shapiro & Morin
2101 L Street, N.W.
Washington, DC 20037

Dear Mr. Garment:

I am writing to express my high praise for your recent article in The New Yorker on the Hill litigation. The perspective of your article, as well as the insights you brought to the personalities involved, made it a fascinating piece for lawyers, as well as a most accessible history for those outside our profession (not an easy thing to do!). Although I am sure I am but one of a score to pass on similar feelings, I believe your article to be of exceptional merit and I wanted to add my voice.

Very truly yours,

C. Evan Stewart

bcc: James H. McGlothlin, Esq.
(I think you will find Mr. Garment's article to be of very high quality indeed.)

CARTER, LEDYARD & MILBURN
Counsellors at Law

Donald J. Zoeller
Of Counsel
•
Direct: (212) 238-8615
Email zoeller@clm.com

2 Wall Street
New York, NY 10005-2072
•
Tel (212) 732-3200
Fax (212) 732-3232

1350 I Street, N.W.
Washington, DC 20005
(202) 898-1515
•
570 Lexington Avenue
New York, NY 10022
(212) 371-2720

May 19, 1999

C. Evan Stewart, Esq.
The Nikko Securities Co. International, Inc.
One World Financial Center
200 Liberty Street
New York, New York 10281-1092

Dear Evan:

Thanks for the article about Garment and Nixon. I enjoyed it a great deal. I was Len's assistant at the Hill trial, and throughout the appeals process. The case was one of the most enjoyable I have ever worked on.

Glad to see you're doing your bit for Fordham. It's a great place. It is my good fortune that neither of the two courses I teach requires an exam.

Sincerely,

Donald J. Zoeller

DJZ:maf

The Nikko Securities Co.
International, Inc.

NIKKO

One World Financial Center
200 Liberty Street, New York, N.Y. 10281-1092

C. Evan Stewart
Executive Vice President
General Counsel

Telephone: (212) 416-5441
Facsimile: (212) 416-5687

May 5, 1999

Donald J. Zoeller, Esq.
Carter, Ledyard & Milburn
2 Wall Street
New York, NY 10005

Dear Mr. Zoeller:

Now that it will no longer be deemed an ex parte communication, I thought you might find of interest an article I wrote a while back regarding two of your former partners (I was told that Len Garment liked the piece). Given our mutual interest in teaching Fordham students, I am also enclosing, FYI, my syllabus (the exam is tomorrow!).

Best regards.

Sincerely,

C. Evan Stewart

C. Evan Stewart

Enclosures

Aug-21-97 04:23P Lois Evans, Tom Evans AUG 21 '97 04:18PM P.01

FAX TRANSMISSION

THOMAS W. EVANS
10245 COLLINS AVENUE
BAL HARBOUR, FLORIDA 33154
305-864-3619
FAX: 305-867-0750

To: C. Evan Stewart, Esq. **Date:** August 21, 1997

Fax #: 212-416-5687 **Pages:** 1, including this cover sheet.

From: Tom Evans

Subject: FBC News

COMMENTS:

Evan: When you wrote me on December 6 of last year, you noted that you were "looking for Len Garment's book in '97." I see from the FBC News that you not only found the book, but have written an article (most enjoyable) about it. When I get back to New York in September, after a Wyoming vacation which begins tomorrow, we can talk about "the rest of the story." If you are interested, please leave word and some mid-September dates on my voicemail at 212-850-2813. In the meantime, you should probably begin thinking about how you will respond to the outcry from our membership re your omission of Garment's unvarnished description of a former president of the Council. All the best.

LAW OFFICES OF

DECHERT PRICE & RHOADS

1500 K STREET, N.W.
WASHINGTON, DC 20005-1208

TELEPHONE: (202) 626-3300
FAX: (202) 626-3334

30 ROCKEFELLER PLAZA
NEW YORK, NY 10112
(212) 698-3500

4000 BELL ATLANTIC TOWER
1717 ARCH STREET
PHILADELPHIA, PA 19103-2793
(215) 994-4000

THIRTY NORTH THIRD STREET
HARRISBURG, PA 17101-1603
(717) 237-2000

PRINCETON PIKE CORPORATE CENTER
P.O. BOX 5218
PRINCETON, NJ 08543-5218
(609) 520-3200

TEN POST OFFICE SQUARE • SOUTH
BOSTON, MA 02109-4603
(617) 728-7100

90 STATE HOUSE SQUARE
HARTFORD, CT 06103-3702
(860) 524-3999

65 AVENUE LOUISE
1050 BRUSSELS, BELGIUM
(32-2) 535-5411

TITMUSS SAINER DECHERT
2 SERJEANTS' INN
LONDON EC4Y 1LT, ENGLAND
(44-171) 583-5353

151, BOULEVARD HAUSSMANN
75008 PARIS, FRANCE
(33-1) 53 83 84 70

THEODORE SONDE
Direct Dial: (202) 626-3340
tsonde@dechert.com

July 10, 1997

C. Evan Stewart
Executive Vice President and
General Counsel
The Nikko Securities Co. International, Inc.
One World Financial Center
200 Liberty Street
New York, NY 10281-1092

Dear Evan:

Len Garment was kind enough to share with me your note and review in the Federal Bar Council News. As you may know, Len joined Dechert a few years ago. We are separated by a few feet and have become close personal friends. I was delighted to see your review and note.

I hope all is well with you. Perhaps one of these days we can get together in the not too distant future. I frequently find myself in New York and will try to give you a call.

Sincerely,

Theodore Sonde

nb

Teaching Letters

6 June 1988

Dear Professor Stewart,

I am writing to formally thank you for what was, without question, one of the best courses in law school. From the beginning, it was clear how much thought and effort you put into developing the course. It was challenging and interesting. Most important, I was always aware of your good will and sincerity of intention in passing on this body of knowledge. It really doesn't get any better than that.

Many thanks and best regards!

Sincerely,
Kim Killion

NIKKO

The Nikko Securities Co. International, Inc.

One World Financial Center
200 Liberty Street, New York, N.Y. 10281-1092

Telephone: (212) 416-5441
Facsimile: (212) 416-5687

C. Evan Stewart
Executive Vice President
General Counsel

June 11, 1998

Kim Killion, Esq.
44 East 92nd Street
New York, NY 10128

Dear Ms. Killion:

Your letter was extraordinarily generous and gratefully received. Thank you!

Congratulations on your fine work and your recent graduation. Good luck on the bar exam this summer, and remember to take a good long vacation before starting in at Cleary Gottlieb. After you get settled there, please give me a call so I can by you lunch and catch up on developments.

Best regards.

Sincerely,

C Evan Stewart

C. Evan Stewart

Kim Killion
44 East 92nd Street
New York, New York 10128

October 10, 1998

C. Evan Stewart, Esq.
Nikko Securities Co. International, Inc.
One World Financial Center - A
New York, New York 10281-1092

Dear Professor Stewart,

Thank you so much for a most enjoyable lunch. I appreciated your words of wisdom and will certainly take them to heart. It is wonderful to have the counsel of someone whose accomplishments and integrity you greatly admire and who is wonderfully funny and generally good company, to boot. (During lunch I was reminded of how, in class, you would deliver these great lines. They were easy to miss -- your facial expressions and tone rarely give anything away. We all *loved* them.)

I do hope you will allow me to reciprocate in the not too distant future. In the meantime, my e-mail address is: kkillion@cgsh.com. Thank you again.

With best regards,

Kim Killion

To my favorite teacher & mentor

I have been so lucky to spend the summer with you. I have learned so much in class & at the firm. This experience has truly been valuable both personally & professionally.

I feel more passionate than ever to pursue the field of law. I know that with hard work, effort, & a little lucky :) I will get into a great law school.

Thank You from the bottom of my heart,
Renée

Keri A. Kilcommons

Evan–

Having found this on the web, I now understand your fascination with *The Godfather*. Stage name and everything! Wow! I apologize for not being more well versed in your pre-legal career pursuits.

~ Keri C

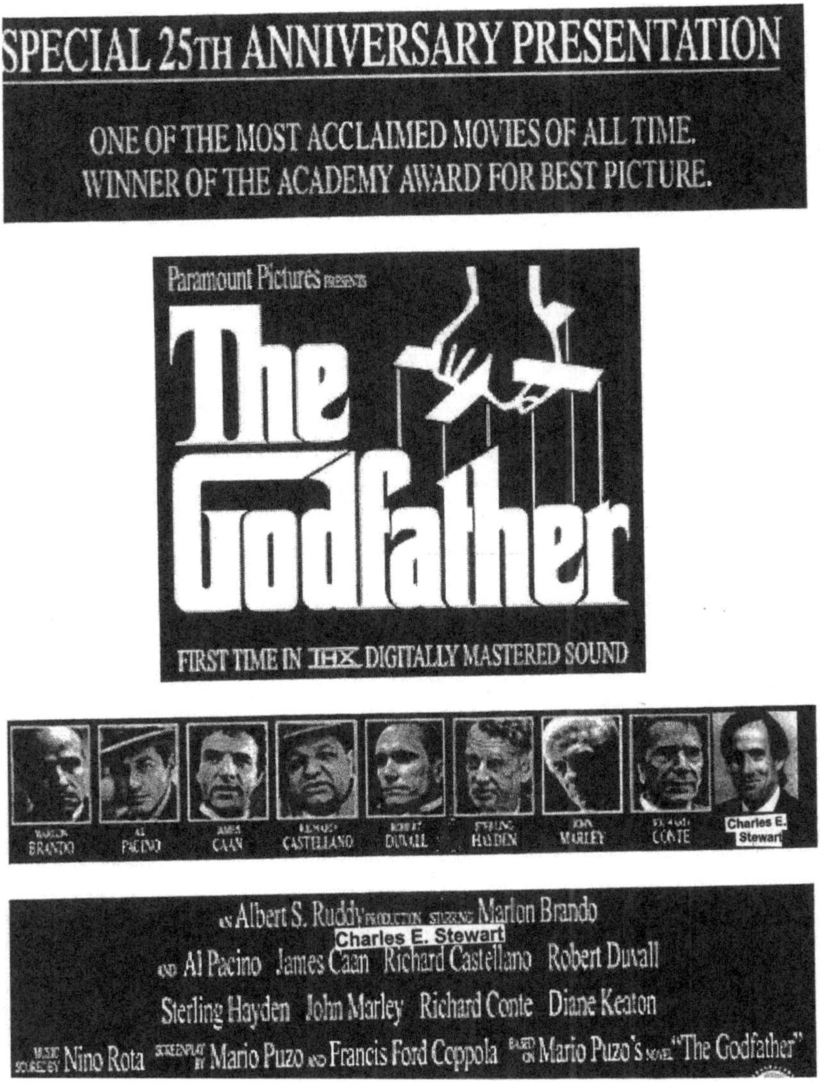
SPECIAL 25TH ANNIVERSARY PRESENTATION
ONE OF THE MOST ACCLAIMED MOVIES OF ALL TIME.
WINNER OF THE ACADEMY AWARD FOR BEST PICTURE.
Paramount Pictures PRESENTS
The Godfather
FIRST TIME IN THX DIGITALLY MASTERED SOUND
BRANDO
PACINO
CAAN
CASTELLANO
DUVALL
HAYDEN
MARLEY
CONTE
Charles E. Stewart
Albert S. Ruddy PRODUCTION STARRING Marlon Brando
Charles E. Stewart
AND Al Pacino James Caan Richard Castellano Robert Duvall
Sterling Hayden John Marley Richard Conte Diane Keaton
Nino Rota
SCREENPLAY BY Mario Puzo AND Francis Ford Coppola
BASED ON Mario Puzo's NOVEL "The Godfather"

05208126

05208126

Institution **Fordham Law School**
Control Code **N/A**
Extegrity Exam4 > 9.3.23.1

05208126-S.-7-7

Course / Session **Stewart - Pro Resp-Corp Counsl**
Instructor **NA**
Section . Page **7** of **7**

V. Extra Credit.

Smokey Robinson: Tears of a Clown. Lyrics: "though there's a smile on my face it's only there to fool the public...don't let this smile I wear, make you think that I don't care."
When a friend of mine suggested that I take professional responsibility with Professor Stewart, they told me that he was a funny guy: he stands on chairs and he gets underneath the table and sucks his thumb. That friend was half right. Professor Stewart is funny and the class discussion was enjoyable; but I walk away with the feeling that Professor Stewart wants us to remember his class for something else: the ethical rules of lawyers present many traps for the unwary and it is a dangerous and unfair world for corporate lawyers especially. Professor Stewart laughed, but he was dead serious. He also cares. I'm convinced that if I ever slip up, he will hunt me down like a dog someday. Thankfully, I'm more aware now than before of all the issues that may cause me to slip up.

C. Evan Stewart

From: Stewart, Evan <Evan.Stewart@gs.com>
Sent: Monday, July 10, 2017 6:08 AM
To: C. Evan Stewart
Subject: FW: Flynn, Kevin - Thank you

-----Original Message-----
From: Kevin Flynn [mailto:kwcflynn@umich.edu]
Sent: Friday, June 30, 2017 6:44 PM
To: Stewart, Evan [Legal]; estewart@cohengresser.com
Subject: Flynn, Kevin - Thank you

Hi Professor Stewart,

I hope this email finds you well.

I wanted to reach out to let you know how thankful I am for all I learned from you these past three weeks. As I look back on my experience, I can appreciate what an absolute privilege it was to learn all I did about the legal system from you. Not only am I grateful for the time you took to speak with me one day after class, but I am especially thankful for the discussion we had on our last day of class about Fortenberry. I am sure that the rest of the class would agree when I say that your message to "care for ourselves" as young associates is something that we will all take with us into our professional careers.

I wish you all the best, and hope to cross paths again in the future.

Thank you very much, Professor Stewart.

Best regards,

Kevin Flynn

C. Evan Stewart

From: Jillian Victor <jlvictor@umich.edu>
Sent: Friday, June 24, 2016 12:31 PM
To: C. Evan Stewart
Subject: Thank you

Hello Professor Stewart,

I wanted to thank you for teaching such a great class. I have never learned so much in such a short amount of time. Because of your class, I truly have a passion for the law. Thank you for being an inspiring professor.

All best,
Ms. Victor

C. Evan Stewart

From:	Dilan Cabral <dilan.cabral@uconn.edu>
Sent:	Saturday, August 03, 2019 4:16 PM
To:	C. Evan Stewart
Subject:	Summer Semester 2019

Dear Professor Stewart,
I hope your summer is treating you well and all has been good. Foremost, I wanted to thank you for an amazing experience this summer. Your class was by far one of the most difficult academic challenges I have faced, due to the nature of the material and the pace at which we progressed through it. However in light of this, I cannot think of another class that has taught me more or pushed me harder to succeed. I had only taken a couple law classes before this summer, but none of them gave me such insight into the actual law profession and law school like your class did. Due to my enjoyment of the material and seeing first hand at my internship how law functions in the real world, I have decided to pursue law school after finishing my undergraduate degree. I understand you have a very busy schedule and I am sure many of my classmates have asked already, but I would be honored if you would be able to write a letter of recommendation for me. I will be applying for law schools in the coming year and a letter of recommendation from yourself would be a privilege and a great addition to my application. Again, I thank you for the enlightening experience this summer and am proud to have been a student of yours. Please let me know if there is anything I can do for you. I look forward to hearing from you soon.
Best Regards,
Dilan Cabral

C. Evan Stewart

From: Madeline Rutowski <mjr444@cornell.edu>
Sent: Tuesday, July 23, 2019 10:59 AM
To: C. Evan Stewart
Subject: Thank You

Professor Stewart,

I just wanted to reiterate how thankful I am for being given the opportunity to work at Cohen & Gresser. I sincerely enjoyed my time there and felt like I learned valuable lessons about what it means to be a good and ethical lawyer.

I am sorry our paths did not cross at the summer outing last Monday, but I took advantage of the sun by the pool and the yoga class! Thank you very much for inviting me. It meant a lot.

Finally, I want to thank you for the class. I am not sure how I did on the exam, but I sincerely believe that I learned more in those three weeks than I have in any other law class previously. I took away so much -- everything from Cardozo's ridiculous opinion in *Palsgraf*, to the true meaning of the "Cf." cite; from the various meanings of latin phrases like "*respondeat superior*" in *Koczwara*, to some much needed education on American cinema. I am very thankful for the foundation of legal knowledge my fellow classmates and I were provided in taking your class. I think this will set us up for success in our first year of law school, a much needed edge in such a competitive field. Thank you again. I truly enjoyed my time.

Best,
Madeline Rutowski
P.S. I have my cartoons, which I am now confident were drawn by you, hanging on my wall at home. They make me smile!

Cornell Letters

CORNELL
UNIVERSITY

Office of the President

300 Day Hall
Ithaca, NY 14853-2801

Telephone: 607 255-5201

April 25, 2001

Mr. C. Evan Stewart
1070 Park Avenue, #3C
New York, NY 10128

Dear Evan:

Thank you for your recent gifts to Cornell for the Charles Thorp Stewart Scholarship for law students. I am sure that your father is honored and touched by your admiration and affection for him. Thank you, too, for your gift to the Ramin Parlor renovations at Sage Hall.

Cornell is fortunate that you choose to give so much of your time and talent on so many fronts. From your role as a trustee, to your leadership with your class, to your work with the Law School and the many other responsibilities you so capably manage, please accept my heartfelt gratitude.

Yours sincerely,

Hunter

Hunter R. Rawlings III

psb

CORNELL UNIVERSITY
300 Day Hall
Ithaca, N. Y. 14853-2801

Office of the President

February 20, 1998

C. Evan Stewart
Executive Vice President
General Counsel
The Nikko Securities Co.
One World Financial Center
200 Liberty Street
New York, NY 10281-1092

Dear Evan:

It was a wonderful treat for Elizabeth and me to join you and your family for the party Saturday evening. We enjoyed ourselves thoroughly and particularly appreciated your tribute to your dad.

The Cornell feeling in the room was palpable to all of us, a real tribute to your family's loyalty and commitment.

Thanks very much for sending the two versions of your article on Jessie Boulton. I shall read them with pleasure and interest.

Best wishes to you and your entire family.

Yours sincerely,

Hunter

Hunter R. Rawlings III

The Nikko Securities Co.
International, Inc.

NIKKO

One World Financial Center
200 Liberty Street, New York, N.Y. 10281-1092

C. Evan Stewart
Executive Vice President
General Counsel

Telephone: (212) 416-5441
Facsimile: (212) 416-5687

February 16, 1998

Mr. Hunter R. Rawlins III
President
Cornell University
300 Day Hall
Ithaca, NY 14853

Dear Hunter:

It was wonderful of you and Elizabeth to join us for the festivities on Saturday night. I know it meant a great deal to my father.

To add to your bedside reading table, enclosed are two versions of the Jessie Boulton article: the short one (as it appeared in Cornell Magazine), and the long one (pre-editing).

Again, my sincerest thanks to you both, and I look forward to seeing you soon.

Warmest and best regards.

Sincerely,

Evan

C. Evan Stewart

Enclosures

CORNELL UNIVERSITY
300 Day Hall
Ithaca, N. Y. 14853-2801

Office of the President

November 4, 1994

Mr. C. Evan Stewart
122 East 82 Street
New York, NY 10028

Dear Evan:

I want to thank you for your tribute to Rosa and me on Friday evening of Trustee Council Weekend. It will remain in our hearts as a lasting honor. Your friendship to us and your service to Cornell will never be forgotten. Seeing you, Trisha and Charlotte again was a memorable delight.

With all good wishes,

Sincerely yours,

Frank

Frank H. T. Rhodes

rg

CORNELL
U N I V E R S I T Y

Cornell University Council

626 Thurston Avenue
Ithaca, New York 14850-2490

Telephone: 607 255-7555
Facsimile: 607 255-8480

November 2, 1994

Mr. C. Evan Stewart
Executive Vice President/General Counsel
The Nikko Securities Company
One World Financial Center
200 Liberty Street
New York, NY 10281

Dear Evan:

Thank you for your wonderful support throughout this year's Board of Trustees and Cornell University Council Annual Meeting. I particularly appreciate your sure-handed moderation of the New Member Welcome and Information session and your eloquence at both the Joint Annual Meeting and the tribute to President Rhodes. You have established yourself as a true leader of Cornell alumni, and it is a pleasure working with you.

As usual, Trish was a delight, and everyone was charmed by Charlotte. It seems fitting that her birthday fell during Trustee/Council weekend: I'm sure one day, she'll make a fine Council Chair herself.

Sincerely,

Joanne Davenport

JD:rbu

CORNELL
U N I V E R S I T Y

Vice President for Public Affairs

303 Day Hall
Ithaca, New York 14853-2801

Telephone: 607 255-5142
Facsimile: 607 255-9412

November 4, 1994

Mr. C. Evan Stewart
Executive Vice President/General Counsel
The Nikko Securities Company
One World Financial Center
200 Liberty Street
New York, NY 10281

Dear Evan:

Thank you for your part in making Trustee/Council Weekend such a success, as well as for the wonderful leadership you continue to provide to Council. Your report at the Joint Annual Meeting was thorough and incisive, and your participation in the tribute to Frank and Rosa lent the evening an air of true warmth and decorum.

Council is fortunate to have so loyal and committed a chair, and I deeply appreciate your efforts on behalf of Cornell.

With thanks and best regards,

Sincerely,

Richard M. Ramin

RMR:rbu

CORNELL
UNIVERSITY

College of Arts and Sciences

Office of the
Harold Tanner Dean
147 Goldwin Smith Hall
Ithaca, NY 14853-3201

Telephone: 607 255-1097
Fax: 607 255-8463
E-Mail AS_Dean@
Cornell.edu

April 10, 1998

C. Evan Stuart
General Counsel
Nikko Securities
One World Financial Center
200 Liberty Street
New York, NY 10281-1092

Dear Evan:

Congratulations on your election to the Board of Trustees! While I've been hoping ardently for this outcome, I must admit that the grouping of candidates prompted me to worry that qualifications would matter less than connections to certain constituencies. Your victory sends a reassuring message about the values of our alumni.

You've picked up a little scheme of mine in spotting and questioning the word "retorsionary." I'm attempting to prompt the lexicographers to introduce it into the English dictionary by using whenever it's appropriate. It can be regarded as a translation of the French term *retors,* which is used to qualify an idea or problem as not necessarily unthinkable or radically insoluble, but nonetheless exceedingly resistant or shifty, owing to its tough, knotted, twisted texture and complicated, sinewy structure. When applied to persons, it qualified them as wily, crafty, sneaky, mobile, elusive, adaptive, resilient, and so forth. The idea you mention does provide, as it happens, a secondary connotation of the adjective in French since the noun *rétorsion* has the meaning of retaliation that you've noted. So far the other person to weigh in on the subject of this word is Archie Ammons, who felt, he said to me, that he ought to have a use for it, so you are in good company.

I look forward to seeing you in May. My best to Tricia.

Yours,

Phil

JAMES D. STOCKER

August 17, 1998

Dear Evan,

Many thanks for your thoughtful note. Pat and I are thrilled to be included among this fine group of Cornellians.

I'm not sure I offered you my warmest congratulations on your election as Cornell's alumni trustee. We alumni are truly well-represented!

I hadn't realized that you were one of the original instigators of the Rhodes Award, but I salute you for this inspiration. It will give even further inspiration to our dedicated Alumni!

I (we) look forward to seeing you in October.

Warm regards and again, Thanks!

Jim + Pat

Cornell Law School

Russell K. Osgood
The Allan R. Tessler Dean
and Professor of Law

April 13, 1998

C. Evan Stewart, Esq.
The Nikko Securities Co.
International, Inc.
One World Financial Center, Tower A
200 Liberty Street
New York,
New York 10281-1092

Dear Evan:

I was very pleased to learn the good news of your election to the Board of Trustees. On behalf of the Law School, my warm congratulations. They've made an excellent choice. I'll look forward to seeing you on campus for Trustee/Council Weekend in October and in the city next month for the DSLC meeting.

My best,

Russell

Russell K. Osgood

/afg

265 Myron Taylor Hall, Ithaca, New York 14853-4901 ~ FAX: (607)255-7193 / Phone: (607)255-3527

THE BEANSTALK GROUP

Seth M. Siegel
Co-Chairman

February 26, 1998

C. Evan Stewart, Esq.
The Nikko Securities Co. Int'l,. Inc.
One World Financial Center-A
200 Liberty Square
New York, NY 10281-1092

Re: Cornell Trustee

Dear Evan:

For the first time in the twenty-plus years that I've been getting these communications, I have had the opportunity to vote enthusiastically for a trustee candidate. Just wanted you to know that you got my vote, and I hope to be reading soon in the alumni magazine of your victory.

Best regards,

Seth M. Siegel

SMS/lbl

H:\USERS\LISA\CORRES98\022698.WPD

The Beanstalk Group, Inc.
101 East 52nd Street New York, New York 10022
Telephone (212) 421-6060 Fax (212) 421-6388

Academic Letters

Yale Law School

KATE STITH · *Lafayette S. Foster Professor of Law*

March 4, 1999

C. Evan Stewart
Executive Vice President and General Counsel
Nikko Securities Co. International, Inc.
One World Financial Center
200 Liberty Street, New York, N.Y. 10281-1092

Dear Evan:

I am so pleased to have met you, too. The breadth and depth of your knowledge gave me comfort that our panel would go well, even as it awes me a bit! You must be an incredibly hard worker and efficient reader and writer, Evan. It occurs to me that you would be a wonderful visitor for my classes up here, and I wonder if you would be interested in coming up sometime. David Fein and I are teaching a course on Investigations in the Fall Term next year. But what I'd really love is to get you for my course on Criminal Law in the Spring Term (especially if you understand anything about corporate criminal liability – all I know is that we indict corporations and they usually plead guilty, and I never really understood why prosecutors do that except as leverage on individuals or as a fall-back when they can't get the people). I'll also be teaching a course in the Spring Term on Advanced Topics in Criminal Law; the topics will be whatever I want, and I haven't put that course together yet. Your own syllabus and exam look daunting and exciting and I appreciate receiving them.

In the meantime, thank you for the *Chronicle* article on Dartmouth. I have loved reading that journal over these last ten years, and I have even considered keeping up a subscription (alas that I would pay for) after I leave the Dartmouth Board in June -- my term is up, I regret. By the way, did you ever get to know Judith Brandenberg (if I'm spelling that right) on Cornell's Board?

José certainly enjoyed talking with you, too. I hope that we can keep in touch one way or another.

Best,

Kate

P.O. BOX 208215, NEW HAVEN, CONNECTICUT 06520-8215 · TELEPHONE 203 432-4835 · FACSIMILE 203 432-1148
COURIER ADDRESS 127 WALL STREET, NEW HAVEN, CONNECTICUT 06511 · EMAIL KATE.STITH@YALE.EDU

NIKKO

The Nikko Securities Co.
International, Inc.

One World Financial Center
200 Liberty Street, New York, N.Y. 10281-1092

C. Evan Stewart
Executive Vice President
General Counsel

Telephone: (212) 416-5441
Facsimile: (212) 416-5687

February 25, 1999

Kate Stith-Cabranes, Esq.
Lafayette S. Professor of Law
Yale Law School
P. O. Box 208215
New Haven, CT 06520-8215

Dear Kate:

It was a distinct pleasure to "panel" with you in Hawaii, as well as it was to get acquainted with you and Jose.

Upon my return, I found the enclosed article in the *Chronicle*, which I am confident you will find of interest. And although my confidence level is less high, I am taking the liberty of sending on the piece about one of the first women at Cornell, as well as copies of my syllabus and last year's final (any professional/pedagogical comments/criticism would be appreciated!). Also enclosed is my "correspondence" with Ms. Dowd, FYI.

Lastly, as to my point about the attorney-client privilege being under attack and being less effective, it is premised upon the critical importance of certainty stressed by Rhenquist in Upjohn and the facts that (i) we have moved away from that certainty by dint of various decisions (e.g., Georgia-Pacific, Neisig, Belvin, etc.), (ii) the privilege is much more likely today to be challenged by the government and private litigants (e.g., the comments of our panel), (iii) the privilege is scrutinized more carefully by judges today (with less judicial deference), and (iv) the foregoing is happening at the same time that judges are paradoxically "finding" privileges that did not have precedent in Anglo-American jurisprudence (e.g., ombudsman, self-critical analysis, etc.).* All of this seems (to me, at least) at odds with careful lawyering in the litigation process and the ability to counsel clients with some degree of certainty. Oh well, I guess if it were easy...!

* Not to mention the odd notion, recognized by the New York Court of Appeals last year, that a law firm's files did not belong to them (rather, they were the "property" of the client). But see In re Murphy, 560 5.2d 326 (8th Cir. 1997).

NIKKO

Kate Stith-Cabranes, Esq.
Page 2
February 25, 1999

I hope the rest of the week was fun, and we will wave to you as we drive to Madison each weekend.

Best regards.

Sincerely,

C. Evan Stewart

Enclosures

UNIVERSITY OF CALIFORNIA, LOS ANGELES UCLA

BERKELEY · DAVIS · IRVINE · LOS ANGELES · RIVERSIDE · SAN DIEGO · SAN FRANCISCO SANTA BARBARA · SANTA CRUZ

DEPARTMENT OF HISTORY
6265 BUNCHE HALL
BOX 951473
LOS ANGELES, CALIFORNIA 90095-1473
tel. (310) 825-4601
fax (310) 206-9630

January 25, 1998

Mr. C. Evan Stewart
The Nikko Securities Co.
One World Financial Center
200 Liberty Street
New York, New York 10281-1092

Dear Evan,

The delightful picture of Charlotte arrived a couple of weeks ago. What a joyous face to look at.

The Seattle meeting went very well. We had magnificent weather the entire time, except for a little snow to see us off on Sunday. Our luncheon with Senator Slade Gorton and University of Washington President Richard McCormick was especially valuable. We got a chance to put forward our case to Senator Gorton about federal funding for the humanities, and he in turn was very frank with us. It would have been nice to have had more DAC members there, but we were happy that Albert Beveridge (who, as you know, is the association's counsel) came.

Orin McCluskey had sent me the names of the CEOs of Amazon.com and Starbucks. I invited them to attend, but neither could, though they responded to the invitation. Maybe we can follow up on these contacts sometime.

John Cooke and I are now planning the fund-raising dinner at Disney Corporate Headquarters with a tentative date of April 15th. Gordon Wood, who is at the Huntington this year, and I are going to do the program on shifting opinions of Thomas Jefferson. The March 11th reception in Cambridge seems to be well in hand, and I heard from Holly Isdale earlier that she was scouting out places for the New York party.

Coming home from Seattle, I had the time to read your articles which I found a wonderful blend of wit, wisdom and information. You are a born writer, not to mention cartoonist! I think I see now why you enjoy history as much as you do, for you have an analytical, yet sympathetic, approach to life which I think the best history must contain. Thank you for sharing them with me.

I hope the new year finds all of the Stewarts well. I am happy to be a past president of the AHA, but plan to keep in touch on DAC matters.

Yours sincerely,

JAC

Joyce Appleby
Professor of History

NIKKO

The Nikko Securities Co.
International, Inc.

One World Financial Center
200 Liberty Street, New York, N.Y. 10281-1092

C. Evan Stewart
Executive Vice President
General Counsel

Telephone: (212) 416-5441
Facsimile: (212) 416-5687

March 10, 1997

Professor Joyce Appleby
University of California, Los Angeles
Department of History
405 Hilgard Avenue
Los Angeles, CA 90024-1473

Dear Joyce:

Thank you for your nice note, as well as for History Wars; the latter recently arrived and I have put it away for safekeeping for my daughter's spring break (a quick perusal suggests it will be an excellent bookend to the Diplomatic History volume devoted to the subject--many thanks!).

Not to suggest that it is adequate repayment, but I am enclosing a piece from the most recent Weekly Standard whereby Professor Saxe weighs in against the AHA, et al. Walt LaFeber does not mind when I flag for him what "other" folks are expressing, and I hope you will not either. By the way, I thought your recent comments in the March Perspectives were on the mark (and I have a special fondness for the word "brouhaha"). Perhaps the AHA should sponsor a get-together with Bartley and his editorial page colleagues and try to reach some common ground.

Again, many thanks for your thoughtfulness. I look forward to our future contacts.

Best regards.

Sincerely,

Evan

C. Evan Stewart

Enclosure

UNIVERSITY OF CALIFORNIA, LOS ANGELES — UCLA

BERKELEY · DAVIS · IRVINE · LOS ANGELES · RIVERSIDE · SAN DIEGO · SAN FRANCISCO — SANTA BARBARA · SANTA CRUZ

'he Nikko Securities Co.
nternational, Inc.

DEPARTMENT OF HISTORY
405 HILGARD AVENUE
LOS ANGELES, CALIFORNIA 90024-1473

Dear Evan,

A copy of History Wars, the book I mentioned to you in New York last month, is winging its way towards you. I hope that you enjoy it as much as I did. It was good having a chance to chat.

Yours sincerely,

Joyce

January 28, 1997

CORNELL
UNIVERSITY

Department of History
450 McGraw Hall
Ithaca, NY 14853-4601

Tel. (607) 255-8862
Fax. (607) 255-0469

February 3, 1998

Dear Evan,

Your Seward essay is really good. Only someone who has worked over the guy can appreciate how much you packed into such a short space, got it in good proportion, and as far as I can tell, got it all right. He is not an easy person to go through. As Henry Adams said, Seward was such a practiced politician at wearing disguises, people soon did not know which was the disguise and which was the real face (I paraphrase loosely but to the point.) I recalled little about the Wyatt case, so was happy to see this. On the Freeman, your use of C. F. Adams reminded me of Gladstone (of all people) saying that Seward's 10-hour sum-up in that case was "one of the great forensic efforts in the English language." Maybe he did not say "one of." For Gladstone to say that is rather incredible, but I imagine he appreciated the cause. I greatly liked the part at bottom of p.8 where in the Van Zandt case Seward nicely works in anti-slavery with progress and more especially the new industrial economy. The guy really knew what was going on around him, and he could put it together systematically -- which was the really interesting part of his thinking. I'd have loved to have heard Seward and Lincoln in a four-hour bull session. Many thanks for recognizing Rachel at the end of your paper. She will greatly enjoy and appreciate that. She recently wrote to say, among others things, that she did have a section on Freeman in her Honors Thesis, which I now do rather dimly recall, but did not put it into the NEW YORK HISTORY piece, which had a different emphasis. She just wanted you to know she had not missed anything, which is her style-- incredibly polite and sensitive, but never one to miss a point or allow others to think she has missed it. If I ever do the short biography of Seward, I'll steal at length from your essay.

The Robert Kagan essay is really scary. He is getting worse and worse. Albright has just spent the past week running all over the Middle East drumming up support, and people in the White House are working 18-hour days to do the same, but if we put ground troops in the middle of Iraq and started after Saddam, all that work would disappear in a minute. I think his point that these Middle Eastern leaders secretly really do want us to get rid of Saddam might be true to a point--but they do not want to be involved in any way and they want to know what is going to follow. And both of those provisos rather rule out what Kagan is recommending.

Speaking of a Kagan reminded me of something you might want to know about because of your invaluable work now with the AHA. Gene Genovese called a week ago and asked me to join the governing board of a new historical organization, called The Historical

Evan, 2

Organization, oddly enough. Gene and some of the other members of the Executive Committee-- including Don Kagan, Jack Diggins, Bill Freehling, and Marty Sklar -- are pretty alienated from the cultural emphasis of the AHA (read: gender, among other things.) They want to have national meetings every other year and regional meetings every other year -- primarily to read and critique papers, including grad student papers. Part of this is that Gene does not have enough to do. But part of it is that he and the others really are alienated and want a forum for talking with each other. (Gene started our conversation talking about "We neocons....") He is also after Joel and the political historians, who in many cases are really alienated from the AHA after the AHA turned down program proposals for next year's meetings. Joel will probably join,but serve on no governing body. I'll probably do the same, in large part because I'd like to be involved in papers that Diggins and especially Marty Sklar write or discuss. I'm a lifetime AHA member, so I'll remain in that organization, certainly (and am even on the program next January, with Akira Iriye, to discuss post-1945 Asia), but with a fee of $20 for dues, I think I can afford to join the new group even though I very much dislike some of the people involved, as well as like others.

Your comment in your January 9 letter about "vast, fundamental changes in the socio-economic life and culture of Japan" made me sit and think for about an hour. I think you are right, entirely, and the shake-up in the Finance Ministry this past week seems to make your point. That Ministry, I don't have to tell you, has been at the center of the entire system in Japan. I'm watching Eisakabura to find out in which direction he heads, but I think even he knows how the wind is blowing -- although he is one of the several people there who will be ingenious in setting up barricades to protect what has made them so successful over the past 35 years.

You were good enough to send along Lloyd Gardner's review of the Vietnam books, and shortly after I told him that he had effective demolished Bob Schulzinger's account, and I was surprised Schulzinger had been so mealy mouthed about Vietnam's effects. Lloyd was surprised I read it that way. I told him there was no other way to read it. He then understood why he had received several letters of congratulations for the review. He did not (to answer your question), know Paul Fussell very well, but thought he was rather strange, which seems to be a consensus view. Thanks especially for the Sherry review of Gaddis. Sherry destroys Gaddis at the most vulnerable--and important---spot: Gaddis's ignorance of U.S. society and economic system. He simply assumes it, unexamined.

So, in all,I owe you a great deal for the recent enclosures. I hope to be able to thank you personally soon. We have not been able to get to NYC for several months, and are heading elsewhere at the moment, but hope to get there in the very near future and to see Trisha and you when we do.

Best Wishes,
Walt

accelerating the strength of an already dominant U.S. economy. These themes reach far back in American history, at least to Seward and the Whigs, and at their center lay the possibilities and problems of new technology.[15]

Seward reshaped American law to ensure that new inventions could be employed to ensure commercial supremacy. In 1843 he agreed to defend James G. Wilson, who owned a patent on a planing machine used to process lumber. Seward broke new legal ground by refusing to base his argument on precedent (which would have worked against his client), and instead argued that patent laws should be interpreted so they would foster genius. Seward instructed the court on the relationship between technology and a vast continental empire: "The American continent, from its icy boundaries on the north, to undefined latitude within the tropics, seems to be rapidly falling under the political sway of our confederacy. The habitations of a hundred million people, and of how many more I dare not conjecture, are to be erected by our artisans. The machine in question [in this case] reduces . . . the labor and expenses of a necessary part of every structure, whether it be raised for use or ornament."[16]

In 1846 the case reached the Supreme Court where Seward was joined by Daniel Webster, who had also studied the new technologies' meaning. Seward and Webster not only won the case, but as C. Evan Stewart has shown, the Supreme Court subsequently adopted the arguments Seward had advocated.[17]

Because of new technologies, the American empire's possibilities now stretched far beyond the continent. When Secretary of State Webster wrote the instructions in 1852 ordering the opening of Japan to the United States, he explicitly stated that he was not acting out of any missionary urge, but because the new steamships opened up immense potential for the China trade, and Japan, located on a convenient route to China, happened to have the coal needed by the steamships.[18] Through nearly four hundred years, Seward declared in 1852, "merchants and princes" dreamed about exploiting "'Cathay,' 'China,' 'the East.'" Now, thanks to steam, this four-century dream was to be realized. As William Earl Weeks notes, "Amazingly the nation's technological development seemed to be able to keep pace with its messianic ambitions."[19]

---

15. Michael J. Hogan, *The Marshall Plan: America, Britain, and the Reconstruction of Western Europe, 1947–1952* (New York, 1987); Lloyd C. Gardner, *Architects of Illusion* (Chicago, 1970); Thomas J. McCormick, *America's Half-Century: United States Foreign Policy in the Cold War and After*, 2d ed. (Baltimore, 1995). For overviews of the Whig approach, or what Walter Licht nicely calls achieving prosperity "through the superintendency and stewardship of the upstanding," see Licht's *Industrializing America: The Nineteenth Century* (Baltimore, 1995), esp. 88–94; and Charles G. Sellers, *The Market Revolution: Jacksonian America, 1815–1846* (New York, 1991).

16. C. Evan Stewart, "William Henry Seward," *Federal Bar Council News* 6 (February 1999): 3.

17. Ibid., 4; also William H. Seward, *The Reaper: Argument of William H. Seward in the Circuit Court of the United States, October 24, 1854* (Auburn, NY, 1854).

18. Walter LaFeber, *The Clash: U.S.-Japanese Relations Throughout History* (New York, 1997), 12, has Webster's quote; Eugene S. Ferguson, "The American-ness of American Technology," *Technology and Culture* 20 (January 1979): 18–19.

19. Seward, *Works* 1: 247–50; William Earl Weeks, *Building the Continental Empire: American Expansion from the Revolution to the Civil War* (Chicago, 1996), 84.

CORNELL
UNIVERSITY

Department of History
450 McGraw Hall
Ithaca, NY 14853-4601

Tel. (607) 255-88[illegible]
Fax (607) 255-046[illegible]

February 4, 2002

Ms. Elise Carlson Lewis
Vice President, Membership and Fellowship Affairs
Council on Foreign Relations
58 East 68th Street
New York, New York 10021

Dear Ms. Lewis:

C. Evan Stewart has been nominated for membership in the Council, and I am delighted to be able to recommend him to you in the strongest terms. I have known Evan since he was an outstanding undergraduate and law school student at Cornell, and it has been a remarkable and rewarding experience to have remained in contact with him over the years. He has not only been highly successful in his profession, but in becoming involved in a wide and important array of political and academic fields, he has enriched them all.

One of the youngest elected members when he joined the Cornell Board of Trustees, Evan has rapidly become one of the most active and respected members of the Board. He has been highly effective in helping to set up processes for the study of ethics relating both to law and biology. As his record indicates, his interest in ethics has been long-standing; he has found time to teach courses on the subject at Brooklyn and Fordham Law Schools. He has also been involved in ensuring Cornell's commitment to undergraduate teaching by spending a good deal of time visiting classes and with faculty, while making the Trustees aware of the needs of the undergraduate teaching program. He has made himself uncommonly informed not only about the usual on-campus and in-instate Cornell activities, but about alumni and fund-raising overseas. A number of knowledgeable people at Cornell believe it is only a matter of time before Evan will chair the Board of Trustees.

Some five years ago when I was on the Executive Council of the American Historical Association – not only the largest such association in the world, but an extraordinarily international group, especially given its members from Europe, Latin America, and, more recently, Asia – the Council decided to invite a dozen members from the private sector to advise the AHA on its political activities in Washington, and to help raise the endowment. I nominated Evan, who rapidly became a leader of the group. He was so impressive that AHA officials asked him to become one of the three Trustees who oversee the Association's affairs, especially its financial positions. Evan has become a vital part of the AHA leadership. This is not surprising. Not only is he highly able, but he has immense commitment to studying – and writing on – topics that are historically oriented. He is, to my knowledge, the one outside officer who can best talk with AHA

Ms. Elise Carlson Lewis
2

members on their own ground. Evan has published many important essays on law. Most of them involve topics currently being debated in the courts and among lawyers. In some of this work – as an analysis of William Seward's law practice in New York during the 1830s and 1840s – he has made scholarly contributions that, for example, provide important background for the development of criminal and copyright law in the United States. (It might be added, moreover, although it is of lesser importance, that Evan has built an impressive, comprehensive, and entertaining collection of political cartoons and memorabilia of the past 150 years. Some of us exploit his collection when we need to illustrate our own publications.)

Evan is already active and highly effective in his chosen profession, Cornell University, the study of ethics (especially as it relates to the law), the largest and most important international historical association, and New York City politics. In his law practice he has been involved in important cases involving other nations. As I know from his extensive comments on my own writing, Evan draws on a wide range of experiences and reading to be able to comment critically and constructively on foreign policy issues, both current and historical. He accomplishes all this, moreover, with a personality that quickly wins both trust and friends who deeply respect and admire him. Already successful in a range of fields, he is going to be even more of a noted and effective leader in these and, given the range of his curiosity and abilities, other important fields as well.

Sincerely,

Walter LaFeber
Noll Professor of History

Stewart, Evan

From: Walter LaFeber [wfl3@cornell.edu]
Sent: Thursday, February 26, 2009 7:13 PM
To: Stewart, Evan
Subject: Many thanks

Dear Evan.

Many thanks for your good articles, which arrived today, and your most welcome note. I'm glad Charlotte found the material on Vietnam to be helpful, or at least understandable, and I'm amazed that you somehow dug out that 1975 or whenever AHR piece on FDR and Vietnam. As for Mary Young, whom you mention, I like her much as a person, and Sandy and I have admired her ability to deal with cancer, surmount it, and continue to flourish -- and, as you may have noted recently, be on the Bill Moyers's PBS program. I was not impressed with her performance with Moyers, but he has had her back, so clearly she impressed someone (him.) I do admire some of her work of a decade or so ago on Vietnam, or, to be more precise, I've found it useful in my own work.

Joel had been patiently awaiting his new book on 1848, and I suggested that it probably would never appear since the publisher had no doubt invested everything with Bernie Madoff. Then after the volume finally arrived, I saw who had published it and congratulated him on having Kansas do it--the Kansas Press has built, rather quietly, a superb record in political history (and constitutional history too--it has published several of Louis Fisher's recent works, including one or two which have moved into second editions and beyond). The Press, and therefore Joel, will do well with his book.

I very much liked your review of Macey's volume, and noticed the slight
relationship between this review, when you noted in passing in several places "the board failures," and your article on how lawyers would be well advised to stay off such boards. I particularly liked your beginning and ending of the latter article, and your use of the Bailkin quote--that quote is really something: egotistical, overstated, and just asking to be kicked. Both of your pieces made me wonder whether there will be an Adolf Berle-type author who, given the current situation from Enron through the present financial institutions, will do an educational and pioneering job on how boards have abrogated their responsibilities and made many of the rest of us pay for it. Berle would be the person to do this, if he were still around, since he and Means understood nearly 80 years ago where the real power could be found given the relative detachment of shareholders from corporate boards. More to the point, I did not realize, but am might impressed by, how much you knew about Tammy Wynette and the country hits of 1978. I'd like to think that Cornell gave you a wonderful education, but I very much doubt whether you learned much about country music from Robert Summers's courses.

It is good to hear you'll be here on April 24-25, but it is sad to say that we unfortunately won't be. Sarah Berger, Sandy and Susan Berger's daughter, is being married down in Virginia that weekend, and we are planning to attend. Sarah was a student in the foreign policy classes here, and she has been helpful to some Cornell students who needed advice about law school and her experience in the non-profit world. Sarah began with Hogan & Hartson (her Father's old firm), and then moved to Teach for

America in New York City, where she was much happier. I think she has now left Teach for America to work for New York State's higher education system in New York City. In any case, she is a good person, and between you and me, I also want to see how Sandy and Susan Berger have survived their own hell of the past 4 years. I've noticed that Sandy has been listed in groups and meetings advising Clinton and Obama, but I'm not sure what that means. In any case, I hope you'll be returning to Ithaca soon after late April so we can get together. It's my turn to buy dinner.

Very best wishes, as always, to Trish, Charlotte, and you.

Walt

CORNELL
UNIVERSITY

Department of History
450 McGraw Hall
Ithaca, NY 14853-4601

Tel. (607) 255-8862
Fax. (607) 255-0469

August 11, 1995

C. Evan Stewart
Executive Vice President and General Counsel
The Nikko Securities Co. International, Inc.
One World Financial Center
200 Liberty Street
New York, NY 10281-1092

Dear Evan:

Now really! A number of these have been circulating up here but no one will tell me their origins. I suspect social historians.

In Ithaca, they are being traded for a Ted Lowi, two Jim Hofhers and a used Fred Somkin. Maybe they should go on ~~to~~ one of the commodities markets.

All the best,

Joel

Joel H. Silbey
President White Professor of History

JHS/jmh

NIKKO

**The Nikko Securities Co.
International, Inc.**

One World Financial Center
200 Liberty Street, New York, N.Y. 10281-1092

C. Evan Stewart
Executive Vice President
General Counsel

Telephone: (212) 416-5441
Facsimile: (212) 416-5687

July 24, 1995

Mr. Joel H. Silbey
President A. D. White Professor of History
Cornell University
450 McGraw Hall
Ithaca, NY 14853-4601

Dear Joel:

I traded a Duke Snider and Willie McCovey to get the enclosed priceless memorabilia. May I please get it autographed so that it may take its place next to your dollar bill?

Warmest and best regards to you and Rosemary.

Sincerely,

Evan

C. Evan Stewart

Joel H. Silbey
Professor of History
New York Giants Fanatic

"PARTY IS EVERYTHING"

MILESTONES

Joel Silbey hangs tough. Born August 16, 1933, he survived growing up as Brooklyn's only Giants baseball fan. Joel later worked on the New York City docks before tackling history and Iowa, where he acquired the hardiness to endure Cornell undergraduate pranksters and the pre- and post-LT Giants era.

Cornell's leading historian of American politics and its contentious pluralism, Silbey is legendary for keeping his rash promise to make the Fall '82 History 311 final exam optional after the Giants finished the season with three consecutive wins. Silbey continues to fantasize about another Giants' Super Bowl victory and an American two party system with smoke filled rooms.

Grandstand 818-992-5642 1995

C. Evan Stewart

From: Angela Olverson
Sent: Monday, July 22, 2019 5:34 PM
To: C. Evan Stewart
Subject: FW: Silbey

FYI

From: Walter F. LaFeber [mailto:wfl3@cornell.edu]
Sent: Monday, July 22, 2019 5:33 PM
To: Angela Olverson
Subject: Re: Silbey

Ms. Olverson,

Thank you very much for sending Evan's 2002 poem about his mentor, Joel Silbey. Please tell Evan that I don't remember him rhyming "factor" with "Don Fehrenbacher," but that it is truly a stroke of poetic genius, and I'll treasure it -- as I do the entire poem.

Walt

From: Angela Olverson <aolverson@cohengresser.com>
Sent: Monday, July 22, 2019 5:23:00 PM
To: Walter F. LaFeber <wfl3@cornell.edu>; Glenn C. Altschuler <gca1@cornell.edu>
Cc: C. Evan Stewart <EStewart@CohenGresser.com>
Subject: Silbey

Good Afternoon:

Attached hereto is an email regarding Mr. Silbey from Mr. Stewart.

Angela Olverson
Legal Secretary

800 Third Avenue
New York, NY 10022
+1 646 398 5302
aolverson@cohengresser.com
www.cohengresser.com

New York | Seoul | Paris | Washington DC | London

1

A Professor Named Silbey

There once was a professor named Silbey
Who said to himself, I think history will be
My profession, my life, and with Rosemary, my wife
I will, ever after, live happily

Influenced by Hays, Bogue, and Benson
Joel analyzed voting behavior, and then some
Soon came Shrine of Party and A Partisan Imperative
With computer analysis and even some narrative

Joel told students that (political) parties are great fun
In particular, when researching years such as 1851
And while Clay, Calhoun, and Webster were all very big
Just remember, that Lincoln was **always** a Whig!

McGraw 165 was the usual place
Where Joel's disciples received a good taste
Of Civil War Synthesis and ethno-cultural forces
All of which made his the most popular of courses

Now some may have called it a "Rude Republic"
And may even have tried to rebut Joel's rhetoric
But it has had no effect, so far as I could factor
'Cause Glenn Altschuler ain't no Don Fehrenbacher!

Joel Silbey taught me a lot, it is true
About research and analysis—a great slew
Joel mentored me in straight forward fashionry
He even taught me how to spell prosopography!

At the end of the day we've been blessed
That for forty years Joel never thought to rest
He's called 'em as he saw 'em, you and I know
Even though the Giants often laid him very low

Tonight we are gathered to pay tribute
To a man whose legacy is his long suit
Great scholar, great teacher, great colleague, great friend
To Joel Silbey we say, God speed and Amen!

April 20, 2002

Stewart, Evan

From: Macey, Jonathan [jonathan.macey@yale.edu]
Sent: Saturday, January 24, 2009 8:50 AM
To: Stewart, Evan
Subject: One thought.....

I love your review. It's extremely punchy and well-written. One thought... you write "Is Macey Chicken Little about boards, or is he correct?" You might want to add a word about what you think the answer to this question is.... from the phrasing of the question it sounds as though you think I'm Chicken Little, but the substance of the text suggests otherwise. All the best Jon ps and most importantly, thanks for doing this! It's wonderful to have my work taken seriously and reviewed by somebody with your gravitas.

Jonathan Macey
Sam Harris Professor of Corporate Law, Corporate Finance, and Securities Law
Deputy Dean
Yale Law School
127 Wall Street | New Haven, CT 06511
203.432.7913
jonathan.macey@yale.edu

-----Original Message-----
From: Stewart, Evan [mailto:estewart@zuckerman.com]
Sent: Thursday, January 22, 2009 1:03 PM
To: Macey, Jonathan
Subject: RE: Harold Wilson

Jon: finishing up a first draft of my review of your opus. Would you like to see it (and/or make changes)? Best regards. evan

-----Original Message-----
From: Macey, Jonathan [mailto:jonathan.macey@yale.edu]
Sent: Sunday, November 09, 2008 10:34 AM
To: Stewart, Evan
Subject: RE: Harold Wilson

I loved it!!! I think that your writing just keeps getting better. The "I'm shocked" analogy is absolutely perfect and hasn't been brought up before, much less with the Casablanca tie-in!

Jonathan Macey
Sam Harris Professor of Corporate Law, Corporate Finance, and Securities Law
Deputy Dean
Yale Law School
127 Wall Street | New Haven, CT 06511
203.432.7913
jonathan.macey@yale.edu

1

New York Law Journal

WWW.NYLJ.COM

©2009 INCISIVE MEDIA US PROPERTIES, LLC An incisivemedia publication

VOLUME 241—NO. 24

THURSDAY, FEBRUARY 5, 2009

Lawyer's Bookshelf

Corporate Governance: Promises Kept, Promises Broken

REVIEWED BY C. EVAN STEWART

By Jonathan R. Macey, Princeton University Press, Princeton, N.J. 344 pages, $35

If there ever were a moment in U.S. history for Jonathan Macey's book, "Corporate Governance: Promises Kept, Promises Broken," it is now. Macey, the Sam Harris Professor of Corporate Law, Corporate Finance, and Securities Law at Yale Law School, is one of America's most prolific writers on and analysts of corporate governance issues. Against a backdrop of the most pervasive corporate failures since the Great Depression, Macey's book is must-reading for those who want to understand how we got into this mess.

Unlike most members of the legal academy, Macey's prose style is straightforward and unencumbered by professional gobbledygook. He has three basic themes, which he sets forth clearly and then proves with telling evidence:

• Corporate governance is essentially aspirational in nature; it is based upon promises. Contrary to what most lawyers (and everyone else) think, corporate governance is not really contractual in nature. Rather, Macey posits that the relationships between shareholders and the corporations they "own" are based on trust (and if that trust is illusory or the promise is broken, investors will not invest).

• Assuming this theory of promises and trust, then Macey puts the challenge to the various institutions and the established corporate governance mechanisms as to how well they have worked to ensure that the promises have been kept and the trust protected. Much of Macey's book is directed to reviewing the Sarbanes-Oxley era and giving a score card on how these institutions and mechanisms have performed.

• Finally, Macey weighs in with the law of unintended consequences. In his view, those institutions and mechanisms that are most effective in ensuring effective corporate governance are unpopular (hedge funds) or have been heavily regulated or been made hard to obtain as a practical matter (hostile takeovers, dissident director slates). And those institutions and mechanisms that are least effective (boards of directors, credit rating agencies) have been given relatively free rein.

As for shareholders' "legal" control of their corporations, Macey demonstrates that the complex and conflicted system of shareholder voting is hardly "a panacea for corporate governance." Macey is also spot-on that we need to enhance legal processes that do not let boards get fat, dumb, and happy; allowing challenges to control does have a causal link to better corporate governance. The negative example of Yahoo's 2008 rejection of a generous "hostile" tender-offer from Microsoft proves that proposition. After the Yahoo rejection, its stock price tanked, top management was overhauled, and the company is slowly twisting in the wind; just exactly how did this episode promote shareholder value?

Macey's criticisms of many of the institutions he reviews, moreover, are certainly on the mark and hard to argue with. For example, Macey has been a long-standing critic of the credit-rating agencies; had we listened a tad more carefully to him years ago, perhaps the subprime mortgage mess and resulting chaotic fall-out to the banks and credit markets could have been avoided.

And contrary to recent criticisms of the SEC over its various enforcement failures (Bernie Madoff), Macey documents that the SEC has historically had an "anemic" record with respect to anticipating corporate governance scandals, even in areas of "its own areas of expertise—disclosure and capital market regulation." Nor can

New York Law Journal THURSDAY, FEBRUARY 5, 2009

the SEC's recent performance be ascribed to inadequate resources; the SEC's resources today dwarf what they were at the start of the Millennium. This record is likely to get worse as the SEC's new leadership is vowing to "take the handcuffs off" and get into the business of regulating hedge funds and credit default swap instruments; query whether the commission has the knowledge, resources, etc. in order to regulate in those spaces.

Even more important is Macey's incisive focus on corporate boards, of which he properly notes "[m]uch is expected." Macey posits that while much of the focus on directors' failings (and accountability) occurs when there has been corporate fraud, the other side of the equation has profound consequences—recent judicial precedent and legislation "suggest that directors will avoid personal liability even when they fail to exercise due care, as long as they are not disloyal to the corporations."

And while the emphasis of corporate governance vis-à-vis directors in the post-Enron era is to "outperform the Enron board," query whether that is the correct test. Has a greater number of "independent" directors being more directly involved in decision making been a godsend? No, says Macey, because even the best boards get "capture[d] by the managers they are supposed to monitor."

Is Macey Chicken Little about boards, or is he correct? Certainly, in his highlighting of the scandal of boards' complicity in executive compensation, Macey is just shooting fish in a barrel. But executive comp is merely the poster child for a larger problem. At the same time boards have been doling out vast sums to a select few, they have been doing so while seeming to be asleep at the switch. Just two examples should suffice. At General Motors, during Richard Wagoner's tenure as CEO, the stock price of what used to be the world's most formidable car company went from $60 per share to $11 per share—and that was before the financial meltdown (it is now around $3.50 per share). Yet in 2007, when GM lost billions, the board increased his compensation by 64 percent to $16 million. And as the company drifted into functional bankruptcy in late 2008, the board (as well as GM's other core constituencies, e.g., the UAW) did Tammy Wynnette proud. What is wrong with that picture?

At least as equally troubling are the board failures at major financial institutions, where huge paydays were sanctioned based almost entirely on leveraged derivative products as to which the directors seemingly had no clue. Put another way, which is worse: that the AIG board understood the credit default swap exposure on its books, or that the AIG board did not understand that exposure?

The foregoing do not arise out of complicity in fraud, malfeasance, or venality. The GM and AIG directors likely believed (and believe) they were "loyal" and discharged their duties as a legal matter. And yet they failed miserably.

Speaking of financial institutions and their boards' failures, said failures in my view are leading to a paradigm shift in corporate governance. With the massive "investments" by the U.S. government in the largest financial institutions, we are on the cusp of a possible nationalization of America's banking system. Although this disturbing notion started out as only a "temporary" program, given the size of the government's investments in Citigroup and in Bank of America, we have already seen the not-so-invisible hand of the government making business decisions for those two corporations. That their boards have been neutered seems clear; supposing that government bureaucrats will be better stewards of these institutions than their management and directors is anyone's guess (but I know where I am betting my nickel). What is certain is that under this new paradigm the concerns of taxpayers and not shareholders will be paramount.

Macey wrote and published his brilliant book before the financial meltdown we are experiencing. For corporations not accepting federal bail-out money, his analyses and conclusions are important. It should be hoped that his well-documented criticisms of those corporate governance mechanisms that investors most heavily rely upon will be heeded; at the same time, I have my doubts as to whether the mechanisms he has identified as more useful in promoting good governance will be embraced. In any event, Macey believes that "the pricing capabilities of capital markets emerge as the greatest corporate governance mechanism we have." Amen.

C. EVAN STEWART *is a partner at Zuckerman Spaeder and handles litigation before the U.S. Supreme Court, the Judicial Panel on Multidistrict Litigation, and other courts.*

Tennis Letters

NIKKO

**The Nikko Securities Co.
International, Inc.**

One World Financial Center
200 Liberty Street, New York, N.Y. 10281-1092

C. Evan Stewart
Executive Vice President
General Counsel

Telephone: (212) 416-5441
Facsimile: (212) 416-5687

March 10, 1998

Ms. Tippi C. Younger
Director of Adult Competition/
Marketing Coordinator
USTA, Eastern Tennis Association
550 Mamaroneck Avenue, Suite 505
Harrison, NY 10528-1618

Dear Ms. Younger:

Per your letter of January 12, 1998 concerning tentative rankings for 1997, I am afraid that the proposed ranking for Mr. Howard Berman (#9) is clearly improper and must be re-evaluated. Not only did Mr. Berman suffer numerous losses to men, women and children considerably less highly ranked (in all age groups), the punishment to be meted out by the USTA for refusing to play challenge matches (see the enclosed August 1, 1997 edition of Tennis Week) has clearly not been factored in, as well. At best, Mr. Berman deserves inclusion in the "Insufficient Data" category; at worst, he should be restricted to using wood racquets exclusively.

Please let me know if you need other pertinent information regarding Mr. Berman's reputation, character or tennis record.

Very truly yours,

C Evan Stewart

C. Evan Stewart

Encl.

cc: Howard J. Berman, Esq.

Howard Berman, a highly ranked 45s and older player based in New York, has been cited by the USTA. The offense: failure to play a challenge match with a former Cornell teammate of Berman's, **Evan Stewart**, for over one year. The USTA Director of Marketing, **Pierce O'Neil**, said that Berman's "fear to play Stewart, while understandable, is no excuse. Under the circumstances, we will have to take drastic steps."

At press time the USTA had not yet decided what formal action would be taken. Sources at the USTA, however, are confident that sanctions will include barring Berman from the U.S. Open until the Millenium and granting Stewart an A.T.P. ranking within the top 100.

Tennis empresario, **Gene Scott**, was quoted as saying that "Stewart has earned the ranking on the merits. And in any event, Berman deserves severe punishment--last time we played, he called the lines out!"

Bud Collins, tennis historian, expressed shock at Berman's no-show: "This hasn't happened since Bobby Riggs failed to defend his Wimbledon title!"

The **ATP Tour** Tel Aviv tournament September 8-14 has been sold to **Sasson Khakshouri**, founder of Moscow's **Kremlin Cup**. Khakshouri will move the event to Tashkent, Uzbekistan, where he owns a Challenger event, keep the same date and upgrade the Challenger to a world series tournament offering $303,000 in prize money. For further information, contact tournament director Ian Froman by fax at (7) 371-264-2720.

Reliable sources say **Ray Benton** and **Sara Fornaciari** are no longer under consideration to take over **Anne Person Worcester**'s position as chief executive officer for the **Corel WTA Tour** in 1998.

World No. 1 Pete Sampras has agreed to represent the United States against Australia in the Davis Cup semifinal in Washington, D.C., in September. Sampras did not play in the first two rounds of Davis Cup this year nor last year, when the USA lost to the Czech Republic in the quarterfinals.

Boris Becker, whose final appearance at a Grand Slam event is expected to be at the U.S. Open, said he would make himself available to compete for Germany in Davis Cup matches in 1998. Becker is starting a coaching career for his German junior team (see Richard Evans' story on page 16).

Brad Gilbert and **Justin Gimelstob** are considering working together on the tour. Gilbert and **Andre Agassi**, whom he has coached since 1994, will discuss whether their relationship will continue; the same goes for Gimelstob

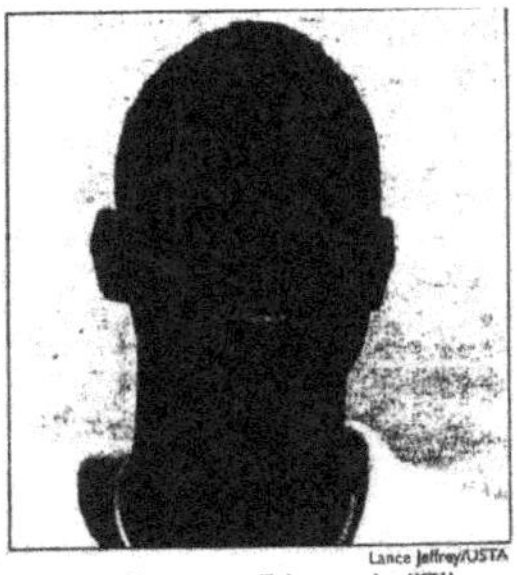

Lance Jeffrey/USTA

Rodney Harmon will become the USTA's director of multicultural development August 11th. Harmon, who is leaving his job as men's coach at the University of Miami after one year, was a former USTA national coach. He is the only African-American besides Arthur Ashe to reach the U.S. Open quarterfinals, which he accomplished in 1982.

and his current coach, **Bobby Banck**. Coincidentally, Agassi stumbled in the opening round against Gimelstob at the **Infiniti Open**, losing 7-5, 6-2.

"Tennis vs. Other Sports", a series of 30-second spots that are part of a **USTA** advertising campaign, compares the challenges and rigors of tennis with professional baseball, basketball and football and promotes the **U.S. Open** at the newly renovated **USTA National Tennis Center**.

The spots premiered July 19th on CBS and will run nationally through August 31st on CBS, USA Networks, CNN, CNBC and locally on ESPN, ESPN2, MTV, VH1, E! and others.

"The primary goal for our new advertising campaign was to present tennis in ways sports fans have never thought of—by comparing the passion, power and athleticism of the game with other professional sports," said USTA Director of Marketing **Pierce O'Neil**.

The advertising spots were created by **Grybauskas Beatrice**, New York.

Chanda Rubin has hired **Brian Gottfried** as her new coach.

photos by Paul Zimmer

Wimbledon champions **Martina Hingis** and **Pete Sampras** were honored at a ball in London when the The Championships ended. For Sampras, the night called for a cigar.

50 TW August 1, 1997

NIKKO

The Nikko Securities Co.
International, Inc.

One World Financial Center
200 Liberty Street, New York, N.Y. 10281-1092

C. Evan Stewart
Executive Vice President
General Counsel

Telephone: (212) 416-5441
Facsimile: (212) 416-5687

December 15, 1993

Mr. Bud Collins
The Boston Globe
135 Wm. T. Morrisey Blvd.
Dorchester, MA 02125

Dear Mr. Collins:

My family and I go back with you a long way: in the late '60s we watched from Maine as you televised Longwood, and laid the foundation for your wonderful career. You later were a highlight of our 1974 trip to Wimbledon when my mother espied you heading down to the practice courts while warbling "The Best Things in Life Are Free"!

Having just purchased your recent Encyclopedia (to add to my large Collins library), I must lodge a small objection. How could you omit Richard L. Stockton from your "Also Served" section, while including virtually all of his peer group (Gottfried, Mayer, Tanner, etc.)? Although Dickie never achieved the potential many (including you) predicted for him (principally because of injuries), he still had an outstanding career: ranking in the world's top ten; reaching the semi-finals of Wimbledon and the French, as well as the quarters of the U.S. Open (twice); finalist WCT Finals; NCAA champion; Davis Cup; outstanding doubles career; etc. (not to mention the U.S. Pro Indoor--of which I have the laser disc; narrated by Bud Collins, where he declares Stockton #1 in the world).

Short of having you pull the Encyclopedia prior to its next printing, would it be possible to get a listing from you of his career (as if he had been included)? If you can fit this into your busy schedule, I promise that my sister will not groan when she sees your pants next July 4th!

Many thanks for all your contributions to our great sport, and happy holidays.

Very truly yours,

C. Evan Stewart

C. Evan Stewart

The Boston Globe

P.O. BOX 2378 BOSTON, MA 02107-2378 (617) 929-2000

4Mar95

Dear Mr Stewart,

Thanks for your kind words -- and your patience. If the Encyclopedia is ever re-printed, your friend and mine, R L Stockton, will get a paragraph. Deservedly. Time and space ran out -- other deserving characters (Hans Nusslein?) will also make it.

Enclosed, please find the data I would work from.

Cheers,

Bud Collins

Collins

WINSTON & STRAWN

35 WEST WACKER DRIVE
CHICAGO, ILLINOIS 60601-9703

43 RUE DU RHONE
1204 GENEVA, SWITZERLAND

444 SOUTH FLOWER STREET
LOS ANGELES, CALIFORNIA 90071-2911

200 PARK AVENUE
NEW YORK, NEW YORK 10166-4193

(212) 294-6700

FACSIMILE (212) 294-4700

www.winston.com

21 AVENUE VICTOR HUGO
75116 PARIS, FRANCE

1400 L STREET, N.W.
WASHINGTON, D.C. 20005-3502

C. EVAN STEWART
(212) 294-4781
estewart@winston.com

April 9, 2001

Ms. Nancy Gill McShea
Tennis Week
341 Madison Avenue, Suite 600
New York, NY 10017

Dear Ms. McShea:

I was pleased to read your USTA/Eastern News column in the April 3rd issue, especially insofar as seeing that Dick Stockton will be inducted into the Hall of Fame. Having been at the Hackley School with "Dickie" back in the 1960s, having played on several teams with him, and having myself played intercollegiate tennis (at a level **far** inferior to his), I have followed his tennis career with interest.

Perhaps you were just being kind to Ms. Jackson and Messrs. Seewagen and Cranis, but I think you underplayed Dick's accomplishments a bit. While a junior (at least until he lost the National 18s to Van Dillen), he was clearly number one (that Davis's record eclipsed his was, in large measure, because of later proliferations of ranking categories); and, in 1986, he was world's number one again (in the men's 35s). In between, in addition to what you correctly listed (although others ranked him higher in 1977--e.g., Lance Tingay), he reached the semis of Wimbledon and the French, as well as the quarters of the U.S. Open (twice); he was also a finalist at the WCT Finals (which was the "fifth" major at that time), won the U.S. Pro Indoor (also a big deal in those days), had a great record in the World Cup (3-1 in singles--his only loss was to Laver--when both had match point!; 2-0 in doubles), won two Grand Slam doubles titles, and at the end of his career (as a wild card) Dick took Lendl (then the World's Number One) to five sets at Wimbledon. Although Dick never reached the potential many predicted for him (principally because of injuries, as well as the change over to slower surfaces in the middle 1970s), he had an outstanding career and it is fitting that he be inducted into the Hall of Fame.

I am only sorry not to be present on April 20th when he is honored.

Very truly yours,

C. Evan Stewart

C. Evan Stewart

bcc: Howard J. Berman, Esq.
P. Nicholas Kourides, Esq.
Mr. J. Pierce O'Neil
Mrs. Anne F. Barnes

June 13, 1990

Mr. Eugene L. Scott
Publisher and Editor in Chief
Tennis Week
124 East 40th Street, Suite 1101
New York, NY 10016

Dear Mr. Scott:

Many thanks for your very nice phone call the other day, as well as for setting the record straight. Justice Burton once wrote that [t]here is something pretty final about a death sentence," and I would not want to presume to be the purveyor of such finality with respect to such a wonderful man as Eddie Moylan.

I did go and check the alleged source. Rather than what was reported to me, it turns out that all that was written was that he had formally retired from the Cornell athletics staff after 28 years. No one should have interpreted that as death!

I regret that I did not use the opportunity of your call to get your reaction to the French finals. I will nonetheless look forward to reading it in the next issue and perhaps, at some future tennis event, I will have the chance to talk with you in person.

Again, I am most apologetic for my error. I take comfort in the old Korean proverb: "Remember, even monkeys fall out of trees."

Best regards.

Sincerely,

C. Evan Stewart

bcc: Howard J. Berman, Esq.

NIKKO

The Nikko Securities Co. International, Inc.

One World Financial Center
200 Liberty Street, New York, N.Y. 10281

Telephone: (212) 416-5441
Facsimile: (212) 416-5600

C. Evan Stewart
General Counsel

June 5, 1990

Mr. Eugene L. Scott
Publisher and Editor in Chief
Tennis Week
124 East 40th Street, Suite 1101
New York, NY 10016

Dear Mr. Scott:

I enjoy reading your "Vantage Point" columns. They focus on timely and important issues in tennis.

With respect to your May 24th piece, I was particularly interested in your comments about Eddie Moylan. As a backbencher for Coach Moylan at Cornell in the early 1970s, I can attest to your description of his playing style. I can also attest to his being a gentleman and a great ambassador for the sport, not to mention his fine teaching skills.

Unfortunately, I must update one aspect of your column. Late last year Coach Moylan passed away in Ithaca.

Very truly yours,

C. Evan Stewart

C. Evan Stewart

bcc: Howard J. Berman, Esq.
(w/article)

6/11/90 - Scott called + said he'd recently talked of Moylan – Mark Twain!

STEPTOE & JOHNSON
ATTORNEYS AT LAW
1330 CONNECTICUT AVENUE, N. W.
WASHINGTON, D. C. 20036-1795
(202) 429-3000
FACSIMILE NO. (202) 429-9204
TELEX: 89-2503

MOSCOW, U. S. S. R.
TELEPHONE: 011-7-095-415-4249
FACSIMILE: 011-7-095-415-2920

PHOENIX, ARIZONA
TELEPHONE: (602) 266-6610
FACSIMILE: (602) 274-1970

CHRISTOPHER T. LUTZ
(202) 429-6440

June 29, 1990

C. Evan Stewart, Esq.
General Counsel
The Nikko Securities Company
International, Inc.
One World Financial Center
Two Hundred Liberty Street
New York, New York 10281

Dear Mr. Stewart:

Many thanks for your letter.

I am afraid I cannot plead confusion as a defense for my mistake. The problem was just faded memory. In the final editing of the article, I tried to find a copy of Levels Of The Game to check what I had said. Unfortunately, few bookstores carry it around here, though I think it is still in print. I even considered at the last moment deleting the word "Wimbledon." It turns out I should have listened to my nagging doubts, but I didn't.

Thanks again.

Sincerely,

Christopher T. Lutz

CTL/fbm

NIKKO

The Nikko Securities Co. International, Inc.
One World Financial Center
200 Liberty Street, New York, N.Y. 10281
Telephone: (212) 416-5441
Facsimile: (212) 416-5600

C. Evan Stewart
General Counsel

June 26, 1990

Christopher T. Lutz, Esq.
Steptoe & Johnson
1330 Connecticut Avenue, N.W.
Washington, DC 20036

Dear Mr. Lutz:

As a John McPhee fan, as well as a former collegiate tennis player, I must proffer one suggestion to you with regard to your recent article in Litigation magazine. The match Mr. McPhee described in Levels of the Game was a 1968 Forest Hills semi-final between Arthur Ashe and Clark Graebner. You may be confusing that book with a coffee table book about Wimbledon, for which he wrote some text. I recommend each highly, although the coffee table book would not be of much use for purposes of your article.

Very truly yours,

C. Evan Stewart

C. Evan Stewart

bcc: Howard J. Berman, Esq.